The German Army
on The Western Front 1915

To my aunt and godmother

Joan Ede

With love and thanks for a lifetime of kindness.

By the same author:

The German Army on the Somme 1914–1916
The German Army at Passchendaele
The German Army on Vimy Ridge 1914–1917
The German Army at Cambrai
The German Army at Ypres 1914
The Germans at Beaumont Hamel
The Germans at Thiepval

With Nigel Cave:

The Battle for Vimy Ridge 1917
Le Cateau

The German Army on The Western Front 1915

by

Jack Sheldon

Pen & Sword
MILITARY

First published in Great Britain in 2012 by
Pen & Sword Military
an imprint of
Pen & Sword Books Ltd
47 Church Street
Barnsley
South Yorkshire
S70 2AS

Copyright © Jack Sheldon 2012

ISBN 978 1 84884 466 7

The right of Jack Sheldon to be identified as the author of this work has been asserted by him in accordance with the Copyright, Designs and Patents Act 1988.

A CIP catalogue record for this book is available from the British Library.

All rights reserved. No part of this book may be reproduced or transmitted in any form or by any means, electronic or mechanical including photocopying, recording or by any information storage and retrieval system, without permission from the Publisher in writing.

Typeset in Ellington by
Phoenix Typesetting, Auldgirth, Dumfriesshire

Printed and bound in England by
CPI Group (UK) Ltd, Croydon, CR0 4YY

Pen & Sword Books Ltd incorporates the Imprints of Pen & Sword Aviation, Pen & Sword Family History, Pen & Sword Maritime, Pen & Sword Military, Pen & Sword Discovery, Wharncliffe Local History, Wharncliffe True Crime, Wharncliffe Transport, Pen & Sword Select, Pen & Sword Military Classics, Leo Cooper, The Praetorian Press, Remember When, Seaforth Publishing and Frontline Publishing

For a complete list of Pen & Sword titles please contact
PEN & SWORD BOOKS LIMITED
47 Church Street, Barnsley, South Yorkshire, S70 2AS, England
E-mail: enquiries@pen-and-sword.co.uk
Website: www.pen-and-sword.co.uk

Contents

Introduction ... viii
Acknowledgements ... xiii
Author's Note ... xiv
Chapter 1   The Winter Battle in Champagne ... 1
Chapter 2   Neuve Chapelle ... 44
Chapter 3   Gas Attack at Ypres ... 81
Chapter 4   The Spring Battles in Artois:
            Arras, Aubers Ridge and Festubert ... 122
Chapter 5   The Argonne Forest ... 164
Chapter 6   The Autumn Battles in Artois:
            Arras and Loos ... 203
Chapter 7   The Autumn Battle in Champagne ... 246

Maps

The Western Front 1915 ... x
Champagne Area ... 2
The Winter Battle in Champagne ... 4
Neuve Chapelle ... 46
Gas Attack Ypres ... 84
Vimy Ridge ... 124
Aubers Ridge ... 130
Festubert ... 146
The Argonne Forest ... 165
Western Argonne Defence Line ... 170
Eastern Argonne Defence Line ... 192
The Loos Battlefield ... 204
The Autumn Battle in Champagne ... 248
The Tahure Counter-Attack ... 281

Appendix I	German – British comparison of ranks	289
Appendix II	Chronology	291
Appendix III	Selective biographical notes	292
Bibliography		302
Index		307

Introduction

The *German Army* series concentrates on description and analysis of the way events unfolded along the Western Front and does not usually pursue consideration of alternative scenarios. However a broader discussion is essential in the case of 1915. This was a seminal year on the Western Front and for the First World War more generally. Despite months of incessant fighting it did not even begin to determine the outcome of the war, but it certainly defined the way it would be fought.

The stalemate at Ypres the previous November brought mobile operations to an end in the west. This forced the German High Command and Falkenhayn in particular to confront the reality of the long-feared war on two fronts and to decide on future strategy. Given the constraints of manpower and equipment it was clear that it would be impossible to maintain large-scale offensives in both east and west at the same time. Priorities had to be laid down and difficult choices confronted. In the event, the decision was to attack on the Eastern Front and to conduct defensive operations along the Western Front. There were only two, relatively limited, exceptions to this policy. Throughout the year, but more especially up until August, the reinforced XVI Corps, commanded by General der Infanterie von Mudra, conducted a permanent offensive, driving in a southerly direction through the difficult terrain of the Argonne Forest west of Verdun whilst, in late April and early May, Fourth Army, commanded by Generaloberst Duke Albrecht of Württemberg, launched a limited attack, preceded by the first offensive use of chlorine gas, which was designed to eliminate the Ypres Salient.

Despite their peculiar impersonal dryness and strange couching in the third person throughout, it is clear from an examination of Falkenhayn's memoirs that he appreciated that the greatest threat was posed by the Allies in the west and that it would be in Germany's interest to conclude a separate peace with Russia. As a result of this line of thought, his first inclination was to deploy the extra forces generated in early 1915 on the Western Front rather than in the east. A combination of training and equipping new units, coupled with a major reorganisation of the field army, including substantial reductions in the infantry available in each of the divisions, made it possible to create eight additional divisions in February 1915 and a further fourteen the following April. All these extra forces, in fact, went to the east, which throws up two questions: why was this done; and, was there an alternative? It would appear that by the end of 1914 Falkenhayn had already decided that the ultimate decision would have to be fought out on the Western Front but that, in the light of the failure the previous November in Flanders and the relative strength of the two sides, this could not be achieved by breakthrough and manoeuvre. Instead, it would have to rely on a policy of attrition, coupled with delaying tactics on the Eastern Front. It could be said that this was another example of Falkenhayn playing a percentage game, rather than risking all on decisive, but possibly risky, action.

It is certainly consistent with the way he chose to fight the battles around Ypres and Flanders the previous autumn. By launching the fresh formations of Fourth Army east-west, parallel to the coast, he ensured that, if there was no swift breakthrough and wheeling movement to the south, there would at least be a defensible line at the end of the offensive. A great captain might well have preferred to have massed his forces along the line of the Lys, allowed the Allies to progress along the Belgian coast towards Ostende then to have driven hard north to the sea, refusing his left flank and so have eliminated the main body of the BEF. Falkenhayn later described the operations in Flanders as a 'gamble', but he was referring to the rushed deployment of his raw troops, rather than risking all his chips on one spin of the wheel.

Throughout 1915 the war in the west comprised more or less incessant French attacks, with the main emphasis placed on the winter battles in Champagne in February and March and the Anglo-French offensives in Artois and Champagne in May and June; September and October. On the Eastern Front the inverse was true, with the forces of *Oberbefehlshaber-Ost* (*Ober-Ost*) [Commander in Chief Eastern Theatre] launching one major offensive after another, which gained great swathes of territory, but influenced the strategic situation not one jot. Although the Argonne offensive, which was maintained throughout the year, was obviously designed to interdict the main railway line to Verdun and thus prepare the way for an offensive against that salient, it was not until February 1916 that operations intended to give substance to Falkenhayn's policy of attrition began. This suggests either that Falkenhayn's plan was never realistic, or that he did not stick to it.

Of the two decisions to deploy forces in the east, the despatch of eight divisions in February is the more difficult to understand. Falkenhayn himself stressed that the situation of the forces of Austria-Hungry, though extremely difficult, did not amount to a crisis and he doubted that two offensives to be launched simultaneously five hundred kilometres apart in Masuria and South Galicia would generate any sort of synergy. Worse, a winter campaign would simply wear out the fresh forces. However, Falkenhayn was up against the widely held view that the war could be won in the east and the belief of the Austrians that the Russians would be more likely to be willing to negotiate if they were first beaten decisively in the field. In addition, the star of Hindenburg and Ludendorff was in the ascendant after Tannenberg and Germany craved victories. Bethmann Hollweg, the German Chancellor, had conspired with them at the beginning of the year to bring about Falkenhayn's dismissal and, although this was not successful, he was weakened. Political pressure built up on Falkenhayn, the Austro-Hungarian situation did appear to be deteriorating and so these eight divisions were sent east where, operating as Tenth Army, they duly made great gains in Masuria until they were, like the army in the Carpathians, brought to a grinding halt, completely exhausted.

Had a more balanced assessment, one based more on straight military considerations, been made of the relative strengths of the three main Allied belligerents, France, Russia and the United Kingdom, it is possible to argue that Falkenhayn, by buckling in to pressure, forfeited a fleeting chance to gain a substantial advantage in the west. It is true that the armies of Austria-Hungary, which had lost over two million men by March 1915, would have required propping up; but there can be little doubt that it would still have been possible to go on the strategic defensive in the wide open spaces of the Eastern Front. Had this been done, there could then have been a serious examination of how best to wear down the Western Allies and force them onto the back foot. Given their ability to draw on the resources of two empires and their maritime strength they could, if unchecked, continue the war almost indefinitely, so speed and decisive action in the west was absolutely essential.

If that factor had been given the weight it deserved, detailed planning could have then considered, for example, whether it would be best during the coming months to operate against the French army and the BEF simultaneously or separately. There would hardly have been sufficient forces or materiel available to engage in simultaneous action and, by early 1915, although France had already suffered a huge number of casualties, it was able to plug the gaps by calling on its colonial forces to make up the deficit. Furthermore, thanks to its system of conscription, it could also continue to bring a great many freshly trained and highly motivated troops into the army, all keen to eject the invading Germans from their territory. That being the case it could certainly have been expected to put up extremely stiff resistance to any German attempts to launch offensives that year and so was not an obvious first target.

The position of the BEF was rather different. It had performed as well as might have been expected for an army neither manned, nor trained, nor equipped for large-scale operations on continental Europe, but it had overdrawn its resources in fighting from Mons to the Aisne and around Ypres the previous year and was in a relatively parlous state in early 1915. It had attracted huge numbers of volunteers to the ranks, but training and equipping them was intensely difficult. There was a desperate lack of men with military skills and experience; whilst units and formations were largely officered by men promoted way beyond their level of knowledge and competence and with no adequate staff to support them. No significant improvement could be expected for months to come and the situation was made worse by the decision to divert men and materiel to the Dardanelles for the misbegotten campaign at Gallipoli: a strategic choice which also put paid to any chance of the French army launching simultaneous assaults in Artois and Champagne in March, thus easing the defensive task of the German army appreciably.

It does not take much imagination to see that had the eight fresh divisions been joined by, say, eight others drawn from reserves in the west, or obtained by thinning out other parts of the Western Front, a powerful striking force, supported by all the heavy guns and howitzers available, launched in March against the British between Lens and Armentières, could have achieved both breakthrough and far-reaching effects on an army which was still struggling to come to terms with major operations against a first class opponent. Naturally, there would have been a violent French reaction, but the winter battles in Champagne would have been disrupted and, let it not be forgotten, a

x   THE GERMAN ARMY ON THE WESTERN FRONT 1915

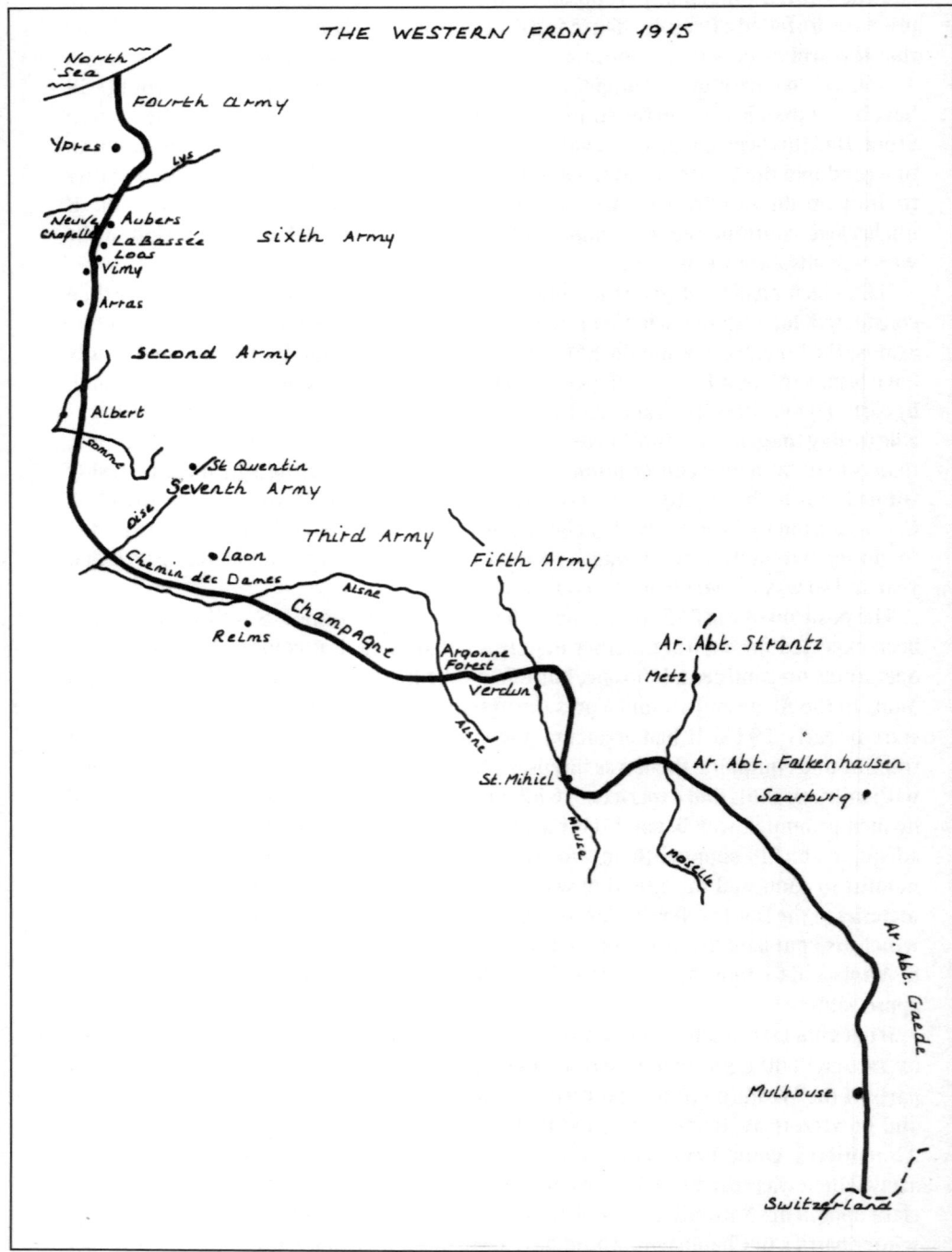

further fourteen divisions which fuelled the great breakthrough in Galicia that spring would have been available very shortly after battle was joined. However, none of these things happened.

The British, the more hated of the Western Allies, because of their pre-eminent position in the world, their maritime strength and the perceived value of their huge empire, were gravely underestimated by those in Germany with decision-making powers. There was an arrogant assumption that, lacking any recent history of land operations by massed armies on continental Europe, it was highly improbable that Great Britain could either develop or field an effective army to rival that of Germany for the foreseeable future. Falkenhayn's personal assessment was that, individually, the British soldier was courageous and possessed of great powers of endurance, but that the BEF, collectively, was so clumsy – to the point of incompetence – that there was, firstly, no possibility of it achieving any sort of decisive success against the German army for the time being and, secondly, that the same problems rendered it vulnerable to a determined German offensive early in 1915. Unfortunately for Falkenhayn, a combination of political and diplomatic pressure, coupled with countervailing military opinion from Hindenburg and Ludendorff who disliked and despised him, meant that his first point was embraced as justification for the priority to be given to the Eastern Front and his second was ignored.

As a result and luckily for the Allies and the future course of the war, the opportunity to eliminate, or at least seriously weaken, the BEF before it could build up its strength, was not taken. The war in the east generated great, but indecisive, victories whilst, in the west, the German army dug in, developing its defence in depth all along the front and perfecting the use of the machine gun as a weapon of defence *par excellence*. Exploiting the excellent interior lines available to it - in particular, the highly developed railway network in Western Europe, it was able repeatedly and with ease to redeploy its heavy artillery and meagre reserves up and down the front to counter the most pressing threats as they occurred. Despite these developments, there was no way that the Allies, France especially, could permit the Germans to sit calmly in their entrenchments, occupying large amounts of French and Belgian territory; so prompt offensive action was essential, both to drive out the invaders and to demonstrate to the Russians that, despite the continuing series of disasters being played out in the east, it was still worth prosecuting the war as a member of the alliance.

This book is concerned with how the Western Allies, with the French taking the lion's share of responsibility and providing the strategic direction, took the fight to the Germans in a lengthy and bloody campaign, which saw French losses in the war to date reach almost two million by December 1915, of which just over one million were fatal. Fighting was more or less continuous in the west throughout the year, but there were peaks in Champagne from mid-February to mid-March and then again in September and October, when the French army launched a series of vain, but ruinously costly, attacks to the east of Reims. A major offensive on the Arras front by the French Tenth Army in the period May-June was also roughly handled by skilful German defenders. A renewal of these attacks in September, timed to coincide with operations on the Champagne front, supported this time by the ill-fated British assault at Loos, was even less successful and was effectively called off after two days. Joffre, foreshadowing equally unwise prophecies by Nivelle two years later, promised both his armies and the whole of France complete success. In fact the German defence, though severely pressed at times, held firm. The consequent dislocation of expectations led to serious doubts about his competence which, when combined with his failure to anticipate Verdun the following year, led ultimately to his removal.

By that time Sir John French, commander of the BEF, had also been removed from command. Ineffective, exceedingly bloody, assaults launched at Neuve Chapelle in March, Aubers Ridge and Festubert in May and Loos in September, which demonstrated to the German army that, for the time being, they had nothing to worry about from that direction and which were treated with complete dismissive disdain by the French High Command, coupled with his own errors and personal limitations, sealed his fate. Superficially, the situation was quite different for Germany as the year drew to a close. It had enjoyed more or less continuous success in 1915. At huge cost, the Allies had made almost no gains in the west whilst, in the east, both the Russians and the Serbs had been put to the sword in no uncertain manner. The Allied response was the Chantilly conference in December, intended to improve the situation by coordinating more closely the attritional offensives planned for the following year.

Almost as if sensing that, despite the encouraging results of 1915, the tide was beginning to turn against Germany and having decided that if he was ever to give substance to his own theories of attrition it would have to be soon, Falkenhayn set in train the detailed planning which would see the Fifth Army, commanded by the German Crown Prince, launch the assault on Verdun in late February 1916. However, the fateful year of 1916 was still in the future when the battles described in this book were fought successfully by a German army still at the height of its powers. Though not perfect by any means, the standard of its command and control and staffwork was uniformly high throughout the period; but the main reason it achieved so much in both major theatres during 1915 was the fighting ability and resilience of the men of the hour who manned its regiments. That year their performance was superlative.

Jack Sheldon
Vercors, France
December 2011
jandl50@hotmail.com

Acknowledgements

Once again, as I prepared this book, I was able to turn to Dr Alex Fasse in Germany for information and explanations concerning a number of obscure references which appeared during my research and I am most grateful to him. Mick Forsyth was an excellent sounding board, as I sought accuracy in translation and I appreciate his assistance with my rendering of difficult words and phrases, though the final outcome is entirely my responsibility. Eddy Lambrecht was kind enough to offer me a selection of photographs relating to Ypres 1915 and also permitted me to publish an extract from a letter in his private collection.

As ever, I am most grateful for the careful editorial work of Nigel Cave, who works hard to keep this continuing project on track and I also appreciate the support of everyone at Pen and Sword Books. My wife Laurie has once more helped me in so many ways. Her meticulous drawing of the numerous maps in the text has been enormously helpful, as has her loving support throughout the lengthy period of research and writing.

Author's Note

Sources used for this book include items from the archives in Munich. The Bavarian 6th Reserve Division featured prominently in French Flanders during 1915, as did reinforcements from the Bavarian II Corps, located to the north in Flanders, so much valuable primary material is available for study. It is undeniable that the loss of almost all the Prussian archival material as a result of an air raid on Potsdam in April 1945 denies us access to what must once have been a wealth of information, but experience has shown that the factual content of German regimental histories written between the wars by authors with access to written documents and the memories of veterans, is generally reliable. In consequence, it is possible to describe these battles from the German perspective, confident that the result is a close approximation to the truth – especially when the descriptions interlock with the published Allied accounts.

Some of the eye witness accounts and other descriptions in the text are linked to a particular place on the various battlefields. Each chapter includes at least one map of the area concerned and, with the exception of the chapter concerning the Argonne Forest, figures which appear on most of the maps refer to the numbers in bold associated with that section of the relevant chapter. Where more than one witness was based in more or less the same place they share a number.

In general the Germans did not differentiate between English, Scottish, Irish or Welsh soldiers and units, referring to them all as *Engländer*. However, so many Scottish soldiers were identified during the battles in French Flanders, that the German eyewitnesses sometimes drew a distinction and this is reflected in the text. With those exceptions, however, the word *Engländer* has been translated throughout as 'British' for all troops from the United Kingdom.

German time, which was one hour ahead of British time, is used throughout the book.

The German Army
on The Western Front 1915

CHAPTER 1

The Winter Battle in Champagne

When the war of movement metamorphosed into positional warfare at the end of the Battle for Ypres and Flanders in November 1914, the German incursion into Allied territory had taken the form of a huge salient, whose flanks were located in Artois and Champagne. The truly great battles, which dominated action on the Western Front throughout 1915, were centred, therefore, on massive French spring and autumn offensives in both regions. Their aim was simple and straightforward. They were intended to reduce the salient and to eject the invaders. Although conventionally regarded as a 1915 campaign, the winter fighting in Champagne was already underway before the turn of the year. An Order of the Day, signed by Joffre on 17 December 1914 and discovered later on the body of a fallen French officer read:

> "For the past three months, countless attacks of the heaviest nature have not enabled the enemy to break through our lines. Everywhere we have fended them off victoriously. The moment has now come when we reinforced both manpower and *materiel* to exploit the weakness they have shown. The hour of the offensive has struck. Once we have been able to hold the German forces in check we must move to break them and finally rid our country of these invaders. Soldiers! More than ever before France is counting on your courage, energy and will power to bring us victory – cost it what it may. You have already been victorious on the Marne and the Yser, in Lorraine and the Vosges. Now you will know only victory on your way to final triumph."[1]

Ever since the lines had solidified in Champagne weeks earlier, the forward regiments had been hard at work improving their positions, increasing their complexity, improving their dugouts and shelters and producing an obstacle belt. Along the VIII and VIII Reserve Corps fronts, as Christmas approached, the preparations were soon to be tested. Early indications of French plans were being picked up for several days in mid December. At nights there was a great deal of noise coming from the trenches, flares were fired regularly and there was a noticeable increase in patrol and artillery fire. Then, on 21 December, all doubts were cast aside as the artillery fire, which had been building for some time, rose to a crescendo and Reserve Infantry Regiment 133 of the Saxon 24th Reserve Division located to the north of St Hilaire-le-Grand on the eastern flank of XII Reserve Corps, was subject to a sharp attack which led to a break in of the forward positions.[2]

They did not remain there for long. An immediate counter-stroke was launched under the command of Hauptmann Götze of 5th Company and supported by engineers armed with hand grenades. After a short, sharp action large numbers of French soldiers (later estimated at approximately 300) of their 78th Regiment were killed and 178 were

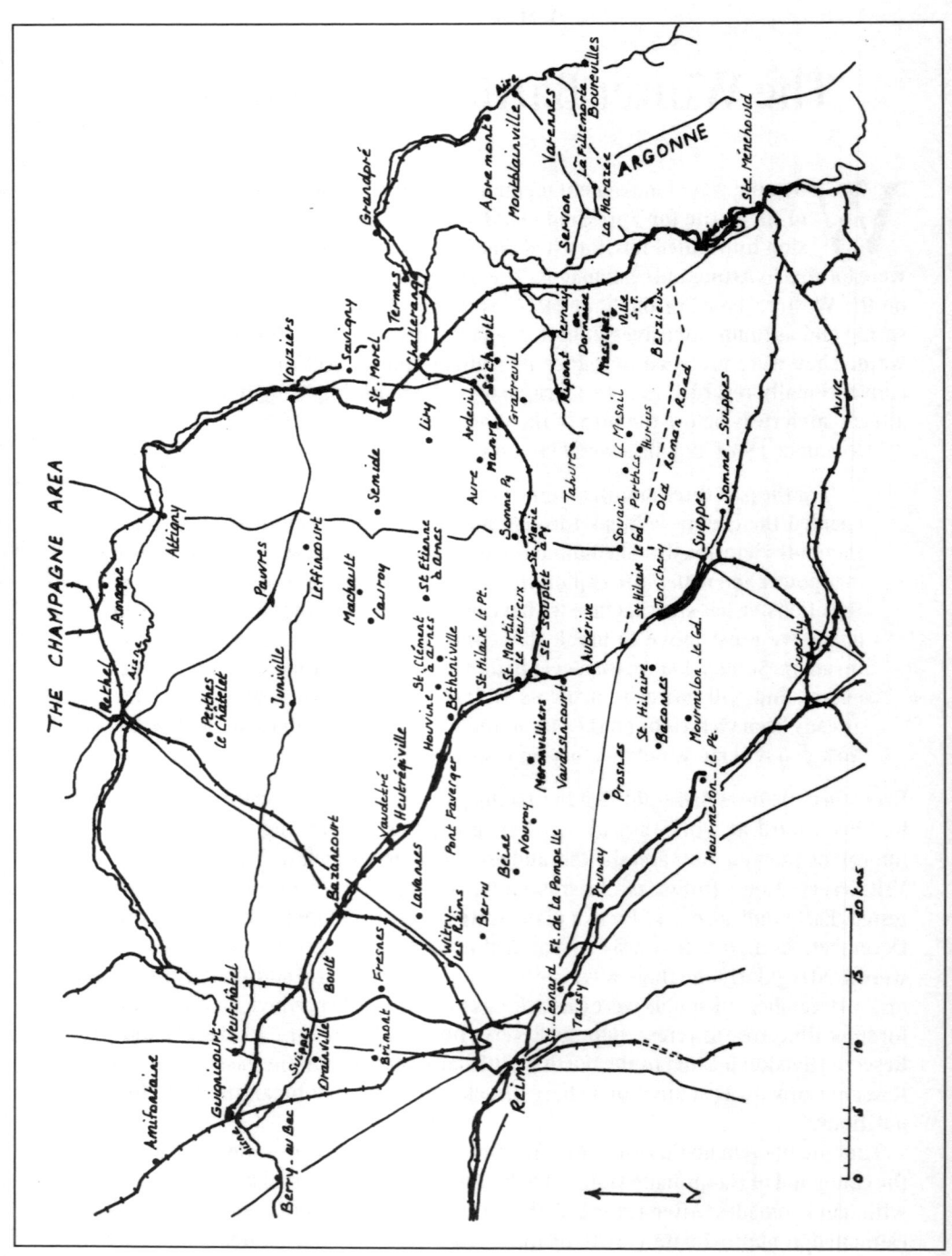

captured. This earned the regiment mentions in Corps Orders, the Army Communiqué for 22 December 1914 and a telegram of congratulation from King Friedrich August of Saxony.[3] There was also heavy fire for several hours that day all along the front, interspersed with numerous French thrusts, designed apparently to test the German defences. Immediately, plans for Christmas celebrations were put on hold. The forward troops were all placed on highest alert. With very few exceptions there was no possibility of thinning out the positions to permit company celebrations behind the lines or gathering for the church services, which were normally an important aspect of life for these God fearing troops. As a result, the padres found themselves under considerable pressure as they rushed around ministering to the forward troops wherever they could.

Pfarrer Zitzmann, Padre 24th Reserve Division[4]

"During the coming days I celebrated the feast of Christmas repeatedly. I had to make use of a car so that I could travel quickly enough from one body of troops to another. The finest scene was played out during a service on New Year's Eve. At 9.00 pm we gathered together, very close to the position held by Reserve Infantry Regiment 104; and, if I am not mistaken, men of Reserve Infantry Regiment 107 and Reserve Field Artillery Regiment 24, who came over from the nearby gun lines, were also present. Thick fog blanketed everything and I marvelled at the ability of our driver to pick his way through the shell holes so we were able at the cost of no more than muttered curses to reach the spot where the service was to take place in our old, worn out wagon.

"Here, too, the fog was so thick that I could only with great difficulty pick out the faces of the worshippers who were standing around, but the new harmonium was there to bind everything together. A shone hand torch helped with reading the music, which swelled powerfully out into the night: 'Direct Thou Thy Ways' and 'Now Thank we all Our God'. I had taken my text from [the Book of] Genesis [Chapter 16, Verse 8], where the angel of the Lord speaks to the weary Hagar by a well in the desert, 'Whence camest thou? and whither wilt thou go?' As the preacher, there was little to add. The recent past spoke for itself and we had to be ready for anything the near future might hold. We knew where we had come from and as for where were going, we should know soon enough. It would certainly be different from anything we had expected."

Skirmishing of varying levels of intensity continued during the next three weeks, as the French completed their plans and began to reinforce the attack sector and build up large stocks of ammunition and equipment. The planning phase was largely complete by mid January then, on the 19th, General Joffre directed the French Fourth Army to resume offensive operations by 12 February. This order was not easy to implement. The Fourth Army was still not in a strong position to do any such thing, the weather was bad and so its commander requested a further delay to complete preparations and the right to choose a period of relatively dry weather for the start of the operations. On 25 January its commander, General de Langle, of whom Joffre had a very favourable opinion, set his

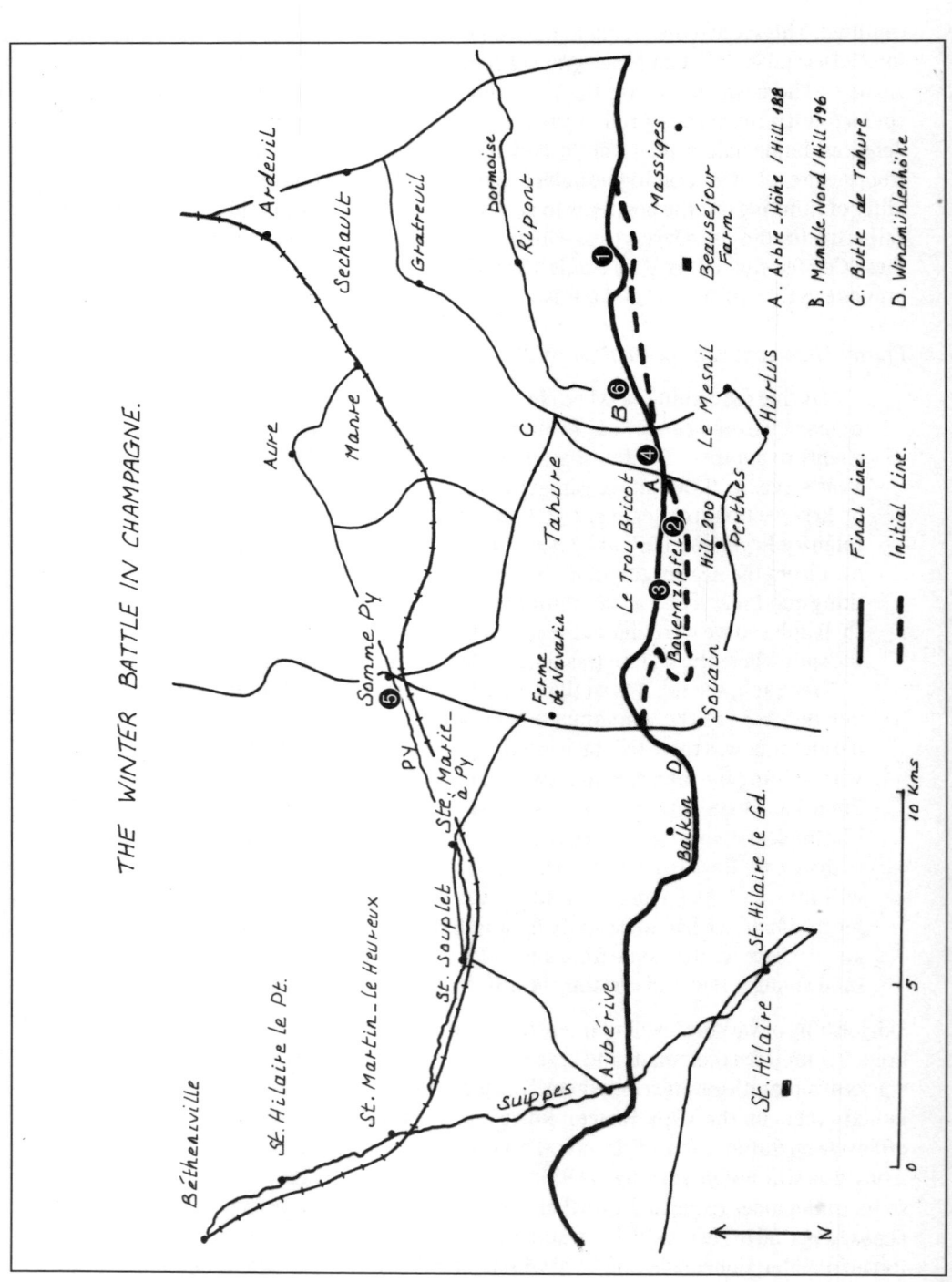

further thoughts down on paper, pointing out that, in a month of operations, lack of concerted effort had produced only localised successes restricted to the narrow thrusts on each of the corps' fronts. Instead he proposed a powerful blow on a wider front, with plentiful reserves on hand to exploit the resulting breach. Specifically his proposal was for a major effort primarily along a five kilometre front from Trou Bricot on the west via Hill 188 to Mamelle Nord.[5] 'Only once the enemy has evacuated their trenches between Souain and Perthes', wrote Langle, 'will we able to deploy onto the Butte de Souain [five kilometres west of Tahure] and directly threaten Somme-Py'.[6]

In the meantime on the German side, with fighting of varying intensity flaring up all along the line in this region, so as to camouflage preparations, everything possible was done to relieve formations which had suffered heavy casualties, to build up stocks of ammunition and to reinforce the existing artillery, with particular attention being paid to numbers of heavy guns.

Vizefeldwebel Haftmann 9th Company Reserve Infantry Regiment 107[7] **1.**

"Already on 28 January 1915 word arrived that our regiment was to be deployed to the east near Ripont, under command of VIII Reserve Corps. Extensive preparations were then carried out. There were inspections of the weapons, parades in marching order and all the platoons were reorganised. From 6.00 pm the 2nd Battalion was ready to move. All kinds of rumours were circulating concerning the situation around Ripont. It was said that heavy fighting was taking place as the French made huge efforts to break through, that the positions were almost non-existent and very badly constructed and the losses amongst the fighting troops were allegedly fantastically high. In particular, Reserve Infantry Regiment 104, our sister regiment, was reported to have suffered very heavy casualties. That was where fate was leading us as we set off at 7.45 am on 30 January 1915, heading for the fighting which military history would later record as the 'Winter Battles in Champagne'.

"Following badly worn roads in poor condition, we soon reached Ripont. From a long way off, we could tell by the thunder of the guns that things were hot here. In addition, the shell-damaged villages of Sainte Marie-à-Py, Somme-Py and Tahure bore witness to heavy days of fighting in the recent past. The billets which awaited us in Tahure were dismal: draughty, damp and cold. During the early hours of 1 February 3rd Battalion moved silently and full of nervous anticipation of the reality, which had been painted in such grim colours by the men of Reserve Infantry Regiment 104, onto the position by way of bottomless, muddy paths and across open country.

"In the order right to left of 12th, 9th, 10th and 11th Companies, we occupied the front line trenches, where our comrades of Reserve Infantry Regiment 104 waited longingly for our arrival, with weak forces, amounting to not more than one platoon per company. The relief took place smoothly and extremely swiftly, because the men we were relieving wanted to be able to turn their backs as quickly as possible on a place which had become Hell on earth for them. As it became light we saw with our own eyes that the situation was just as had been described to us. The trenches were so narrow and shallow that it was almost impossible to move about in them. The actual fire trenches so lacked depth that it was impossible to move about upright in them and the trench floors were one great morass of liquid mud, so we sank thirty centimetres deep into sticky, clinging slime. This made moving about very difficult and it was far from rare for boots to remain stuck in it.

"There were no dugouts or any form of protection against enemy artillery fire. The closest to shelter were a few modest structures in the reserve position a few hundred metres behind the front line, but it could not be said that they offered protection from either the weather or enemy fire. Some comprised a few rough planks with earth on top, others were just a groundsheet or a piece of corrugated iron supported by a few rifles placed across the trench. That was all there was between the men and enemy shells. It was a matter of sheer luck that the French lacked high angle howitzers in this sector and, because of the fact that the reserve positions were located on reverse slopes, they offered a certain amount of protection from low trajectory fire".

By mid February German total holdings of guns had reached almost 850, with more than one hundred of calibres over 100 mm, though not all these weapons were available in forward firing positions when the offensive began on 16 February. The two French corps most closely involved - I and XVII - had been reinforced by an infantry division from II Corps and the whole of I Cavalry Corps. The condition of the ground and the weather was, however, still extremely bad. There were shortages of every type of trench stores and the roads and tracks had suffered badly from the increased traffic, being reduced in many cases to one great sea of mud.

Despite the need to conserve stocks of artillery ammunition so as to have sufficient to support the forthcoming offensive, the forward positions were all kept under constant bombardment. When the regiments of 19th Reserve Division arrived to relieve the men of 1st Guards Infantry Division they discovered that gunfire had caused losses of fifteen to twenty five men per day in each of the forward battalions – a sobering thought.[8] Taking over the positions just to the north of Perthes, they found that the trenches were almost shot away and heard from their predecessors that for weeks there had been nothing but heavy bombardments, interspersed with infantry assaults on the dominating wooded Hill 200, 1,500 metres west of Perthes.

Reserve Hauptmann Wilhelm Kellinghusen Reserve Infantry Regiment 92[9] *2.*

"In the early morning of 5 February, Hauptmann Bangert[10] and we company commanders went forward to carry out a reconnaissance. Initially our route took us through a dense wood to the south of our camp, but this ended some 250 metres before the *Arbre-Höhe* [Lone Tree Hill – astride the Perthes – Tahure road]. From here the way forward was along a communication trench, which soon forked. The right hand branch led to the right flank of the regiment whilst, off to the left, was the sand pit to the north of Perthes. The trench was very muddy, shot up and so full of water at the lower end that we practically had to swim through it. Lost boots or soles of boots, together with miscellaneous pieces of equipment, were bobbing about in the water. We followed the right hand arm as far as the location of 1st Company on the right flank, with the aim of traversing the positions from right to left.

"The position presented a less than appealing appearance. Troops from the Rhineland who had fought the Christmas battles here had been relieved by the Guards at the beginning of January. During the month of January the French had bombarded the new positions on a daily basis and had also launched several infantry assaults, though the Guards had successfully beaten them off on each occasion. The Guards had suffered heavy casualties so that wherever we went through the position there were dead guardsmen, whom it had so far prove impossible to bury, lying in and behind the trenches. This was due to the fact that by day the trenches were under constant bombardment and each night had to be spent repairing them.

"Alongside the guardsmen were already some men from our 1st Battalion. Here and there body parts, or complete corpses, were sticking out of the walls of the trenches or shell holes. In the hell of this battle not even corpses were left to rest in peace. The situation was even worse in the middle in the 2nd Company position, because the bombardment had been heavier and the casualties higher. The trenches belonging to 3rd Company on the left, by the sandpit, had also been more or less flattened, but there had been fewer casualties than was the case in 2nd Company. The men in the companies made a rather depressing impression, because for days they had had to withstand drum fire of previously unparalleled intensity. They were encrusted with a thick layer of clay and chalk, whilst their hands, faces and uniforms were frequently stained yellow with the explosive fumes from the enemy shells".

Meanwhile French preparations continued at a rapid rate. In order to maximise the chances of success (and in agreement with Joffre), Commander Fourth Army had decided to launch several simultaneous thrusts against the German lines with the aim of breaking through on a fairly wide front. The main axis of advance was to be launched by I and XVII Corps along a corridor, now finally planned to be eight kilometres wide, between Beauséjour Farm and the woods to the west of Perthes. A subsidiary attack was also planned for 60th Reserve Division to the east of Souain. In order to camouflage the precise sector where the blow was scheduled to fall, increased artillery shoots were laid on by adjoining formations and the French Third Army received orders to press forward in the Argonne as and when it could.

For this renewed effort the Fourth French Army had amassed, '155,183 rifles, 7,999 sabres and 879 guns, 110 of them heavy'.[11] This provided the French with an overall two to one superiority in almost every category and although there had been considerable German reinforcement of the various positions, the initiative and, therefore, the ability to concentrate much greater force against short sectors of the front, conferred a distinct advantage on the French. Acting on intelligence reports, Supreme Army Headquarters signalled the German Third Army in Vouziers at 5.00 pm on 14 February, 'A general French offensive is expected on 15 February. Prayers will be said in French churches and the people have been called on to fast in support of it ... '[12] Despite this assessment, the whole of 15 February passed relatively quietly and certainly with no evidence of a major assault. However, this was nothing but a lull.

During the early morning of 16 February, shortly after morning stand to, an enormous weight of fire crashed down on the sectors of VIII and VIII Reserve Corps, all along a sixteen kilometre frontage line from Beauséjour Farm as far as Souain. It was perhaps fortunate that the weather was bad – raining and overcast – so aerial observation was not possible. Nevertheless, as the morning wore on, the bombardment was extended east and west of the main sector, to include the areas of adjacent defending divisions and so camouflage further the width of the attack frontage. During a two hour period of intense fire, trenches were flattened, obstacles swept away and German casualties began to mount. According to a member of 3rd Battalion Reserve Infantry Regiment 74 of 39 Reserve Infantry Brigade, located on the left flank of 19th Reserve Division just to the north of Perthes, 3.

> "Suddenly – it must have been 9.00 am – the storm broke out. Had the Gates of Hell opened? An insane rate of concentrated fire began to come down on our trenches. We were literally covered in masses of earth and showered with red hot glowing iron splinters. It was, as we later discovered, the first example of drum fire of the entire war. All we could do was to remain there helpless and let it wash over us. There was never a fraction of a second without the noise of gunfire or the crash of an exploding shell. In amongst all this great mortar rounds landed on or around our trenches, but nobody paid them any heed. Pressed hard against the walls of the trench or cowering on the ground, white faced and tense, we awaited death. Not one of us believed we should ever escape unscathed from this Hell. Over there one comrade cried out, threw his arms in the air and collapsed. Here another sank silently to the ground as a shell splinter a quarter of a metre long pierced his helmet and split his skull open. A third, drenched in his own blood, shrieked, 'Help, help mother, mother!' and his cries blended terribly with the raging fury all around.
>
> "Our faces were contorted in agony. When would I be hit? This was the only question which occupied us and our thoughts turned swiftly to home, wife and child; father and mother – but these did not last, because it would all be over soon. There was simply no way out. Minutes went by; we did not know how long. We had abandoned hope of life, so what was time to us?" [13]

Finally, at about 10.00 am, in accordance with a well coordinated plan, the fire lifted abruptly onto the trenches and approach routes in rear of the forward defenders. 19th and 16th Reserve Divisions then found themselves under attack by the French I and

XVII Corps respectively. In order to facilitate the advance, mines were exploded under the forward trenches of 39 Reserve Brigade, the right forward [western] brigade of 19th Reserve Division. The report of Reserve Infantry Regiment 74 continues:

"All of a sudden there was a dull roar. The earth upon which we were standing quaked. We were thrown in the air then fell back down with a thud. Sandbags from the barricades rained down on us and the walls of the trenches collapsed. To our left, barely one hundred metres away, a huge fountain of earth was projected into the air before falling back down to ground with a crash and burying everything around it. "But what was that? Human voices? Yes, the sound fell faintly, but clearly, in our ears. '*Urrah, Urrah*'! With their long bayonets fixed, they came running at us, ''*Urrah, Urrah*'!

"Everything now occurred in a split second blur. Forgotten was our fear of death and feelings of hopelessness simply seemed to blow away. Rifle to shoulder and – bang! The closest Bluecoat fell then next to him another; more and more of them as they got closer Flashes and the crash of shots came from all along our smashed trench line. Already they were hesitating over there and throwing themselves flat to the ground. Whoever raised his head provoked a storm of fire. We were now not under artillery fire. They assumed over there that we had long since been dealt with and overrun. We used this breathing space to free our legs from the soil which had buried them. We then scrabbled around feverishly in the loose soil for sandbags which we threw up hastily in front of us. Taking cover behind them we waited to see if the French would renew their attack.

"This was the situation at one point of our position, i.e. the extreme right flank of 10th Company, but what was happening to the other companies? The 9th Company was more or less intact and it had cleared the position on the right. It had not come under direct frontal assault. Mines had gone off on the left flank of 10th Company. The entire 3rd Platoon was blown sky high and hardly anyone survived. The great fountains of earth, one hundred metres from us, had buried them deeply. Instead of a trench there was now a great mine crater, into which the French were flooding. No resistance was being put up. Further to the left, Trenches III and IV were partly blown up, partly completely flattened. The men of 11th and 12th Companies who had been manning them were completely rubbed out, right to the last man.

"Nobody returned. Most were killed; their bodies torn apart beyond recognition. The tiny remainder, wounded but still alive, fell into the hands of the enemy after putting up a desperate defence. Amongst them was Leutnant Roth, officer commanding 11th Company. He was a forester by trade and an outstanding shot. Despite a serious leg wound, he remained on his feet, firing and firing until he was completely surrounded. Eventually his smoking rifle had to be ripped out of his hands. But all this courage was in vain. For the time being the position was lost."[14]

Anticipating the risk of such thrusts, the commander of 19th Reserve Division, General der Infanterie von Bahrfeldt, ordered energetic counter-strokes by his reserves. This was almost completely successful in the forward area of 31 Reserve Brigade, where the original front line was almost fully restored by nightfall; but north and west of Perthes, in the left forward brigade sector, this was not possible and a savage close quarter battle, which lasted a full seventy two hours, began.

As always on such occasions, the reaction from the chain of command was swift and very soon reserves and counter-attack forces were being deployed all along the attack sector. Until the previous evening 1st Battalion Reserve Infantry Regiment 92 had been in the line, but had been relieved and was looking forward to a two day break. The commander of 4th Company found himself at Regimental Headquarters and about to discuss some routine matters with the commander.

Reserve Hauptmann Wilhelm Kellinghusen 4th Company Reserve Infantry Regiment 92[15] *2.*

"I was just about to deliver a briefing when he [the commander] received a telephone call, informing him that the French had tunnelled beneath the positions of Reserve Infantry Regiment 74 on *Arbre-Höhe* and blown them sky high. Simultaneously they had launched attacks against the 74th and our regiment. Reserve Infantry Regiment 74 had lost two company positions whilst, in our sector, our outpost line on *Arbre-Höhe* had been overrun and [the enemy] had broken into the *Sandgrube* [Sand Pit] position. [Furthermore] it was said that the French had captured the entire Sand Pit Position and had already reached the hill to the north of the Sand Pit, which was an extension of our main defensive line on *Arbre-Höhe*. At that Bangert's [i.e. 4th] Battalion was stood to and despatched forward.

"My company was in the lead. Leutnant Heinemeyer was even more pleased than ever before and was once again his old enthusiastic, happy self. Towards midday, when we emerged from the woods north of *Arbre-Höhe* where the communications trenches began, I was ordered to assault and recapture the position of the Sand Pit company north of Perthes. I moved my company under heavy artillery fire – the shells were whistling just over our heads – behind a small hillock, just in front of *Arbre-Höhe* as far as a track which led from the bivouac site to Perthes and which became a sunken road in front of the Sand Pit. This way I was able to pick my way forward to the enemy out of sight. In fact we got to within two hundred metres of them completely unseen. They were already dug in on our Main Defensive Position II on the hill north of the Sand Pit.

"Together with Leutnant Heinemeyer, I went a bit further forward, so that we could obtain a good overview of the situation. I then ordered Heinemeyer to take his One Platoon to the right (west) of the track and to form up for the assault in a short section of trench. I myself would lead Two Platoon left (east) until we drew level, then, on my signal, we would attack simultaneously. For the time being Three Platoon was to remain under cover along the line of the track until further orders then was to be ready, if necessary, to launch an independent attack. Once the platoons had formed up along the start line, I raised my small spade, which I always carried in the attack, then gave the time honoured signal for the attack, just as once General Seydlitz had done with his pipe during the wars of Frederick the Great. With rifles sloped and shouts of *Hurra!* we doubled up the hill towards the French infantry.

"No sooner had the French spotted us than their artillery brought down a wall of shell fire between us and their own infantry. This defensive fire covered almost every square metre, but we did not allow it to stop us. Instead we charged on determinedly through the shelling, though a number of brave lads were torn from us by the fire. One man, storming forward about half a metre from me, was decapitated, sending two great gouts of blood up from his carotid arteries. At this, Unteroffizier Senger, attacking on the far side of the dead man, cast a worried look in my direction. I received a very small splinter from the same shell in my left upper arm, but it gave me an enormous blow as though I had been hit by a heavy sledgehammer. The assault went on.

"Suddenly I heard a different battery opening up on the enemy and realised from the howl of the shells that we were just about to run into the impact area. I made a decisive move backwards, taking those nearest to me along and, sure enough, the shells landed right where we had been. If we had not pulled back we should have right in amongst where they landed. Then we quickly doubled forward once more. Again and again shells impacted left and right of us but, by good fortune, we got through and closed up on the enemy. At the last minute the French leapt up out of their trenches, weapons in hand and ran towards us, as though they were trying to carryout a counter-stroke.

"This even caused a few of us to hesitate, but that lasted only a few seconds because the French threw away their weapons and came towards us with their hands up, begging for mercy and shouting, *Je suis marié, Je suis marié* [I am married]. They then passed through our ranks and made their way towards the rear. In so doing they were forced to move through their own defensive fire, which left some of them sprawled by the roadside. With that the hilltop position north of the Sand Pit was in our hands but, down below in the Sand Pit itself, the position was still occupied by the enemy. Our two platoons then set about launching a second assault against this position and, by 2.00 pm, it was firmly in our hands once more. By then about 150 Frenchmen had been captured.

"Unfortunately losses that day were very high. About half of [the men of] the two platoons fell victim to the defensive fire of the enemy artillery. Just as we launched the second assault against the Sand Pit and Leutnant Heinemeyer leapt into the trench just ahead of me he was shot twice in the stomach by rifle fire from the right coming from a trench out on a flank. Severely wounded, he collapsed in the trench. Unteroffizier Graf, a member of his platoon, administered first aid and, on my orders, remained with him until evening. I received a terrible shock when I saw him lying there in the trench. Initially I hoped that his wounds would not prove to be too severe and that he would survive and to begin with he was most cheerful, so I was able to devote my entire attention to my duties as company commander.[16]

"Unfortunately we could not move him to the rear by day because, although we were not under very much fire in our forward positions, the artillery continued to come down throughout the afternoon on the hill to our rear. Apparently the artillery observers must have been on the hill and were captured along with the infantry, so the enemy guns had to fire without direction for the remainder of the day. It is also possible that the fire was directed in rear of us to prevent reinforcements from being moved in to the Sand Pit and so make it easier to drive us away by means of a further concentrated attack. The remainder of the Sand Pit position to the right of the actual Sand Pit and the flanking trench were still densely occupied by the enemy. We attempted to attack for a third time over the top to capture these positions, but it was not possible for us because, as soon as one of us appeared out of the trench, he immediately came under rifle and machine gun fire. It was obvious to me that there was no point in trying to continue in that way.

"In the meantime, moving along the track, either side of which we had originally attacked, came, first, reinforcements from 12th Company and, later, from 8th Company. Just as I was discussing with the company commander of 12th Company how we might recapture the remainder of the position, against all expectations a lucky chance came to our assistance. Some men of 12th Company had come across a Frenchman in a short sap which led down from the Flanking Trench to the Sand Pit. He was sent back by us with orders to return with his comrades as prisoners. To begin with he did not want to but, finally, he went and returned with five others, who were immediately despatched to the rear, so as to get clear of the danger zone. I held on to the last man and told him that he was to go and fetch more prisoners.

"This one took longer to return. We could hear the French debate the matter then he arrived with about twenty Frenchmen. Once again I kept the last man back and told him to round up the rest of his comrades. He refused, however, saying, *Je ne comprends pas* [I do not understand]. At that I placed my pistol on his chest and said, *Quoi donc? Tu ne comprends pas? Tu sera tiré tout à l'heure, si tu n'apporteras pas aussitôt tes comrades pour prisonniers.* [How come? You say you do not understand? You will be shot at once, unless you bring in your comrades as prisoners immediately.] The result was striking, because he was quick to assure me, 'Yes Sir, I understand'. At that he ran back swiftly and brought in, literally, every one of the Frenchmen, including a lieutenant, who were occupying the Flanking Trench. Altogether we rounded up between seventy and eighty men from this trench and were able to reoccupy it without incurring any further casualties.

"There remained only the right half of the main position which abutted the French position and was separated from them only by a wall of sandbags. The French located there were unwilling to surrender. Demands to do so went unanswered and, whenever we showed ourselves, we were shot at. We attempted to drive them back from firing bay to firing bay with rifle and bayonet, but that did not work. They had erected successive sandbag barricades at each traverse and opened fire at us from good cover each time. In the process we lost several excellent men and one particularly good NCO – Unteroffizier Göbel who, in attempting to drive the French back, was bayoneted in the nose and chest and then wounded by a shot which killed him. At another time one bullet killed two of our comrades who were standing one behind the other and were both shot through the head.

"The only thing left was to launch a hand grenade attack, so we sent to the rear for supplies. Half an hour later we had twelve of them. These were thrown by a young kriegsfreiwilliger, Diedrich Pähr from Aurich. With his long arms he was able to throw them from one traverse to beyond the next, which meant that he himself was never in danger. The effect was absolutely superb. The first grenade fizzed over behind the next barricade which concealed eight Frenchmen. An instant later came load shouts and shrieks from the Frenchmen and two of them suddenly appeared on our side. The other retreated to another sandbag wall in another traverse. We followed up quickly and a second hand grenade whizzed over. This produced the same effect as the earlier one. In this way we pushed the French back from traverse to traverse , capturing them and taking more and more of them prisoner.

"Finally we came across some rifle grenades on the position and fired these at the French. Because the range was much greater than for hand grenades, we were able to threaten the Frenchmen who were located much more to the rear and the effect of bursting rifle grenades was a lot greater than that of hand grenades. Very soon we had recaptured our entire position, including the old sandbag filling point, which was where our position met the old French one. At this point a number of Frenchmen, who had been under cover, in our position or near our barbed wire, surrendered. Altogether we now had about a further fifty prisoners. So, at about 4.00 pm, the whole of our old position was back in our hands.

"About eighty Frenchman had pulled back into their old Second Position and I did not want to let them escape either. Together with twenty to twenty five men, Leutnant Richard Fressel, commanding 12th Company, Leutnant Ummen of 8th Company and I pushed our way into this trench. To start with the French fired at us but, once we had closed to twenty metres and shouted *Hurra!* as we charged, they put their arms up as one and gave themselves up as prisoners. They also had a lieutenant with them. It took a whole section of our men to conduct them to the rear. I wanted to push on with about two sections into *Arbre-Wood* and from there force a way into the old enemy First Position ... To that end, I requested reinforcements from battalion and sent word to the two companies on our main position on *Arbre-Höhe*, so that they would be informed about my intentions.

"I informed them that we would begin our assault by shouting *Hurra!* and that, when they heard us, they should launch frontal bayonet charge at the enemy. Sadly, despite the fact that it could have been laid on easily, nothing came of this plan. On the one hand I received no reinforcements from battalion and the garrison of the Sand Pit was so weakened that we could not withdraw any manpower from it; on the other the cooperation of the two companies on *Arbre-Höhe* was not forthcoming because my message did not get through to them. Nevertheless I attempted it with just two sections, but we could not get further forward than the wood edge. At that point the French were reinforced from Position III, so a further advance with so few men would have been folly; it would have been too easy for the reinforced French to surround the wood and capture us all.

"Despite the fact that it was hard on us after our victories to do so, we pulled back to our trenches, taking as many French arms from their trenches as we could carry and smashing the remainder in half. Amongst other items we took a machine gun and a grenade launcher. We had already captured a second French machine gun. Just as it was going dark, we captured a French sergeant major, who had been hiding in a shell hole in front of our opposition and who was carrying a strong box containing 550 francs in gold."

This vigorous counter-action by Bangert's company commanders had led to the capture of no fewer than three hundred French prisoners but, despite the local success, the overall position was still precarious in the extreme. Over on the right [western] flank of Reserve Infantry Regiment 92 the fight for *Arbre-Höhe* went on more or less continuously. Once word reached the regimental commander at about 1.30 pm of its loss, 6th Company was immediately tasked with its recapture. Taking under command three sections of 8th Company Reserve Infantry Regiment 74, commanded by an offizierstellvertreter, Leutnant Walsemann set about carrying out the necessary assault. Even with the extra men, such had been the earlier losses that he only had about fifty riflemen at his disposal. Despite this, the small group lunched a virtually suicidal attack. No sooner had they broken cover than they came under fire frontally, not only from *Arbre-Höhe*, but also from flanking machine gun fire. One by one, the assaulting troops were hit and fell dead or wounded to the ground. The offizierstellvertreter from Reserve Infantry Regiment 74 was hit in the head, followed a short time later by Leutnant Walsemann, who also collapsed with a head wound. At that the entire impetus drained away from the attack. Only eight men returned unscathed, a harsh lesson in the consequences of launching hasty, ill-prepared attacks against dug in defences.

Despite this, the recapture of *Arbre-Höhe* was being seen as a matter of honour, so the commander ordered a repetition at 3.30 pm, this time by elements of 6th and 9th Companies under Leutnant Kortejohann. This attack was once more hit by French small arms fire, but also ran into problems from ill directed German artillery fire. Amazing to relate, Kortejohann and about twenty men succeeded in closing right up on the French positions before he was mortally wounded and once again the attack failed. This time a mere ten men returned; the majority were missing, believed killed.[17] As soon as elements of Reserve Infantry Regiment 29 arrived to take over the task of reserve for Reserve Infantry Regiment 92, 11th Company, under Leutnant Brinkard, was also sent forward, together with platoons from 5th and 6th Companies and deployed.

A party commanded by Leutnant Henze of 9th Company worked its way forward along a series of smashed trenches until it closed right up to the French positions then, at about 4.00pm, a fresh assault, commanded by Leutnant Scharnhorst of 10th Company, and with the participation of elements of three other companies as well as his own was launched. Once again poor shooting by the German guns led to heavy casualties and the attack petered out with nothing to show for it but a depressing increase in casualties, amongst them, Leutnants Barthel and Schumann killed and Leutnant Reuter of 10th Company missing. Profiting from these successive failures, the French launched an attack of their own against Reserve Infantry Regiment 74 at about 5.00 pm. Reserve Infantry Regiment 92 brought down flanking fire against this thrust as best it could, but the French attack brought it once more as far as the Second Position and in a position to pose a distinct threat to the flank of Reserve Infantry Regiment 92.

Wehrmann Rohlje 8th Company Reserve Infantry Regiment 92 [18] **2.**

> "We looked out over the bank behind which we were sheltering and there we saw the Frenchmen, who were already almost level with us and heading towards the *Sandgrube* and our 2nd Company. We poured fire into them; some of the men jumping up into the open to engage them from a standing position. There were shouts of, 'Calm down and aim properly!' This bore immediate fruit; we had long ago learned not to squander our ammunition and we brought down one Frenchman after another."

Darkness fell, but the battle continued. Three companies of Reserve Infantry Regiment 29 were sent up into the line to relieve men of 2nd and 3rd Battalions of Reserve Infantry Regiment 92, 150 of whom were concentrated into an attack force which had yet another attempt at *Arbre-Höhe* at 8.30 pm. This attack was pressed with great determination but, well equipped with flares and well laid machine guns, the French defenders beat off this attack, though not before there had been hand to hand fighting and grenade battles in some places. Such were the demands of this battle that Commander VIII Corps, General der Infanterie Riemann, was forced to feed in two complete regiments and numerous smaller reinforcing units from the neighbouring 15th Infantry Division in an effort to contain the crisis. Assessing that this particular battle was unprecedented in both its scale and intensity, he pressed Third Army to despatch substantial reinforcements forward.

Time passed, there were sporadic bursts of fire as clashes took place in the dark then, towards 11.00 pm, yet another attack, this time commanded by Hauptmann Larenz and with three companies of Reserve Infantry Regiment 29 under command was directed at restoring the front line of Reserve Infantry Regiment 74. A communications trench, which marked the boundary between the two sectors, was used as a forming up point but it became clear, as the moment for the assault approached, that the enemy were occupying different positions, so the attack was cancelled, but not before the company on the right flank has suffered heavy casualties from flanking fire. Even this problem did not put an end to the aggressive policy of commander Reserve Infantry Regiment 92 and Major Dziobek gave out orders at 2.30 am on 17 February for a fresh attempt on *Arbre-Höhe* to be made at 3.30 am.

Bearing in mind that this was a night attack against an alert enemy, the plan was overcomplicated. Leutnant Henze, with his own platoon from 12th Company, reinforced by a platoon of 5th Company Reserve Infantry Regiment 29 and supported by engineers carrying grenades, was to advance on the right. One platoon from 4th Company Reserve Infantry Regiment 92 was to attack frontally, whilst Leutnant Schumacher's platoon from 11th Company had the task of advancing on the left. The composition of the assault force makes it clear that this was cobbled together from whatever resources Dziobek could lay his hands on. Command and control of these disparate elements was going to be very problematic and the chances of success were slim before the attack even began.

In the event, both Schumacher and Henze got to within a few metres of the enemy position before their attacks withered away in intense small arms fire and enemy hand grenades. Casualties, including Schumacher killed outright, were very high. This was still not the end of the attempts. At 5.30 am, Leutnant Peitz of 5th Company led yet another attack on *Arbre-Höhe*, was mortally wounded and died the next day. Six hasty attacks had achieved nothing but huge casualties. The French remained in command of this key feature, Reserve Infantry Regiment 92 was so worn down that it was hard pressed to hold on forward for a further forty eight hours before relief. It is hard to escape the conclusion that a bit more thought and careful preparation might have led to a single, coordinated, counter-attack with more prospect of success.

In the 16th Reserve Division sector, Generalleutnant von Altrock, who had only been with the Division since the beginning of January, when he received the promotion in recognition of his skilful handling of 60 Infantry Brigade during the battles around Ypres the previous autumn, was confronted by assaults directed primarily against his centre and left [eastern] flank. This led to several separate breaks into his lines. Nevertheless, during the course of the afternoon of 16 February, all were closed, with the exception of a so-called 'Frenchman's Nest', right in the centre of his front. One member of Reserve Infantry Regiment 107 located on the far left flank later wrote a detailed description of the events of the day.

Vizefeldwebel Haftmann 9th Company Reserve Infantry Regiment 107[19] **1.**

"During the early hours of 16 February I had the task of taking half of Three Platoon forward to relieve some of our comrades in the front line. Just before I set off I was ordered to report to the commanding officer, Major Roth, who shook my hand in a comradely manner and stated that he was pleased to see that I should be in the front line because, according to French deserters, who had brought the news, a strong French attack was to be expected. Even the relief was more difficult than normal, because artillery fore was coming down on the approach trenches, *Schanzzeug-Graben* and *Stobbe-Graben* ...

"There was hardly time to post sentries and for me to give my orders for the expected attack than the enemy artillery began to bring well directed fire down on our trenches ... and, by 8.30 am the entire position was one single mass of crashing and whirring [shell fire]. How it howled, cracked, flashed, roared, screamed and hammered. Fuzes whistled through the air and embedded themselves in the mud and filth nearby. We had never known such a hellish situation ... We all longed for this hail of iron to stop and for the infantry assault to begin ... It must have been about 9.30 am when we observed signals being given with red flags in the French trenches. The artillery fire was lifted more to the rear and hundreds of enemy soldiers emerged from their trenches. In great masses, bayonets fixed, they charged towards our positions.

"The first man to climb out of the right hand sap, directly opposite my men, was a French officer, signal flag in hand. Other soldiers followed him rapidly. Apparently they believed that they would only encounter weak resistance. How disappointed they must have been, therefore, to find German bullets whistling past their ears. We did not greet the enemy with rapid fire; rather with well aimed individual rifle fire. Every shot hit its mark. Not a single man reached our lines, though the distance was only twenty to thirty metres. Enemy corpses piled up in front of the sap and acted as a warning to those who were to follow. Instead they tried to drive us out of the trench by sending over 'twittering robins'.[20]

"Because lack of troops meant that the left hand sector of our company position could not be defended, the enemy soon broke in there. However we did not allow them any time to get established. Assisted by a few men and home made hand grenades, without waiting for reinforcements I began immediately to clear along the trench. Soldat Albert Müller II and Unteroffiziers Zinke and Ballschuh particularly distinguished themselves and, within a short time, the whole of the 9th Company position was completely in my hands once more. I captured seven unwounded prisoners. Other enemy elements escaped in the left hand sector into the trenches of 10th Company. Initially they had a tight grip there. They secured their flank to us by means of the erection of a substantial sandbag barrier, greeting us with rapid rifle fire and, initially, preventing us from advancing further ...

"The runner, whom I sent back immediately the enemy attack began, was caught by enemy artillery fire coming down on *Schanzzeug-Graben*. Shell shocked, he could not make himself understood, so the wait for reinforcements was prolonged, but we were filled with joy when Leutnant Bornmüller arrived with the remainder of Three Platoon and elements of One and Two Platoons. It was not before time. We were already under fire from three sides and it was all we could do to save our skins. Gradually, however, the company reserves succeeded in driving them back to the trenches of 10th and 11th Companies. A general attack to recapture these trenches was ordered for 4.00 pm. 9th and 11th Companies were to launch flanking attacks from their trenches, whilst the company reserve was to attack frontally from the rear trenches.

"Because not all the preparations for this attack could be completed in time, it was postponed until 5.00 pm. I was ordered, together with my Three Platoon (Leutnant Bornmüller, the previous platoon commander, had, in the meantime, been wounded), to attack the barricade between 9th and 10th Companies. A shout from us telling them to surrender was replied to with rifle shots. From then on we engaged the barricade with rapid fire and, under cover of the fire, we readied ourselves for the assault. Watch in hand and sitting amongst dead and wounded, I waited with my men for the ordered time. Suddenly it was 5.00 pm! A quick look confirmed that the reserves had climbed out of their trench and were running into the attack over the top, led by Leutnant Behr.

"With shouts of *Hurra!* and the throwing of grenades over the obstacle, we had soon closed up to it. Follow-up troops tore it down in short order. Horror-struck and totally demoralised by the effect of our grenades, the French cowered behind the barricade and ceased to defend themselves. There was an instant response to my shout of 'Hands up!' Some of the French nevertheless rushed off down the communications trenches, pursued by our rifle bullets. About fifteen prisoners remained in my hands. The entire position of 3rd Battalion was completely recaptured in the concentric attack.

The situation was much the same on the front of Reserve Infantry Regiment 65 and Infantry Regiment 157. At about 11.30 am 16 February, an extremely concentrated assault on a frontage of only 150 metres saw French incursions into the sectors of 2nd and 8th Companies. However a two company immediate counter-stroke enjoyed complete success. The whole position was soon firmly back in German hands and thirty French prisoners were making their way to the rear. Despite heavy artillery fire, which continued to come down throughout the afternoon, the regiment rushed a further five reserve companies forward. The reinforcement was in place none too soon because, at about 6.00 pm, the artillery fire lifted to the rear and two strong French assault columns attacked. Once again there were break ins and Hauptmann Brieger, the local commander, was forced to pull back to the Second Position, having suffered heavy losses. Attempting to inspire his men, he stood up on the parapet of the trench to direct the fire of his men and fell, mortally wounded in the head.[21] Hauptmann Ritter was on hand to take over and Hauptmann Engelien arrived on the scene with two companies of reinforcements. Reserve Infantry Regiment 65, noting what was happening, also despatched three reserve companies to assist and participate in another immediate counter-stroke. 12th Company Infantry Regiment 157 managed to recapture a section of trench, but the Reserve Infantry Regiment 65 attack was swiftly in trouble. Two of the company commanders fell, one killed, the other seriously wounded and the attack stalled. The survivors were rallied by Hauptmann Engelien and, because this stabilised the situation to some extent, Major Mund, Commander of Infantry Regiment 157, decided to launch a planned counter-attack with all his remaining reserves as dawn broke on 17 February. Commanded by Hauptmann Engelien, this was completely successful and two hundred French prisoners were taken.

Although Mund had managed his slim resources carefully, relieving the worst hit forward units during the morning, the constant fighting and the total lack of hot food and water for more than forty eight hours had exhausted his men. As a result, after yet another heavy bombardment during the afternoon and a repeated French attack at about 3.45 pm, a combination of general exhaustion and heavy suppressive fire meant that it was impossible to react immediately and the French had time to barricade themselves into their newly won trenches. Nevertheless, drawing on the assistance of three companies of Reserve Infantry Regiment 65 under Oberstleutnant Meersmann and two others of Reserve Infantry Regiment 68 under Major Hiepe, Major Guhr launched yet another attack after a short bombardment at 11.45 pm.

Thoroughly alert, the French defended themselves vigorously and progress was extremely slow and costly. After three hours of close quarter battle with severe casualties on either side, including Hauptmann Brünner and Hauptmann Reinhold of Infantry Regiment 157, most of the lost trenches had been recaptured. However, at that moment, extremely concerned about the weak state of Infantry Regiment 157, 16th Reserve Division, directed that it was to be relieved immediately by the newly arrived Infantry Regiment 30 of 34th Infantry Division. Further attacks were immediately suspended but, so great was the confusion, that forward elements could not be relieved for several hours. When the survivors eventually rallied at Ripont Mill they presented a sorry sight. Hats were missing, uniforms and equipment in shreds and many were barefoot, having lost their boots in the mud. Well over two hundred had been killed[22] and more than four hundred wounded. Initially there were a great many missing and though stragglers continued to rejoin for some time subsequently, the ultimate figure was still in excess of two hundred.

Occupying the left forward [eastern] flank of the 16th Reserve Division sector was the Saxon Reserve Infantry Regiment 107. It had been heavily engaged, but with not quite the same intensity as the regiments at the inter-divisional boundary, so it was able for the time being to remain in position and conduct internal reliefs of the most hard pressed sub units.

Vizefeldwebel Haftmann 9th Company Reserve Infantry Regiment 107[23] **1.**

"At 6.00 am we conducted internal reliefs within the company, but the French granted us no rest. If we had believed that we should be allowed some well earned sleep, we had not taken the enemy into consideration. Between 8.00 and 9.00 am a heavy barrage came down once more. Both sides fired as fast as they could load their guns. The French increased their rate of fire minute by minute until the fine detail of events was lost in one great torrent of hissing, spitting and roaring – drum fire! Between 9.00 and 10.00 am we received a report that the enemy was attacking our front line yet again. At the same time I was ordered, together with my third platoon, to advance in support. Swiftly, my much reduced little group was assembled and off we went along the *Schanzzeug-Graben* through the swirling dust and smoke and into the crazy confusion of fire, iron and flying clods of earth and ear-splitting racket.

"Greeted heartily at the front by Leutnant Schwarze, we experienced the exact same situation as we had the previous day. The sole difference was that this time the French had also captured the 9th Company position, with the exception of a few nests of resistance, and had barricaded themselves into our trench. An immediate attack was ordered and I was entrusted with its leadership. We soon spotted that the enemy had deployed fresh troops for this attack. They had attacked with great élan but, initially, had enjoyed only slight success, which they were defending fiercely. Nevertheless, we succeeded during a battle, which we conducted, first with grenades and then hand to hand and which went on for several hours, in forcing the French troops who had broken in back hard against the left flank, where it was only a matter of throwing a final heavy shower of grenades before what was left of the trench garrison threw away their weapons and surrendered to us, with their arms in the air. Large numbers of prisoners could be led away.

"Unfortunately six of my best men paid for this victory with their lives and ten wounded increased the number of casualties. At the same time, the adjacent trenches, belonging to 10th and 11th Companies, were recaptured by 7th Company under Hauptmann Holthausen and the remainder of 12th Company led by Leutnant Behr. On 18 February 9th Company was relieved by the 8th. Beause of the heavy losses the 9th Company had to be reorganised into two platoons. Leutnant Schwarze took over the first and I the second.

"The artillery battle continued in undiminished strength throughout the day, rising to drum fire in the afternoon. Wild rumours flew around that the front line trenches had been abandoned, so I was sent forward to reconnoitre and was able to report that the men of 12th Company were holding their positions firmly, but that in the trenches of 9th Company, which had formerly been held by 8th Company, only three men were still alive. Later, a report arrived stating that the enemy had once more forced their way into our trenches. Reserves which were despatched forward at once found that they were, in fact, deserted and they occupied them. The attack had been nipped in the bud by our courageous artillery, in particular by the 210 mm heavy howitzers".

Very early on in the attacks, numerous French prisoners were captured; initial interrogation confirming that not only had the attack involved the entire French I Corps, but that strong reserves were also at readiness a tactical bound to the south. In response, VIII Reserve Corps directed two resting reserve regiments in the corps rear area to be ready to move at 7.00 am on 17 February, which, some noted grimly, was Ash Wednesday. Reporting up the chain of command, its commander, Generalleutnant Fleck, assessed the situation as serious and requested reinforcement.

Responding with commendable speed, Supreme Army Headquarters released large quantities of ammunition to Third Army and directed Fifth Army to despatch an improvised brigade with artillery support down to the battle area. Built up around Infantry Regiment 144 and a battalion of guns from Reserve Field Artillery Regiment 20, this force was soon assembled and on the move. Once it arrived in the forward area, it came under the command of Headquarters 38 Reserve Infantry Brigade. Simultaneously, Headquarters XII Corps, deployed to the west of the main thrust, was ordered to launch a feint attack in an attempt to draw forces away from the VIII Corps sector and, in addition, warning orders shortening notice to move were sent to several other formations.

None of these measures had a pronounced effect on the battlefield in the short term, 17 February being marked, as has been described, by a renewal in undiminished strength of the attack between Perthes and Beauséjour Farm. Despite being hard pressed, the defence managed to hold these latest assaults, though there continued to be local successes on the *Arbre-Höhe*, which was still being defended by sub units of Reserve Infantry Regiment 92. Increasingly concerned about the turn of events, the Army Commander, Generaloberst von Einem,[24] concentrated every available reserve behind the threatened front. The *ad hoc* 38 Reserve Brigade was subordinated to VIII Corps and despatched to a holding area between Somme-Py and Tahure, whilst an infantry regiment furnished by VI Corps moved under command of the same corps and was sent to cover the corps right [western] flank near the village of Ste Marie à Py. Additional resources were drawn from XII Reserve Corps, whilst 37 Infantry Brigade of X Reserve Corps was despatched to relieve the worn down 39 Reserve Brigade as soon as it arrived by train. In a precursor of the later use of *Eingreif* troops in the counterstroke role, General von Einem directed his reinforcements, including both infantry regiments and 38 Reserve Brigade, to be prepared to launch forward and counter-attack in the event of a French breakthrough.

Some of the prisoners captured during the fighting on the 19th Reserve Division front were channelled to the rear by members of Reserve Infantry Regiment 65, who searched an officer and discovered a copy of an order which should not have been carried into battle. According to this, the assaults were all part of a large scale offensive involving three of four French corps and, significantly, according to part of it, General Joffre had stated that he wished the French troops to have secured the important local route centre of Somme-Py by the evening of 18 February.[25] Stubborn Geman resistance had thrown the timetable out badly and it was small wonder that the final French assessment of the opening phase of the offensive was that, 'Despite the valour of the troops, the gains from these three days were very slight'.[26]

Although losses had been severe, there was still plenty of fighting power left in I and XVII French Corps. Nevertheless, General de Langle quickly decided to throw fresh forces into the battle. This was the start of a pattern which was to continue for a few more weeks and at once detailed French staff work began, being devoted to how best to make use of IV French Corps once Joffre could be persuaded to release it.[27] On the German side, confirmed knowledge of the immediate French aims reinforced the need to strengthen the greatly weakened front line and reinforcements were once again rushed forward. So that evening 2nd Battalion Reserve Infantry Regiment 68 found itself moving into action to relieve the left battalion of Infantry Regiment 68, which had been manning the inter-corps boundary and had suffered badly in the process.

There was little reliable information, other than the fact that there had been serious casualties and that the trenches were largely shelled out of existence. The commanding officer, Major Meinardus, decided, therefore, to send up 5th and 6th Companies to relieve the men of Infantry Regiment 68, whilst 7th and 8th Companies, heavily laden with digging implements and trench stores, set about clearing the communications trenches and restoring the battle trenches as far as possible. Luckily nightfall saw a diminution in the gun fire, but there was no time to lose if the position was to be effectively defensible the following morning when, inevitably, the attacks would be renewed. In other parts of the front 18 February was relatively quiet, but this was certainly not the case in this particularly vulnerable place.

Showered all day with high explosive and shrapnel, the forward companies suffered considerably so that, when the attack finally came in at about 4.00 pm, there was some doubt about the Germans' ability to hold the French attack. A courageous runner got back through the hail of fire and the commander ordered a platoon of 6th Company, under Reserve Leutnant Fricke, to move up and reinforce. Despite the fact that the men had to pass straight through the French barrage, most of them managed to reach the front unscathed and the combined efforts of all enabled the position to be held, though there were penetrations on both sides. The Reserve Infantry Regiment 68 companies swapped roles during the night and yet again there was no sleep as the entire hours of darkness were spent digging out collapsed trenches.

If 18 February saw a relative reduction in the frequency and scale of the French attacks, that was merely a lull before a sharp resumption of the fighting on 19 February. Fortunately, though with great difficulty in places, the night 18/19 February had seen a great deal of activity behind the German lines as the depleted units which had withstood the first of the assaults were replaced with fresh troops. They had little time to settle in, however. By 9.00 am the artillery battle was rejoined in earnest east and west of Perthes – Infantry Regiment 65 describing it as 'Hell on Earth'. After ninety minutes of incessant drum fire, the commander of 7th Company, Leutnant Hoitz, reported major activity and concentrations of fresh attacking forces in the French lines. Back in support,

5th and 7th Companies loaded up with ammunition and prepared to move then, at about 11.30 am, the sound of massed small arms fire could be heard coming form the front line.

During the next ninety minutes, no fewer than four successive French mass attacks were launched at the inter-corps boundary, but all were beaten back with terrible losses and no French soldier succeeded in getting into the German position on this sector. In places the fighting was at very close quarter and there were innumerable acts of gallantry on both sides: the bravery of sixteen year old Kriegsfreiwilliger Bruns of 8th Company coming in for special mention subsequently.[28] Pockets of fighting went on well into the night, but there was good interaction between the fresh infantry forces and their supporting artillery and, once more, the French were frustrated in their attempts to break though.

Meanwhile, Reserve Infantry Regiment 78, which was rushed back to its parent 19th Reserve Division from a training period near Laon when the full extent of the latest French attacks became known, soon found itself occupying extremely vulnerable positions on and around the critical *Arbre-Höhe – Sandgrube* position north and west of Perthes, where it was subject to extremely violent French bombardment and assault on 19 February.

Major van den Bergh, Commander Reserve Infantry Regiment 78[29] **4.**

"The first day of battle developed into a critical day of the first order. The left hand sector, which we had by no means managed to take over in an orderly manner, was a permanent danger point, but, initially, the right hand sector was hardest pressed. Days earlier the French had broken through to the right [east] of the regimental position, so our right flank was threatened from the side and the rear and there they exerted all their pressure. Throughout the day the 3rd Battalion sector was under almost permanent gun fire of the heaviest variety and, on three occasions, it came under attack from different directions. For the first time our men made the acquaintance of the infamous drum fire. From 10.00 am to midday, from 1.00 pm to 2.00 pm and from 4.30 pm to 5.30 pm there was such a weight of fire of all calibres coming down on the trenches that it was impossible to distinguish the individual shells. It just sounded like a massive drum roll.

"Great clouds of black, poisonous smoke hung over the trenches, which had been transformed into a scene from Hell. Then, at the appointed time, the enemy lifted the fire to the rear, so as to interdict the move forward of supports. Simultaneously, dense assault columns launched forward so as to capture the trenches which, it was assumed, housed nothing still alive. However our daring men of the Landwehr and young kriegsfreiwilligen had withstood the artillery onslaught. Coolly, they manned the side of the trench and extracted the machine guns from half smashed dugouts.

"Calm, well aimed fire hammered into the assault columns and the field was covered with uniforms of blue and red, The attack stalled, then disintegrated. Those of the enemy who reached the trenches were brought down in hand to hand fighting or captured. Hardly one Frenchman returned. This made such an impression on the enemy that the second wave either did not exit their trenches or soon ran back to them. There were attacks like this on three occasions that day. Battalion losses amounted to about two hundred men, but the enemy suffered several times as many."

A little further to the east, 16th Reserve Division enjoyed a slightly easier day but, by around 4.00 pm on 19 February, it appeared to be facing a crisis as waves of French attackers piled into and through the outer crust of its defences. With all its ammunition for its heavy howitzers fired and resupply uncertain, with some of its forward defenders allegedly falling back, VIII Corps requested and received the services of 38 Reserve Infantry Brigade from Third Army. In the event the reporting had been over-pessimistic. There had been a sharp French thrust, but concentrated fire from the organic artillery of 16th Reserve Division from both flanks had brought the advance to a halt once more. Nevertheless, it was deemed expedient to leave almost two regiments of reinforcements at the disposal of Generalmajor von Altrock and, in addition, Third Army requested and received the services of a further *ad hoc* three battalions, which were held near to Bouconville. At the same time it directed XII Reserve Corps to concentrate all its remaining reserves near St Souplet.

XII Reserve Corps raised objections to this. They had had to fend off an enemy attack directed against Aubérive earlier that afternoon and, although this was probably intended as a diversion, continuing heavy fire on the forward positions of 24th Reserve Division suggested that a renewal of the assault was a distinct possibility. In the event there was a brief operational pause. The first two days of fighting had seen concentrated efforts by troops of the French I and XVII Corps, with an intervention by substantial elements of IV Corps on 18 and 19 February, yet none of these assaults had led to the hoped-for breakthrough. Nevertheless the utmost watchfulness was required of the German defenders, who were aware from prisoner interrogation that the French II Corps was assembled in rear, ready to be deployed forward to renew the offensive.

In response, as fresh French assaults were awaited, the German army continued to reinforce the threatened sector and Infantry Regiments 28 and 29 of 16th Infantry Division were deployed right forward by VIII Corps to relieve the worn out Infantry Regiments 68 and 69 of 19th Reserve Division. Thus far the fighting had been marked by attacks by wave after wave of French infantry, generally over the same ground and frequently reinforcing failure, rather than attempting to exploit success. The defenders were genuinely puzzled about the French tactics, which were certainly putting them under pressure, but at huge cost to the attacking troops. It was not just a matter of highly motivated troops striving to drive a hated invader from French territory. The discovery of yet another operational instruction by the French GQG on the body of a dead French officer who fell in battle on the 16th Reserve Division sector showed that the assaulting troops were simply following orders issued at the highest level:

"Copse B.C.D and [a specified sector of front] are to be stormed and captured. To that end, storm columns are to be assembled during the previous night. The attack is to be repeated as often as necessary until the objective is taken. Troops manning the forward trenches are to secure the start lines and to provide flank protection by occupying adjacent trenches. Reserves will follow the storm columns. These will be organised as follows: The battalions are to be organised into two waves, each of two companies and the companies are to deploy formed into as few columns as possible. Gaps are to be made in the enemy wire obstacle. In the copse this is to be carried out using 'Melanit' hand grenades;[30] in other sectors, it is to be achieved by artillery and machine gun fire. While this fire is taking place, commanders are to remain located alongside artillery observation officers, so as to satisfy themselves concerning the success of this fire. The leading platoon of each assaulting company is to station itself immediately opposite these breaches. The direction of attack is to be confirmed, in order that this may be carried out without loss of time. At the appointed time the assaulting companies are to leave the trenches, with the leading platoons led by their commanders and the remaining platoons following up as closely as possible. The commanders of these follow up platoons are to move in rear of their troops in order to maintain order and cohesion. The movement must be carried out swiftly and silently, but the troops are not to be exhausted [in the process]. Flanks will be secured as follows: in the copse by the troops who are manning trenches on the edges of the clearings; in other places by troops in the front line trenches. As soon as the assaulting columns have gained a lodgement in the enemy trenches, they are to reorganise themselves to meet the enemy machine guns. Those elements of the trench garrisons who have been able to hold on between the traverses must be driven off with grenades. Engineers for this purpose will follow up infantry attacks. The enemy must be prevented from re-capturing the trenches through a counter-attack. To that end, saps must immediately be driven forward towards the enemy; not only at the extremities of the trenches, but also at points in between. Machine guns are to be placed in the sap heads and sand bags to facilitate this may be used. In addition trenches are to be adapted immediately to cover the new front. The necessary material for this is to be taken forward. Once the forward enemy line has been captured and consolidated, the attack will be pressed forward by fresh troops. The greatest care is to be taken with flank protection. The enemy is to be attacked at the point of the bayonet and every effort is to be made to bring about encirclement. Attacks over open ground will be conducted in accordance with the valid principles and will be accompanied by a diversionary attack."[31]

Luckily, Infantry Regiments 28 and 29 did not have to fend off attacks on 19 February. There were attacks to the left and right but they themselves only had to suffer incessant artillery fire and they attempted to orientate themselves in the blasted landscape and repair the worst of the damage to the defences. During the afternoon of 20 February, however, there was a determined series of French thrusts, most of which were beaten off, but there were incursions on the front of Infantry Regiment 28 which were still not cleared twenty four hours later. To add to the difficulties in this sector, there was strong French push on 21 February by the French 5 Brigade of II Corps, which had been placed at the disposal of I Corps.[32] The previous afternoon elements of 1st Guards Infantry Division began arriving in the Third Army sector, having been released by Sixth Army. Placed by him towards the east of his area of responsibility, so as to strengthen his threatened left flank, General von Einem felt that he was now well placed to rebuff further attacks on that part of his line. He was confirmed in this view when the French launched a series of somewhat half-hearted assaults throughout the day on 22 February. It appeared to the commanders of both VIII and VIII Reserve Corps that the French attacks had run their course and, by that evening of that day, Third Army released 38 Reserve Infantry Brigade back to Fifth Army and Fusilier Regiment 73 and its supporting artillery to Seventh Army.

The move was somewhat surprising and rather premature, especially in view of the losses the worn down ground holding front line troops had suffered and the appalling state of their trenches and other defences, which had been badly smashed by all the artillery fire. However, work went ahead feverishly to repair the damage and to replenish stocks of ammunition and other combat supplies – tasks made more difficult by the fact that there was no let up in the rate of harassing French artillery fire twenty four hours a day. To this must be added in the dreadful weather, the exhaustion of the infantry and immense problems of rationing these poor unfortunates who were suffering badly from the conditions as they clung on to their positions, soaked to the skin and frozen to the bone. Despite this, the Third Army assessment was that French strength was draining away from the front and artillery was being withdrawn, prior to being reallocated.

It came as a rude shock, therefore, suddenly to be subjected during the afternoon of 23 February to a huge weight of gun fire all along the VIII and VIII Reserve Corps frontages. It was the precursor to further serious heavy fighting, whose hallmarks were extraordinarily heavy artillery bombardments, but only isolated infantry assaults. There was no return to the massive frontal attacks all along the Third Army frontage, such as had characterised the early clashes. According to prisoner statements this was an attempt by the French to exploit a policy of 'artillery conquers; infantry occupies'. Be that as it may, so narrow was the front that masses of defending artillery fire could be directed in turn to each of these attacks as they came in, thus rendering them even less effective than they otherwise might have been.

The French official view of these defensive measures was that, 'the reinforcements introduced by the enemy and successive physical defensive measures which they had created, rendered the task of the assaulting troops ever more difficult on the XVII Corps front'. This led in turn to a further division of the assault sector of the French Fourth Army as General de Langle, in a supreme effort to force a decision, deployed ever more troops and altered the command responsibilities, placing I and II Corps under the orders of General Gérard and IV and XVII Corps under the command of General Dumas.[33]

Despite all French efforts, the stereotyped nature of their operations was proving to be a serious weakness. Most days saw a build up of artillery fire during the morning and the middle of the day, followed by infantry assaults from late afternoon to early evening, presumably with the intention of allowing the attackers to consolidate any gains during the following hours of darkness. Nevertheless, all this constant shell fire took a severe toll on the defending infantry, as did continuing local attacks. Both Infantry Regiment 28 and 29 suffered badly during these days, Infantry Regiment 28 to such an extent that, by 25 February, it could no longer control events fully in its sector. Fusilier Regiment 73 had to be rushed forward to relieve it, by which time the French had established a pocket of resistance between one hundred and one hundred and fifty metres wide in the centre of its position.[34] One of the members of the regiment later recalled the final move forward.

Gefreiter R Philipp 5th Company Fusilier Regiment 73[35] **5.**

"The train halted with a hard, unfriendly jolt. There was no shrill trumpet call, just a short, almost grumpy, shout of 'Everybody out'! ... We stood on the platform of the station at Somme-Py then, gradually, we stirred into life and marched off, through an absolute mud bath, accompanied by snow squalls. A gunner stood in the doorway of a house ... and called out [in thickly accented dialect], *'Willt ji ok in den Hexenkettel? Kinners, dor danzt dem Düwel sin' Großmudder!'* [Are you also heading for the witches' cauldron? Lads, the Devil's dancing with his grandma there!]. We did not bother to reply. In silence, depressed by the ugly, damp darkness and accompanied by the distant roar of the battle, we stumbled onwards – endlessly – endlessly – accompanied by occasional quiet thoughts of the Devil's grandmother.

"The road was covered by white mud. To the right just off the track were wagons, convoys which had returned from the front earlier that night. White mud dripped from the axles, was sprayed on the boxes and balled up in the spokes of the wheels. Tiredly, we pushed on up the road. We had been thrown in here to bring relief to the front, men who were going through the same Hell as we should be tomorrow. We felt as though a pitiless fate had placed us where we should fulfil our destiny. Our way must be followed to the end; just as last night; just as in the one to come; as always, right until the final moment and nobody knew when this final moment might arrive for him. Our way into an appalling defensive battle roused no fiery heroic feelings. Here only the iron call of duty applied.

"Now for a brief orientation: everywhere there were deep holes, which were only passable by crawling. We found refuge in these holes in the ground. The softened earth clung to our boots and we were greeted by mouldy, wet straw. The situation was not improved by the weight of our mud-encrusted boots. But we lay down where we were, almost one on top of the other in the divisional bivouac near Somme-Py. The sound of battle [reached us], as we stood on a hillock near the camp and stared towards the front. A ghostly silhouette danced before us. Painted in grim outlines, fists lunging up to the sky, a toppling giant – it was as though the spirit of a fallen soldier could find no rest; as though, in his final fury, he could only go on fighting grimly. So it lived on, shrieked, groaned and crashed. Thus the battle ground on and the gaping muzzles roared on dully, as though a thousand headed monster was reaching out for young lives."

By 26 February Fusilier Regiment 73 was in position forward, attempting to establish itself and deciding how to tackle the French incursion. This was far from straightforward. The forward trenches, where they existed at all, were in a terrible state, the parapets had all been blown away and a degree of flank protection could only be obtained by judicious placement of sandbags. This exposure made it almost impossible to place machine guns effectively and, each time it was attempted, shell bursts either knocked them out or buried them with flying earth and rendered them unserviceable. There was a crying need for grenades but, at this stage of the war, they were all improvised and the French were much better equipped in this respect.

Despite the difficulties, the forward companies – 9th and 12th – had to prepare to put up a vigorous defence. From 2.30 pm, gun fire increased until it was only just short of drum fire and the barrage was maintained for a full three hours before the French came storming forward once more. Desperate close quarter fighting, coupled with hasty counter-strokes, then began. The German lines were threatened with outflanking and only a decisive intervention by 3rd Battalion brought relief. Nevertheless, and despite the fact that some trenches were recaptured, the outcome was a further expansion of the French pocket of resistance. Bombardment and sporadic firing went on late into the night, but there were no further French infantry assaults. The hard pressed 9th and 12th Companies were relieved by 10th and 11th respectively; then came the order from 16th Infantry Division, 'The Frenchman's Nest is to be captured!'

Hurried preparations were made then, after the precise size and shape of the French position had been illuminated, it was subject to a short hurricane bombardment at 8.00 am, then attacked at 8.25 am by 10th, 4th and 7th Companies Fusilier Regiment 73. There was no success on the left, but on the right flank sixty metres of trench line was recaptured. Naturally this was insufficient and a renewal of the attack was ordered for later in the day. Before that could occur, however, the French also laid down a bombardment and counter-attacked with almost one thousand men in a great mass at 3.30 pm. Luckily for the French assault force, all communications between the German front line and their guns was broken, otherwise this would have made an excellent target for concentrated gunfire.

The French attack succeeded once again in gaining ground and would probably have expanded the pocket of resistance even more. However a bold counter-stroke led by Hauptmann von Frese disrupted their efforts and went a long way towards restoring the overall situation. A special tribute to Frese, who was killed, along with several others, during this close quarter battle was published later.[36]

"Of the numerous brave deeds during the 'Day of Perthes', the charge forward by Hauptmann von Frese and the men of the reserve of 3rd Battalion Fusilier Regiment 73 was by far the most outstanding. During the morning of 27 February, elements of 4th, 7th and 10th Companies had stormed the wide French pocket of resistance to our front, but in vain. The attack was to have been renewed during the afternoon, but this was pre-empted by the enemy. Suddenly, at 3.30 pm, an overwhelming weight of drum fire was brought down on our sector, then an assault was launched and they succeeded in pushing their infantry on into the central section of our positions, where there were almost no trenches.

"At that, the enemy tried to push on deep into our right hand sub sector, apparently with the aim of uniting the platoons pushed forward here with the mass already established in the middle and so being able to operate against the rear of our forward trench garrison. In the event some enemy troops, at least several platoons in strength, did manage to press forward as far as our reserve position. Spotting the danger, Hauptmann von Frese assembled his battalion reserve of about one and a half companies, rushed the enemy who had broken in and put them to flight. This thrust in behind the enemy and the ensuing panic were exploited by Hauptmann von Frese, who took advantage of the flank protection offered by the forward companies to storm the nest of resistance.

"Frese was brought down by artillery fire. It is not known if it was enemy fire or our own. His adjutant, Reserve Leutnant Heitmueller, and many of his men also met a hero's death, just as did the courageous commander of 12th Company, Reserve Leutnant von Wallmoden, right at the start of the attack. The daring stroke succeeded in neutralising the extreme ferocity outlined above and ensured the special place granted to Frese in the history of the regiment."[37]

A combination of French predictability, coupled with the willingness rapidly to learn and apply lessons, meant that the German response to these later attacks was more sophisticated and very much more effective than had been the case earlier in the battle. It was decided, in view of major difficulties with reconnaissance and target acquisition, that the effort put into counter-battery fire was not very cost effective. Instead, almost the entire effort of the guns was shifted to countering the infantry. As soon as an attack threatened, the French front line was brought under fire by every gun within range and, on many occasions, the attackers not only were unable to leave the trenches at all, they were also forced to pull back or disperse to avoid the fire. In addition, some sections and batteries of guns were pushed right forward where, firing large quantities of shrapnel, they had a devastating effect on assaulting infantry, making the mopping up of attacks a much simpler proposition for the defending trench garrisons.

Counter-battery fire was not ruled out completely, but it was mainly conducted on rare days when the weather was clear and there was some chance of aircraft and balloon observation. Quite apart from the need to conserve ammunition and to use it in the most efficient manner, the defence lacked guns: the entire thirteen kilometres of the frontage of VIII Corps, for example, was only covered by twenty two batteries of field guns, nine of heavier calibre and one of heavy howitzers. To compound the difficulties, much of the ammunition being supplied by the rapidly expanding armaments industry was of poor quality, leading to many duds and damage to guns (including a disproportionate number of breech explosions). This had a bad effect on the crews and caused a rapid decline in the number of fully operable weapons at times. At the beginning of March, for example, 19th Reserve Division reported that twenty five per cent of its guns were out of action at one point.

At about the same time, the ammunition shortage made itself painfully felt. All formations were ordered to keep the expenditure of shells to an absolute minimum. The order, though understandable, had a bad effect on the morale of the forward troops, who had to hold their positions, despite the French rate of fire climbing to above 60,000 rounds per day in some divisional sectors. Trench mortars were rushed into service in an attempt to boost fire power in the front line, but their presence, though welcome, was hardly compensation for the flexibility of well handled guns with plenty of shells to fire. There is little doubt that, had the French been able to continue with attacks on a broad front, the German defence would have been severely stretched. As it was the main effort, which had been the sector between Perthes and Beauséjour Farm when the battles of mid February were raging, shifted by the end of the month to the Le Mesnil area, though there were diversionary thrusts near Perthes from time to time.

Increasingly, Hill 196[38] became the focus of the worst of the fighting and the scenes on and around this hill as the battle wore on were indescribable. Constant shelling and bad weather combined to turn the trenches into a flattened morass of isolated defended localities where groups of attackers and defenders, frequently separated only by the thickness of a wall of sandbags, hung on grimly amidst scenes of death and destruction. The physical situation was equally bad for attackers and defenders but the French, due to superiority of numbers, were able to introduce fresh troops constantly, whilst there was no such luxury for the hard pressed defenders. As has been mentioned, within Fusilier Regiment 73, Frese's deeds might have been singled out for special praise, but this deployment witnessed many more and extraordinary endurance, as one of the company commander later noted:

Reserve Oberleutnant Hermann Otto 4th Company Fusilier Regiment 73[39] **6.**

" 'It is beyond description; it is simply impossible to find words to describe the position your regiment is in the process of taking over. Not insignificant numbers of the men are being driven mad by the utterly appalling weight of enemy artillery fire.' These, roughly, were the words spoken to me when I occupied the position with my 4th Company by an engineer hauptmann who had been operating in the area for several weeks. I took him for a Job's Comforter, but the following days taught me that he was certainly not wrong in his statement. The artillery fire really was indescribable. In amidst the thunder of countless simultaneous shots, it was impossible to distinguish individual explosions. The firing signatures, the crashes as the shells impacted, the whizzing, whirring and whistling of fragments flying through the air, caused a hellish racket. My brave lads performed wonderfully through all this dreadful fire.

"Despite serious casualties, my 4th Company survived its baptism of fire brilliantly as we were moving along a ravine which was hit by numerous shells during our march forward by night onto the position – then how they proved themselves afterwards as they hung on obstinately in heavy artillery fire, but also conducted themselves with dash. 'Oh, come on', shouted Unteroffizier Friedrichs (who was standing next to me as we fought our way along the trenches towards the 'Frenchmens' Nest'), to one of the engineers who was standing next to an enemy barricade and who was being somewhat reluctant to act, 'leave it to me'. Saying this, he grabbed the hand grenades out of his hands and launched a vicious attack against the enemy garrison manning the trench beyond the barricade. Kriegsfreiwilligers Jansen and Voigtmann sprang to his side and soon the French trenches were full of crashes and smoke, making it impossible for any of the enemy to remain in a lengthy stretch of trench. Instead they began shooting at the obstacle that we were occupying from long distance.

"A few steps away from me, Friedrichs collapsed on the ground, shot in the head. Jansen was shot through the arm and suddenly – this all happened in a flash, Voigtmann, whom I had just praised, 'Bravo Voigtmann', was standing with a fresh grenade in his hand when he threw his arms up and fell backwards to the ground dead: almost at my feet. He had been shot straight through the centre of his head. His body was recovered later by Kriegsfreiwilliger Henkel and some others. Unfortunately there was insufficient time to recover Friedrichs, though we did take his personal effects with us. I did, however, request Leutnant Graf of Infantry Regiment 69, who relieved me, to do everything possible to recover Friedrichs' body.

"Six other members of my company – altogether there were thirteen of them during this period – lie together in a communal grave right by the trench which my company held. A memorial in the shape of a simple wooden cross which carries the names of the fallen (including Friedrichs and Sus) adorns the hill."

The battles along the remainder of the front continued naturally, but at a lesser intensity, so Third Army was able to take advantage of the fact and, husbanding its forces carefully, arranged for the relief of hard pressed formations with fresh ones and increased the strength of the defence in places by thinning out those sectors which were less threatened. The release of reinforcements by adjoining armies and Supreme Army Headquarters meant that, though badly pressed at times, the defence was able to hold on into March, despite continuing bad weather. This was particularly important around the key terrain of Hill 196, north of Le Mesnil, where repeated assaults were beaten back over a period of several days of intense fighting, albeit at the cost of high casualties and swift exhaustion of the defending troops, as they strove to keep a grip on this exposed place.

1st Guards Infantry Division had been located in and around Douai for a number of days, resting and training when the call came for a redeployment swiftly to Champagne. Immediately on arrival, the battalions of Footguard Regiment 4 were moved forward under command of 31 Reserve Infantry Brigade and thence to shore up Reserve Infantry Regiment 29, which was under immense pressure, having taken substantial casualties on and around Hill 196. For about forty eight hours the battalions were assigned different tasks depending upon where the crisis of the moment was deemed to be then, during the night 3-4 March, elements of the regiment and also of Footguard Regiment 2 were ordered forward to recapture trenches lost around the so-called *Hiepewäldchen* [Hiepe Copse], primarily the *Schwerk-Weg*, which ran forward over Hill 196. The attack proved to be extremely difficult, drawn out and costly. It stalled more than once but, eventually, the Guards prevailed and that part of the battlefield was wrested back finally from the French. One of the company commanders from 2nd Battalion later described it from his perspective.

Leutnant von Kienitz 6th Company Footguard Regiment 4[40] **6.**

"During the bombardment the French had brought the entire rear area under heavy fire and more or less flattened the *Schwerk-Weg*. In these circumstances it was difficult to bring up reinforcements. At approximately 1.00 pm the barrage stopped and the French fire was lifted to the rear. At the same instant the French launched forward against the *Sackgraben*, manned by 6th Company. However, because we were on the alert, we beat them back immediately. Everything happened quickly and we even had hand grenades left over. They had apparently made an unpleasant impact on them. On the other hand, the trenches were only thirty to fifty metres apart, so it took very little time to cover the distance in between. This situation was to be very problematic when the French launched their second attack, because it was difficult to bring much fire to bear in such a short space of time. Once these first assaults had stalled, the French fire died away somewhat, concentrating on the re-entrant just behind our trench, so as to interfere with the move forward of supports. Reserve Oberleutnant Berndt, commander 5th Company, had already been killed. Despite the fact that he had ducked down in a hole beneath the base of the trench, a shell had torn both his legs off. He was also buried up to his neck and died as he was being dug out, but not before declaring, 'We were once Grenadiers!'[41]

"Until 2.30 pm all was quiet then, suddenly, the French artillery fire came down with equal intensity once more. It can be reckoned that every half hour they fired between 4,000 and 6,000 shells at the two trenches. The loopholes and banks of earth that had been destroyed, then rebuilt, were wrecked again in no time. Reserve Leutnant Gaedtke was hit in the right cheek by a shell splinter and I was buried up to my chest as I moved through the position. Immediately afterwards the French launched their second attack [at] 2.55 pm. This was directed straight at 5th Company. The French stormed forward in dense columns, each in about battalion strength, which were met by only sporadic fire from the company, which had been seriously weakened, but there was heavier enfilading fire from 6th Company and, at that, they chose to run back to their trenches.

"However, at that moment, the French artillery fired on their own trenches, so they attacked once more – this time 6th Company. They must also have broken into the right [western] flank of 5th Company and they pressed forward against 6th Company. Because I was there [at the key point] I was able to rally elements of 5th and 6th Company and get them back into the battle. That the French were unable to penetrate further was largely thanks to Unteroffizier Radestock, Range Estimater Balzereit and Grenadier van Eß, because, as Radelstock and I fired shot after shot at twenty to twenty five metres range at the Frenchmen, who were advancing along the trench, Eß directed the fire of fifteen to twenty riflemen at the flanks of the French who were still streaming forward out of their trenches.

"Balzereit built a sandbag barricade in the trench, whose foundation was two corpses lying on the floor of the trench – but there was no alternative. Finally we succeeded in preventing the enemy from advancing any further. Another barricade of French corpses had also built up in the trench because at such a short range, every round was on target. Unfortunately Radestock was creased by a head wound after he had halted this advance. I had been hit by a shell splinter in my left side right at the beginning of the action then a short time later I was shot in the cheek and could not stay at my post. I handed over the company to Reserve Leutnant Gaedtke, who was still alive at that time. The Frenchmen who had broken in were totally destroyed."

Falkenhayn, on his return from a tour of inspection of the Eastern Front arrived at Headquarters Third Army in Vouziers for discussions with the Army Commander. They both agreed that it was better to fight hard to maintain their current positions and so the order went out that there was to be no further retreat in the Le Mesnil area. To that end an immediate programme of evacuation of French inhabitants of villages and hamlets behind the lines began in earnest, whilst large numbers of Landwehr and Landsturm units were rushed forward to dig all manner of additional trenches and dugouts in rear of the front line and so increase both the strength and the depth of the positions. Nevertheless, by this time the strain on the forward troops was so great that they had to be relieved, severely worn down at ever shorter intervals. Those released headed for the rear hoping that they would never see Hill 196 or its surroundings again, but often that was not the case, as this diary entry by a member of Footguard Regiment 2, who had been involved in the costly counter-attack of 4 March explains:

Leutnant Fromme Oficer Commanding 7th Company Footguard Regiment 2[42] **6.**

"During the day [5 March] the company was relieved by 5th Company (Hauptmann von Volkmann) and headed for the familiar dugouts in the *Küchenschlucht*.[43] I paused for a while at the battalion command post where I, like everyone else who returned utterly exhausted from the position, was greeted by Major von Holtzendorf and his adjutant, Leutnant von Heister, in the most calming way possible and reinvigorated. Nevertheless, I was so worn out that I could have slept standing up. Down below in the *Küchenschlucht* I met up with Leutnant Gropius, who was just about to go forward with his company to relieve. After the unprecedented heavy casualties of the past few days, to meet up with a familiar face was an unexpected pleasure.

"I had just parted from him and had entered a dugout where I could lie down and catch up on some much needed restorative sleep, when an order arrived. 'Company Fromme is to move immediately to Gratreuil and act as a reserve.' On the face of it, it would have been pleasant to be able to rest for a few hours outside the area swept by fire but, at that particular moment, given the generally exhausted state of the company, the prospect of a three hour march was not exactly inviting. However, orders were orders and we duly marched off. Because of the unbelievable state of the tracks we did not reach Gratreuil until 6.30 am, then the company found quarters in some large, but not exactly inviting, huts.

"I found space in a somewhat dismal shack, which already housed five officers lying on straw on the floor. Amongst them were a good acquaintance, Landwehr Leutnant Möckel of 5th Company, who was on his way from the Homeland back to the regiment; and three members of the regiment who were ill: Reserve Oberleutnant Graf Luckner, Leutnant Graf von Schwerin and Reserve Leutnant Grabbe. I sank onto the straw next to them and slept the sleep of the dead. When I awoke it was almost 7.00 pm. After cleaning myself up thoroughly, I had an evening meal and then went back to sleep.

"When I awoke once more it was already nearly 11.00 am. This is the way that we gradually become human once more. During that day I remained together with the company in Grateuil and we worked on the weapons and equipment, which attention was sorely needed after a week of the Champagne battles. A rumour gradually spread that the entire regiment was to be relieved by tomorrow evening. Given the exhausted and decimated state of the troops, relief seemed to be urgently necessary. However, things generally turn out differently than we imagine, or hope. Instead of the expected relief, orders arrived that Company Fromme was to report to the *Küchenschlucht* by 11.00 pm.

"Understandably the news was not greeted enthusiastically. Soldiers are quite happy to be sent to different theatres of war and they embark on battle, be it offensive or defensive, without complaint. The spur of the new, the great and the unknown is mightier than the inclination against danger, privation and emergencies of all types. There is only one situation which leads to disinclination which is hard to over come and that is repeated deployment in the very same place which has proved itself to be Hell on Earth and a witches' cauldron. There is only one means of countering such rebellious impulses: resort to the strict discipline hammered home with attention to detail and drill in peacetime training. There is nothing which can replace it.

"Possibly there are individuals who have no need of such training, but an army can never neglect it. Thank heavens our men are still outstanding, even though some of them might have been overwhelmed by the impressions and events of previous days. Promptly, at 7.30 pm, we marched forward via Ripont."

Meanwhile there was renewed French activity further to the west and it appeared that a fresh thrust was in preparation east and west of Souain along a line from the *Balkonstellung* [Balcony Position], through *Windmühlenhöhe* [Windmill Hill] to the vulnerable *Bayernzipfel* [Bavarian Point].[44] It certainly was the intention of the French to develop operations further between Souain and Perthes. The task was entrusted to a newly formed formation, comprising the French XII and XVI Corps, reinforced by 60th Division, under the command of General Grossetti. The attack was launched on 7 March, enjoying a certain amount of initial success when several minor breaks were made into the German lines. However, vigorous counter-action largely restored the opening situation then, on 8 March, General von Einem sought and was given, agreement by Fifth Army to assist in the launching of a diversionary attack on the left flank of VIII Reserve Corps.

This desire to recapture the initiative was held widely within Third Army. A staff officer, despatched by Supreme Army Headquarters to investigate the situation in the sector of 16th Reserve Division, was sent back with a very robust message:

Generalmajor von Altrock, Commander 16th Reserve Division [45]

"The French have been worn down badly, but we are not seeing the benefit because the enemy is constantly deploying fresh forces. There can be no question of relinquishing ground or the German positions voluntarily. This would simply be a major boost to the confidence of the enemy and be a blow to the morale of our troops. We simply have to hold out, though it must be expected that the French will make gains here and there. With the forces we have on hand we cannot think of launching an attack ourselves. It would be possible if we were sent strong forces and if we were able to dominate the enemy artillery."

It is possible that Altrock was reacting to strongly worded reports from his brigade and regimental commanders because the previous day the commander of Footguard Regiment 2, Oberst von Estorff, under the distinct impression that divisional headquarters was asking the impossible of his worn out men by continuing to insist – without making available the necessary support and without correcting the hopelessly inaccurate fire of the German artillery – that yet another attempt be made to push the French out of minor gains they had made on and around Hill 196, had sent the brigade adjutant an extremely strongly worded private letter.[46]

> "I should not bother to report anything other to the Division than a clear cut statement of the failure of the work of our artillery. Everything else can be the subject of a detailed account to be rendered later. It looks as though the intention is to keep us here until we are wiped out! Furthermore, Footguard Regiment 2 is at the end of its strength. I have reported and justified this often enough already and I hereby declare that I am no longer willing to take responsibility for the consequences. I wish you to pass on this last point to the Brigade Commander."

The forward troops continued to report that friendly artillery fire was landing well to the rear of the French enemy positions. 16th Reserve Division was convinced otherwise and all the protests from the regiments cut no ice, 'The Brigade will not be relieved until after the position has been restored', it declared. Elstorff insisted on reinforcement and received the services of three companies of Reserve Infantry Regiment 30, so just before dawn on 9 March yet another attack was launched on the approaches to Hill 196 and enjoyed a certain amount of success, before a violent French counter-attack later that morning pushed the men of Reserve Infantry Regiment 30 out once more. Brigade and Division lost no time in demanding yet another counter-attack from the worn out men of Footguard Regiment 2, but Elstorff stood his ground and, eventually, Division relented. An exceedingly bitter Elstorff reported at 1.00 pm,[47] **6.**

> "The French are established on Hill 196. Our second line is located about one hundred metres behind it. The French position can only be captured by a counter-attack, but it is beyond the capability of the exhausted troops. For the time being the only thing possible is to defend the Second Position (the so-called *Artillerie-Stellung*). We occupy it and it is defensible. The arrival of fresh troops is urgently necessary. Precisely what was predictable has occurred."

Eventually, Reserve Infantry Regiment 65 arrived forward to carry on the battle and the foot guards, together with the worn out deployed elements of Reserve Infantry Regiments 30 and 63, were relieved.

Surprising to relate, given the intense battle raging overhead, March saw a continuation and intensification of mine warfare, which had been a feature of the area for months already. In fact, of course, despite the constant fighting, in many cases the lines had been restored almost to their original starting positions. Infantry Regiment 160, for example, observed a brief hurricane bombardment on 7 March, followed by a mine going up in the area of *Windmühlenhöhe*, just to the west of Souain.[48] 'At 2.30 pm', they reported, 'the earth heaved. The ruins of the mill disappeared and almost two companies of the 65th [Infantry Regiment 65] were buried under mountains of chalk.'[49] This was not absolutely accurate. In fact 5th Company bore the brunt of this massive mine. Losses were heavy and the subsequent immediate counterstroke launched to eject the French from the crater formed by the explosion cost the regiment one experienced battalion commander, Hauptmann Wilhelm Meinardus, killed and over fifty others killed or wounded.[50] Taken together with at least forty men of 5th Company killed in the explosion, this was a bad day for the regiment.

Of course the effects were not just felt by the German army. Reserve Infantry Regiment 74, returning to the line to relieve Reserve Infantry Regiment 73 of 19th Reserve Division in its original locations, after a brief period of rest and recuperation following the mauling it had received in mid February, commented that, in general, the battle intensity was lower, but that artillery fire was still troublesome and French mortars were a constant irritation. In addition,

> "Mine warfare was driven on zealously by both sides. It having been established that the French were driving forward right under our trench, on 8 March at 10.30 am our engineers blew in a gallery. There was a large dull thud, the earth trembled and a new sight confronted us: it was a large crater, which was particularly deep in the centre. The engineers concluded that it had completely succeeded in crushing the enemy's gallery. This gave us a pleasantly calming feeling. One hour later our engineers conducted another operation, when they blew a gallery of their own which they had driven forward under the French trench. Prior to this our artillery, so as to deceive the enemy, had fired a concentration on this sector, so suggesting that we were about to attack it. This caused the French to move troops forward into the endangered section of trench, so this explosion was a complete success also."[51]

As might be expected, the overall lack of success was discouraging for the French army; it certainly led to discussion about how the offensive should be further developed. General de Langle, of whom Joffre had developed a favourable opinion, favoured a surprise thrust by XVI Corps north of St Hilaire le Grand, but his commander in chief, after lengthy reflection, decided on powerful attacks around Le Mesnil under the command of General Grossetti. In order to achieve maximum impact, considerable regrouping was deemed to be necessary. All artillery within range was placed under his command, together with strong formations from I, II and XVI Corps and the assault was to begin by 12 March at the latest.

After an immense effort to be ready on time, major operations recommenced during the late morning of 12 March. This led to some success, but within VIII Reserve Corps, where the main blow had fallen, the commander, Generalleutnant Fleck, arranged for several fresh regiments to be rushed forward and to be thrown into the battle. The aim was not simply to parry the blow, but also, in an early example of the *Eingreif* tactics used to great effect later in the war, to disrupt the French attacks and eliminate pockets of resistance which the attackers had established. Despite these efforts, the broadened offensive continued right across the VIII Corps frontage and against the right [western] flank of VIII Reserve Corps the following day. The combined efforts of 15th Infantry Division, 19th Reserve Division and the newly-arrived 2nd Guards Reserve Division, succeeded in blunting the attacks on a day when the Third Army estimated that over five French corps were committed to the battle.

The main effort still seemed to be going in against the high ground north of Le Mesnil, where retention of the key terrain was causing German casualties to mount alarmingly and this was confirmed the following day when, at about 5.00 am, the French mounted yet another strong, but abortive, assault on Hill 196 to the north of Le Mesnil. Infantry Regiment 68, which had fought a desperately hard battle during the operations in mid February and had had to be relieved, reorganised and reinforced twice already, found itself ordered forward to begin the relief of the hard pressed and worn down Grenadier Regiment 101 in positions it had been occupying a month previously. This task was undertaken by its 2nd and 3rd Battalions, whilst its 1st, having previously been deployed elsewhere, moved in to the adjacent sector to strengthen the weakened Infantry Regiment 29.[52]

These initial moves were the preliminaries to the full assumption of responsibility for the sector on 14 March. The state of the position was a shock to the regiment. The entire area had been ploughed up by shells and the woods were reduced to pathetic collections of stumps (known universally in the German army as *Zahnstocherwälder* [toothpick woods]). Much more serious was the fact that the French had driven a large salient, hundreds of metres wide, into the centre of the sector, had dug in strongly and were developing additional trenches and saps in the direction of the intermediate position in the depth of the German lines. This attack was followed later in the day by serious attacks east and west of Perthes against 19th Reserve and 2nd Guards Reserve Division. These attacks were also beaten off, but there was a loss of terrain on the left [eastern] flank of VIII Reserve Corps. Once more, however, it was the right [western] flank of VIII Reserve corps which suffered the most. At about 9.30 am French troops were spotted massing for an attack and there was an immediate call for artillery fire to break them up.

Unfortunately for the defenders, the resulting concentrations of fire were too weak to achieve a decisive result and, following a French bombardment, a massed attack by colonial troops was launched on the battered German positions at about 2.00 pm. A spirited defence held back the attackers, causing them severe losses for most of the afternoon but, at about 5.00 pm, flares shot up demanding the heaviest defensive artillery fire and alarming reports were passed up the chain of command by 2nd Guards Reserve Division that masses of French infantrymen were swarming up the slopes of Hill 196. Reacting immediately, General von Altrock despatched forward every reserve unit he could lay his hands on to prop up his threatened right [western] flank. More than two tense hours passed, then information arrived that the reinforcements had succeeded in outflanking the attackers and driving them back to the line of the Perthes – Cernay track. It had been a close call.

The Winter Battle in Champagne 39

Urgent steps were taken to organise a counter-attack by 16th Reserve Division the following day, but the time for preparation was too short. Launched at 4.00 am, before dawn, in the face of dreadful weather and stiff opposition, it failed in its mission and bitter close-quarter fighting ensued all along the heights north of Le Mesnil during the next two days. Later, on 17 March, Supreme Army Headquarters released 112 Infantry Brigade of 56th Infantry Division to Third Army in order that a further attempt could be made to recapture Hill 196. It was a task that this formation, which had only been raised less than two weeks earlier and which was armed with captured Russian weapons, found to be beyond its capability. There was to be 'thorough preparation', so the attack did not go in until 19 March, but it still failed.

Surprise was meant to be the order of the day, with H Hour set for 7.10 pm and the operation to be preceded by no more than a hurricane bombardment lasting ten minutes. Unfortunately, possibly due to the rawness of the new formation, the attack preparations were observed. The French reinforced the opposing trench garrison and brought down a hail of artillery fire and enfilade machine gun fire from both flanks against the forming up places. Such was the French response that many of the German front line troops believed that the French themselves were preparing to attack. When H Hour arrived, some battalions were under such heavy fire that they could not advance at all but, south of Ripont, one regiment did succeed in overwhelming a French centre of resistance and taking prisoner 300 men of the French XVI Corps. This success, however, was attributed not to a mass assault, but to skilful work by grenade teams advancing up parallel trenches and from cover to cover until the position was outflanked and then surrounded.

Had the defenders but realised it, this was almost the last significant act of this long drawn out struggle. From the French perspective, on 18 March, the day that the French and British fleets assembled in the Mediterranean under Vice Admiral de Robeck prior to attempting to force the Dardanelles, the French winter battles in Champagne finally officially came to an end. This was not immediately apparent to the men of Reserve Infantry Regiment 29 of 16th Reserve Division, who had arrived the previous day to relieve Footguard Regiment 3 on Hill 196. As far as it was concerned, 6.

> "18 March was a major day of battle. At 1.45 pm heavy artillery fire came down on our sector and increased to the most intense rate by 4.00 pm. At 5.00 pm there was an infantry assault. 5th and 6th Companies had to pull back and 4th Company rushed forwarding support, but it was not needed. The enemy were beaten off and retreated to their trenches. The French, who broke into the 2nd Battalion sector, were all captured. The effect of our trench mortars was excellent. A number of direct hits with their consequent appalling blast effect caused the enemy to give up.
>
> "We also suffered casualties. Leutnant Bürstinghaus was killed, shot through the head and Leutnant Schwerling received a serious stomach wound. 3rd Battalion, attempting to advance through the barrage, lost sixty men. Although the enemy penetrated into the *Hindenburggraben*, defended by 2nd

Battalion, it was possible to hold on to *Brigadegraben*. 7th Company then charged down the hill, brought rapid fire down on the enemy who had broken in and ejected them from the position with grenades. At 5.40 pm, there was a general assault forwards and the recaptured trenches were occupied ... A Zouave officer and several Zouaves were captured, but a great many more lay dead in and in front of the trenches."[53]

So, as can be seen, the intense, close quarter hand to hand combat for the key terrain marked the entire campaign from start to finish. The French offensive had opened with optimistic expectations, but any hopes of a breakthrough had faltered and then foundered in the face of bad weather and stubborn German resistance. The French Commander in Chief summed up the campaign later and, putting the best possible gloss on what must have been a major disappointment, wrote:

Marshal Joseph Joffre [54]

"Despite persistent bad weather, the troops had acquitted themselves admirably. I was particularly pleased by the fact that we had succeeded though continuous effort to counter all the enemy actions. This success, modest and incomplete though it was; nevertheless seemed to me to amount to the first step towards the victory that we should achieve once our equipment and tactics were sufficiently refined. I made a point of expressing my particular satisfaction to the 51st Regiment, which had been the first to break into the depth of the enemy position. I had the regiment march past in review a few days after it had been withdrawn from the battle and I thanked its commander, Colonel Brion, 'in the name of France'.

"As far as General de Langle was concerned, he had confirmed my favourable impression of him. Calm, thoughtful, methodical in his actions, benevolent in his treatment of his subordinates, loyal and correct in his dealings with me, he had brought this first major action to a successful conclusion and I was able profitably to apply the lessons [learned] during the battles to come."

By 10 March the German Supreme Army Command had in any case decided that all fighting of significance was over and published this final communiqué, somewhat prematurely.

"The reports of the fighting of today and the past few days, indicate that the 'Winter Battle of Champagne' has been brought to such a point that no minor flare up can alter the final result. As we reported on 17 February, the origin of the battle lay in the desire of the French high command to provide relief for the heard-pressed Russians in the area of the Masurian Lakes by launching an attempt at breakthrough towards the town of Vouziers, regardless of cost. As the outcome of the Masurian fighting has shown the [main] objective was not achieved and the attempted breakthrough was a complete and utter dismal failure. Contrary to all claim made in the official French publications, nowhere did the enemy obtain the slightest significant advantage.

"For this we must thank the heroic conduct of the troops stationed there, the vision and determination of their commanders, especially Generaloberst von Einem and his corps commanders, Generals Riemann and Fleck. During ceaseless fighting by day and night since 16 February, the enemy has launched six reinforced corps one after the other again an eight kilometre front defended by only two weak divisions from the Rhineland. Extraordinary quantities of ammunition of their own and American manufacture, frequently more than 100,000 shells in a day, [were fired]. Unshaken, the Rhinelanders, reinforced by the Guards and other units, not only stood firm in the face of attacks delivered at odds of six to one, but often pre-empted them by means of powerful counter-strokes."

So this four month battle came to an end. The German casualties were serious; the French ones simply dreadful and this was merely the first round of a year of intense fighting all along the Western Front. Third Army casualties amounted to a total of about 1,100 officers and 45,000 other ranks; whilst the French losses over the same period were said by one French source to have totalled 240,000.[55]

Notes
1. Kellinghusen *Kriegserinnerungen* p 184.
2. In fact the French date the start of the offensive to 20 December 1914. See FOH 2 p 289.
3. Heintz History Reserve Infantry Regiment 133 pp 39-41.
4. Anspach History Reserve Infantry Regiment 107 pp 296-297.
5. Known to the German army as Hill 196 and scene of the most bitter fighting of the battle.
6. FOH 2 p 414.
7. Anspach *op. cit.* pp 301-303.
8. Kellingusen *op. cit.* p 183.
9. *ibid.* pp 185-186.
10. For reasons which are not entirely clear, Reserve Infantry Regiment 92 was organised at this time into four battalions, each of three companies, instead of the more usual three battalions of four companies. Bangert commanded the 4th Battalion, comprising 4th, 8th and 9th Companies. See History Reserve Infantry Regiment 92 p 114.
11. FOH 2 p 425.
12. *Der Weltkrieg Vol 7* p 42.
13. Bauer History Reserve Infantry Regiment 74 pp 133-134.
14. *ibid.* pp 134-135.
15. Kellingusen *op. cit.* pp 196-202.
16. In fact Leutnant Christian Heinemeyer succumbed to his wounds the following day. He is buried in the German cemetery at St Etienne-à-Arnes Block 5 Grave 436.
17. Leutnant Erich Kortejohann is buried in the German cemetery at Souain Block 1 Grave 928.
18. Blankenstein History Reserve Infantry Regiment 92 p 110.
19. Anspach *op. cit.* pp 304-
20. This somewhat obscure slang expression is believed to refer to improvised grenades of some description.

21. Guhr History Infantry Regiment 157 p 42.
22. This included seven officers killed in action: Hauptmanns Brieger, Brünner, Schulz and Reinhold, Reserve Leutnant Nagel and Offizierstellvertreters Reinicke and Böhm. In addition a further nine officers were wounded, some of them seriously. Of these officers, only Reserve Leutnant Fritz Nagel has a known grave. He is buried in the German cemetery at Berru Block 3 Grave 368.
23. Anspach *op. cit.* pp 304-
24. Einem's full name was von Einem gen. von Rothmaler, but he tended to use only the abbreviated form.
25. Krall History Reserve Infantry Regiment 65 p 76.
26. FOH 2 p 411.
27. See FOH 2 pp 430 – 434.
28. Krall *op. cit.* p 78
29. Möller History Reserve Infantry Regiment 78 p 77.
30. These grenades were improvised at or near the front and comprised a slab of explosive with detonator and safety fuze wired to a wooden stick. Their effect was unpredictable; the risk of injury or worse being almost the same for thrower as for target.
31. Anspach *op. cit.* pp 67-68.
32. The other principal reinforcement between 19 and 24 February was the release to the French XVII Corps of 8th Division of IV Corps. See FOH p 411.
33. See FOH 2 p 411.
34. Wellman History Infantry Regiment 29 p 311.
35. Voigt History Fusilier Regiment 73 pp 255 – 256.
36. *ibid.* pp 259 – 260.
37. Of the fallen, only Reserve Leutnant von Wallmoden has a known grave. He is buried in the *Kamaradengrab* of the German cemetery at Sommepy – Tahure.
38. Hill 196 was known to the French army as the Mamelle Nord.
39. Voigt *op. cit.* pp 278-279.
40. Reinhard History Footguard Regiment 4 pp 69-70.
41. The regimental history hints strongly that this was a deliberate reference to the play *Fuimos Troes* (Aeneid 2) [The True Trojans], attributed to the English writer Jasper Fisher 1591 – 1643. *Fuimos Troes* [We were Trojans once; we have known better days] has heroic connotations.
42. Rieben History Footguard Regiment 2 pp 239-240.
43. This was known to the French as *Ravin de la Goutte.*
44. One of the meanings of *Zipfel* is 'tongue', a good choice for this very distinctive, narrow tongue-shaped salient jutting out south west from the German front line in the direction of Souain.
45. *Der Weltkrieg Vol 7* pp 49 – 50.
46. Rieben *op. cit.* p 242.
47. *ibid.* p 246.
48. This is also marked as *Windmühlenhöhe* [Windmill Hill] on some maps.
49. History Infantry Regiment 160 p 73.
50. Krall *op. cit.* pp 81-83.
51. Bauer *op. cit.* p 152.
52. Pafferath History Infantry Regiment 68 p 129.
53. Hillebrand History Reserve Infantry Regiment 29 pp 49-50.
54. Joffre *Memoirs* p 61.

55. *Der Weltkrieg Vol 7* p 53. The estimate of French losses is quoted from Palat Général *La Grande Guerre sur le Front Occidental Tome IX 'Les Offensives de 1915'* p 149 Paris 1922. It should be noted, however, that the FOH 2 (p 481), published some years later, puts the losses at 1,646 officers and 91,786 other ranks, of whom 820 officers and 42,000 other ranks became casualties during the period 16 February – 20 March. This still amounts to an offensive/defensive loss ratio of at least two to one and is, in fact, very close to a German Third Army estimate of 11 March, 'Our losses are indeed heavy, but amount at the most to one third of those of the enemy. The French have lost more than 45,000 men. The German front in Champagne is stronger than ever.' See History Infantry Regiment 29 p 315.

CHAPTER 2

Neuve Chapelle

Following preliminary discussions between the French and British commanders in chief in late December 1914 and subsequent exchanges of letters and messages, in mid February 1915, Joffre had sought specific British support in connection with his planned major offensive in Artois. The request was for the British to attack and capture the heights around La Bassée and also advance on Warneton and Messines, with a view to threatening the German hold on Lille. This ambitious plan was coupled with efforts to persuade the British to relieve, at the very least, the ground holding French IX Corps so that it could be withdrawn from the line and used to bolster the fighting strength of the French Tenth Army. Unfortunately, from the British perspective this had to be dependent on the timely arrival of the regular British 29th Division and 1st Canadian Division in France and, at more or less the same time, word arrived that the 29th Division, which had been earmarked for the Western Front, was instead to be deployed down to the Dardanelles for the invasion of Gallipoli, being replaced by a territorial division.

As a result, French wrote to Joffre on 18 February stating that, if the British I Corps was to remain where it was for the time being and because a lower standard territorial division was not due in theatre until the beginning of March, he would be able to participate in a joint attack but not to carry out the desired relief until later. This was not what Joffre wished to hear and he caused the French government to press for the appearance of the 29th Division in France, because any other solution would put in jeopardy his plans for an offensive in Artois, which was designed originally to coincide with operations further south in Champagne.[1] Simultaneously, he wrote once more to French, stating his view that the BEF must be strong enough to relieve the French IX Corps but, once more, French refused to contemplate any such action, adding in a letter of 23 February that the 46th Territorial Division would not begin arriving in France until 28 February and that, even after its arrival, it would require a period of advanced training, so it was unrealistic to expect the British army to take over more of the front until 1 April. Joffre maintained his pressure but, eventually, he was forced to accept that the British would not be moved on this issue and, finally, on 7 March, he had to inform French that, for the time being, the Tenth Army offensive could not take place.[2]

It is quite clear that the situation was an embarrassment to the British Commander in Chief, who felt that there was a need to demonstrate to the French that the British were reliable allies, who could be relied upon to deliver more than simply a line-holding capability to the joint effort. Thus it was that the final decision was taken to conduct, with maximum effort, an independent assault aimed at breaking through the German lines either side of the small, insignificant, village of Neuve Chapelle in French Flanders. Already, whilst the battles in Champagne were still raging, away to the north British army operational planners had been taking the first tentative steps towards this aggressive action against the invaders, which was designed not only to break the German lines, but also to improve their standing with the French and to help to take some of the pressure off the Eastern Front, which was to be the scene of almost all German offensive action throughout the year.

In view of the perceived importance of the project and despite competing demands for manpower, equipment and ammunition, the British First Army concentrated what, for the period, was a huge assault force opposite the salient formed by the village of Neuve Chapelle. Possession of the built up area itself had no value tactically or operationally, but it held the key to an advance of some ten kilometres onto the line Illies – Herlies on Aubers Ridge, from which high ground there was considerable potential for developing the offensive. At this stage of the war the German defences were not especially well developed. There had been little time to dig elaborate defensive works and, in any case, with the water table very close to the surface, there was considerable reliance on a single line of sandbagged breastworks less than two metres thick, which were easily penetrated by even light shells. Wire was beginning to appear along the front, but in this area it was still very sparse – the most vulnerable points being protected by what the Germans referred to as *Spanische Reiter* [wooden knife rests reinforced by spikes or barbed wire]. There was still only one main defensive position; indeed there were specific orders from Falkenhayn against the construction of a second line of defences, so as to ensure that forward defending troops would fight resolutely in the defence of the front line. Nevertheless, some work was taking place and there were already, for example, reserve gun positions in depth when the battle began.

On the German side, early in March, VII Army Corps, which was responsible for the defence on this sector of the front, had had to give up Infantry Regiments 53 and 158 of 14th and 8th Infantry Divisions respectively. These regiments, together with Fusilier Regiment 39 of 14th Reserve Division, left to form 100 Infantry Brigade of 50th Infantry Division, which was raised on 10 March 1915. It is unclear if it was reckoned that greater risks could be taken on those parts of the Western Front where they faced the British but, in the event, the timing could hardly have been worse. Regimental frontages had to be adjusted, leaving the sector defended from north to south, approximately along the line Beaucamps, Aubers, Piètre, Neuve Chapelle, Richebourg, Festubert and Givenchy, by only six regiments and one jäger battalion, in the sequence Infantry Regiments 55, 15, 13, Jäger Battalion 11, Infantry Regiments 16, 56 and 57. In view of the size of the blow that was about to fall, from the point of view of the size of the trench garrisons, this was overall a weak defensive position, especially because when the attack was launched it was bounded more or less by the left flank of Infantry Regiment 16 and the right flank of Infantry Regiment 13 – a very short distance.

However, these weaknesses were counterbalanced to some extent by certain additional defensive features which had been constructed, such as a line of concreted machine gun firing points, located about one kilometre in rear of the front line, where they could provided covering fire over the intervening flat ground and which were designed to be occupied in an emergency. In addition, the German army, after some

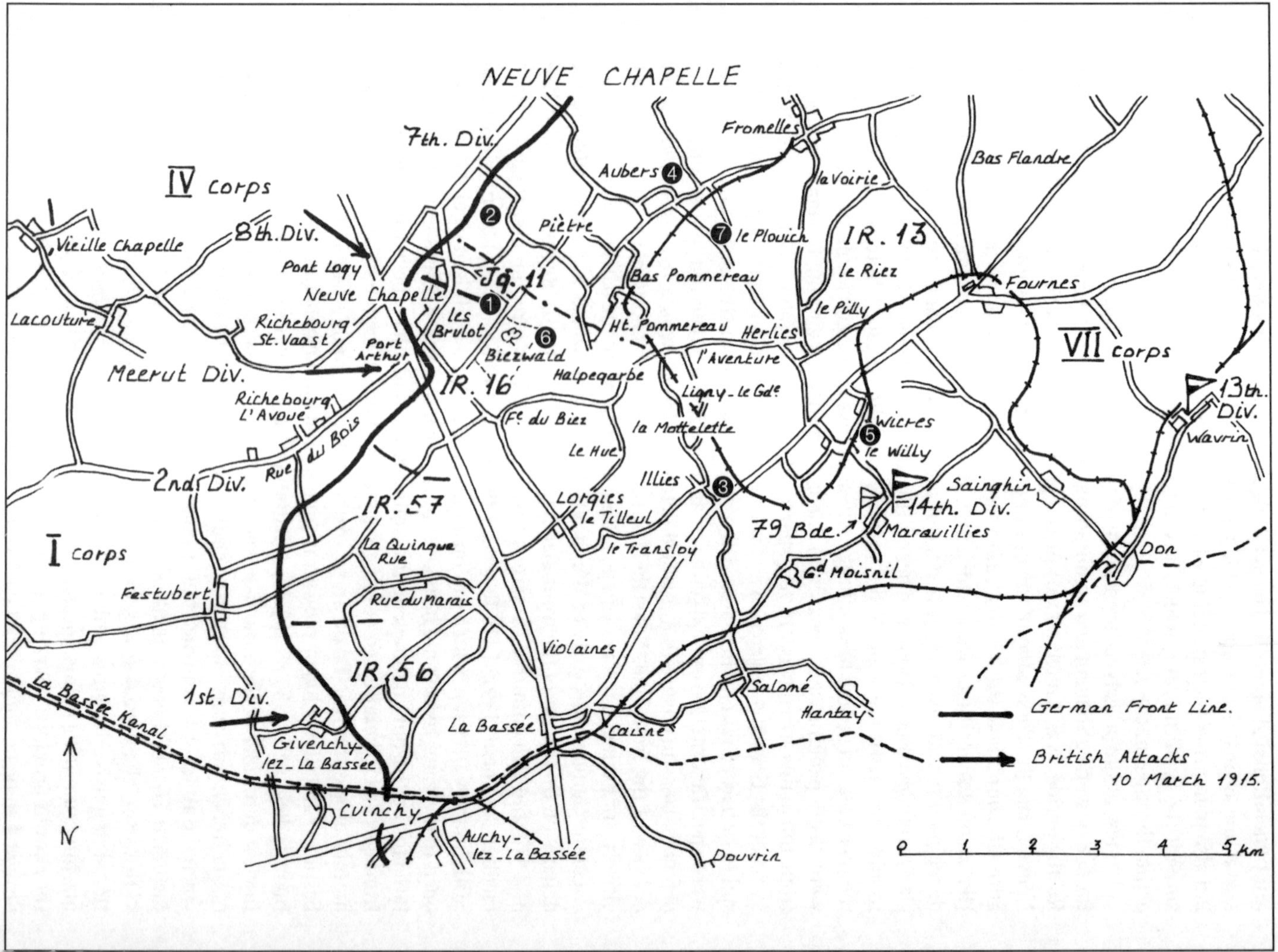
NEUVE CHAPELLE
7th. Div.
IV corps
8th. Div.
Vieille Chapelle
Pont Logy
Neuve Chapelle
Jg. 11
Lacouture
Richebourg St. Vaast
les Brulot
Port Arthur
Biezwald
Meerut Div.
IR. 16
Richebourg L'Avoué
Rue du Bois
2nd. Div.
IR. 57
I corps
Festubert
La Quinque Rue
Rue du Marais
IR. 56
La Bassée Kanal
1st. Div.
Givenchy lez_La Bassée
Cuinchy
N
Auchy-lez_La Bassée
La Bassée
Violaines
Aubers
Piètre
Fromelles
la Voirie
le Plouich
Bas Pommereau
Ht. Pommereau
Halpegarbe
Herlies
l'Aventure
Ligny_le Gde
la Mottelette
Fc du Biez
le Hue
Illies
Lorgies
le Tilleul
le Transloy
IR. 13
le Riez
le Pilly
Wicres
le Willy
Bas Flandre
Fournes
VII corps
13th. Div.
Wavrin
Sainghin
14th. Div.
79 Bde.
Maraquillies
Gd Moisnil
Don
Salomé
Hantay
Caisne
Douvrin
German Front Line.
British Attacks
10 March 1915.
0 1 2 3 4 5 km

months of experience of positional warfare, was already developing techniques of defence in depth, which provided considerable flexibility and greater robustness than numbers alone might suggest. To take the layout of Infantry Regiment 13 as an example, the three battalions were each allocated a sector about 750 metres wide, but the front lines were only held by two companies forward. The remainder were located in support or reserve up to between five and seven kilometres to the rear.

Its left forward (3rd) Battalion, commanded by Hauptmann von Brunn, defended the front between the Chapigny – Piètre Road and the *Wasserburg* [Moated Grange], but only maintained two companies forward manning the breastworks. Its third company was back on the eastern edge of Piètre itself, almost two kilometres in rear, with the fourth company another three kilometres to the east at L'Aventure. To complement this defence in depth, in corps reserve were 4th and 7th Companies drawn from the 1st and 2nd Battalions Infantry Regiment 13 respectively, together with 2nd and 4th Companies of the adjacent Infantry Regiment 15. This group was held back in Fournes. Given the size of companies at the time, this corps reserve amounted to approximately 1,000 all ranks. Commanded by an experienced officer, Major Strippelmann of Infantry Regiment 15, it was capable of bringing considerable force to bear when deployed.[3]

The dispositions of Infantry Regiment 53 prior to its relief had been similar. There had been three battalion sectors, with some companies forward and others held in rear of the *Biez-Wald* [Bois du Biez], poised ready to man the machine gun posts forward of the wood and the remainder back near Les Brulots. However, when Infantry Regiment 16 arrived, with Jäger Battalion 11 in support, the commander made some changes. The Jägers placed two companies right forward, adjacent to Infantry Regiment 13, with the remainder of the battalion in reserve at Halpegarbe. This enabled 1st Battalion Infantry Regiment 13 to remain in divisional reserve eight kilometres away at Le Marais, whilst 3rd Battalion had all four companies forward and 2nd Battalion two, with one company in support at Ferme du Biez and the other at Halpegarbe.

The overall scheme for defending the Neuve Chapelle salient was for the forward companies to hold firmly while the supports either moved forward to reinforce or to block the flanks of any breakthrough by exploiting the potential of the line of machine gun posts and manoeuvring around them. The calculation was that this would prove to be sufficiently strong to hold up any advance until further reserves could be rushed to the area. In direct support were the guns of Field Artillery Regiment 7. There was provision for the neighbouring Field Artillery Regiments 22, 43 and 58 to superimpose their fire as required and there were also some heavy 210 mm field howitzers within range, namely three batteries of 1st Battalion Foot Artillery Regiment 7, commanded by Major Richter. It is, perhaps, indicative of the manpower pressures on the German army and, perhaps a faulty assessment of British offensive intentions, that it was willing to face up to the potential threat with so attenuated a force, because there is evidence that intelligence had been available for several days, suggesting a forthcoming attack.

According to Infantry Regiment 16,[4] a group of Indian soldiers had deserted to Infantry Regiment 13 the previous week and had warned that extensive preparations were being made behind British lines for an assault 'within the next few days'. It does appear that there was no appreciation of the size of the blow that was about to fall and there is no doubt that tactical surprise was complete. Forty eight battalions, effectively 30,000 men, from the four divisions of the Indian Corps and the whole of the British IV Corps, supported by 400 guns and howitzers of all calibres, were to launch an attack on a front of only two kilometres and there had been no special arrangements made by the defenders to prepare for it.

The night 9/10 March was remarkably quiet though, just as it went dark, there was a sudden concentration of about twenty heavy shells, which landed just in rear of the trenches of Jäger Battalion 11. This was the merest hint of what was to come when, at 8.00 am on 10 March, a bombardment way beyond anything in the experience of the jägers came down on their forward positions and those of the neighbouring 3rd Battalion Infantry Regiment 13. In all more than 3,000 shells crashed down in half an hour and, in no time flat, the front line trench was in chaos and enveloped with smoke and dirt flying in all directions. Shells and mortar bombs landed in dizzying quantities whilst above came the more or less continuous popping of shrapnel pots. Sandbags and timber reinforcement were thrown around, together with knife rests and other element of the obstacles. Within moments one machine gun, together with all its crew, received a direct hit and was buried, whilst another heavy shell smashed through the overhead protection of a battalion dugout, killing all the signallers.

The elaborate system of dams and channels, which reduced the amount of water flowing into the trenches, was soon wrecked and a sea of filthy mud and water cascaded into the position, immediately rendering parts of it completely untenable. Whilst British aircraft circled low overhead, Neuve Chapelle itself disappeared behind a torrent of fire, as did all approach routes, rear areas and known battery positions. Casualty figures mounted alarmingly then, at about 9.00 am, eight battalions of troops from the Meerut and 8th British Divisions charged forward. For some minutes a great weight of fire had been concentrated on the jägers, falling in particular on 3rd Company in the middle sub sector and on the one communication trench available to the battalion. Dense masses of attackers bore down on them and the right flank of Infantry Regiment 16 to their left, with Scottish troops seen to their right and Indian to the left. 1st Company Jäger Battalion 11, right forward, was attacked in two waves, but not quite so heavily; whereas 3rd Company was utterly overwhelmed, its men buried alive, killed or wounded, almost to a man; and the situation was broadly similar for Infantry Regiment 16.

1st Company Jäger Battalion 11, profiting from the fact that the attack on them was slightly less intense, rushed to get their surviving machine guns into action. Having done so, they poured fire into the advancing British troops and forced at least some of them back to their start line with heavy losses. A bare half hour later, the attack was resumed on the by now depleted 1st Company and soon a close quarter battle developed, sustained on the British side by the arrival of reinforcements at the critical point. It was completely impossible to get troops forward to assist the jägers, even if any had been available close at hand, so they were forced to give ground and the survivors to take up positions in the Infantry Regiment 13 sector, where they moved to be co-located with the left flank company. Due to this rupture in the front line there were now serious concerns about the guns of 1st Battalion Field Artillery Regiment 7, which were located in and around *Biez-Wald* and fully engaged in maintaining a high rate of fire. Leutnant Mohr, machine gun officer with Jäger Battalion 11, who was wounded already, assembled the remnants of 1st and 3rd Companies of the jägers and moved them to where they could bring down fire to their front and protect the guns which were still maintaining a high rate of fire.

It was at this point that errors of both planning and execution by the attackers began to come into play and grant the defenders precious time to react to this serious breach in their lines. Directed to halt for a quarter of an hour about 200 metres beyond the line of breastworks, so as to allow time for further bombardment of Neuve Chapelle itself before the forward troops advanced into it, the main beneficiaries were the German formations. Reacting quickly to the crisis, by 8.30 am Major Graf Soden, commander of Jäger Battalion 11, had alerted 2nd and 4th Companies and directed them, together with the cycle company and a further machine gun platoon, to make for the northwest corner of *Biez-Wald* and to take up hasty defence west of 1st Battery Field Artillery Regiment 7. The move was far from straightforward. The moment the troops moved forward of Halpegarbe they encountered heavy harassing fire designed to prevent reinforcements from reaching the forward battle area. Reacting automatically, as they had been taught, the jägers doubled or trebled their spacing and pushed on amidst a hail of shrapnel and high explosive shells which burst above or among them and thinned their ranks drastically. Despite the losses, most came through and found themselves working their way forward through the wood, which was under equally heavy fire.

Branches and twigs showered down on the advancing reinforcements, bullets cracked past and shells burst, but they pressed forward, clear of the western edge of the wood and took up positions close to the lost village of Neuve Chapelle. The heavy fire continued to take a toll. 4th Company, on the right, lost Leutnant Totzeck seriously wounded and Offizierstellvertreter Strack mortally wounded, whilst two of the platoon commanders were also wounded. 2nd Company on the right lost its commander, Leutnant von Küster, immediately on arrival, then, in quick succession, three platoon commanders, including Leutnant Baumbach von Kaimberg.[5] There was nothing for it but to dig down rapidly for protection, making use of all existing trenches. Under the command of Oberleutnant Prinz zu Solms this was done; the heavy incoming fire providing all the incentive necessary.

Meanwhile heavy fire was maintained on the village of Neuve Chapelle then, when the attempt was made by British troops to press on east of the village, they were met by a torrent of well-aimed fire, especially from the machine gun platoon, located on the right, who cut swathes through the advancing lines as they moved across the open ground and as they attempted to pass the crossings over the Layes Brook. 1st Battalion Royal Irish Rifles, which had moved forward from support, suffered particularly badly at this point, as did 2nd Battalion Rifle Brigade and the British advance stuttered and then stalled.[6] The first part of the defensive plan had worked smoothly. Both flanks of the breakthrough had been effectively reinforced and, gradually, the intervening gap was covered as more troops were moved up out of reserve.

The surviving pair of guns of 1st Battery Field Artillery Regiment 7[7] maintained a rapid rate of shrapnel fire all the time their ammunition lasted and the combination was sufficient to force the attackers back into the shelter of the village, though the cost to the gunners was high. Hauptmann Frings, its commander, collapsed, shot through the lower abdomen by a rifle bullet and command devolved on Leutnant Weber, whose face and hair had been dyed bright yellow by a shell exploding very close to him.[8] Firing went on, there was a direct hit on one of the guns and the numbers of dead and wounded lying next to the position increased alarmingly. In the meantime all reserves in range were also being directed to force march forward. Such was the extreme urgency of the situation that, although they only arrived in dribs and drabs, they were immediately sent forward to where the need was greatest. Amongst the first to arrive were men of 3rd and 4th Companies Infantry Regiment 16, commanded by Hauptmann Courtin, who took up positions north of *Biez-Wald* to provide additional support for the jägers and the hard pressed gunners of Field Artillery Regiment 7. Gradually, numbers increased until, at about 2.00 pm, Graf Soden was able to order a renewal of the attack. Despite the casualties and in the face of very heavy fire, a position was established to the west of the Layes Brook, thus securing the bridge.

The corps reserve, the equivalent of a further battalion, namely 4th and 7th Companies Infantry Regiment 13, together with 2nd and 4th Company Infantry Regiment 15, were next to arrive during the late afternoon. Major Strippelmann was in command but, early on, he was mortally wounded by a shell splinter hitting his right arm and command had to be assumed by one of the surviving jägers, Oberleutnant Swart.[9] As it was beginning to go dark two companies from Infantry Regiments 56 and 57, together with a further three machine guns, arrived under the command of Hauptmann Prösch and were placed to cover the left flank, whilst the cycle company of the jägers was pulled back into close support of 1st Battery Field Artillery Regiment 7 once more.

On the Infantry Regiment 16 front, the men manning the forward positions had noticed a great deal of aerial activity early in the morning. It may have been a coincidence but, at 8.30 am, an aircraft flew over their lines and threw out a bag of shredded paper. This seemed to be the signal for a torrent of fire to be brought down on them. Of all ill luck, this occurred as the commander, Oberstleutnant von Hassel, was on his way to visit Hauptmann von Nerée, commanding 3rd Battalion and, in addition, the telephone system was almost immediately shot up and failed. The regiment was, for the time being, leaderless. Major Wenbourne stepped into the breach, ordering 1st and 2nd Companies to move into reserve at Halpegarbe and 6th Company, which was there at readiness, to move forward to reinforce.

It was not a moment too soon, because elements of 3rd Battalion, manning the so-called Sector II, were in the process of being overrun. 11th Company, which had suffered badly in the past few days, now lost its commander, Leutnant Jersch, seriously wounded, together with many other men.[10] The enemy broke straight through its lines, forced their way into Neuve Chapelle and turned with a view to rolling up the German front line. Throughout the day the trenches remained under heavy shell fire. Men were continually being buried alive, the trenches were smashed in and casualties mounted alarmingly. However, the enemy did not succeed in developing their attack southwards and it proved to be possible for 1st and 2nd Companies to work their way right forward to compensate for the gaps which had been torn in the ranks of the trench garrison.

Severe pressure was maintained, however, with close quarter fighting reaching its climax in the early evening when the shattered remnants of 10th, 1st and 2nd Companies had to yield a certain amount of ground. Darkness then fell, which put an end to the enemy thrusts and advantage was taken of the hours of darkness to rush reinforcements forward to bolster what had by then become a vulnerable point in the defence. Elsewhere, despite the fact that 2nd Battalion Infantry Regiment 16 had not been attacked directly, it had suffered severely from the bombardment and continuing harassing fire, so 4th Company Infantry Regiment 139, under Oberleutnant Nicolai, was moved into position to reinforce its thinned ranks.

To the north of Neuve Chapelle and on the right of Jäger Battalion 11, 3rd Battalion Infantry Regiment 13 was under a great weight of fire, which stretched back right to the Rue d'Enfer [Road of Hell], which was a particularly well named road that day. Once the village fell, there was an immediate crisis on the left flank of Infantry Regiment 13, which was now in the air. Initially 10th Company, commanded by Leutnant Rudloff, had managed to beat off the attack, but it was outflanked relatively quickly and forced north sometime around midday, despite putting up a spirited close range defence with grenades. Firing to the very last minute, Gun Commanders Stock and Overgoor managed to save their guns, less the mounts but the third, which was kept in action by its commander, von Bremen, until the very last moment, by which time both commander and crew were lost, had to be thrown into the river.[11]

Recognising the danger, 11th Company, commanded by Leutnant Aistermann, swiftly set about barricading its trench with sandbags. Having established a stop, the point was defended resolutely with grenades, whilst British troops poured into Neuve Chapelle. They were brought under small arms fire but, at ranges of around 1,200 metres, it was not possible to achieve a decisive result. Nevertheless, the check was sufficient to enable Infantry Regiment 13 reinforcements to be rushed forward and to establish a hard shoulder of resistance facing south to cover the open flank from the hamlet of Piètre as far as the Layes Brook. Once again this deployment was made in the nick of time. There were constant British attempts to develop their attack in this direction but, for the time, being they were all beaten back. The onset of night and falling rain did not bring matters to a halt on this sector of the front, however. Sentries from 11th and 5th Companies, on full alert, strained to see through the darkness then, profiting from the guttering light of flares, were able on several occasions to raise the alarm and to assist in beating off attacks throughout the night.

Infantry Regiment 15, manning trenches to the south to cover Aubers and Fromelles, were not under direct attack but their 2nd and 4th Companies, only recently withdrawn from the front line and forming the reserve of 15 Infantry Brigade at Fournes, were soon involved.

Vizefeldwebel Brockmann 4th Company Infantry Regiment 15[12] 1.

"Shells were landing with an extraordinary racket on the village. Alarm! The Tommies have launched an attack! Everyone was gathered together, including the sick, then we forced marched to Brigade Headquarters. Generalmajor von Brauchitsch got us together and explained the situation. The field kitchens arrived, steaming away, so food and iron rations were distributed. Everyone ate his fill and crammed his pouches to capacity. We topped up with ammunition from an ammunition wagon and set off, commanded by Major Strippelmann, with each man carrying two extra belts of ammunition round his neck and singing, 'We're not afraid of the thunder of the guns' ...

"We came under shell fire at Herlies for the first time and from then on it was bloody awkward. We broke down first into platoons and then into sections. During the afternoon an ammunition column of the 58th [Field Artillery Regiment 58] came racing past at a full gallop, rushing to take shells to a battery hidden away in some bushes. Just before it reached its destination it was hit by an enormous concentration of fire and practically wiped out. Honour its memory! Towards the close of day we arrived. Accompanied by the crack of bullets and casualties everywhere, night fell. At the entrance to the village, near the Layes Brook, we dug in, a mere one hundred metres from a farm occupied by the Tommies. The road was barricaded, whilst off to the left 2nd Company also dug in. Each man dug a small trench as best he could and we sent out reconnaissance patrols because the intention was to capture the farm at 6.00 am."

Also present near Neuve Chapelle on 10 March were the engineers of 3rd Company Pionier Battalion 7, who had been deployed there for some time to carry out numerous specialist tasks. Their diarist noted,[13] 'We had been working here for five months. Now a rumour was circulating to the effect that, as soon as everything was complete, 14th Infantry Division would be relieved and the trenches would be occupied by Landwehr formations, whilst we moved elsewhere to attempt to contribute something decisive to the war effort. Things were to turn out differently.' On the day the battle opened, they were located forward, working on a new project on the eastern edge of *Biez-Wald* and certainly not equipped to give battle. 'Already, the previous day, we had noted that the British artillery had fired the odd shell into the wood, but we had not recognised them as ranging shots by newly arrived assault batteries. Now there was suddenly a violent, indescribable, racket and the place was thrown into chaos. It was soon impossible to differentiate between firing signatures, the roar of shells in the air and the explosions as they crashed down. Everything was subsumed into a great symphony of terror. Within a very short time the entire area was shrouded in powder smoke.' Immediately, the engineers took cover in buildings nearby then, at about 10.00 am, they were ordered to pull back to Halpegarbe because they lacked weapons and ammunition. This situation was soon changed and, suitably equipped, they were ordered forward once more to plug gaps in the line. There they could observe ruefully the destructive effect of all the artillery fire on their handiwork. They were split into three groups, the first, commanded by Fähnrich Hattingen, moved to assist the threatened left flank of Infantry Regiment 13, the second under Unteroffizier Landwehr deployed to the remnants of Jäger Battalion 11 and the third group to Infantry Regiment 16. Thanks to their intimate knowledge of the ground, they all succeeded in reaching their appointed places unscathed and then spent the night helping to make hasty repairs and improving the existing defences.

The amount of time which had been granted to the defence on the first day of the battle so that it could begin to move reinforcements and so counter the thrust was, in large measure, due to British mistakes and deficiencies in the planning and execution of the operation. It has already been noted that the pause before the village itself was occupied provided a crucial opportunity but, thereafter, hold ups on the flanks and the choking effect of great masses of infantry unable to get forward meant that the contact battle was being conducted by only a fraction of the attacking force. Compounding these problems was the fact that control of the operation was held back at corps level. Whereas the situation was crying out for dynamic and forceful leadership right forward, the decisions concerning the way to react to the various checks had to be taken several kilometres to the rear of the British lines and literally hours were lost whilst this was done.

In the meantime the German defence, exploiting the strength of the concreted machine gun posts and the excellent fields of fire, more than held its own. Infantry Regiment 13, regretting the small quantities of shells held forward, which meant that the guns fell silent quite early on and were denied the opportunity to inflict huge damage on the mass of British infantry jammed in and around Neuve Chapelle, nevertheless made excellent use of its machine guns to engage British columns as they approached Neuve Chapelle. The survivors of 11th Company, under Reserve Leutnant Aistermann, did particular damage with engagements out to a range of 1,200 metres. This and similar actions as the immediate reserves rushed forward, bolstered the defence, prevented the breach from being exploited systematically and allowed time for the potential of the machine gun posts to be exploited as pivots around which the defence could be conducted.

During the evening the situation improved even more as two companies of Infantry Regiment 104, together with one from Infantry Regiment 139, reported to Major Graf Soden of Jäger Battalion 11and were then joined by a second company from each of Infantry Regiments 56 and 57. This meant that the first crisis had been dealt with and thoughts could turn to regaining possession of Neuve Chapelle the following morning. In addition, there was a considerable amount of the improvisation for which the German army was famous. Such was the urgency of the situation that a wide variety of sub-units were pressed into service by VII Corps. Commanded by Hauptmann von Beulwitz of Infantry Regiment 139, XIX Corps arranged for the formation of a composite battalion. This was built up from 11th Company Infantry Regiment 133,[14]

40th Infantry Division, 4th and 11th Company Infantry Regiment 139 and 5th Company Infantry Regiment 179 of 24th Infantry Division.

To add to this, the following day 1st Battalion Field Artillery Regiment 77 (less 1st Battery), 3rd Battery Field Artillery Regiment 78, plus its staff and 6th and 7th Batteries Foot Artillery Battalion 19 were also rushed to the area, where they were subordinated to 13 Field Artillery Brigade of 13th Infantry Division.[15] The batteries of Field Artillery Regiment 77 were, however, used in piecemeal fashion to fill in crucial gaps in the gun lines, which must have made resupply extremely difficult. 1st Battery remained in reserve near Herlies at the disposal of the divisional commander and 2nd Battery took up positions, adjacent to the Le Plouisch - La Cliqueterie road, about 200 metres southwest of the Herlies – Aubers road. 3rd Battery, on the other hand, was split into its constituent sections and placed by Aubers, with the 2nd Section, commanded by the battery commander, located along the Rue d'Enfer at the northwest end of Aubers. Quite how the fire of the battalion was controlled is difficult to say, but it played a full part in the bombardment of Neuve Chapelle and the British depth positions as this description shows.

Away to the north, in the German XIX Corps area, the news of the attack on Neuve Chapelle had been greeted with some concern, lest it be the precursor of an attack on its own positions. The thought of a breakthrough at that place, leading to a threat to Lille itself, was so serious that both 24th and 40th Infantry Divisions dug deep into their own resources on 11 March and each produced a composite battalion to go to the aid of the hard pressed VII Corps. For 24th Infantry Division, the task was given to Infantry Regiment 179 of 47 Infantry Brigade. Only its 2nd Battalion was in reserve at the time and it could not be sent complete, so a weak battalion was assembled under the command of Hauptmann Tempel as follows: 5th Company, Offizierstellvertreter Schöne with 120 other ranks; 6th Company Leutnant Hertzsch and sixty one other ranks; 7th Company, Reserve Leutnant Goldmann and 123 other ranks and 8th Company, Leutnant Haase and 122 other ranks.[16] The total of 431 all ranks did not even amount to half a battalion under normal circumstances, but the circumstances were not normal and in the current emergency it represented the best that could be done. The call had come about midday and that same afternoon Tempel's men entrained at St André and taken to Marquillies, from which point they marched forward via Illies and Halpegarbe before digging in behind elements of Infantry Regiments 16 and 104.

For their part, the men of 2nd Battalion Infantry Regiment 104, 40th Infantry Division, had just been beginning the third day of a rest period at Quesnoy-sur-Deûle on 10 March. It was in the process of starting to train three hundred battle casualty replacements who had arrived the previous day when, at 11.30 am, the commanding officer, Hauptmann Facius, received a telephone order from regimental headquarters, 'The battalion is to stand by, ready to move, immediately!' At first, because all was quiet in their area, the assumption was that it was a test but the first warning order was followed by a written one from divisional headquarters, 'The battalion is to be made ready for entraining. A train will be available at Quesnoy station at 1.00 pm. Plentiful supplies of small arms ammunition are to be taken. The battalion heavy transport is to make its way to Fournes, fifteen kilometres south of Armentières. The battalion commander is to report immediately to Headquarters 14th Infantry Division'.[17]

There was an immediate scramble to get ready, especially for 8th Company, which was out on a route march when the order arrived. Nevertheless, at the cost of a rationing problem for this company, the train was boarded in record time, because the station was under shell fire, an occurrence which was blamed on the presence of a British aircraft circling overhead and spotting movement through breaks in the cloud. On arrival at Marquillies the battalion was met by a staff officer from headquarters 14th Infantry Division, extremely pleased to find that a complete battalion of 1,100 men had arrived, when Hauptmann Facius reported to him. 'Thank heavens the Saxons are here', he is reported to have said. 'Who is the senior company commander? He is to lead the battalion to Illies. Here is an unteroffizier to act as a guide. You yourself and your adjutant are to move immediately to meet the divisional commander.'[18]

The situation was much the same for the various artillery regiments which were pressed into service.

Wachtmeister Franz Brückle 7th Battery Bavarian Reserve Field Artillery Regiment 6[19]

"In Toufflers it was 11.30 am 10 March 1915. The telephone rang! Feldwebelleutnant Eberle, who was standing next to me, answered it, '7th Battery here – then announced. Battalion order! Prepare to move immediately!' There was no need for further questions and, in a short time, the battery was assembled on the parking area ready to move. The signallers quickly reeled in the telephone wire because we did not want to leave this valuable material behind. Then we set off. Battery morale was high. We assumed it was just a practice alert and never thought that anything serious was happening. About 3.00 pm we arrived at Lannoy [two kilometres southeast of Roubaix] where we met up with the staffs of the regiment and the battalions which had also been alerted. It then became clear that this was no practice alert. As was always the case when something unexpected happened, rumours were flying about. One person maintained that the population of Lille had revolted, another claimed that we were about to be transported to the Eastern Front. Just before Lille there was a lengthy pause in our movement; priority apparently had to be given to other troops. We then continued through the blacked-out streets of the French town of Lille. We could remember its wrecked station and the Rue de la Gare from October 1914. Slowly we travelled through the cold March night through Lille and Loos to Haubourdin, where we arrived about midnight and were told to find billets near the Grande Place. 7th Battery was accommodated in a tile works on the main road between Lille and La Bassée. The road was crammed with traffic moving to and from the battlefield. Ambulances filled with wounded and other vehicles transporting British officers passed by ceaselessly. In the darkness the best we could do was to get the horses under cover, then we made ourselves as comfortable as possible in the office, bedding down on some damp straw that we had obtained somewhere. Battery orders were to remain on the alert and to await further orders. There was no chance to rest. Heavy artillery and machine gun fire could be heard very close by, so it was obvious that we should soon be coming to the aid of our hard-pressed comrades. Eventually we discovered that the British had attacked in overwhelming strength near La Bassée and that our 13 Reserve Infantry Brigade was already heavily engaged. There was an extremely tense atmosphere as we contemplated what was to come."

The original aim was to launch a counter-attack at 6.00 am, all along the line and without artillery preparation, but doubts as to the viability of this course of action led to a last minute postponement. Word arrived in some cases only thirty minutes before the attack was due to jump off; in others, the information never arrived and so the assaulting troops were faced by the worst possible combination of circumstances. Luckily for the forward troops manning the Infantry Regiment 16 start line, the news was in time, but this was not the case to the north of Neuve Chapelle and, in the words of the history of Infantry Regiment 13, 'The companies which had been ordered to attack, stormed forward without any artillery preparation. Because the troops to the left did not advance, the attack withered away in a storm of flanking fire.'[20] For the reinforcements from Infantry Regiment 15, it was almost the same story. They had actually stepped off when the signal to break off the attack reached them.

Vizefeldwebel Brockmann 4th Company Infantry Regiment 15[21] **1.**

"Slowly the moment approached. Rifles were unloaded and bayonets fixed silently. We crept out of our holes and worked our way forward noiselessly towards the farm. At the very moment we were about to charge it came the trumpet call to break off and return [to the start line]. That put the Tommies on the alert. I heard the order 'Give fire!' [*sic*.] and a machine gun opened up not twenty metres away. However it fired everywhere but at us, so we kneeled up and fired back. It went quiet immediately opposite and we crawled back through the morning mist, though a number of us were killed or wounded.

"When it became light a hellish rate of fire began. However, it cannot be compared with that which we experienced later on the Somme or at Chavignon.[22] One sulphur shell[23] after another sent pillars of yellow smoke skywards. In between, incendiary rounds smashed down, covering the area with black clouds and, over it all, came the sound of machine guns firing. A row of burning houses cast a flickering light over everything, casting an image which was at the same time both fascinating and appalling. Over our heads at one point circled a German airman. It was Leutnant Max Immelmann the *Adler von Lille* [the Eagle of Lille], who was surrounded by white clouds of bursting shrapnel ... The enemy launched attacks several times, but wherever their lines appeared, we shot them up. A number of Tommies tried to take cover behind this wall. Very quickly it was holed like a sieve. Our ranks were thinned too. The major was dying, Oberleutnant Kuipers, commanding 2nd Company, was killed,[24] Bavarians, Hessians and Saxons came pouring in during the night. The plan was to assault Neuve Chapelle in the early dawn, but our company was scattered to the four winds and torn apart … "

Typical of the hurried, improvised nature of the riposte, was the order to 3rd Battalion Infantry Regiment 133, which was in regimental reserve, to supply a composite company under command of Reserve Leutnant Bössneck, commander 11th Company. Having arrived by train, it was thrown straight into action. The plan was for it to complete its march forward through the cold and rain of a March night in unfamiliar territory and to be in position to join the counter-attack the following morning. In the event and unsurprising to note, it got lost in the mud and the rain, was unable to participate in the ill-fated attack, but ended up spending the next two days holding forward positions and losing heavy casualties in the process.[25]

In the event, the 11 March was a day of inconclusive attacks, primarily by the British army, which was attempting to give substance to First Army Operation Order No.11 issued at 11.30 pm [British time] on 10 March.[26] Essentially this directed a resumption of the offensive by IV and the Indian Corps from 7.00 am [British time] on 11 March. Clearly, the British did not want to give up on broader aspects of the original plan but it was highly optimistic – to put it no more strongly – to attempt to storm a German position which was now manned considerably more strongly than the original line of breastworks had been. Orders had also been given on the German side by Commander VII Corps for a counter-attack by 14th Infantry Division to commence at 11.00 am. It is not clear how serious this intent was, because by then the possibility of surprise had been lost and German doctrine dictated that a full scale counter-attack had to be preceded by appropriate preparation. This direction superseded earlier orders to launch an attack at 5.30 am under cover of darkness and without artillery preparation as soon as sufficient reinforcements had been moved forward to the line of *Biez-Wald*.

Unsurprising to note, given the confusion, the change to the attack orders did not reach all formations and units, so there was a half-hearted assault by some sub units of Infantry Regiment 13 at 5.30 am which, being unsupported on either flank, soon withered away in British enfilade fire. The story was similar for the Bavarians. Held in forward assembly areas where they were subject to increasingly heavy British harassing fire, it was decided to press on with the attack and, taking heavy casualties as they advanced, the companies, arranged in several waves, attempted to close on the British positions. Eventually there was some limited progress and 3rd Battalion closed up on trenches held by the Indian Corps, 1st Battalion reorganised around a group of houses near to Piètre and 2nd Battalion got quite close to the area just northeast of Neuve Chapelle itself. This was a poor return for the effort expended and risks run. It was not only the British army which was experiencing difficulties with the passage of information and command and control. Nothing came of the German 11.00 am idea in any case, because a series of uncoordinated British attacks began at 8.25 am, when an attack with some artillery support came in against the right flank of Infantry Regiment 13, where its 1st and 2nd Companies succeeded in beating it back with heavy losses; no enemy troops got within eighty metres of the German lines.

A similar British attack was launched at 9.30 am and was also driven off. A British observation aircraft, flying low in an attempt to counteract the ground mist and direct fire onto the line of strong points accurately, was also shot down by Infantry Regiment 13 at about this time. One crew member was killed and the other captured.[27] On this day the mist was definitely to the advantage of the defence. It was effectively impossible to locate the German defensive positions, either from the air or the ground. This neutralised much of the artillery effort and, furthermore, it also disguised the fact that any further British advance would only succeed in the attacking troops penetrating even further into the defensive killing zone, which was becoming stronger with each passing hour. If to this is added the hopeless British command arrangements, which meant that moves were being directed by headquarters in rear completely ignorant of the actual situation at the front and suffering from delays between reporting and the issue of orders of from six to eight hours, it is small wonder that the attacks launched during the afternoon enjoyed no more success than the earlier ones. The orders arrived late, were frequently irrelevant or inappropriate and the defence had no trouble at all in both shooting them to a standstill and also in launching numerous low level trench clearing actions on both flanks. Eventually the coming of dusk brought the curtain down on a day of battle which had produced nothing but lengthening casualty lists and the German troops defending more or less the same positions that they had been twenty four hours earlier, but by now very much more securely.

Crown Prince Rupprecht of Bavaria Commander Sixth Army Diary Entry 11 March 1915[28]

> "According to the morning reports the enemy have broken into our positions near Neuve Chapelle and north to the road by Moulin au Piètre on a frontage of almost three kilometres, occupied old British trenches just forward of the eastern edge of the village and have attempted to protect them with obstacles. One section of our trenches between the Moulin au Piètre road and the parallel road to the north of Neuve Chapelle is still in our possession. Just before 2.00 pm a captured Order of the Day by Sir Douglas Haig, commander of the British First Army, dated 9 March, was brought to me. The order stated that the preconditions for an attack were extraordinarily favourable. The French had achieved success in Champagne and the Germans, who were suffering from hunger and unrest at home, had to weaken their front. The British would be deploying the heaviest guns ever used in a land battle and forty eight battalions were poised to attack a sector defended by only three German battalions. The British aim was to do battle and eject the German barbarians.
>
> "Because Haig's Army contains seventy two battalions, it is believable that forty eight battalions were in fact concentrated for the attack on Neuve

Chapelle. Whereas yesterday evening, when VII Corps was requesting the subordination of another division, I felt that the enemy was being overestimated, I was now of a different opinion and directed that the seven-battalion 86 Reserve Brigade was to be moved from Roeselare to Don and that it was to arrive there during the course of the night. I also gave orders to the neighbouring corps that they were to release to VII Corps as much of their high-angle artillery as they could spare, the aim being to have twenty batteries of howitzers in position to bring down fire before Neuve Chapelle.

"I then drove to Marquillies. The artillery fire that was coming down ceaselessly during the morning had dwindled significantly since then. It was now possible to distinguish each shell. General von Claer, who had stayed at [Headquarters] 14th [Infantry] Division whilst orders for the recapture of Neuve Chapelle were being issued, returned a little later. He stated that the attack was to go in at dawn the following day. On the right would be the Bavarian Reserve Brigade Scheler [14 Bavarian Reserve Infantry Brigade of 6th Bavarian Reserve Division, commanded by Generalmajor z.D. Scheler]; on the left was Brigade von Obernitz (14th Infantry Division). In addition, two Saxon battalions would take part, together with a Bavarian Reserve Regiment (initially to remain in reserve). The inter-brigade boundary was the line La Russie – Piètre and the regiment of 6th Bavarian Reserve Division, which was acting as corps reserve, would be located in Halpegarbe.

"It seemed to me that this attack, planned to go ahead with inadequate artillery preparation, was a somewhat risky enterprise and I drew attention to the desirability of delaying the attack until the guns had had a chance to bring effective fire to bear. General von Claer countered that he had only just heard about the approaching artillery reinforcements and that it would not be possible to make use of all the available batteries, due to a lack of suitable observation points, which had already forced several batteries to place their observation posts together in one place. At most he could deploy sixteen batteries and he would be forced to leave some of those in stand by locations. In addition it would be impossible to delay the start of the attack, due to the impossibility of moving reserves forward in daylight.

"*Biez-Wald* was under constant heavy fire, because our opponents assessed that reserves were located in or behind the wood. To the front of this wooded area were two Saxon battalions which were deployed yesterday evening and have been rather badly shaken up and others, also located there, were only roughly dug in. If the attack was to be postponed, it would have to take place at dawn the day after tomorrow and these troops would have to be withdrawn tonight. This would mean that the enemy would be granted a further twenty four hours to consolidate their hold on the captured position and it would then be necessary to conduct a full scale counter-attack, whose preparation would take weeks.[29]

"Despite my approval of the desire to attack, I regard it as a mistake that yesterday, before sufficient reinforcements had arrived, troops were all placed and allowed to remain forward of the strong points between the first and second positions. If they had occupied the strong points they would have been in prepared positions and would have been able to await the arrival of the remainder of the troops with far fewer losses. In addition, if the enemy had attempted to follow up, they could have been attacked in much more favourable positions. It proved to be impossible to withdraw the troops manning the front line because, whilst I was still in discussions with General von Claer, there was an enemy attack. Tomorrow's operation is certainly risky, especially because a significant part of the artillery due to arrive during the evening will not be able to provide fire support to the attack until it is well underway. It does appear, however, that our enemy was not feeling particularly aggressive; otherwise they would have pressed on with their attack."

When the battle began on 10 March, the men of Bavarian Reserve Infantry Regiment 21 had just arrived in Tourcoing, where they were supposed to be embarking on an extended period of rest and retraining. Instead of that they soon found themselves on trains heading rapidly towards Neuve Chapelle via Wavrin. It was a similar situation for Bavarian Reserve Infantry Regiment 16.

Reserve Leutnant Carl Stiegler 1st Company Bavarian Reserve Infantry Regiment 16[30]

"We were Army Reserve and, if we were lucky, we might be here for several weeks. But we had no such luck. Around midday [10 March] the cry of 'Alarm!' went up. One hour later 1st Battalion marched off to the station. Rumours flew about. 'We are off to Russia.' 'No, we are heading for the Vosges.' 'We are returning to our old positions.' We knew nothing and we were told nothing. Crammed to the roof, the blacked out trains snaked their way through the Flanders countryside. Night fell. We sat silently and shivered in the dark carriages. Suddenly there were blinding lights – Lille.

"The train rolled onwards. Suddenly, our ears pricked up and our pulses quickened. It was the dull, heavy rumble of distant guns. We arrived at a lit up station and the train halted briefly. There we saw wounded men with white bandages and caught snatches of sentences. 'British have broken through.' 'Trench lost.' Then we continued on our way. The train came to a halt and, after a short march we reached a village which had been abandoned by its occupants. There we paused for the night. Before us was the front, the sky above it illuminated by the light of countless flares. The roar of the guns was constant, [as was] the rattle of machine guns."

At 1.00 am on 11 March, some elements of 6th Bavarian Reserve Division began to march forward via Sainghin, Wicres and Herlies to Halpegarbe. 3rd Battalion Bavarian Reserve Infantry Regiment 17 had already been rushed forward on arrival and, together with 3rd Battalion Bavarian Reserve Infantry Regiment 20, was retained at the disposal of 79 Infantry Brigade in Halpegarbe, but the remainder of the advanced group, which was meant to be ready to begin the attack prior to dawn had had such an extremely difficult approach march that this proved to be impossible. It had taken them so long to move up that dawn was already breaking before they could reach their start lines and, because, as already discussed, there were insufficient forces both to hold the line of strong points and also attack, the operation was cancelled.

Instead, the formations of 6th Bavarian Reserve Division bivouacked hastily in the rear areas. Following discussions involving the regimental commanders and higher authority, a plan for the eventual assault on 12 March was worked out and reconnaissance parties moved forward at 7.00 pm, with orders being issued to the battalions at 10.00 pm. Already during the afternoon 3rd Battalion Bavarian Reserve Infantry Regiment 21 had been moved up to the *Biez-Wald*, prior to being moved to reinforce the defences in the sector of Infantry Regiment 56. There they encountered a totally confused situation, with elements of Infantry Regiments 56, 57, 104 and 139 completely jumbled. Major Graf Soden of Jäger Battalion 11 was placed in overall command and he directed a reorganisation of the defences; *viz.* right flank, anchored on the northern edge of the wood: Jäger Battalion 11 and 10th Company Bavarian Reserve Infantry Regiment 21 under Hauptmann Prinz zu Solms; centre, 11th and 12th Companies Bavarian Reserve Infantry Regiment 21 and 2nd and 4th Companies Infantry Regiment 57, commanded by Hauptmann Bauer of Bavarian Reserve Infantry Regiment 21; left flank as far as the southern edge of the wood, 1st Battalion Infantry Regiment 56 and 9th Company Bavarian Reserve Infantry Regiment 21, commanded by Hauptmann Prösch of Infantry Regiment 56.[31] Needless to say this reorganisation took a great deal of time. Nevertheless, eventually some rough order was restored and these troops stood by, ready to participate in the attack on 12 March.

Finally the moment for the counter-attack arrived. Not all the artillery reinforcements promised were yet in position, but most were and some were told off for particular support duties, which posed a variety of problems for those involved. Luckily there are several accounts to draw on, so we have a good overview of how this aspect of the counter-attack was organised and conducted.

Reserve Hauptmann Carl Windhorst Field Artillery Regiment 58[32] *2.*

"During the afternoon of 11 March, 3rd Battery received the following order:

'By tomorrow the battery is to furnish a gun, commanded by an officer, in the sector held by 2nd Battalion Infantry Regiment 13, in order to accompany our infantry and assist in the recapture of the trench which was lost yesterday. There is to be an immediate call for volunteers because the gun is to be deployed [forward] this evening. The officer is to report at once to regimental headquarters for further orders.'

"Commanded by Reserve Leutnant Wolbrecht, a gun team comprising one unteroffizier and seven gunners was assembled then, as dusk fell, the gun and an ammunition wagon were driven along the Piètre road as far as the command post of 2nd Battalion Infantry Regiment 13 (about 150 metres in rear of the infantry front line). From there it was pushed forward by hand, with the ammunition carried by a few sections of infantry made available for the purpose. The move forward of the gun took place under the most difficult of conditions. Despite the fact that the wheels had been muffled with straw, so as to make the move forward as silent as possible, the British were extremely alert. They fired flares constantly and kept the road under machine gun fire all the time. In these circumstances it took almost two hours to move one hundred metres. There could be no thought of digging in here so far forward. There was just a hedge to provide cover from enemy view.

"About 2.00 am the gun crew received orders from the battalion to start bringing fire down at 5.30 am on a communication trench directly in front of the gun, which was occupied by the British then, having engaged that, to shift the point of fire to the main enemy trench in the direction of the *Wasserburg*. Our infantry assault was due to begin at 6.00 am and, at exactly 5.30 am, the first shots rang out from the gun. At a range of between forty and eighty metres, every shell landed in the trench, which had been dug forward about head height into No Man's Land. Soon all that could be heard were the shrieks and groans of the wounded in the enemy trench.

"Two platoons of 4th Company Infantry Regiment 13 stormed forward from their trench at 6.00 am and overran the communication trench with no casualties. Because of the gunfire the British had evacuated it. Unfortunately, the attack stalled right in front of the enemy main position ... After the failure of our counter-attack, the enemy launched forward once more at 10.00 am in renewed strength. They succeeded in breaking into the positions to our right and captured a few hundred prisoners. The situation at this moment was critical, because a large gap had been created immediately next to the gun and no reserves were available to fill it.

"Luckily the enemy was not fully aware of the situation and our batteries in rear filled the gap immediately with concentrated defensive fire, so the worst was prevented. This, in turn, meant that the gun could once more bring down fire, this time into the flank of the advancing lines of enemy infantry. At very close range, this was entirely successful and the remaining 188 shells were fired off rapidly. The enemy attack simply withered away with high losses in the defensive fire of our batteries."

Wachtmeister Franz Brückle 7th Battery Bavarian Reserve Field Artillery Regiment 6[33]

3.

"We spent the whole of 11 March at immediate notice to move. Thick fog cut the visibility right down. Not until about midday did the sun peep through; then it turned into a fine spring afternoon. From the front came a report that the British thrust had been halted and it was therefore questionable if the battery would actually be sent into action. Just before it went dark, the battery was called together once more and the battery commander, Leutnant Weinberger, reminded us of the need for endurance and to do our duty. About midnight I was awakened by the battery commander, who had brought with him the order that the battery was to be ready to move at 4.00 am, so there was no possibility of further rest. At 3.00 am I woke the men and, by 4.00 am, the battery was lined up in the yard, ready to move off. The advance went via Erquinghem, Beaucamps, Fournes and Wicres to Chateau de Warneton, where we paused briefly. The 16th [Bavarian Reserve] (List) and 17th [Bavarian] Reserve Regiments were to our front. Our light ammunition column was already in position here. Onwards! Flares arcing through the sky and the chatter of machine guns showed how close we were to the front.

"The 8th and 9th Batteries of our battalion were deployed to the right [north] of Halpegarbe and were already in action. The main road Lille – La Bassée was crammed with troops marching forward. Finally the battery found some space and, at the trot, passed through Illies, where British shells were exploding. Just before Neuve Chapelle the battery took up position in a tobacco field. The whole area was blanketed in fog, which protected us from observation by enemy aircraft. We unloaded all our ammunition. Shrapnel and high explosive shells landed all round us [but we did not let them] disturb us, because the infantry needed our help. The Prussian officer, who was there to brief the battery, told me where the limbers were to move to and drew my attention to the need to avoid selecting a position near the main road. Having unloaded the vehicles we pulled back through Illies, trotting and occasionally galloping. Eberle and I placed the teams in an orchard by the road to Gravelin. The owner complained about [damage] to his well-tended orchard, but we could only shout, *'C'est la guerre!'* in reply. Alongside us was the light ammunition column of [Bavarian] Field Artillery Regiment 7 and right behind us a 210 mm howitzer battery fired over our heads. It could be assumed that we should not be able to remain here very long. Contact was maintained between battery and echelon by means of despatch riders.

"A terrible battle was taking place around Neuve Chapelle. Infantry reserves continued to march forward. Some were battalions with new equipment so, apparently, they had not been in the field for long. The empty wagons were refilled from the ammunition trains at Illies Station and a never ending stream of limbers and ammunition wagons replenished the battery. The empty wagons were then used to transport the wounded to the rear, so as to get them out of the hellish fire as soon as possible. Despite the pain of their wounds, they were delighted to have escaped the destructive fire. Towards 10.00 am came a report that the Bavarians had retaken the village of Neuve Chapelle from the British – but at what cost?[34]

"Until about midday the echelon location was undisturbed by the enemy, but all that time the main road to our front was under enemy shrapnel and shell fire. I directed Ries, the battery chef, to prepare a meal for the battery from the tinned food. There was no field kitchen available for the purpose, just a large cauldron. Steam was soon rising from it and our stomachs were looking forward to something hot inside, but the evil enemy were not going to allow us this meal. Heavy shells began to land around us, one ammunition wagon had already been damaged and we could soon see that we could not remain here any longer. We set off for Le Willy farm, which necessitated passing along the main road under constant heavy shell fire. Due to the heavy traffic, we could only make slow progress. However, we succeeded in reaching our new position without loss and information regarding the new position was passed immediately to the battery. Our meal continued to cook gently [in the old location] because, in his haste, our chef had forgotten everything. When we later went back to look, all we found was an empty cauldron. We were unable to say if it had been tipped over by an enemy shell, or emptied by other comrades. If the latter, then we did not begrudge it them, though we could certainly have used it ourselves."

Reserve Oberleutnant Schober Officer Commanding 3rd Battery Field Artillery Regiment 77 [35] **4.**

"At 10.00 am on 11 March the battery, which was billeted in Despres, was alerted and was the first of the battalion subunits to arrive that afternoon in Herlies. 1st Section, under Reserve Leutnant Schettler, was deployed at 1.00 pm to the most advanced artillery sector at the northeast exit to Aubers along the Rue Deleval. The reconnaissance of this position, in particular the passage of Aubers, took place under heavy enemy fire, which rendered it very difficult. 2nd Section, commanded by Leutnant Schabbehardt, was ordered to take up position as it went dark, along the Rue d'Enfer, with special instructions to provide direct support to the Westphalian Infantry Regiment 13 and the Marburg Jäger Battalion [Jäger Battalion 11]. During the night the section moved into position behind a road embankment on the Rue d'Enfer, about 800 metres behind the front line trench. Any other location was out of the question, because, to the right and left of the road, the entire countryside was under water. The battery personnel dug all night and, in order to clear fields of fire, twenty tall elm trees had to be felled.

"At 6.00 am our infantry launched an attack against Neuve Chapelle. Simultaneously, our section opened fire on the British who were occupying the village. With only brief pauses, fire was maintained throughout the day against Neuve Chapelle, Pont Rouge and the British trenches ... Calmly and courageously each man served the guns, though the soft ground meant that everyone was covered in the dirt and mud which was thrown up. During the afternoon the ammunition ran out. One platoon of the 1st Ammunition

Column under Leutnant Schulze worked its way through hellish fire to the centre of Aubers, but could get no further; rubble from the smashed houses was blocking the road. There was nothing else for it but for the gunners to fetch the ammunition from there. Moving through this crazy fire, darting from house to house, snatching a quick breather occasionally, then rushing on again with the shell baskets, they eventually arrived at the guns sweating profusely.

"In the meantime the British launched another attack and the infantry urgently needed artillery support. Displaying remarkable daring, the gun commander, Unteroffizier Arnold, and Gefreiter Richter served Number 3 Gun, whilst Unteroffizier Sperling and Gefreiter Ohmann operated Number 4. All remaining personnel were fully occupied fetching ammunition. At long last the enemy fire slackened off at 7.00 pm and, by 11.00 pm, the gunners could have a short break. But it was only short, because it was essential to spend time improving the gun positions, especially against flanking fire and then, the following morning, the battle started once more. The section was directed to bring down fire between Chapigny and the *Wasserburg*. There was a tall, broad elm in the line of fire and no time to deal with it amidst all the heavy enemy fire. A quick decision was taken and it was chopped down by a direct hit. It crashed down across the road, luckily not on the gun. The new sector was dominated by a high house on the western exit, so an observation point was established there, together with a chain of runners. The enemy brought down very heavy fire on Rue d'Enfer and Aubers, so there were the crashes of light and heavy shells landing in front of, behind and either side of the guns.

"An infantryman, dripping with sweat and without weapon or headgear, came running up. 'Have you got a telephone? We need support at once; the British have broken into our trench!' A short time later an officer arrived, bearing the same news. The link from the section back to battalion was the only intact line in the whole infantry sector. The report was passed on swiftly and, a short time later, Bavarian reserves advanced via 'Haut' Pommereau. A large number of enemy aircraft appeared and reconnoitred our positions. Some of our guns fell silent so as not to betray their positions. An enemy pilot circled constantly over the section. The gun position officer ordered, 'Fire is to be maintained, come what may. Our infantry needs us urgently.' The enemy brought fire down on the section, with aerial observation! – so ran a report from the guns. 'Keep on firing!' ordered the gun position officer.

"Just after that came the report, 'Direct hit on Number 4 Gun! Firing will continue regardless! Direct hits on Number 4 Ammunition Wagon and amongst the shell baskets of Number 3 Gun! Keep on firing! Three shells have landed in the protective cover of Number 3 Gun! Firing is be continued!' Thus were the exchanges between the reports from the guns and the orders of the gun position officer. There was such a hellish rate of fire that it was impossible to hear the guns firing from the observation point, which was only 120 metres off to one side.

"Unfortunately, the courageous Unteroffizier Kurt Brunner, who had distinguished himself previously at Thin le Moutier and L'Epinette, was killed here.[36] Despite all the fire, Leutnant Schabbehardt and Fähnrich Töpfer provided remarkable examples of courage. As Fähnrich Töpfer and Kanoniers Lachmuth and Gallschütz were sitting fuzing shells, a pile of shell baskets were shot away from beneath them. Every officer, unteroffizier and man did his duty to the best of his ability. At 6.00 pm the enemy fire began to slacken off. The enemy strength was spent; the attempt at breakthrough defeated. On our side fresh batteries and infantry regiments closed up. The enemy had suffered such high casualties that they did not attempt another breakthrough."

One of the officers of Field Artillery Regiment 78, who was deployed forward during the night 12/13 March to act as liaison officer to Infantry Regiment 13 and observe and correct the fire of 3rd Battery, also wrote a detailed account of his experiences after the battle.

Reserve Leutnant Reiling 3rd Battery Field Artillery Regiment 78[37] **2.**

"Accompanied by my batman, I made my way to Cliqueterie Farm where I was given more detailed orders and despatched in the general direction of Moulin Piètre and the trenches of Infantry Regiment 13. We moved through Aubers, which was burning, then left the road, which bore the magnificent name Rue d'Enfer, then stumbled in pitch blackness through the mud of Flanders. Flares and rifle fire showed us the way towards the enemy. Looking ghostly, we made out Moulin Piètre. It was the devil of a job to find our way by night through completely unknown terrain. The odd figure loomed up left and right. I must have been somewhere around the so-called *Wasserburg*, when my batman called out something to me. Suddenly a German infantryman was at my side, telling me in a low voice to keep as quiet as possible because out to the front was a section of trench which had already been occupied by the British. Rifle bullets whizzed to and fro and the sound of English voices was carried to us on the west wind.

"So as to avoid making too close an acquaintance of the Tommies, I set off in an arc to the right, went forward once more and jumped down into a trench. A soldier was sitting there on a rough bench, rifle tightly gripped in his hand and apparently asleep. As I bent over him, I realised I was looking into the face of a dead man. I carried on. At long last I heard, 'Halt! Who goes there? It was a sentry belonging to Infantry Regiment 13 from Münster and I asked him for directions to the company commander. The regiment had been manning this position for two months and during the past few days had, with great courage but high cost, held back the British, who outnumbered them considerably. The section of trench appeared to me to be still in quite good condition. It was well supplied with sandbags and revetted with wickerwork. It was, however, very wet and had to be pumped out constantly. This was the very front line. The courageous Westphalian comrades made me very welcome. Continual small arms fire made it impossible to get any rest, then at dawn we drank a cup of coffee.

"The situation was not exactly rosy. To our left, the British had broken into our lines on a battalion frontage. They are bound to do everything possible today to expand that. I made early contact with the battery and was able to range them in on the British trenches. The British infantry is only eighty to one hundred metres away. Small arms fire has been incessant and now artillery fire is coming down at an unprecedented rate. The dugouts are only lightly constructed, offering protection against shrapnel only. The best protection is still that afforded by the parapet. The walls of the trenches are trembling and heaving and exploding shells are hurling masses of earth and stone into the trenches. I have been hit several times by large pebbles and am learning something of the lot of the infantryman who has to hold on, sometimes for days, ready for anything, despite heavy fire. If an enemy assault was to come in now it would almost be a relief. But that is something which the enemy is apparently not risking.

"Already breaches have been shot here and there. Apparently the aim is to make our trench ready to be assaulted. In front! Behind! In front! Behind! Then came a huge explosion in the trench itself. Piles of earth and planks covered several of our brave lads, who were all dead when they were pulled out. Wounded men were carried off in groundsheets. A further explosion tore a huge gap in the parapet and swept away the barbed wire obstacle. Everywhere the holes blown by the huge shells were turned into miniature ponds. The company was now down to about half its peacetime strength, but they were fine lads. They came from Westphalia and were men of few words, but all were ready to give the Tommies a hot reception. I noted with pleasure that the gunners were very welcome in their midst. At such times support by one's own artillery is a great comfort to the man in the trench.

"The telephone link to the rear was cut. The fire was weaker around midday. It was as though the Tommies were concentrating on their lunch. We opted to do the same and ate a good humoured, but sparse, meal in a dugout. That afternoon the Anglo-French [sic.] drum fire began once more. A heavy shell hammered into the ruins of a house to the rear of the trench and flattened it completely. The worst aspect of it was the fact that it was impossible to evacuate the wounded to safety or recover the fallen. The company medical orderly went round giving injections of morphine. At long last evening fell. We sat there in a dugout, muddy, covered with dirt and drowsy, but our attempts to sleep were barely possible, due to the frequent bursts of firing. It was there that I heard that Leutnant Weber had been sent forward to the front line trench to act as a second liaison officer. On the way he was hit in the head by a shrapnel ball and died a hero's death."[38]

If the troops in and around *Biez-Wald* had problems shaking out and preparing for the assault on 12 March, the remaining reinforcements, which were to move up during the night 11/12 March, faced even greater difficulties. The blacked out rear areas were a scene of complete chaos as marching troops, guns and vehicles jostled for space on the roads and tracks. In fact the situation was so bad and the roads leading forward were crammed to such an extent with troops, guns, vehicles and other impedimenta, that it was impossible to move in formed bodies and the men had to pick their way forward by squeezing through the jams on an individual basis. That fact, coupled with the pitch darkness and unknown territory, meant that hours passed with little progress and when the time for the assault came, for example, only three companies of 2nd Battalion Bavarian Reserve Infantry Regiment 21 were in the correct place. Of the 1st Battalion there was no sign and, when it was finally located, its commander, Major Eberhard, who had been directed to go and receive orders at Brigade Headquarters, was still missing and Hauptmann Riederer of 1st Company had to assume command.[39] Even those who attempted to move cross country had immense difficulty. Bavarian Reserve Infantry Regiment 16 later described the conditions as, 'dreadful'. 'The bog in and around the *Biez-Wald* will be remembered for ever by those who survived. Some lost their boots and marched on barefoot. Others could only keep up by discarding their equipment'.[40]

In the event, 12 March was a frustrating day of attack and counterattack which produced nothing but large numbers of casualties and can be swiftly summarised. Bavarian Reserve Infantry Regiments 20 and 21 of Bavarian 14 Reserve Brigade were deployed to the right of the surviving elements of Jäger Battalion 11, which had been continuing to pass upwards pessimistic reports of the chances of ejecting the British from their newly won positions. 'The enemy is already too well established', they reported.[41] Murky conditions enabled the German assaulting troops to get fairly close to the British positions before they were spotted, but all initial attempts were beaten back, as were the occasional sorties launched by the British. Towards midday there was increased British artillery fire and a final British attack began at about 2.00 pm, but enjoyed no success. All the German artillery reinforcements added their weight of fire to the battlefield and began to have an increasing effect and put a complete stop to any British thoughts of further offensive activity for the time being, especially after leading elements of the British 2nd Cavalry Division were driven back sharply by concentrated German gunfire in mid afternoon.

Part of the responsibility for the German counter-attack was shouldered by the survivors of Infantry Regiment 16, who had spent a grisly thirty six hours in the *Biez-Wald*, being shelled constantly and suffering casualties from splinters, both steel and wooden, as the trees were felled and splintered on all sides. This was hardly the best preparation for a vigorous assault, though the arrival of hot food during the night 11/12 March came as welcome relief to men who had gone hungry for forty eight hours at that point. Once the attack was launched, these Westphalians attempted, alongside the

Saxon and Bavarian reinforcements, to get forward, but they too were beaten by British artillery and small arms fire. 2nd Battalion Bavarian Reserve Infantry Regiment 16 attempted to fill a gap in the thin line of Jägers and to press on, but it was all in vain.

A determined early effort by the British directed against *Biez-Wald* was thwarted by a resolute defence put up by 9th Company Infantry Regiment 57 and 10th Company Bavarian Reserve Infantry Regiment 17 whilst, off to the north, a force, including 6th and 9th Companies Infantry Regiment 104 and 8th Company Infantry Regiment 179, pressed right up against the British trenches but the attack could be developed no further, once the contact on the left flank with the Jägers was lost and the threat of being deeply outflanked increased sharply. Not even a further determined attack by Bavarian Reserve Infantry Regiments 20 and 21 could prevent the assault force falling back. Although a few isolated pockets held out for the remainder of the day, it did not affect the overall outcome and very few members of the northern force survived the day.

A scratch force in the southern sector, led by Oberleutnant Schroer of 2nd Company Infantry Regiment 16 and including elements of the 7th and 10th Companies, temporarily commanded by Leutnants Dönhof (of Field Artillery Regiment 7) and Gropler, did make reasonable progress towards the former trenches of 10th Company. Elements of 11th and 12th Companies Bavarian Reserve Infantry Regiment 20 moved up alongside and Schroer's men were able to hold their positions throughout the rest of the day, regardless of British pressure. Having withstood constant shelling and machine gun fire, as well as several infantry assaults, this outpost was withdrawn. Orders were given to suspend offensive operations in the south. Both sides had fought themselves to a temporary standstill and both made use of the hours of darkness to consolidate their positions and dig in to the extent possible in this waterlogged area.

On the German right flank, once 6th Company Infantry Regiment 13, under Leutnant Herrmann, and 2nd Battalion Bavarian Reserve Infantry Regiment 20 had deployed, the remaining members of Infantry Regiment 13 also lunged forward. The temporary commander of the remnant of 9th Company Infantry Regiment 13, Vizefeldwebel Weide, went down with a very painful arm wound[42] and his remaining men were taken under command of Leutnant Aistermann of 11th Company and the attack continued – but not for long. The more progress it made, the more it came under heavy fire until, eventually, the combined fire of six British machine guns from a house forward of Neuve Chapelle broke it and forced the few survivors back to their start line. One unnamed eyewitness from 11th Company Infantry Regiment 13 later described the situation in a letter home:[43]

> "Our Leutnant Aistermann led the entire operation. He was everywhere – giving advice, encouraging and inspiring. When 9th Company, which was occupying the start of the former communication trench, did not immediately storm forward – probably as a result of a misunderstanding, our Leutnant climbed quite alone out of cover. Never in my life will I forget this uplifting, extraordinary sight. All alone, coat blowing in the breeze, without a weapon and swinging his usual walking stick high in the air, he stood there, master of

the field, oblivious to any personal danger and he led 9th Company into the assault. What a leader! He was hero of a type very seldom encountered; one of the calmest, most active and able officers of the entire regiment."

There are suggestions[44] that there were examples of misuse of the Red Cross flag in this area; that some British forces either donned German uniforms in an attempt to deceive, or drove German prisoners in front of some of their attacks as human shields, but it is difficult to give much credence to these ideas. It is far more probable that they arose out of a misreading of a confused battlefield, with all manner of different activities taking place simultaneously.

Initially, 1st and 2nd Battalions Bavarian Reserve Infantry Regiment 17 of 12 Bavarian Reserve Brigade were held back in reserve, but its 3rd Battalion, together with 1st and 3rd Battalions Bavarian Reserve Infantry Regiment 16, were subordinated to the Prussian 79 Infantry Brigade for the counter-attack. There was a role for the commander of Bavarian Reserve Infantry Regiment 16 but, initially at least, regimental headquarters Bavarian Reserve 17 had nothing to do, a fact bemoaned by Bavarian Reserve Infantry Regiment 17 later, 'Once more, exactly as at Wijtschate, circumstances had torn the regiment apart and caused it to have to deploy under strange commanders.'[45] It was a further contribution to what was already a thoroughly confused and confusing situation, some idea of which can be gained from this account by a member of one of the Bavarian regiments.

Reserve Leutnant Carl Stiegler 1st Company Bavarian Reserve Infantry Regiment 16[46]

"During the evening [of 11 March] we were informed that the British had broken through at Neuve Chapelle and that, at 6.00 am the following day, we reserves were to launch a counter-attack. Night fell. We continued to lie on straw in the farmhouse kitchen with its broken windows. To my left was Jakobus; to my right Max Müller. Both were fast asleep and silence reigned. I packed my knapsack carefully. Logs burned in the open fireplace, casting wild shadows on the walls. Cigarettes smouldered. Gradually the fire died down and we lay wrapped in our blankets, using our knapsacks as pillows. The guns rumbled incessantly, like lions roaring after meat. I slept – no, I lay awake – because I was so cold.

"We marched off at 3.00 am, following a blazing torch, which cast its light on a forest of grey helmet spikes. Ambulance vehicles, artillery convoys and machine gun wagons [were everywhere]. To the front it was the calm before the storm. A shot up village. Sandbags were distributed. A wood loomed up. Terrible sodden countryside, criss-crossed with drainage ditches. Pitch black. Clinging clay added pounds to the weight of each boot. The company shook out into three assault lines and advanced. From then on events just cascaded over me like a kaleidoscope. 6.00 am. Suddenly violent small arms and gun fire crashed out. The assault lines got mixed up. There was wild rushing about. Here and there someone went down.

"Shell holes. Tree trunks. Folds in the ground. I ducked down behind a fold. A farm. Through the fruit trees cracked machine gun bullets. I crawled off to one side in a narrow ditch. Wounded men shrieked. The guns opened up. Salvoes of shrapnel. Bursting shells bloomed out in the darkness into great fiery flowers. The machine guns rattled away endlessly. The enemy was totally invisible. To the left was a meadow with trenches. Occupied by our men. Out front just white fog. Gentle rain. From the sound of the machine guns, I eventually worked out where the British were located. And I spotted that the shells were also British. Tching – boom; tching-boom, came the salvoes of shrapnel rounds, sending bullets spraying through the branches of the fruit trees. I leapt into the trench which ran from the farm to the edge of the wood. Because it was knee deep with water, like everyone else I dug down and took cover in the spoil heaped up above it. Bullets cracked just overhead.

"To my left were members of a Saxon regiment; to my right, men of a different battalion of my regiment. There was wild confusion. A comrade from 4th Company was shot through both hands. Tching-boom – more shrapnel. A few spent balls rattled against my mess tins. A man of my company was crawling to the rear with a leg wound. I called out to him, 'Have you been hit?' Just then I received a dreadful blow, my head hit the clay and I lost consciousness. When I came round, streams of blood were running down my face. My helmet lay off to one side. It had been pierced by a large shrapnel ball, but the metal Bavarian lion insignia had taken the force, otherwise I should probably already have been invited to join the valkyries in Valhalla."

At around midday, drum fire crashed down on 11th Company Infantry Regiment 13 and the right hand [northern] defensive flank. In view of the totally inadequate level of protection provided by their defensive works, once more there were serious losses and the nerves of those still unwounded were badly affected. A British charge gained some ground, 9th and 11th Companies Infantry Regiment 13 fell back and, as a result, the left flank of 5th Company was extremely vulnerable. The company commander, Leutnant Fritz Philippi, was first wounded by a round which penetrated the viewing slit of a steel infantry shield and then killed when a shell crashed into his dugout[47] and Leutnant Ekey had to take over and try to hold his position near to Piètre. For some time the situation was extremely precarious, but 10th and 11th Companies Infantry Regiment 55 were rushed forward from Pommereau and the front stabilised once more,[48] though this was not finally the case until Generalleutnant Scanzoni's 6th Bavarian Reserve Division was formally inserted into the front between 13th and 14th Infantry Divisions later that afternoon and the German artillery, now fully deployed and supplied with plentiful stocks of ammunition, pounded every worthwhile target in range.

Wachtmeister Franz Brückle 7th Battery Bavarian Reserve Field Artillery Regiment 6[49]

5.

"The battle by artillery and infantry continued until dark. The British tried everything to break through here and the German wall sagged in places but never broke and the arrival of reserves repeatedly checked their progress. Our battery brought down rapid fire on British cavalry, scattering it like bees from an upended hive. From Le Willy we could follow the course of the battle easily. For a spectator with no responsibilities, this would have been a great pleasure, but it was not for us. 11 and 12 March cost 6th Bavarian Reserve Division many lives and much blood. The lightly wounded headed to the rear in groups almost the size of companies. We could recognise them at a distance by their white dressings. Countless motorised and horse drawn ambulances transported the seriously wounded to the hospitals. Only those who have seen it with their own eyes can really appreciate the blood and misery of battle. Darkness fell, but the battle raged on. Now was the moment for the field kitchens as they brought food forward to the hungry comrades. Many of our brothers in arms were not there to receive the food; they lay dead on the battlefield, having done their duty to home and Fatherland. May they rest in peace!

"During these days the performance of the battery under pressure was beyond all praise. The drivers, in particular, had been outstanding. Our dear paymaster, Schletter, brought cash forward that evening, so on the gun line we were able to distribute rations and pay. We had no idea what the coming days had in store for us. Even at night the British brought fire down on our approach routes and it was mere chance that we got back to the echelon position unscathed. About 1.00 am the British troubled us again with heavy shells. Our only thought was that today or tomorrow it would be our turn [to be hit]. We spent the entire night out in the open. The following day, that is to say 13 March, the fighting reduced in intensity somewhat. Now we realised fully what the enemy had been attempting and what our troops had achieved. There were tears in our eyes when the remnants of the *Marburger Jäger* [Kurhessisches Jäger Battalion 11] rallied near us. All the time the support vehicles of this battalion were alongside us, only eleven men reported in. At Ypres I had once seen the remains of a battalion of Bavarian Infantry Regiment 9 commanded by a Fähnrich, but the sight of the heroes of Neuve Chapelle, stained yellow from the sulphur fumes of the shells, their uniforms hanging in tatters, was even more pitiful. Our fallen lay in rows in the military cemetery at Illies. May God grant that these heroes rest in peace!"

Everywhere lay the dead and wounded. It was dangerous for the slightly wounded to attempt to move, but even more risky not to make the attempt, as artillery fire continued to crash down, raking over the entire battle area.

Reserve Leutnant Carl Stiegler 1st Company Bavarian Reserve Infantry Regiment 16[50] **6.**

"I jumped down into the water-filled trench and waded to the farm. About twenty Saxon men were sheltering in this dismal mud shack. Two of them bandaged me up roughly. The shell fire grew heavier. I feared that any second the farm would be hit by a 240 mm howitzer and wiped off the face of the earth, so I decided to get out of it. I dashed over the meadow into the wood. The meadow was littered with long rows of discarded knapsacks, dead and wounded. Men of my regiment were digging in the wood. Out of a ditch crawled an old grey haired soldier, bleeding dreadfully from a stomach wound, and dragged himself into bushes by the edge of the wood, just like a deer wounded by a hunter. There was a dead man from a Saxon infantry regiment, with an appalling gash in his skull.

"A few sections of our men went forward, but some tumbled to the ground like hares, hit by machine gun fire. There was an unteroffizier from 2nd Company, his shin bone split open by a shell splinter. A comrade from 3rd Company was hit in the arm. A sanitätsunteroffizier organised some of us to carry back his comrade who had the shin bone wound. We sat him on a rifle and carried him back gently though the wood, though we ourselves were utterly exhausted because of loss of blood. Four or five British machine guns now opened up on the edge of the wood. Then it all started! They sent over complete salvoes of shrapnel and high explosive. Our uniforms were stained yellow with the smoke from the picric acid of the British shells. Tree trunks crashed to the ground, branches splintered, the seriously wounded groaned. Engineers were carrying heavy mortar rounds forward. Heavy projectiles crashed endlessly into the wood. It was as though giant monsters, howling and screaming, were falling on us from a great height.

"Gritting our teeth, wounded ourselves, we carried our seriously wounded man further. Around us, above us and at our side, Death howled, screamed and plucked at us. The leafy wood was transformed into a Hell full of flame and fire, splintering trees, appalling detonations, branches and masses of earth tossed high into the sky. Everywhere there were the terrible screams of the dying, intermingled with blood, smoke and the stink of powder. At long last we got clear of the girdle of fire. In Halpegarbe emergency dressings were applied then we were taken in straw-lined cattle trucks to Lille. The grey streaks of dusk filled the sky as we arrived in this rear area town. The lamps in the boulevards were flaring and the streets were filled with the colourful bustle of a city. Yet, only a few kilometres away, filthy and soaking wet, our brothers were facing danger and death."

At about 8.00 pm, Sixth Army sent the following report to Supreme Army Headquarters in Mezières:

"The British attack was conducted by two complete corps which are still in place. In the face of this superiority a continuation of the attack with the forces available stands no chance of success. Therefore, for the time being, the Army intends to issue orders to hold the positions it has won and to initiate no further action."[51]

Following a somewhat tense telephone conversation between General Konrad Kraft von Dellmensingen, Chief of Staff Sixth Army and General von Falkenhayn, the Army commander summed up a disappointing day in his diary.

Crown Prince Rupprecht of Bavaria Commander Sixth Army Diary Entry 12 March 1915[52]

"VII Corps reports that the enemy attack yesterday evening was unsuccessful. The attack to recapture Neuve Chapelle began at 6.00 am and the enemy artillery began to return fire about fifteen minutes later. According to the initial reports which came back, the brigade of von Obernitz and, later, that of Scheler, penetrated into Neuve Chapelle and that the attack was making slow progress. Following a request, Corps Headquarters was permitted at 8.00 am to move 86 Reserve Brigade [43rd Reserve Division] forward to Herlies and Illies[53] and the corps has also moved to Ligny the Saxon light field howitzer battalion which it claimed yesterday could be spared. At midday reports indicated that trenches in front of Neuve Chapelle had been captured – nothing more was being said about the village itself and, by 2.00 pm, the sugar refinery to the east of that place came into our possession.

"By the same time there had already been 1,500 admissions of wounded into the field hospitals. Later VII Corps requested that 86 Reserve Brigade be released to them and this was approved. During the evening the sad, but unsurprising, news arrived that the attack had failed. With the exception of one regiment of 86 Reserve Brigade, every other formation had been deployed. For the most part they were now located back on their start lines but, in the centre, they were forward of their strong points. The corps commander in his evening report stated that he believed that he would be able to hold out but that, if the enemy launched another attack, further support would be needed.

"I was unable to guarantee that from within [Sixth] Army resources, so had to pass the request on the Supreme Army Headquarters. [It] responded by informing us that a brigade, currently in Second Army reserve and located in Nesle, would detrain in Don and Wavrin by tomorrow night. General von Falkenhayn was extremely worked up about the loss of Neuve Chapelle and also expressed the opinion that the counter-attack should not have been conducted. However, this did provide the advantage that the enemy did not press home their own attack and took no ground during the day."

Nightfall on 12 March may have seen an end to the major thrusts and counter-thrusts of the two sides, but it took some time thereafter before things returned to normal trench routine. 'There has been no action at all from the enemy infantry at Neuve

Chapelle, who are strengthening their defences.' wrote Crown Prince Rupprecht on 13 March, 'This does not indicate an intention to renew the attack.'[54] Naturally, exchanges of fire, occasionally heavy, continued for some time, defences were improved by both sides, the original hard pressed and much reduced formations of 14th Infantry Division were relieved and there was a steady flow of casualties for several days to come.

Reserve Leutnant Reiling 3rd Battery Field Artillery Regiment 78[55] **7.**

"Day dawned on 14 March, the worst day [for me] of the Neuve Chapelle breakthrough battle. During the early morning I was summoned to the newly repaired telephone with a view to ranging in the guns of the battery and, luckily, I took the company commander with me out of the dugout so that he could orientate me. To that end, we went about twenty paces along the trench to the right and began to range the guns. Suddenly heavy drum fire began again on our trench and, just as we were pressing ourselves against the parapet, the dugout we had just vacated took a direct hit and flames belched out of it. In the midst of the racket of the gun- and rifle fire suddenly we heard the tak! tak! tak! of a British machine gun which, in the course of a few bursts, wrecked the protective parapet in front of our machine gun, destroyed the weapon and killed or wounded several of our brave lads who were attempting to save the gun.

"The commander of a neighbouring Bavarian battery had just arrived in our trench to discuss something with us, when he was hit in the head by a shrapnel ball and badly wounded. We took him into a dugout on the right flank of the company but, hardly had we arrived, than this section of trench also came under violent drum fire. The wounded man was given some cognac, then crawled with us into a dugout whose supporting beams were shaking. As the fire slackened a little, I noticed a few young lads gathered in front of the dugout. I was just about to call out to them that they should remain under cover when a shell landed right there and tore them apart. I was literally thrown back into the dugout by the overpressure and I was sprayed with so much of their blood that it was assumed initially that I was wounded. This severe test of our nerves lasted for hours.

"Outside in the trench the situation was awful. The water had risen so high that it was no longer possible to pump it out; whilst the yellowish, clay laden liquid was stained in places red with blood. The company strength was so reduced and the trench so damaged that the very thought of an enemy attack was a source of great concern. However over there the casualties were also not slight and the hope was that the desire to attack had ebbed away. Our artillery fired constantly. From the rear of Aubers Ridge, where my battery was also located, concentration after concentration was fired at the British lines. It was melody that my Gunner's heart could warm to. The heavy, dull thuds of the firing signatures could be heard from beyond Aubers. This was followed by the dull humming roar of the 210 mm shells of our heavy howitzers, which landed in the British positions with violent crashes.

"Whenever one of these shells came down in a British trench, I could see beams and fascines being thrown into the air as high as a house. These impacts even made our dugouts shake and hurled rocks from over there at us. It must have been anything other than a happy experience on the other side and that was a great comfort to us. We began to think that if the enemy did not assault after this sort of preparation, then the great breakthrough would come to nothing. It really was getting quieter over there and the situation became much easier. News was passed down the trenches, 'Infantry Regiment 13 is to be relieved this evening'. I bid my bold comrades farewell, because I had to remain in the trenches longer. The performance of the courageous 13th was beyond all praise. When the rather sparse army communiqué was published, those back home understood a lot less than us who had seen what these grossly outnumbered troops had achieved in the muddy trenches near La Bassée against the British army and its coloured supporting people. In place of the 13th came the Darmstadt Grenadiers.[56] The battle continued to die away and late that afternoon orders arrived directing me to rejoin the battery."

One week later, his regiment having redeployed to a quiet sector, a member of Bavarian Reserve Infantry Regiment 16 wrote home, describing in a way entirely typical of this battle what he had experienced.

Vizefeldwebel Josef Wenzl 2nd Company Bavarian Reserve Infantry Regiment 16 [57]

"At 7.00 pm [11 March] our battalion commander told us that we were to be deployed against Neuve Chapelle at 6.00 am the following day. Despite the situation we were all full of confidence. The following morning at 6.00 am all those deployed were engaged by a hellish rate of fire from artillery, machine guns and riflemen. They were forced to dig in behind the hedge just to their front and then to try to work their way forward through heavy fire in small groups. Large numbers ended up lying dead or wounded in a trail 250 metres long. The forward trenches were full of water. Despite this, even men with leg wounds and others bathed in sweat, threw themselves into the cold filthy water and had to stick it out until evening.

"The men advanced on Neuve Chapelle, despite the fact that the enemy brought down rifle and machine gun fire every time the tip of a helmet was seen. To the right the troops there attacked and, despite the dreadful fire, managed to reach Neuve Chapelle in weak numbers. Immediately the enemy brought down an appalling bombardment, which shrouded the entire landscape with one great smoke cloud. The noise of firing and exploding shells sounded as one and our artillery did not seem to be able to make any effective reply. The roaring and thunder of the enemy guns must have continued at full intensity for a good two hours. The earth shook, bits of houses flew in the air, whilst trees and branches were thrown about around the wood. I thought that my last hour had come; not even the end of the world could possibly be worse. The fire had such a deadening effect on the nerves that men fell into an exhausted sleep.

"We were up to our chests in water. To the right, in order not to be cut off and captured, the Germans had to pull back once more. All we could do was watch them being driven back; we were powerless to do anything. Those who returned occupied a position which they held against all attacks and despite the heaviest of fire. Without being able to help we had to stand and watch whilst the British captured prisoners. Because we could move neither forwards nor backwards and were threatened by flanking fire, we decided to defend to the last man. The British forced their way into a trench off to a flank. Once it went dark, we made our way back to where [Bavarian] Reserve Infantry Regiment 16 was manning a defensive position and there, despite being soaked through, we had to hold out by day and night."

Despite the fact that his earlier misgivings concerning the counter-attack of 12 March has proved to be fully founded, on 14 March Commander Sixth Army drew a line under Neuve Chapelle when he signed a special Order of the Day, directed at all participants.

Crown Prince Rupprecht of Bavaria Commander Sixth Army 14 March 1915[58]

"Soldiers! Having employed forty eight battalions against three German ones, the enemy succeeded in capturing a section of our defences, despite the heroic defence put up by its garrison. Attempts to re-take it were not successful, but your attack broke the offensive will of the enemy. Two enemy corps did not dare to thrust forward from the captured village, whose possession is of no significance.[59]

"I wish to express my warmest appreciation and thanks to each and every one of you for your sacrificial courage."

Neuve Chapelle was a short-lived, but bloody, battle, which cost both sides in excess of 10,000 casualties. In its way it is extremely interesting, because it illustrates clearly the problems that static positional warfare posed to the attacker who sought a breakthrough. Given suitable concentration of force, especially in guns, a break in was relatively easily obtained but, thereafter, when communications inevitably failed, it was almost impossible to maintain the impetus, to reinforce local success and to avoid the isolated attackers forward of the friendly positions from being first stopped by long range machine gun fire from depth positions, then pounded by artillery and finally forced back whence they came by a build up of defensive strength on the flanks and determined counter-attack.

The setback at Neuve Chapelle nevertheless came as a shock to the German army, which was quick to draw the appropriate lessons and amend its defensive methodology and tactics. It was a shock, too, to the British army, which had been shot to a standstill in the assault during the encounter battles along the Aisne heights the previous September, but believed that careful planning, concentration of force and the bravery of its infantry would lead inevitably to breakthrough. Its disabuse must have been a painful experience, which no subsequent assertion, amounting almost to bluster, about how close it allegedly came to success or what effect it was said to have had on the morale of the German army could have eradicated. The hard, but inescapable, fact of the matter is that it came nowhere near to succeeding – not even as a means of impressing the French by a display of British battlefield prowess. Joffre, whilst acknowledging the results obtained on the first day, then curtly dismissed their significance, *'Mais ce fut un succès sans lendemain.'* [But it was a success which led to nothing.][60]

Notes
1. This was not the first time in 1915 that Joffre had lobbied the French government for its support in obtaining British reinforcements. See Joffre *Mémoires* p 57 in which he refers to his letter No. 4230, dated 15 January 1915 concerning this very matter.
2. See BOH pp 71-73 & GOH pp 56 – 58.
3. Groos History Infantry Regiment 13 p 76.
4. Baldenstein History Infantry Regiment 16 p 73
5. Leutnant Karl Baumbach von Kaimberg is buried in the German cemetery at Lens-Sallaumines Block 8 Grave 167. Leutnant Alfred von Küster succumbed later in the month to his wounds and is buried in the German cemetery at Seclin. Block 4 Grave 24.
6. BOH pp 96-97.
7. Two guns of the four gun battery had been put out of action by the preliminary British barrage and a third was hit later in the action.
8. Henke History Field Artillery Regiment 7 p 105.
9. Major Alex Strippelmann was evacuated to a field hospital where he died of his wounds nine days later. Riebensahm History Infantry Regiment 15 p 104. He is buried in the German cemetery at Lille- Süd Block 2 Grave 391.
10. Leutnant Frans Jersch, who was twenty one when he died, succumbed to his wounds in a British hospital six days later. He is buried in the German plot of Merville Communal Cemetery Block 1 Row L Grave 3.
11. It is possible that this is the incident referred to in their after action report by 2nd Battalion Berkshire Regiment of 25 British Brigade. See Bridger *Neuve Chapelle* p 34.
12. Müller-Loebnitz *Das Ehrenbuch der Westfalen* pp 161-162.
13. *ibid.* p 162.
14. This in turn was a composite company, comprising one platoon from each of 9th, 10th, 11th and 12th Companies Infantry Regiment 133 under Reserve Leutnant Bössneck. In the event it played a relatively small part in the attempted counter-attack forward of the *Biez-Wald*, but its casualties were, nevertheless, high. See Niemann History Infantry Regiment 133 p 34.
15. Baumgarten-Crusius History Infantry Regiment 139 p 106 & Bolze History Field Artillery Regiment 77 p 26.
16. Goldammer History Infantry Regiment 179 p 63.
17. Wolff History Infantry Regiment 104 p 136.
18. *ibid.* p 137.
19. Dellmensingen *Das Bayernbuch vom Weltkriege II. Band* pp 200-202
20. Müller-Loebnitz *op. cit.* p 162.
21. *ibid.* p 162.

22. This is probably a reference to the battles fought on the Aisne in 1917 by 13th Infantry Division and, in particular, to events at Chavignon on 23 October of that year.
23. This is a common way for German eyewitnesses to describe normal British shells filled with lyddite.
24. Oberleutnant Georg Kuipers is buried in the German cemetery at Wicres – Route-de-la-Bassée Block 1 Grave 185. This is a most unusual cemetery. Laid out in 1915, complete with surrounding stone wall, as the burial place of the fallen of Infantry Regiment 15 and Reserve Infantry Regiment 15, the majority of the 584 men buried there were from those two Westphalian regiments, though the French authorities moved a number of solders from 6th Bavarian Reserve Division to this place after the war. Each man has an individual grave and only thirty are unknown.
25. Niemann History Infantry Regiment 133 p 34.
26. BOH p 392.
27. Groos *op. cit.* p 78.
28. Rupprecht *In Treue Fest* pp 310-313.
29. Crown Prince Rupprecht's chief of staff, General Krafft von Dellmensingen, later added a file note to the diary entry for that day; *viz.* 'His Royal Highness, nevertheless, continued to maintain that the attack would not be sufficiently prepared until the following day. At that General von Claer proposed that he asked once again if the divisions deployed forward could hold out until then. The response, predictably, was negative. At that, the Crown Prince granted reluctant permission for the attack to go ahead in accordance with General von Claer's plan – i.e. earlier. If, on the other hand, the troops had been directed to hold out until the postponed attack was launched, they would have been able to achieve it. All officers from the Army Headquarters who were present had the impression that the attack was over-hasty and they were concerned about its likely outcome.'
30. Solleder *Vier Jahre Westfront* pp 116-117.
31. Braun History Bavarian Reserve Infantry Regiment 21 p 26.
32. Windhorst History Field Artillery Regiment 58 pp 88-89.
33. Dellmensingen *op. cit.* pp 200-202
34. Of course this report was quite wrong, but it is typical of the faulty information passed to the rear in the heat and confusion of battle.
35. Bolze *op. cit.* pp 136-138.
36. The body of Unteroffizier Kurt Brunner was recovered and he is buried in the German cemetery at Illies Block 4 Grave 457.
37. Funcke History Field Artillery Regiment 78 pp 64-67.
38. Leutnant Hans Weber is buried in the German cemetery at Wicres Block 2 Grave 95.
39. Braun History Bavarian Reserve Infantry Regiment 21 p 27.
40. Solleder *op. cit.* p 107.
41. Müller-Loebnitz *op. cit.* p 162.
42. It was claimed later that this had been caused by a Dum Dum bullet, which is highly unlikely. It is far more probable that this serious wound was caused by a ricochet.
43. Groos *op. cit.* p 80.
44. Müller-Loebnitz *op. cit.* p 163.
45. Großmann History Bavarian Reserve Infantry Regiment 17 p 26.
46. Solleder *op. cit.* pp 114-115.
47. Reserve Leutnant Friedrich (Fritz) Philippi is buried in the German cemetery at Fournes en Weppes Block 5 Grave 18.
48. Poetter History Infantry Regiment 55 p 21.

49. Dellmensingen *op. cit.* pp 200-202
50. Solleder *op. cit.* pp 115-116.
51. GOH Vol 7 p 59.
52. Rupprecht *op. cit.* pp 313-314.
53. 86 Reserve Brigade had been located in Roeselare acting as Fourth Army reserve but, when the order came to move south during the afternoon of 11 March, Reserve Infantry Regiments 203, 204 and Reserve Jäger Battalion 15 were soon moving into position by train. See Schwedt History Reserve Infantry Regiment 204 p 39.
54. Rupprecht *op. cit.* p 314.
55. Funcke *op. cit.* pp 64-67.
56. This must be a reference to the Leibgarde-Infanterie-Regiment (1. Großherzoglich Hessisches) Nr 115, whose garrison town was Darmstadt and which was certainly deployed in the reinforcing role to Neuve Chapelle, As an elite regiment, its 3rd Battalion was referred to as the Fusilier Guard Battalion, but it is not clear why Reiling referred to the newcomers as 'Grenadiers'.
57. Solleder *op. cit.* pp 118-119. Wenzl was killed later on in the war in Artois, on 6 May 1917 and is buried in the German cemetery at Lens-Sallaumines Block 2 Grave 238.
58. *ibid.* p 113.
59. Tactically this may have been the case but, nevertheless, Falkenhayn was exercised throughout the battle by the symbolism of the loss of the village to the BEF.
60. Joffre *Mémoires* p 71. The French perspective is perhaps best illustrated by the fact that Joffre devoted a mere six lines of his memoirs to the battle.

Chapter 3

Gas Attack at Ypres

For the first quarter of 1915, the German army was under severe pressure, mainly due to the demands of the winter battles in Champagne and an attempt by the French army to pinch out the St Mihiel salient, but the failed British attack at Neuve Chapelle was also locally important for a few days. Gradually it became clear that the German defence had in every case held the line and, for better or worse, following a lengthy debate at the highest level, senior German commanders had decided that, for the foreseeable future, there was no possibility of the Allies achieving any decisive results on the Western Front. This finally persuaded a reluctant Falkenhayn to take the formal decision on 13 April to shift the German point of main effort to Galicia for the time being.[1] Despite the commitment to give priority to the Eastern Front, however, it was also decided that even though there could be no question of a major German offensive in the west, that was no reason to permit the Allies to rest undisturbed on the defensive, so thoughts turned to opportunities to prosecute the war within the constraints of available resources.

During the early weeks of 1915, whilst the daily life of the men manning the waterlogged positions in Flanders was one of monotonous trench routine, the staffs were hard at work planning one of the more ambitious local attacks to be launched that year by the German army. What transpired seems to have been no more than a large scale experiment to determine the value of the use of gas on a large scale.[2] Experiments and trials had begun in Germany weeks earlier, as had the production of rudimentary protective face masks. As early as January, Falkenhayn had made 6,000 full size cylinders of chlorine available to Fourth Army, together with instructions to plan on using them in the Ypres area. Orders were also placed for the manufacture of a further 24,000 smaller cylinders, which would be easier to handle than the unwieldy commercial types. A main depot and filling station was established near Kortemark and the filled cylinders were then moved forward by rail to unloading points where the infantry had the unenviable task of manhandling the heavy and unwieldy cylinders forward to where the experts of Pionier Battalion 35 could emplace them. After a long period of preparation and awaiting the correct meteorological conditions, Falkenhayn finally spoke to the Commander Fourth Army, Generaloberst Duke Albrecht of Württemberg, during the morning of 21 April and directed him to launch the attack at the first opportunity. The instructions were not to lay down a distant objective, but to give priority to early implementation of the plan.

These instructions conformed neatly to Duke Albrecht's intention, ever since the front solidified in November 1914, of exploiting the tactically unfavourable Allied positions in order to strike a severe blow around Ypres. This was later explained in a Supreme Army Headquarters report as follows:

> "Forcing the enemy back from its salient against or across the Ijzer would reduce the Army frontage and further restrict the amount of Belgian territory still in enemy hands. In addition, after a lengthy period of positional warfare, a major attack would certainly have a significant effect on [enemy] morale. The main attack had to be planned to take the enemy positions along the Ijzer Canal into account. Because the positions to the south of Ypres had already been pushed to within four kilometres of the town, whereas in the north they were twice as far distant, an attack from that direction appeared to be most appropriate.[3] Every effort was to be made to hold the enemy for as long as possible at the eastern end of the salient. That being the case, the main attack could not be extended too far to the east and it was also the task of the remainder of the forces on the Ypres front to fix the enemy troops opposite them. This was the thinking behind the attack of 22 April."[4]

In parallel with the physical measure needed to launch the gas attack and in an early form of psychological operations, accusations concerning the use of asphyxiating gases were underway before the cylinders were ever opened. The British believed (incorrectly) that gas shells had been employed on Hill 60 on 18 April.[5] The Germans levelled the same charge at the British almost simultaneously. This, in turn, led to the inclusion of this comment within a British communiqué, which the Germans read on 21 April:

> "There is no truth in the assertion contained in a recent German report (17 April) that we have been making use of suffocating gases. It is probably intended as a justification for the frequent use of these gases by the enemy, including during its attacks against Hill 60. It should not remain unmentioned that Germany is a signatory to the clause of the Hague Convention which forbids the use of asphyxiating gases."[6]

In a further attempt to spread baseless rumours about Allied use of poison gas, or possibly to provide a covert warning more generally within the German army, Supreme Army Headquarters issued this directive to all army headquarters on the Western Front:[7]

> "In recent days there have reports from various points along the front that the enemy have been using *Stinkgeschosse* [gas shells]. All specialists, chemists and doctors stationed along the front are to attempt to determine what chemicals are being used or are to recover and forward shell fragments complete with contents. Protective equipment for our troops is being procured but, prior to its distribution on a large scale, it is recommended that all troops manning the front line carry a wad of damp cotton waste with them at all times, pressing it against mouth and nose as soon as incapacitating gases are detected. In most cases this should provide adequate protection."
>
> Signed: von Falkenhayn

Although the main German attempts to justify gas warfare came later in the war, on the very day that the gas attack took place, Supreme Army Headquarters issued an extraordinary, rather rambling, statement, whose sophistry was only matched by its bare faced effrontery. An extract reads:

> "In a publication of 21 April the British Army High Command has accused Germany of contravening all the laws of civilised warfare during their attempts to recapture Hill 60, southeast of Ypres, by having made use of shells which generate asphyxiating gas when they land. As has been noted in the German official communiqués, our opponents have been using this type of war *materiel* for many months. Apparently, they appear to be of the opinion that we are not entitled to make use of something which is permissible for them ... They do not accept that the development of German chemical science means that we are in a position to deploy far more effective methods than is the enemy. In any case, references to the Laws of Warfare are not appropriate.
>
> "The German [army] does not fire any, 'Shells, whose sole purpose is the dispersal of poisonous gases', (Hague Declaration of 29 July 1899) and, even though the gases produced on the explosion of German shells are much more unpleasant than the gases from normal French, British or Russian artillery shells, they are much less dangerous than those. None of the smoke generators used by us in the close quarter battle contradict the provisions of the Laws of Warfare; they create no more potent an effect than that which may be obtained from burning straw or bundles of wooden branches. Because the smoke so produced can be detected clearly, even during dark nights, there is nothing to prevent any person from removing himself in a timely manner from where it is being used.
>
> "This brief explanation, which covers the actual situation exhaustively, should serve to convince any unprejudiced person. If, despite this, our enemies continue to issue accusations, then it simply proves that the French and British actually made use of suffocating gases long before us. A closer look at history and the sense of the Hague Declaration of 1890 will place the 'indignation' of our enemies in its correct light.
>
> "For many months the French and British have been using shells which produce asphyxiating gases when they explode and it can be demonstrated that, for their part, the use of suffocating gases, far from decreasing, has actually increased considerably ... We draw attention to the Supreme Army Headquarters communiqués of 13, 14, 16 and 17 April, which include official announcements that the French at Suippes and Verdun and the British at Ypres have once more made use of shells, mines and bombs which produce asphyxiating gases. The report of 16 April states expressly: 'French use of bombs which produce asphyxiating gas and explosive bullets has increased.' ... "[8]

According to the meteorologists on 21 April, it appeared that the atmospheric conditions were likely to be suitable the following day and H Hour was laid down for

84 THE GERMAN ARMY ON THE WESTERN FRONT 1915

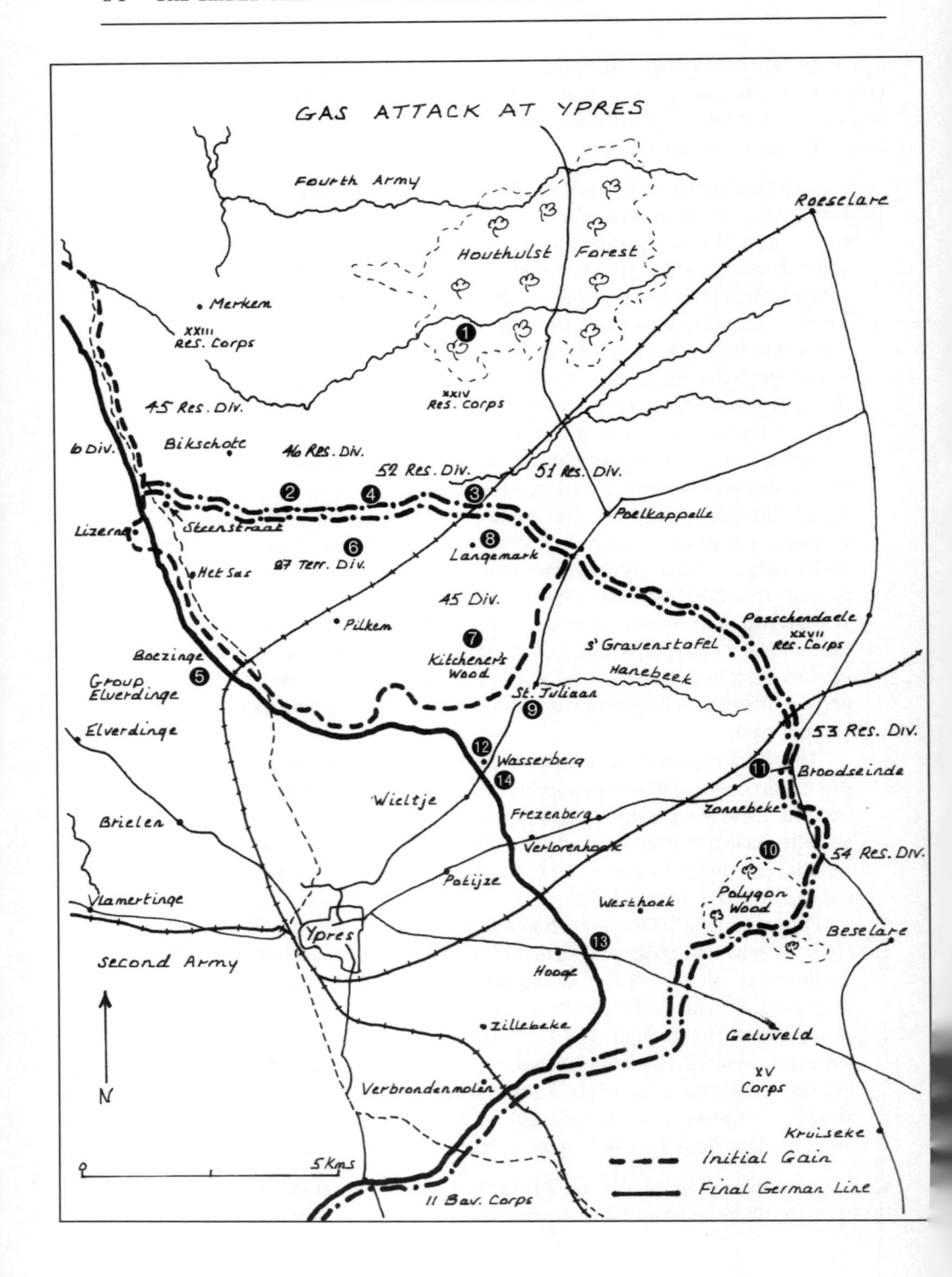

6.00 am. Despite previous requests, with the sole exception of elements of 43rd Reserve Division, there were no reserves on hand to exploit any possible success.[9] Had its commanders but realised it, the German army was sleepwalking to a propaganda disaster without even the chance of taking some significant operational advantage from its dabbling with a novel form of weapon. In the event, there was absolutely no wind at the appointed time on 22 April, so the surprise attack, which was to be supported by the release of clouds of chlorine gas from thousands of pre-positioned cylinders, could not be launched until that evening.[10] Two reserve corps, attacking from Drie Grachten to Beselare, were involved: XXIII and XXVI, which were commanded by General der Infanterie von Kathen and General der Infanterie Freiherr von Hügel respectively. At a later point, formations of XXVII added their weight to the attack. In the first phase, the Yser/Ijzer Canal was crossed, whilst Steenstraat, Het Sas, Pilkem and Langemark - all of which had resisted extreme German pressure during the battles of the previous November - were captured. Northeast of Ypres, the thrust reached St Juliaan and the high ground just west of it.

Because of the sheer amount of labour involved in moving gas cylinders forward and placing them, the planned use of this novel weapon was known about widely, especially when the early, crude facemasks - the so-called *Riechpäckchen* [Stink Packages] - were issued to protect the men against leaks from damaged cylinders and 3,000 sets of Dräger mine self-rescue equipment were made available in the Ypres area. The concomitant risk to operational security was compounded further as the attack drew closer, because specific instructions and information concerning the characteristics of the gas had to be made available on wide distribution. According to the French Official History, nick-numbers to be used in association with the operations were also issued: '222', Prepare Operation; '333', Full Alert; '8888', Release the Gas and '7777', Reduce the State of Alert.[11] This short description by the officer in charge of the release conveys a good impression of the practical difficulties involved.

Oberst Peterson Commander of the Gas Troops[12]

> "The installation of the gas cylinders in the appropriate places was not straightforward. The high water table meant that in places only shallow trenches could be dug and the defences stood out proud of the marshy ground, camouflaged with plants and shrubs. The waterlogged floors of the trenches were mostly equipped with duckboards. In many places the cover provided was extremely poor; often the parapets did not even provide protection from small arms fire and nowhere was there sufficient cover from artillery fire. As a result, the gas cylinders had to be installed vertically under the floors of the trenches – an extremely difficult task with the large cylinders. The completed batteries [of cylinders] were then protected by layers of sandbags.
>
> "The transport and digging in could only be done at night; the latter task taking two gas engineer companies the seven nights from 5 – 11 April to complete. The total numbers involved were 1,600 large and 4,130 small

cylinders. It proved impossible to install several [planned] batteries in only one place, namely a section of the front line south of Bikschote where the cover was smashed by artillery fire on a daily basis. The cylinders for these batteries were stored instead in a shell proof depot behind a ruin, approximately eighty metres in rear of the front line and were placed in position the night before the attack. In order to facilitate the manning of the installed batteries, it was necessary to reinforce the two companies of Pionier Battalion 35 with hastily trained personnel. The other two companies, with about half of the available equipment, were down to the south of Ypres which was the original choice of front for the gas attack, so they were not available on the northern front.

"Because of the mixture of large and small cylinders, the length of time of the discharge was determined by the time taken for a large cylinder to empty. This varied from six to eight minutes, so the small cylinders, which had a much shorter discharge time, were opened sequentially so as to harmonise with the larger ones. Because the exact wind direction could not be determined whilst the cylinders were being placed and in order to avoid endangering sections of our own position, we had to plan for the fact that certain battery positions would be redundant. To that end, special plans were drawn up and copies relating to their particular sectors were given to each engineer officer.

"We encountered one particular problem. This was that all along the frontage of the gas attack there were no reserve positions, no suitable place where reserves could be held. As a result, the attacking troops had to be called forward at night to positions right up behind the parados of the trench then, on the actual day of the attack, they had to remain forward. As a result, the forward trenches were absolutely crammed with infantry. This made the passage of orders to the different batteries extremely difficult and complicated their actual operation considerably."

52nd Reserve Division was deployed near Langemark during the lead up to the assault. A newly joined musketier, whose baptism of fire this was, later wrote an interesting account of the transition from routine in the line to all out attack.

Musketier Johannes Kauven 5th Company Reserve Infantry Regiment 240[13] **1.**

"In those days the three battalions relieved each other from front to rear, so that one battalion was manning the position near Langemark, one was in reserve based in railway wagons hidden in Houthulst Wood and the other was resting in billets in Vijfwege [a village located just southeast of Houthulst Wood]. We were in reserve and, apart from the fact that the accommodation was anything but homely, were able to get along quite well in the wood during these early spring days ... Already when we were still in Staden we had noticed that every soldier was wearing a fist-sized package attached to his jacket. In response to our questions we learned one of the greatest secrets of the Western

Front: at Ypres there was to be an attack with a previously unknown weapon; namely gas.

"In recent days, gas cylinders had been dug into the trenches and we were waiting for favourable *Stinkwetter* [gas weather] in order to release the poisonous contents for the enemy to breathe in. The *Riechpäckchen* were our counter measures to protect us from the gas. These gauze packages, filled with cotton wool, were designed to be soaked with a liquid and then had to be kept moist. Naturally, after that, trenches and the gas attacks were the only topics of conversation. The feldwebel and our other NCOs kept drumming in to us, 'Every man must have a *Riechpäckchen!*' ...

"Returning from the range [one day] we received the order, 'Prepare for battle!' It sounded as though everything was in order. An iron ration was issued to every two men. They split the contents and packed them separately. Ten sandbags per man were rolled up in our coats. Our mess tins, filled with iron rations, were attached and the remaining rations were jammed into our bread pouches. We paraded from 7.00 pm until 8.00 pm and final preparations were completed. Anything which could not be fitted into our assault equipment went into our knapsacks, which were marked with our names, placed in platoon stacks and were to be brought forward to us later.

"When a men is faced with serious action, his entire spirit seems to be weighed down, a feeling which transmits itself to his physical being. Nobody could sleep that night; [the waiting] got on our nerves. I wrote a little by candle-light. Somebody brewed a chocolate drink. These little actions took our minds off things to some extent. Just to be doing something was helpful. Some others were playing cards and the clock was crawling towards midnight ... then came the call, 'Stand to! Stand to!' ... Soon the company was ready. Hand grenades were distributed, together with white armbands, so we could distinguish friend from foe. In addition to our usual 120 rounds, we were each given a bandolier with seventy more, which we each had to hang around our neck ...

"To our front and off to both sides gun fire could be heard and every so often small arms fire came from the front ... we came ever closer to the front. The nerves of the newcomers were stretched and all our senses became almost too sensitive. Nobody spoke out loud; everything was conducted in whispers. The tension in the air was almost tangible. But, what was that? The engineers were coming back, yet we had to be very close to the trenches ... then a French flare went up. If they had spotted something then God help us! Slowly the hovering flare burnt itself out, but nothing happened. No riflemen fired, no machine gun loosed off death and destruction from its barrel. If the French had had any idea at all about what was happening, the outlook for us would have been desperate.

"The order came to pull back to our train billets which we reached, tired out in body and spirit, at 5.00 am. Later we heard that the wind was not blowing in a favourable direction. What we did not hear about then and only much later, was the fact that August Jäger of Reserve Infantry Regiment 234 had deserted to the enemy, taking with him the secret of the gas attack. The French had clearly not attached much credence to his story or everything would not have gone so well on 22 April. As it was, it all came out years later and, on 17 December 1932, Jäger was sentenced to ten years' imprisonment by a court in Leipzig and ten years *Ehrverlust*.[14]

Interesting to note, the relevant volume of the French Official History, published in 1930,[15] has nothing to say about Jäger. Instead, quoting a report of the Belgian GHQ, it states:

> "On 16 April, Belgian General Headquarters informed our High Command that the Germans had caused to be produced gauze pads to cover the mouth and nose which, when impregnated with an appropriate liquid, was intended to protect their men against heavy asphyxiating gas which they proposed to direct at our lines. The men of 26th Reserve Corps [*sic.*] had received special training on the handling of gas cylinders which were to be placed in batteries of twenty cylinders every forty metres."

It seems clear, therefore, that one way or another the secret of the intended use of gas was beginning to filter out. Quite apart from accidental or deliberate disclosure, there seem to have been quite variable attitudes to the question of operational security. For example, part of a private letter written on 10 April 1915 by Leutnant Max Stober of Fliegerabteilung 3, based at Menin, reads, 'Unfortunately we are still waiting for a rare easterly wind to blow, so there has been no attack. Everything is ready. To attack would be great! The latest tests have shown that the gas is effective out to five kilometres! So blow you East Wind!!'[16] In the event, the possession of this information from whatever source made no difference. It was not acted upon and surprise was complete when the moment came to attack.

The experience of the men of 46th Reserve Division was similar to that of those of 52nd Reserve Division. Charged with advancing to secure the Pilkem area, its subordinate formations encountered the same pre-offensive problems.

Hauptmann von Hammerstein 1st Battalion Reserve Infantry Regiment 213[17] **2.**

> "The period before the attack was a time when the physical and mental demands were totally unprecedented. It was fortunate that the French shelling barely disrupted our nightly work. The French airmen were not as well trained as they were later, otherwise they would doubtless have spotted our extensive preparations. At 3.00 pm on 21 April '333' [Full Alert] was ordered once again. That evening, therefore, I marched my battalion from Melaene Cabaret to Bikschote. Here everyone assembled once more. My regimental commander, Oberstleutnant Brink, and the regimental adjutant, Oberleutnant Dumas, spent the night in the old battalion dugout. I had arranged for the construction of a new one where I spent the night asleep. My adjutant, Leutnant Hay, as outstanding a man as he was a soldier, oversaw the deployment of my six

companies, whilst the medical officer, Dr Bornstein, completed all the preparations for the reception of the wounded. The company commanders were located forward with their companies.

"The second attacking wave, 10th and 11th Companies under Hauptmann Spamer and the third wave, 1st Battalion, commanded by Hauptmann Wenderoth, were packed tightly into the area immediately to our rear. We spent almost the whole of 22 April crowded together, but suffered no casualties. At long last, at 5.40 pm on the 22nd, the order to attack arrived. At 6.00 pm all the gas cylinders were opened simultaneously and the lead piping was laid out on the parapets. An indescribable, unforgettable scene for all who took part in this first gas attack then unfolded. A greenish cloud developed to our front and began slowly to roll towards the enemy. Gradually the whole sky seemed to have turned green. This sinister turn of events had an astonishing effect on the enemy. The front line troops reacted in total confusion and, casting aside weapons and equipment, bolted in large numbers. Only the obscuration of the air and heavy enemy artillery fire, which came down very rapidly, prevented us from bringing down effective fire against the fleeing enemy.

"By 6.10 pm the cylinders were empty and, at 6.15 pm, I gave the order to attack. To the trained military eye, the effect of my order was simply magnificent. Everywhere the company commanders hurled themselves forward, followed by their men. A general competition began. The second wave did not wait, but went forward with the first line. Under enemy artillery fire, my position was somewhat uncomfortable, but I dashed forward, emerged from the fire and watched the attack flood forward towards the canal ... About two and a half kilometres to our front was our intermediate objective, Het Sas. Several lines of French trenches were overrun. We received as good as no fire from the front; only from Steenstraat on the right [western] flank did we come under very unpleasant enfilade fire. In that sector, Reserve Infantry Regiment 215 made only slow progress, because no cylinders had been installed there.

"Everything went like a peacetime manoeuvre. Where the enemy showed resistance, not much time was wasted with lengthy fire fights. Instead we went straight in with the bayonet. Because of this unbroken surge forward, the enemy had no time to destroy the bridges over the Yser Canal. These fell into our hands intact, so there was no problem crossing ... Once I had handed over responsibility for the home bank of the canal to Hauptmann Spaer with 5th and 10th Companies, I crossed over a lock gate with Leutnant Hay and took over command of all companies on the far side of the Yser Canal."

Hammerstein was wrong about there being a lack of cylinders opposite Steenstraat. A normal quantity had been placed, but the wind direction sent the gas either rolling past Steenstraat or back into the German trenches. Further to the east, men of Reserve Infantry Regiment 234, 51st Reserve Division, unaware of Jäger's treachery, were also fully involved in the build up to the attack and the assault itself.

Leutnant Speyer Commander 2nd Company Reserve Infantry Regiment 234[18] 3.

"In the early part of 1915, mysterious figures moved through the trenches carrying even more mysterious steel cylinders. Some thirsty individual thought, 'That is great. They are obviously opening a bar and have already brought the oxygen forward to dispense the beer!' Unfortunately this never appeared!' Sadly, the engineers began instead to dig deep holes in our beautiful trenches. The cylinders were placed in them, then carefully covered up with sandbags. It was then that we received more exact information. The cylinders contained a gas which attacked human mucous membranes and which would be released on the enemy when the wind was favourable. We were issued with protective equipment and made all necessary preparations for the attack. Unfortunately, the correct gentle northeast wind was a long time coming.

"We were resting in reserve at Oostnieuwkerke when the wind became favourable. We were alerted several times but, on each occasion, dense fog interfered with artillery observation, so we had to return to our billets. Then we were called forward once more during the night 21/22 April and this time it looked as though it was going to be serious. Having spent an entire half a year in position by Poelkapelle, we were now about to attack once more where the the Koekuit – Langemark road crossed the Kortebeek [Broenbeek on the modern map] and where we had been thrown back the previous October. It was a special quirk of fate that we were to be given the chance to complete our earlier assault. This time we just had to succeed!

"However, as night faded into day the wind dropped and the fog rose. All for nothing again! Extremely annoyed, we got back in our trenches and hardly hoped for an improvement by evening. We had been told that release would take place punctually at 6.00 pm, but we had already been disappointed too often. A German aircraft flew very low over the enemy and received a torrent of fire. I looked up and wondered what the strange rushing sound was. My glance settled on the foremost trenches and - *Donnerwetter!* It really had started. Thick yellowish-green clouds, fraught with danger, rolled towards the enemy trenches. For a short time the enemy did not react, but then they opened fire with everything they had.

"Barely had the first enemy shells burst, however, than our artillery brought down fire like the hammers of Hell. We could hardly hear ourselves speak. The enemy fire faded away, weaker and weaker and almost stopped completely. Then, just as the cylinders had emptied, the first assault waves rushed forward. With laughing eyes and joyful shouts of *Hurra!*, Leutnant Ohl and his men raced past 4th Company and leapt into the first enemy trench. Some of our comrades were killed in the process; others were wounded, but this German surge was not to be halted. Soon we found ourselves in the enemy trenches and we could only laugh as we saw the pathetic nature of the makeshift defences, for which we had showed so much respect during the past six months. We had spoken of concreted dugouts, of mines and electrified obstacles. There was no sign of any such thing, just a wall of earth, with a minimal wire obstacle and a few planks of wood; hardly sufficient to keep the rain out. That was the lot!

"Our gunnery and the gas had had a good effect on the assorted races which faced us. Many dead lay around and all those who were unable to run like the wind surrendered to us without resisting. One Indian[19] was so afraid that he had jumped into a water-filled crater formed by one of our 210 mm shells. Nothing could be seen of him, other than his head, which floated like a lotus blossom on the surface. He looked at us, his face contorted with fear, but all we could do was laugh. He laughed too, then, shivering with the cold, he crawled out of his bath."

The formations of 52nd Reserve Division also participated in the initial assault on 22 April, which was observed by one of its officers, who was in reserve for the first phase of the attack.

Leutnant Lennartz Adjutant 2nd Battalion Reserve Infantry Regiment 240[20] 4.

"2nd Battalion Reserve Infantry Regiment 240 was in the second wave for the attack. We should have preferred to have been out front because we were quite clear in our minds that once the initial surprise was over the enemy artillery would concentrate its fire on the reserves ... The tension was enormous. When would it all begin? There were some senior officers who had no sympathy with this type of warfare. They thought that it was unmanly and that we should renounce the use of this type of weapon. Basically they may have had right on their side, but was the use of 280 mm delayed action shells against concrete bunkers, or even the British blockade itself any more humane? We were no longer in that period of history when armoured knights clashed in solitary combat with sword and lance ...

"The attack began at 6.00 pm. A green cloud hovered all along the horizon, hanging low over the Flanders countryside. It was an extraordinary, heart-stopping sight. Our gun fire hammered down on the enemy battery positions and on Ypres itself as the battalion deployed for the attack. The gas crept like a dense green liquid over the enemy, who appeared to be completely surprised. To begin with no shots were fired but, a short time later, a number of machine guns opened up, as did the artillery from beyond the green wave, which brought down fire on the rear areas. We had certainly expected the situation to be worse and we advanced with only light casualties.

"The first of the prisoners came into view. They were a pitiful sight. With hands held high, they begged for mercy. Deaths or damage to health through the gas seem to have been a rarity (in contrast with the gases used in subsequent gas attacks). The enemy were French, mostly Moroccans. The attack went forward easily. The line ordered was crossed and the attacking battalions dug in on Hill 29. That evening 2nd Battalion was called forward to occupy the front line. There was a huge amount of activity there. Digging was being pushed forward energetically and defences against expected attacks were prepared. Battalion headquarters was established in a farmhouse about fifty metres behind the front line. A runner rushed up, most concerned and reported, 'There is a cellar full of heads!' [but investigation showed that] they were large beets, covered with straw!"

The gas had been released opposite the French 87th Territorial Division and their 45th Infantry Division. Blown forward on a northerly wind measuring two metres per second, the gas cloud, some two kilometres wide by 700 metres deep and two metres high, rolled towards the enemy trenches. The French estimated its area of maximum lethality at up to one kilometre from the points of release.[21] Even before the cloud reached the forward lines, defenders were seen to be firing a few shots then turning and fleeing away to the rear. A certain amount of French artillery fire came down on the German trenches, but already the first wave of attackers was launching forward. Confused reports were soon being sent to the rear by French front line troops. One such was received by the commander of the French 90 Infantry Brigade which, with its Zouaves and other African battalions, was deployed near Langemark. Rumours of a strange event reached him in his command post in Elverdinge Chateau to the west of the Yser/Ijzer Canal and then he received a more definitive report.

Colonel Henri Mordacq Commander French 90 Brigade[22] **5.**

"I was just about to set off when, at about 5.30 pm [6.30 pm German time], I received a telephone call from Villevalaix, commander of the 1st Rifle Regiment. Coughing and croaking to such an extent that his voice was barely understandable, he reported to me that he was being attacked heavily and that monstrous yellow pillars of smoke had been seen coming from the German trenches and spreading out to cover the entire area. His men had begun to leave their trenches and were racing to the rear to escape, though many were suffocating and collapsing.

"I must admit that when I heard these words and the tone of his voice I wondered for a moment if the commander had lost his head or had been gripped by panic; something I had often seen at the start of the war of manoeuvre, especially during the battles around Chipotte. Certainly the thought of a gas attack never entered my head. I should never have believed it possible and I had never heard a whisper of any such thing ever since my arrival in Belgium. Almost at the same moment I heard the sound of rapid rifle fire, accompanied by the roar of the guns. Quite clearly something unusual was going on and it could well be an attack.

"Almost simultaneously I received another telephone call, this time from de Fabry, one of the commanding officers of 1st Rifle Regiment, who spoke in the same agitated way as Villevalaix. He told me that he would have to evacuate his command post. It was impossible to breathe. Entire sections had been knocked out, either through suffocation, or because they had fallen victim to the artillery fire which the enemy was bringing down on the reserve positions. The positions could be held no longer. They were caught between gas and shellfire. Finally I received another call from Commandant [Major] Villevalaix, 'Everyone is collapsing around me, I am leaving my command post' I could not catch the end of his sentence, then the telephone went dead. This time I was determined to go [forward]. I leapt onto my horse and rode at a full gallop.

"The rattle of small arms fire increased constantly, gun fire was coming down all over the neighbouring sector and our own guns were firing ceaselessly. The general impression was that this was landing accurately, but it did not continue for long. The further forward we went, the greater the noise of small arms fire, but the less [our] guns fired then, eventually, they stopped altogether. I was immediately very concerned and sent off urgent messages to my command post in Elverdinge; firstly, that all battalions of the brigade were to be alerted and despatched forward into our sector and, secondly, that Division was to be asked to provide us with the support of 91 Brigade. I felt sure that the attack was serious; our troops, both territorial and African, were flooding to the rear on all sides ...

"Beyond the canal, individual yellowish clouds could be seen then, having proceeded to about three to four hundred metres from Boezinge, we experienced a sharp prickling sensation in our noses and throats. Our ears began to roar, breathing became difficult and we were overcome by the unbearable stench of chlorine. We had to dismount, because the horses, suffering, refused to either gallop or trot. We arrived at Boezinge on foot and headed for the ridges. The sights to our front were pitiful, really appalling. Everywhere men were running for their lives in complete disorder: Africans, riflemen, Zouaves, territorials and gunners without their weapons. Holding the skirts of their open coats, their collars ripped open, they raced like madmen for safety. Crying out loudly for water, coughing up blood, some rolled on the ground in agony making desperate attempts to breathe.

"Before my eyes I shall for ever have the sight of an African who, in a state of collapse, cried out for milk, then, seeing me, called out 'Colonel, these blackguards have poisoned us!' In short, it was like a scene from Dante's inferno, though the Italian poet never described anything so appalling in his masterpiece. Since the beginning of the war, I had seen panic in Lorraine and around Arras, but never before had such a scene of utter desperation as unfolded in front of me. It was out of the question to halt the fleeing troops; we did not even try. They were no longer soldiers, these poor fleeing beings who had been driven mad at a single stroke. It was the same all along both banks of the canal, where masses of distraught men sought relief from their agonies in the water."

Most of the front line territorial troops of 87th Division located between Steenstraat and Weidendrift, that is to say on a four kilometre front, were affected more or less badly by the gas and pulled back in panic towards Boezinge. This spread to men occupying depth positions and the gun lines, who disappeared rapidly in the direction of the west bank of the Ijzer. As might be expected, however, the gas was not equally effective all along the line. Forward of Steenstraat, on the left flank of XXIII Reserve Corps where Generalleutnant Schöpflin's 45th Reserve Division was deployed, for example, it had little effect and the troops had to fight their way forward slowly, suffering a considerable number of casualties in the process. At least part of the explanation was provided later by the regimental historian of Reserve Infantry Regiment 212.

> "The gas engineers were stood to, ready to remove the sandbag protection from the gas cylinders and to lay the lead piping over the parapet. Off to our left [east] a greenish-yellow gas cloud developed and rolled forward on the wind towards the enemy ... Comrades from our left neighbouring regiment leapt up onto the parapet and fired at the fleeing enemy before setting off to storm the enemy lines. The gas released from the battery of cylinders opposite Steenstraat did not roll into Steenstraat itself but was blown past it. Because of the wind [direction] the gas in the cylinders located immediately in front of Steenstraat, that is to say in the sector of our 1st Battalion, could not be released, because it would have blown back into our own positions.
>
> "Engineers who did make the effort to release gas here were badly gassed themselves and lay around helplessly. The enemy artillery opened up with great violence, strewing death and destruction in our trenches. Machine guns, firing from Steenstraat, hammered into the ranks of Reserve Infantry Regiment 215 which was storming forward. Meanwhile our own artillery attempted to neutralise the enemy artillery and so to smash the enemy positions that they would be ripe for attack. Our objective, Steenstraat, simply had to be captured ..."[23]

One anonymous Belgian grenadier who observed the attack from a position near Steenstraat later reported:

> "It was a beautiful spring day. A gentle breeze blew from the north. Everything was so calm that we were almost able to forget the war. Then, suddenly, at about 6.30 pm, we saw dense smoke rising from the German trenches opposite. Surprised and curious we stood rooted to the spot. Nobody had any idea what it all meant. As the clouds of smoke thickened, we thought that the German dugouts must have caught fire. Then the cloud began to roll slowly towards us, but then, due to the wind, it was driven off to the right over the French lines. Only the faintest whiff of vapour reached us. It was not at all thick, but it gave off a vile smell and irritated our throats so much that at first we thought we would choke. Suddenly, I heard shouts all round. 'It's an attack, the Boches have arrived!'[24]

In contrast to the tone of many of the German reports, Leutnant Rudolf Binding, the German writer and thinker, who was serving in the salient as the commander of a cavalry squadron with one of the newly raised reserve divisions, had some doubt about the action that had been taken; doubt which he expressed in a letter on 24 April.

> "The consequences of the successful gas attack are appalling. To poison human beings – I do not know about that. Indeed, the whole world is going to be enraged and then copy us. The dead lie on their backs with clenched fists. The entire battlefield is yellow. It is said that Ypres will fall. It can be seen burning – not without regret for the beautiful town. Langemark is a pile of rubble and all rubble heaps look the same. There is no point in trying to describe each one. All that is left of the church is the main door, dated 1620."[25]

Reserve Infantry Regiment 211 and its 2nd Battalion in particular, suffered heavily from enfilade fire from the right [west] as it advanced along the line of the Ijzer Canal. Its problems were further compounded by the fact that it had to cross an unexpectedly broad drainage ditch on its way to the objective and the bridging materials carried forward against such an eventuality proved to be insufficient to cope with the width of the gap.[26] However, even here, by late evening Steenstraat was in German hands.

Aware of the importance of the Steenstraat bridgehead, the French had fought extremely hard to defend it. Pushing forward in full view of artillery observers on the west bank, casualties due to accurate shelling were also high. Subsequently, there was general agreement that the success of the operations in this sector were due almost entirely to the outstanding leadership and personal example of Feldwebelleutnant Weste of Reserve Infantry Regiment 212. He was later awarded the Iron Cross First Class for the part he played in the storming of the canal bridge and the following night, when no fewer than five separate French counter-attacks were beaten off, as the German troops raced to dig in against the inevitable heavy, accurate shelling expected as soon as it became light the following morning.[27]

Hauptmann von Hammerstein, Reserve Infantry Regiment 213, later summed up the events of the day, stating, 'The day cost the enemy a great many casualties, but not many were due to our gas, however. The gas had a colossal moral effect, but I saw hardly any fatal gas casualties. Their very considerable casualties were caused by small arms fire and the taking of prisoners.'[28] Further to the east, the formations of the French 45th Division, deployed between Langemark and the left of the British line, evacuated the area, having suffered heavily and withdrew to an area southeast of Boezinge, but still east of the canal. So, the result of the 'great moral effect' was that XXIII Reserve Corps had thrown the enemy back across the canal between Steenstraat and Het Sas, capturing a total of eleven batteries of French guns in the process[29] and XXVI Reserve Corps had advanced to a line running from a point south of Pilkem to the area just northwest of St Juliaan. Reserve Infantry Regiment 239, part of 52nd Reserve Division, was tasked with the advance on Pilkem itself. One of its members left a colourful description of the events of the day on its front. **6.**

> "Suddenly the watches showed that it was 6.00 pm and from the regimental aid post came the cry, 'It has begun! The lines of infantry are already

advancing!' Sure enough tiny dots, which represented the widely deployed companies approaching from the rear, could be seen disappearing behind folds in the ground, as though they had been swallowed up, only to reappear, silhouetted, on the next rise. Apparently the weather station of XXVI Reserve Corps was not in contact with that of XXIII Reserve Corps because, suddenly, our companies saw the gas cloud rise in front of XXIII Reserve Corps and the troops there begin to move. For the reserves of 52nd Reserve Division that was also the signal to move and they set off without further orders.

"Now the cylinder squads stationed at the gas batteries co-located with Reserve Infantry Regiment 239 began to open individual cylinders. [They did this] without waiting for the orders of the weatherman [whose task it was to decide if] some series of cylinders, because of their placement, the wind direction and their direction of discharge, would be better left unused. As a result, some of the gas blew back into our own trenches and caused a number of casualties to 11th Company before we even set off. At about the same moment the telephones came to life. From the front came the news, 'The F [gas] batteries have been discharged. The battalion is to advance.' Where there had been nothing but an empty dismal vista, where there had only been shot up walls, dark cellar entrances and open landscape, now suddenly teemed with men as holes, trenches and dugouts discharged their occupants into the light of day.

"The general and his staff climbed on to a roof, whilst the companies set off from their strong points. 'Pick up your equipment! Tie on your face masks!' Squads of men rushed in all directions, companies formed up in section columns, whilst the Divisional Padre, Sander, made the sign of the cross over them. The assault troops set off in ordered and tight formations and yet they swept forward like a mountain stream swollen with rain, their eyes full of enthusiasm. They was no holding them back . . . How little had the waiting during the winter months affected their dash in the attack - so, forwards! It was but a short distance from the forming up points to the front line trenches, whose garrisons had already departed, taking the protective shields with them to be used in developing the new positions. Forward!

"It was an extraordinary sight. The setting sun hung like a ball of fire in the firmament above the countryside, green with the spring. The flaming red of the sky was full of white clouds edged in pink. Everywhere could be seen grey shadows storming forward, the light reflecting and glinting from their rifle barrels and fixed bayonets. To the front of the assaulting lines of infantry was the yellowish-green gas cloud. Great swirling clouds crept forward like a wall across the green fields, ready to swallow up everything in their path as they sunk into the trenches and overwhelmed the batteries. High above in the sky, dozens of aircraft buzzed around like birds of prey. Shrapnel burst overhead, painting the red of the sky with small white clouds.

"Shouts of *Hurra!* could be heard coming from left and right as shells crashed down, sending up pillars of earth, broken masonry and shattered trees into the air, as high as houses. From somewhere came the sound of machine guns and batteries galloped by ... The gas cloud had still not cleared from the first enemy trenches when the first of the assault troops arrived like a thundercloud following lightning. Reserve Infantry Regiment 239 went forward in four columns. 2nd Company aimed for the Kortekeer – Pilkem road with 1st, 11th and 12th Companies just next to it. Enemy fire began coming down on the forward trenches. Press on and get beyond it! Meanwhile 4th, 3rd, 9th and 10th Companies hurried forward from their forming up places, pausing to collect shields and other equipment from the waiting piles and followed up the leading companies.

"The first enemy positions were already overrun; the enemy were fleeing in panic. Within fifteen minutes, the first prisoners were being sent back. The second enemy line! Up on the parapets lay Frenchmen who had vomited the contents of their stomachs as a result of the gas. Prisoners became ever more numerous. Weaponless, hands held high, they needed no escorts as they made their way alone to the rear ... Bullets whizzed through the air from the left, coming from the farmsteads around Pilkem. A machine gun was firing from one particular house. In we went and smoked it out with grenades! Because some of the companies had been delayed by the necessity to storm particular buildings and strong points en route, because Reserve Infantry Regiment 216, attacking to the right of Reserve Infantry Regiment 239 came too far to the left, the battalions were entangled and mixed up with other units.

"Pilkem was traversed and the enemy fled in panic, leaving behind letters which had been started and abandoned on the tables, where the evening meal, which had just been served, was sill warm. Equipment, official manuals and files lay strewn around ... By 7.00pm we were on the Pilkem heights. 'Halt! Dig in', shouted Major Drigalski."[30]

As a result of this shock advance, the French were reduced temporarily to weak forces southeast of Boezinge and some further troops intermingled with Canadians around Kerselaar. Already significant captures had been made: about 1,800 Frenchmen and a handful of British soldiers had been taken prisoner. Furthermore, fifty one guns, four of them heavy, and almost seventy machine guns, had fallen into German hands.

There was a wide gap in the defences between the canal and St Juliaan, which contained only very weak Allied forces. There was no question of a continuous line of defence being in place and, with all the bridges and rear areas near Ypres under heavy German fire, the situation for the Allies was verging on the desperate. The gap between the French and the British was at least three and a half kilometres wide so, for the time being, the route to Ypres was effectively wide open. About the only immediate attempt to counter-attack was launched on the order of the commander of the French 45th Division, General Quiquandon, who ordered a regiment from army reserve to launch an attack at 9.00 pm to recapture lost ground around Pilkem, but this half hearted effort had no discernable effect on the situation, as it stalled and withered away in heavy German fire.

It was just as well for the Allies that no such success had been envisaged, Fourth Army originally having planned only to clear out the Langemark salient as far as the canal. Now, however, emboldened by the swift progress, it issued orders during the early hours of 23 April to develop operations 'in the direction of Poperinge'.[31] To that end, XXIII Reserve Corps was directed to advance on the line Pijpegale – Boezinge, whilst XXVI Reserve Corps was to drive south, right flank on the canal, to threaten the rear of the Canadian troops opposite XXVII Reserve Corps. There were almost no reserves, so this order was highly optimistic, but elements of 43rd Reserve Division, under Generalmajor von Runckel, were placed under command of XXIII Reserve Corps and two marine regiments were called forward from the coast to assembly areas between Staden and Houthulst Wood. In fact any thought of advancing to Poperinge was swiftly abandoned when Supreme Army Headquarters intervened. Written instructions to Fourth Army that, 'For the time being there is no question of Poperinge being an operational objective. [Operations are to be] limited to eliminating the Ypres salient',[32] were not issued until 29 April, but had been passed verbally on 23 April. This was confirmed after the war by the then chief of staff, Fourth Army, Generalmajor Ilse.

Additional Allied counter-measures to the German advance were put in place swiftly. During the night 22/23 April, General Foch placed a further regiment and two batteries of 75 mm guns under General Quiquandon and 186 Brigade of 87th Territorial Division was alerted and moved forward in motorised transport. Other reserves were also stood to and moved into position so, by 23 April, the newly captured German positions came under increasing pressure as attacks went in against them. If nothing else these attacks distracted the German formations then, during the night, there were several attacks in varying strengths directed against the left flank of 45th Reserve Division. Although the German defence was successful, the formations involved were no longer in any position to press the attack with the necessary force. As a result, progress during 23 April was strictly limited to a minor advance south of Steenstraat. The situation was similar for 46th Reserve Division. Having managed to cross the canal at Steenstraat, an attack was launched during the evening against the right flank of the Belgians, but it was driven back and further attempts to cross the canal by boat in the Belgian 6th Division sector also failed completely. French reinforcements rushed forward during the night managed to establish a rough line of defence just to the west of the Lizerne – Boezinge road so, once again, little ground was gained.

In the XXVI Reserve corps sector, much of 23 April was devoted to holding off hasty counter-attacks. Reserve Infantry Regiment 236 of 51st Reserve Division had the task of guarding the threatened left flank of 52nd Reserve Division, where a gap had opened up northwest of St Juliaan. Eventually, during the night 23/24 April, this was done, as Reserve Infantry Regiment 236 thrust against a fortified farmhouse position between Reserve Infantry Regiments 234 and 235. Despite serious casualties and thanks to good work from their machine gun company, the position was taken and the gap closed.

Kriegsfreiwilliger Mathar Machine Gun Company Reserve Infantry Regiment 236[33] **7.**

"During the assault on the British [sic.] position, the machine gun platoon found itself in the so-called *Granatwäldchen* [Shell Copse]. Here we were subjected to the fire of sulphur-filled shells[34] to an extent we had never previously experienced. The poisoned clods of earth and pieces of wood which showered down on us left ugly yellow patches on our uniforms. Our platoon commander, Leutnant Alvermann, crawled almost to the edge of the wood, accompanied by the two gun commanders. A short time later they made their way left and right then waved to the crews, 'Mount gun!' The crews were barely able to carry the heavy guns, suffering as they were from minor injuries caused by the falling clods and wood and having breathed in the air laden with gas and sulphur. Only by exerting all our efforts could we get the guns into position.

"One gun was placed on the left hand [southeast] corner of the wood, with arcs of fire towards St Juliaan. The other gun, located further to the right, fired in the direction of Wieltje. Densely occupied British trenches were located about fifty metres to our front, but the trenches had apparently been dug very rapidly and the heads of the garrison were sticking up everywhere. Under cover, we had a good opportunity to mount our guns high and, firing from the kneeling position, direct our fire directly against the trenches. After we had fired several thousand rounds at them, the small arms fire from there died away. We could still see their heads. We could see several little white flags placed on the parapet. Spotting this and exploiting the moment, we rushed over with our machine guns and were the first to occupy the enemy trench.

"A few infantrymen from 6th Company followed us and then an entire skirmishing line charged through the copse. However, the trench at which we had fired contained only a few wounded men, all that was left of the garrison. Man after man, mortally wounded in the head, lined the front of the trench, some still with their rifles at the aim. [That shows] what a terrible effect our fire had."

The men of 51st Reserve Division, however, did not have things entirely their own way. There had been an intention by the French 45th Division to launch a counter-attack in the direction of Pilkem and a request arrived via a liaison officer for the Canadian Division to conform. In response, the Canadians launched a two battalion night attack at the so-called Kitchener's Wood, about one kilometre to the west of St Juliaan. Although the attack was pressed with great gallantry and some prisoners belonging to Reserve Infantry Regiment 234 were captured, the commanding officer of the 10th Canadian Battalion, Lieutenant Colonel RL Boyle, was mortally wounded and command devolved onto Lieutenant Colonel RGE Leckie of 16th Canadian Battalion. Unfortunately German machine gun fire in particular had a devastating effect on this counter-attack so, with Canadian numbers reduced to under 400 men from the two battalions combined and their positions both isolated and in considerable danger, because no French attack had materialised, there was nothing else for it; the Canadians had to withdraw once more.[35]

It had been planned originally that an attack on 23 April by XXVII Reserve Corps against the northeastern tip of the salient would be preceded by a major release of gas but, because a southwesterly wind stubbornly refused to blow, this was dropped. However, in order to enable the Corps to contribute to the battle, a special assault force in brigade strength and commanded by Generalmajor von Schmieden was organised. This was drawn from all the formations of 53rd Reserve Division. The infantry comprised 2nd and 3rd Battalions Reserve Infantry Regiment 241 and 2nd Battalion Reserve Infantry Regiment 242 (Regiment Reußner) and 2nd and 3rd Battalions Landwehr Infantry Regiment 78 and 2nd Battalion Reserve Infantry Regiment 244 (Regiment Wilhelmi).[36] Dedicated formations also included 1st Battalion Reserve Field Artillery Regiment 54, two Landwehr batteries from Fourth Army Reserve and a dedicated engineer platoon. A further assault regiment from 54th Reserve Division (Regiment von Heygendorff), comprising 3rd Battalion Reserve Infantry Regiment 245, 3rd, 4th and 9th Companies Reserve Infantry Regiment 246 and 2nd Battalion Reserve Infantry Regiment 247, was in XXVII Reserve Corps reserve, placed behind the right [northern] flank of the corps and subordinated to Schmieden for the operation.[37]

On 24 April, following a further discharge of gas on a one kilometre front, the brigade launched an attack against the line St Juliaan – 's-Graventafel and managed to capture Hill 32 one kilometre northeast of St Juliaan and the cross roads northwest of 's-Graventafel. Despite the fact that they had no anti-gas protection, other than damp towels or handkerchiefs, Canadians from the 8th and 15th Battalions managed to stand and fight, which severely limited the German advance.[38] Pressing forward the following day, Schmieden's men advanced a further 500 metres, inflicting heavy casualties and suffering 446 themselves. The brigade went into hasty defence and beat off Allied counter-attacks during the coming days. Meanwhile, the unengaged elements of 53rd Reserve Division were brought to readiness and moved forward. By 5.00 am 25 April, their formations were on the road and advancing west via Passchendaele and Wallemolen. The aim of the day was to renew the attack before nightfall. Despite cold, driving rain, good progress was made. Advance parties and reconnaissance groups were soon operating forward of the main body, which continued on towards Poelkapelle.

As was often the case, this village formed a significant bottleneck and the regiments arrived to find it teeming with personnel from the infantry, artillery and marine infantry. Wounded were being moved or treated, prisoners marched to the rear and a stream of batteries moved through constantly, all competing for road space. Despite the confusion, about 2.00 pm orders were given that as soon as the direct support batteries were in a position to engage the enemy breastworks, the attack would be launched by the divisional composite regiment. About an hour later it moved off in a southerly direction, in the order 3rd Battalion Reserve Infantry Regiment 245, 2nd Battalion Reserve Infantry Regiment 247, with the sub units of Reserve Infantry Regiment 246 following up. An old German position was occupied temporarily, then a battery of 150 mm howitzers arrived to supplement the fire of the direct support battery, which was already battering the British trenches just to the north of 's-Graventafel.

"Initially the Reserve Infantry Regiment 245 Battalion was moved onto the start line, but it was felt to be too weak for the task, so the men of the 247th were moved up as well. There, glimpsed over the protective parapet, was the old British trench which had been captured the day before yesterday. There could be seen shell holes, sandbags, fascines, protective shields and wire obstacles. Crump! crump! went the shells, as we took a short breather behind a hedge. Now the shells of the 150 mm howitzers roared over – crash! crash! crash! – they smashed into the earthworks.

"The artillery must cease firing. We want to assault!' We waved at them, we shouted. At long last we made ourselves understood. They ceased fire and a wild cry went up. 'Up and at the British! Go! *Hurra! Hurra!*' There was no stopping us now! Off and through the hedge; over the sandbags and the trenches! A shot up farm hove into view. 'More to the left! – there they are: there and there!' They were running now. 'Hey, shots from the right! A British machine gun! Flanking fire!' Now and then someone collapsed to the ground, but by then we were in the enemy trenches. 'Go left!' 'What a gruesome sight these smashed corpses make! The earthwork is captured. We have taken about 200 prisoners and six machine guns."[39]

Following on from indecisive battles during the previous two days, as the French 153rd Division, commanded by General Deligny, attempted to eliminate the German bridgeheads over the Ijzer, there was still some fighting west of the Canal on 26 April. General Roy of 87th Territorial Division released some of his surviving units to reinforce 153rd Division and local skirmishing continued for possession of Lizerne. Little was achieved, due to the fatigue of the troops involved and, in any case, the emphasis of the battle by then had swung firmly to the northeast sector of the salient, where pressure continued to be applied northwest of Zonnebeke. There were extensive captures of Canadian troops, bringing the combined total for the first three days of battle to around 5,000, together with nearly fifty assorted artillery pieces. The following day, 27 April, it was the turn of the Allies to launch attacks designed to dislodge the Germans from their newly acquired positions. Preparations were deficient, all formations had been weakened by the events of the past few days, there was a great lack of artillery support and the German troops had had ample opportunity to consolidate their gains and recover captured enemy materiel.

Leutnant Rudolf Binding[40] **8.**

"Tonight, together with my dragoons, I salvaged three captured enemy guns, which were under fire, not fifteen hundred metres from the new enemy trenches. There was moonlight and, in addition, the enemy constantly illuminated the battlefield with irritatingly bright flares. We grafted away all night, continually disturbed by violent salvoes and flares; we had to press ourselves flat on the ground whilst they were burning. Before dawn we had brought all three guns, including their limbers and ammunition, into a place of safety. One of my men was shot through the heart because, in a burst of enthusiasm, he had attempted to bring back a suckling pig, which he had found squeaking in a sty, ownerless. So he sat with it up on a limber, whilst the other comrades, ducked down, pushed at the wheels. Suddenly he sank lifelessly between the wheels still clutching the piglet.

"Forward of our brigade lies a sleeping army, man by man; lying next to one another, never to reawaken: Canadian divisions [sic.]. Enemy losses are gigantic. The battlefield is appalling. A uniquely sour, heavy and penetrating stink of corpses hangs over everything. We ride over one plank bridge, supported in the middle by the body of a long-dead horse. Without it the bridge would be lying in the water. Fallen from the October battles lie half in the bogs and half in the yellowing beet fields. The legs of a British soldier, still encased in puttees, are sticking out from the wall of the trench into which the corpse has been built. A soldier has hung his rifle on them.

"A little stream runs through the trench; it is used by everyone for washing and drinking. It is, in fact, the only water supply. The fact that a few steps upstream a bleached British soldier is rotting away in it does not bother anybody. In Langemark cemetery, a mass grave was piled high; the dead lay higher than the surface of the surrounding earth. German shells began to land and an appalling resurrection of the dead began. In one place twenty two horses, still in harness, were stretched out, together with a few drivers. Half decayed cows and pigs lay around; smashed trees and avenues of stumps; fields and tracks full of craters. That was the six month old battlefield … "

Attempting to press forward against a line running from the Ijzer, via St Juliaan to 's-Graventafel, the French army made no progress at all, apart from at Luzerne, where the village was recaptured.[41] The brigades of the Indian Lahore Division, already reduced in strength because of previous assaults, suffered extremely serious casualties and had to be pulled back later from even their very modest gains. Effectively, they had been left high and dry due to panic amongst French African troops who, having been subjected to gas shells, had fled to the rear during the early evening. The main problem, however, was the fact that the salient had been squeezed to such an extent that German guns, firing from positions southeast of Ypres, now had the range to hit the Indian troops virtually from the rear. It was plain that the situation was unsustainable and, for the first time, the British were forced to consider a significant withdrawal; orders to this effect being issued that same day.[42]

None of this was known in any sort of detail to the German army, though it had intercepted a British radio message on 27 April transmitted *en clair*, which stated, 'The situation of our troops, both the British forces and also the French army formations around Ypres, is very serious. We must prepare ourselves for bad news.'[43] The message was interpreted by Headquarters Fourth Army as Allied acceptance that retention of the salient was becoming ever more difficult with each passing day and that the maintenance of pressure might lead to decisive results. In the meantime, however, it was content to maintain its gains, simply noting on 28 April that there had been further attempts to retake lost ground and that one particular attack, conducted astride the Ypres – Pilkem road, had withered away in a torrent of fire two hundred metres short of the German lines. This was followed later in the day by a further thrust more to the east, which suffered the same fate. The following day, the emphasis shifted back to the west, where the German defenders were subject to constant shelling and waves of attacks around Steenstraat and Het Sas, which were unsuccessful, as were additional attempts launched the following day. This was something of a disappointment to General Foch in particular. Despite the emphasis which the French army was at that time devoting to final preparations for the offensive of its Tenth Army further south around Arras, it had nevertheless managed to produce significant reinforcements of heavy artillery rushed north to Flanders to support a renewed effort to regain ground in the direction of Langemark. Unfortunately, the effort was largely in vain and little progress could be made. For the time being it appeared that the fighting was stalemated but, whilst the British decision to withdraw was postponed repeatedly due to French pressure, and local operations continued, formations of XXVII Reserve Corps prepared another attack designed to drive in the northeast tip of the salient.

Whilst this attack was being prepared, Anglo-French discussions continued. Field Marshal French travelled to Cassel to meet Foch during the morning of 29 April to try to reach agreement. French wished to begin his general withdrawal towards Ypres the following night, Foch to press the assault on Langemark. Both agreed that the current position was untenable, but they differed in their approach. After a lengthy meeting, it was agreed that there would be a joint attack on 30 April. French reserved the right to begin his withdrawal if it did not enjoy success, whereas Foch, with his eye on matters of greater importance to the south, wished to delay any such manoeuvre until the Tenth Army offensive was launched.

The plan was for the French to continue offensive operations around Steenstraat, for General Quiquandon's force to attack from the Boezinge area and for the main effort to be a joint attack between the Ijzer Canal and the Ypres-Langemark road, with the ultimate aim of reaching Pilkem. In the event the attacks were delayed by early morning fog and were not in progress the length of the selected front until 11.15 am. The results were disappointing. The German defenders had no problem defending against the various efforts, which lacked cohesiveness and failed to generate momentum. In an echo of similar British accusations at the time, the French, whilst acknowledging the efficient cooperation of the British artillery, claimed that the only contribution by the British infantry was a half-hearted attempt by the Sirhind Brigade to move against Hill 29, due north of Turco Farm. For their part, the British stated that the French right flank did not advance, so the Sirhind Brigade, which by now had a majority of British troops assigned to it, was not able to either.[44]

It is hard to escape the view that the British were not wholehearted supporters of these continued attacks and that the French were too worn down from their earlier losses to achieve much either. Alarmed at the prospect that the British would carry out their planned withdrawal following a further abortive day of operations on 1 May, Foch travelled to Hazebrouck to meet French and managed to persuade him to delay any move for a further twenty four hours. For the sake of Allied unity this was done, but not enthusiastically, because to delay further was simply to accept increasing casualties from German artillery fire, which rained down on the vulnerable British position from three sides throughout the day.

Despite these Allied difficulties, which saw huge casualties incurred for little or no return, nevertheless the German army did not have everything its own way. The formations of 51st Reserve Division, after several days of intense fighting with serious losses, found itself on standby once more near St Juliaan to conduct a fresh assault supported by another release of gas. Reserve Infantry Regiment 236 was heavily involved in one of the attacks, which was to be launched in the approximate direction of Fortuinhoek. 500 cylinders of chlorine had been buried along the regimental front line and the regiment was on full alert from the evening of 29 April. Fog delayed the operation then, during the morning of 30 April, it rained heavily. The weather forecast was also poor for the following day, but eventually the front passed over, the conditions improved markedly during the afternoon of 2 May and, with the wind believed to be favourable, the cylinders were opened at 6.00 pm, just as they had been on 22 April.

In contrast to the earlier events, however, this time the gas achieved nothing. It was a windy day with strong gusts, so the clouds pillared upwards and did nothing to the enemy, other than to alert them. No sooner had the first wave stepped off than all hell broke loose as murderous flanking fire was opened from the direction of Fortuinhoek, supplemented by heavy rifle and machine gun fire from the area of Vanheule Farm. There was nothing the attackers could do but to dig in for cover and this they did between the Wieltje road and the Hanebeek. 7th Company then remained where it was, some three hundred metres beyond the start line, whilst the reminder pulled back there as soon as it went dark. This was not the end of the story, however. Reinforced by two companies from 3rd Battalion, the attack against Vanheule Farm was renewed at about midnight. The aim was to conduct a silent (i.e. no artillery preparation) night attack and to attempt to seize the farm in a *coup de main* operation.

Initially progress was steady and the right flank of the attackers had already passed the line of the farm when their presence was discovered. Immediately, a torrent of fire was opened and they were forced back once more with serious losses, including Leutnant Kissinger of 12th Company who was killed. It might be thought that after two failures and the Allies under severe pressure anyway, the project would have been abandoned or at least postponed – but not a bit of it. 7th Company was ordered to renew the attack during the morning of 3 May. The sole survivor of this suicidal mission recalled his experiences later.

Gefreiter Ebeler 7th Company Reserve Infantry Regiment 236[45] **9.**

"A beautiful May morning dawned and 3 Platoon of 7th Company, led by Vizefeldwebel Leo, which was occupying a freshly dug trench, prepared to attack the farm. Weary from lack of sleep, chilled and worn down by the battles since 24 April, we waited for the signal to storm forward. After our heavy artillery had landed eighty shells on the farm, we launched forward from our position at 9.00 am. Carrying full battle loads, we shook out into a long line and assaulted the farm. Not a shot was fired then, suddenly, about fifty metres short of the farm, we came under a hail of rifle and machine gun fire from the front and both flanks. Quick as lightning we threw ourselves down. Nobody knew where his neighbour had gone; but the occasional scream or shout indicated that the enemy fire had been all too accurate.

"My sole aim now was to regain the start line. Tall grass prevented me from observing the situation and the surrounding ground, but I was dimly aware of a comrade who was attempting, just as slowly as me, to crawl back. Every movement was accompanied by bullets whistling by – the British were keeping a bloody good look out. Because my knapsack on my back presented too good a target and the leather helmets no protection against fire, I slowly removed my knapsack and pushed it in front as a shield. Again and again I pulled my knapsack and rifle backwards and crawled like a crab at a snail's pace to the rear ... Overhead and to my left and right, bullets cracked through the air. I prayed to almighty God to permit me to emerge alive from No Man's Land. Moving my head carefully, I saw that our trench was only ten metres behind me. Now came the hardest bit. Three metres short of the parapet I hurled my knapsack into the trench, then threw myself and my rifle in too. The return had taken three hours. I was utterly exhausted, drained and filthy dirty.

"That which I had experienced, however, was only a grim foretaste of what was to come. A little later I noticed something fall into the trench to the right of my position. As I ran over, I saw to my great joy that it was my friend and comrade Kriegsfreiwilliger Christian Schmitz from Cologne. We had marched away together in 1914 and he, too, had come out of it alive. Schmitz had seen that our platoon commander, Leo, and our section commander, Unteroffizier Süß, had been killed, but knew nothing of the fate of our other comrades. We sat tight in our trench. Far and wide there was not a sign of friend or foe. The British then began to bring down revenge fire at about 2.00 pm. One shell after another landed to the rear of our empty position, but they were all duds.

"Despite the seriousness of the current situation, we jeered at the artillery ammunition and speculated that they must be American shells.[46] Then, all of a sudden, the enemy opened fire with sulphur shells,[47] which also impacted just to our rear. The clouds of sulphur smoke, which swirled into the trench and slowly dyed our uniforms yellow, were unbearable. After a brief pause, a fresh battery began to engage our trench and, all too soon, the shells began to land accurately in and around the trench. We raced like disturbed wild animals from one end of the trench to the other. Suddenly we heard another shell. I hurled myself at the parapet and pressed against the wall of the trench, with my comrade Schmitz crouched tightly beside me. The shell had impacted on the parapet and I felt his arms pull on me. As I looked carefully around, I saw that my dear friend had been hit in the head by a shell splinter. With tears in my eyes, I gently pulled away from the dead man and laid him on the floor of the trench. The British fired salvoes ceaselessly at the already half smashed trench, so I left this dangerous place, ran in short dashes to the St Juliaan road and took cover in the ditch. Creeping backwards along this, I rejoined the company towards evening. There I discovered that, apart from me, only Kriegsfreiwilliger Kleckers, who died a hero's death the following day,[48] had returned intact from the assault on Vanheule Farm."

Elsewhere on 3rd May, Schmieden's Saxon brigade, reinforced this time by Heygendorff's assault regiment from 54th Reserve Division, attacked once more, capturing a field fortification in a copse near 's-Graventafel and the heights around the village itself. There had been careful preparation and a large allocation of heavy artillery in support. This particular assault was followed by a crumbling of the Allied front. This was not really a surprise for the German chain of command. There had been a realisation for some time that the largely vain Allied attempts to attack had weakened their front line troops and made them increasingly vulnerable to determined German thrusts. Anyone could see that there could be no long term future for the salient in its current shape and, furthermore, already on 2 May German aircraft had spotted the move west of small detachments and defensive works being prepared just to the east of Ypres.

The pressure which had been built up by XXIII and XXVI Reserve Corps and which led the British decision to relinquish ground voluntarily, brought into the battle formations of XXVII Reserve Corps, whose formations had only played a limited role up until that point. Elements of Reserve Infantry Regiments 245, 246 and 247 of 54th Reserve Division, which had formed an *ad hoc* regiment to act as corps reserve, had found itself deployed around 's-Graventafel during the early days of the battle but, by early May, all these units were back with their parent formations and thus were involved in the general advance which began early on 4 May. 53rd Reserve Division pursued the retreating British troops in the direction of Westhoek, whilst the formations of 54th Reserve Division followed up slightly to the north, advancing between the northeast corner of Polygon Wood and Zonnebeke.

There had been signs during the night 3-4 May that something unusual was happening. In numerous places, the front line troops reported small fires burning in the enemy trenches, whilst both the use of flares and small arms fire died away gradually. Cautiously, patrols were pushed forward to try to establish exactly what was happening.

Hauptmann Nuber Commanding Officer 2nd Battalion Reserve Infantry Regiment 248[49]
10.

"During the night 3-4 May, 1st Battalion was located right forward, with 2nd Battalion left forward and 3rd Battalion resting. During the night enemy fire was weak. At 3.00 am there were a few isolated shots and a dugout was set on fire opposite the Sandbag Position. Out to the west, in the distance, further fires could be seen. Then, between 3.00 am and 4.00 am, Unteroffizier Kortner, who was in a lie up position as part of an officer's patrol led by Leutnant Seeger of 8th Company, discovered that the enemy front line trench had been evacuated! This was reported immediately to regiment, who ordered the battalions to follow up – something they had already set in train – and the resting battalion to stand to, ready to move. That which we had longed for had occurred. Pressured by the success of XXVI Reserve Corps, the enemy were pulling back in the direction of Ypres.

"Who could possibly have held back? We were about to discover the secrets of Polygon Wood and the race course! With patrols and scouts feeling their way out forward, 1st and 2nd Battalions advanced. We were, alas, not totally free of casualties. A land mine killed an unteroffizier who was advancing with insufficient caution and also wounded two men. Smashed telephone systems and the fact that very little *materiel* had been left behind showed that this was a planned withdrawal. The poor condition of the trenches and overhead cover was very striking, as were the leaf-covered shelters built by the Canadians.

"By 8.00 am we were at the northwest corner of Polygon Wood. There the battalions consolidated and waited for the neighbouring troops to swing off to the left. In the meantime our sister arm had not been idle. Reserve Field Artillery Regiment 54 was quickly on the scene at Polygon Wood and was sending its iron greetings to the hill and dips in the ground east of Ypres. From the shot up buildings northwest of the wood there was a wonderful view to the west. In the distance the towers of Ypres drew our gaze whilst, further away, Mont Kemmel stood out like the Promised Land. Pillars of smoke marked where our artillery was doing its work and wave after wave of our infantry made their way forward in the undulating terrain, through dips and along hedges, initially barely disturbed by weak and aimless enemy artillery fire. The shortening of the front due to the capture of Polygon Wood meant that 53rd [Reserve] Division moved in front of us. On Brigade orders we were held in reserve to begin with, once it became clear at 12.30 that the enemy had dug in 200 metres west of Eksternest."

When the withdrawal began it was on a significant scale. The north, east and southern sectors of the salient were evacuated on a fifteen kilometre frontage between Fortuinhoek, Broodseinde and Klein-Zillebeke to a depth of between 500 metres and three kilometres. As soon as it was light the following morning, troops of 53rd Reserve Division pressed forward hard on the heels of the withdrawing units, maintaining close contact and bringing heavy aimed artillery fire to bear every time an attempt was made to make a stand. Reserve Infantry Regiment 242 of 53rd Reserve Division, which had been heavily involved a few days earlier in the fighting around Kerselaarhoek, two kilometres southwest of Passchendaele, was closely involved in the pursuit towards Zonnebeke, an advance which was described later by an anonymous member of its 3rd Battalion.[50] **11.**

"It rained heavily throughout 3 May, a most unpleasant situation for those who had no shelter ... Suddenly, it was 2.00 am [4 May] and a green flare went up. What was that? What could it mean? Our eyes strained even more through the viewing slits of our firing positions. One or two of our comrades jumped up onto the firing step and observed over the parapet, their rifles at the ready. We all thought that the only possible explanation was an imminent enemy night attack. At that time the use of coloured flares was such a rare occurrence that their use was of much greater significance than was the case later. However the expected attack did not materialise. Everything remained totally quiet. Enemy firing died away even more and almost no flares were being used. That in itself was significant! Could it be that the British had withdrawn? That hardly seemed possible!

"Nevertheless, the shelling had been intense during the past two days and our comrades had achieved considerable success in open battle. It seemed possible, therefore, that the Tommies had chosen to leave their trenches at night and in the fog and to occupy prepared positions further to the rear. However, there was still the odd shot from the over there. What could be going on? Time would tell. Day dawned on 4 May. It seemed as though another overcast, rainy day was in store. We drew our groundsheets even tighter around ourselves, to act as makeshift raincoats which, however, restricted our movements somewhat. We manned our posts, but now that it was daylight we no longer thought that an enemy attack was probable.

"At about 8.00 am our new company commander, Oberleutnant Hohneck, came along the trench ... and asked, 'Who is willing to come on patrol towards the enemy? The enemy trench is thought to have been abandoned.' We were still amazed [at the news], but a number of men had already volunteered. With Oberleutnant Hohneck, armed with a short hand axe and a revolver, in the lead, the patrol advanced along an old sap towards the British lines then, at its head, jumped up into the open. We manned the parapet tensely, waiting to give covering fire to the patrol, because their bold action made them easy targets for any alert sentry post. To our great surprise, not a shot was fired from the enemy trench. Our patrol then pushed on, shouting back, 'The trench is empty, follow us!'

"At that, we all set off. Our feelings were indescribable as we climbed out over the parapet, casting the encumbering groundsheets aside and headed for the enemy trenches. What would it look like? We were curious to see how the enemy had organised themselves in their trenches. What we found made a dramatic impression on us. Dug deep and wide, there was no revetment except here and there where chain link fencing had been used to stop the walls collapsing, whilst everywhere there were deep water-filled holes caused by the direct hits of the past few days. There were dead enemy soldiers lying around, but there were no dugouts; nowhere were there any signs of construction. How on earth had the enemy managed to pass the winter in such a place?

"After we had spent a few minutes looking around the position, we continued on. Naturally our activity had not gone unnoticed by the neighbours. They also climbed out of their trenches so that, wherever we looked to the left and right, German skirmishing lines were advancing. Our equipment etc was still in the old trench but, with bayonets fixed, ammunition in pouches or in belts hung around us and our caps on, we set off. It was marvellous to be snapping at the heels of the enemy and to capture long disputed ground. Advancing, we were able to examine the ground which the enemy had been holding. Their withdrawal must have been hasty, because we came across complete supply dumps for rations, ammunition and engineer equipment. The enemy had been occupying a series of trenches arranged in depth and it would have been far from easy to have driven them out of these positions if we had had to fight for them.

"About two hundred metres in rear of the front line, they had dug into the walls of a sunken road to provide dugouts. This is where the majority of the garrison must have been accommodated. The many empty food tins lying around bore witness to this. We helped ourselves to small quantities of tinned meat and jam which tasted excellent later in the day. After moving through fields ploughed up by shells, and others full of sugar beet, whose leaves transferred large amounts of water to our clothing to accompany the heavy rain, we arrived soaked to the skin about an hour later in Zonnebeke. This was the same place which had been fought over so heavily in autumn 1914 and which the enemy had held up to now.

"What a state the little place was in! The shells had wrought terrible destruction. Not a building was intact. Of the magnificent church, only the bare walls remained and the churchyard which surrounded it was ploughed up. Gravestones were smashed and the vaults were laid open. The entire place presented as dismal a scene of war as is rarely encountered ... Soon reinforcements from the reserve battalion arrived to press on [whilst we recovered our personal equipment]. From the rear we witnessed the general advance. The artillery left their former positions to take up new ones forward. Ammunition columns raced up and a railway repair company, summoned hastily, worked feverishly to repair the destroyed track. We of 9th Company had nothing more to do that day. Having helped with the railway repairs for a few hours, we returned to Zonnebeke and went into reserve."

The situation was much the same in the 54th Reserve Division sector, though some units were a little slower to pickup the signs of the withdrawal.

Leutnant Eith 7th Company Reserve Infantry Regiment 246[51] **10.**

"The first reports of our patrols came in at 4.00 am: 'The first trench is free of enemy'. Then, at 4.15 am came, 'The second trench has also been abandoned'. At 4.45 am, an officer's patrol under Leutnant Eith and comprising two unteroffiziers and sixteen men, went forward and sent back the following reports: '5.15 am. We have reached the racetrack.' '5.30 am. The northern edge of Polygon Wood has been occupied.' The patrol then pushed on as far as the copse immediately to the east of Westhoek.

"We had all thought that the enemy would have dug themselves in very strongly in Polygon Wood, but this was only the case along the Polygonbeek Position five hundred metres to the rear [west] of the wood.[52] The front line was very poor; in places, the standard of work was rubbish. Most of the enemy obstacles were very badly constructed. The whole situation was indescribably chaotic: nowhere were latrines or drainage ditches to be seen. There was a large sandbagged position opposite our right hand company ... and a mine gallery had been driven ten – fourteen metres forward towards the dugout of one of the platoon commanders of the left hand company.

"The dugouts we came across were extremely poor quality. Behind the *Tabakhaus* [Tobacco Shed] there was nothing but a few half covered, half rotting Frenchmen buried in the parapet or in the trenches themselves. The entire position, into which dead and semi-decomposed French men had been built, would certainly have been untenable in summer."

Eith's remarks on the state of the Polygon Wood and the positions which the regiment had just inherited were echoed later by a member of 5th Company.

Unteroffizier Ingelfinger 5th Company Reserve Infantry Regiment 246[53] **10.**

"A few metres in rear of the enemy trench, by the so-called 'Tobacco Shed', lay three dead cows, which were spreading such a vile stink that it was impossible to stick it out there. A drainage ditch had been dug right past the cows; proof that it ought to have been possible to cover them up. The position was always well manned. Very close by, also behind the trench and, therefore, easily accessible, was an unburied Frenchman. In three places where water had flooded into the trench, three dead men were simply floating in the water. In another place a Frenchmen had been buried in the wall of the trench, with one of his knees sticking out into the trench. The beaten path in the trench floor showed that the French were in the habit of swerving to the left or right to avoid it.

"In one twelve metre stretch seven Frenchmen lay just where they had been killed. From the look of the corpses, they must have been there for months. About three metres forward of the enemy trench was a sapper who appeared to have been killed whilst erecting a wire obstacle. By night he could easily have been pulled into the trench. It was not unusual to see shallow trenches from which a stray hand or foot might be sticking out. I hardly need to mention that all the fallen were immediately covered up where they lay.

"Our accessible graves had long since been tidied up; now we were able to attend to those we had not been able to approach without the risk of being fired on. These were marked properly and wreaths were laid. All reports confirmed the dreadfully unhygienic condition of the enemy positions. If we came across properly laid out burial places, they were all British graves, marked with the inscription 'Killed in Action.' ... On the far side of the butt was a British stand by position. It comprised dismal little holes, arranged in layers and so squashed together that no German soldier would have tolerated them for an instant. These holes teemed with vermin; the floors were strewn with half-mouldy straw. We had thought that the British would have been a cleaner lot. That the French and their black brothers were not, we knew beyond doubt."

The condition of the Allied defensive positions was every bit as bad in the northern sector.

Leutnant Rudolf Binding[54]

"The French are shockingly indifferent. They have not buried their corpses, even though they have been lying for months in the trenches which we have now captured. These are poor and badly constructed. In contrast, ours are like salons. They even leave officers lying about. I collected an identity disc as proof of this peculiarity. It strikes me as strange that a forty six year old officer could fall in the front line and not be moved to the rear. Unfortunately his rank and regiment could not be determined. Even where the fallen have been buried, they seem to arrange things so that soon the graves are indistinguishable from the surrounding earth. They are marked with tiny crosses, not more than the breadth of two hands high, usually made of a few twisted twigs and I have but rarely read a name. If the French government was disinclined to publish casualty lists they could ascribe to all unidentifiable fallen the term 'missing' and imply that all these missing were prisoners of the Germans – and just shrug their shoulders. It is certainly striking how many German graves one sees and how few French. Only by looking hard is it possible to detect that their losses are definitely not lower than ours."

The scenes on 4 May were almost completely novel on this previously static front. German skirmishing lines followed by columns of infantry pushed forward everywhere, accompanied by artillery batteries and their subordinated ammunition columns. In a few days the salient, which had had a length of twenty five kilometres and a depth of nine, had been reduced to one a mere thirteen kilometres by five. This dramatic reduction further eased the task of the German artillery which found it extremely easy henceforth to concentrate a great weight of fire on any chosen part of the salient. However, as the advancing German troops butted up against the new hasty defences, they were soon brought to a halt once more. On 5 May, for example, there was heavy fighting northwest of Frezenberg, especially around the *Wasserberg* [Shell (later Mouse) Trap Farm], but there was rather less action and little additional progress further south.

Hauptmann Nuber Commanding Officer 2nd Battalion Reserve Infantry Regiment 248[55] **12.**

"There was not much change in our position between 5 and 7 May, though 1st Battalion suffered more and more from gun fire. 2nd Battalion had pushed forward once more into Nonnebossen, constructing overhead cover and obtaining material for the front line trenches. 3rd Battalion in brigade and then divisional reserve was given a clearance task and collected in all captured British *materiel* from the abandoned positions. Unfortunately, there was no immediate further advance on the enemy and they took full advantage of the opportunity to dig in and construct obstacles on Hill 50, southwest of Eksternest

Following the dramatic change in the battle situation, on 6 May 'Regiment Heygendorff' was disbanded and its constituent parts returned to their parent formations,[56] just in time to become involved in preparations for a renewal of the assaults on 8 May.

Gefreiter Gräfe 7th Company Reserve Infantry Regiment 242[57] **12.**

"During the early hours of 8 May we were told that we should be attacking once more later in the day. We found this hard to believe, because we were not exactly sure where the main enemy position was located. About 5.00 am our commanding officer, Hauptmann Meißner, came up to us in our trench and observed the ground for a long time with his telescope. We were on edge waiting to hear what was to happen. 'Yes, the attack goes in today!' Now we knew for sure. Our company commander then briefed us. '2nd Battalion attacks today. 6th and 7th Companies will form the first wave, with 5th and 8th following close behind as a second wave. The ruined buildings must be captured and held at all costs. There will be no withdrawal. We have sufficient reserves. Once the ruined buildings are in our hands, we press forward. New orders will be issued for that.'

"The platoon commanders then explained the operation in fine detail and there were numerous questions, so as to ensure that everything would go according to plan. For many comrades this would be their baptism of fire. Watches were synchronised. On the word 'Go!' the first two platoons of the company were to go over the top, with the third platoon, acting as a second wave, ten metres in rear.[58] Our artillery fired a preliminary bombardment from 8.00 am to 10.30 am. Initially they had problems ranging in. The first shell roared overhead to land a long way in rear. The second landed shorter and third yet shorter. We felt the violent air pressure of the fourth shell, which struck with a shattering crash between us and the ruined buildings. We looked anxiously at one another. If they landed them any closer, the next one would come down in our trench! Suddenly there was a salvo. There was one direct hit in the ruined walls which sent tiles spraying in all directions.

"It was barely 8.00 am. Only our 210 mm [howitzers] were firing, but we adjusted our equipment, replaced our caps with *Pickelhauben* and we loosened the fastenings of our spades, whose value had become very clear to us these last few days. Our entire artillery then opened up and shells whizzed over our heads towards the enemy, roaring and groaning. Realising what we were doing, the enemy immediately began to engage our lines with shrapnel and high explosives. We crouched low, jammed together in our rough trenches; never knowing if we should receive a direct hit. The guns roared. Right behind us were the light field guns and, just to our front, shrapnel pots burst and fuzes and shell fragments whirred past our ears, Shells landing in quick succession made the ground tremble. We looked repeatedly at our watches, but time passed at a snail's pace. Some comrades scribbled a field post card to loved ones at home – perhaps for the last time.

"Suddenly the artillery fire died away. We looked over the wall, but the enemy machine guns had already begun their tack! tack! It was 9.45 am. 'Fix bayonets!' came the order. Our artillery opened up again; this time firing much more rapidly. The light field guns were fired red hot. Then we heard, 'Stand by!' We were all absolutely convinced that we should capture the enemy trench. We had complete trust in our capable commanders and were determined to 'show the British a thing or two'. We suppressed any gentle thoughts of loved ones far away or our dear homes. This was no time for softness! Our company commander stood up and raised his hand. 'Go!' raced through the ranks like lightning, a few sandbags were torn from the parapet, we leapt up – and stormed forward!

"Our leaders were slightly in the lead, the third platoon was right behind us, just as we had practised on the barrack square. It was only the rattle of machine gun fire and the whistling and cracking of bullets which showed that this was real war. 'Take cover!' We were under heavy machine gun fire from the left flank. Spotting the danger, our company commander swung part of the first wave towards the left. The remainder of us pushed straight ahead. The second wave was right up with us and, with loud shouts of *Hurra!* we rushed the trench. The garrison, which had initially defended itself bravely, now wished to surrender, but one of the scoundrels hurled a hand grenade at us, so we made short work of them. The trench was ours and we pushed on.

"At this point information reached us that our bold commander,

Oberleutnant Dependorf, had been killed.[59] At that crushing news, we halted briefly, but Leutnant Rose urged us on. Once again we came under machine gun fire from a copse to our front, but we soon silenced it with rifle fire. There were a few dugouts in the wood, which were being defended by some British soldiers, but we cleared them quickly. Beyond the wood we had to dig in because those advancing left of the railway had not been able to make progress as rapidly. Fairly swiftly we had managed to develop a reasonable trench and enemy artillery fire did not disturb us in the least as we searched the dugouts. It was a veritable ration dump, [which contained] large quantities of tinned food, white bread, various types of jam, condensed milk and an ample sufficiency of cigarettes.

So, following on from the bloody work, we enjoyed a shared breakfast. As it went dark we discovered that there were no Very pistols or flares for the entire line and the British made a serious attempt in the middle of the night to recapture our newly won positions. We could not see a thing, but we fired rapidly, supported by our two machine guns and the attack broke down. At daybreak we found the evidence. They had closed right up to us and there were about forty killed and several wounded men near the position ... The attack had cost us all our company commanders: Hauptmann Grahl 6th Company, wounded; Oberleutnant Dependorf 7th and Leutnant Müller 5th Company killed and Leutnant Halbach, 8th Company, wounded ... On 10 May, the mortal remains of the fallen were laid to rest in the regimental Cemetery of Honour by the railway station between Passchendaele and Moorslede".

Hauptmann Nuber Commanding Officer 2nd Battalion Reserve Infantry Regiment 248[60] **13.**

"8 May was a hard day for 1st Battalion, under Hauptmann von Legl. He had succeeded gradually in closing up to an assault position. A bombardment, which lasted several hours, prepared the way for a general attack all along the XXVII Reserve Corps frontage. The infantry launched their assault at 10.30 am. This suffered greatly from enfilade fire but, by about 11.00 am, the enemy trenches on the edge of Hill 50 had been taken. These were immediately 'turned around'. One machine gun and twenty five British soldiers were captured, but the cost to 1st Battalion was one officer, four unteroffiziers and fifty two other ranks killed, with four officers, nine unteroffiziers and 117 other ranks wounded.

"2nd and 3rd Battalions were held back initially as a divisional reserve in the *Eisenenkreuzwäldchen* [Iron Cross Copse] near Westhoek. Two companies of the latter battalion were subordinated to 1st Battalion during the evening of 8 May and 2nd Battalion, commanded by Hauptmann Nuber, was called forward to Nonnebossen. There, at 9.00 pm, it received orders to leapfrog 1st

Battalion, link up with Reserve Infantry Regiment 247 and capture the wood north of Bellewaarde Lake. With 5th and 6th Companies in a first line and 7th and 8th Companies plus battalion headquarters forming a second line, at 5.00 pm, under heavy enemy artillery and small arms fire, the crest and western slope of Hill 50 was crossed.

"The companies in the front line worked their way forward to the western edge of the boggy copse (*Seewald* = Lake Wood) to the north of the lake. The companies in the second line remained as a rearguard by the long hedge to the east, which dominated the entire forward area to the east. There they developed the existing fox holes into a continuous trench – *Heckengraben* [Hedge Trench]. A further advance was not possible for the time being, due to flanking fire from positions half left of the lake."

So with the advance stalled at Bellewaarde Lake and short of Hooge, on 9 May formations of XXVI Reserve Corps and the right flank of XV Reserve Corps also launched further attacks which made little progress, whilst up along the coast XXII Reserve Corps launched small diversionary attacks of only minor importance. These failed completely in the face of determined opposition, but not for lack of courage on the part of those involved. One of these attacks was launched by elements of 44th Reserve Division in the Nieuwpoort area. Reserve Infantry Regiment 207 had been detached earlier to reinforce in the Ypres area, so the attack was conducted by Reserve Infantry Regiments 205 (south) and 208 (north). The divisional orders, issued on 8 May, stated:

"Fourth Army is conducting an enveloping attack around Ypres today. Tomorrow, Division Dorrer will attack. The objective is to seize the eastern bank of the Yser/Ijzer, north of Nieuwpoort. H Hour 2.00 pm."[61]

During the hours of darkness, gaps were prepared through the barbed wire, antipersonnel caltrops were cleared and large quantities of ammunition were distributed. At 5.00 am on 9 May the German artillery opened up, but only at normal harassing fire rates. However, from midday, the rate was increased considerably and the assault was launched promptly.

Kriegsfreiwillige Unteroffizier Neumann 2nd Company Reserve Infantry Regiment 205[62]

"About midday we found out at long last that an attack would be launched the length of the divisional sector at 2.00 pm. All we experienced comrades were well aware what sort of sacrifice an attack in broad daylight would mean. According to our orders, 'At five minutes to 2.00 pm, the company is to be ready to move, bayonets fixed, in the trench. At exactly 2.00 pm the company will leave the trench.' We quickly exchanged details of the addresses of our relatives; our thoughts turned momentarily to parents, siblings and fiancée; our hopes to survival and the success of the assault.

"Suddenly our artillery fell silent and, simultaneously, the enemy literally sprayed our positions with lead. At 2.00 pm precisely the first sections went over the top, with 1st Company to the right [north] of 2nd Company. The remaining reserve companies of the battalion moved forward to occupy the vacated front line positions. That which the experienced comrades had predicted became reality. The enemy, who had ranged in to perfection, cut dreadful swathes in the lines of attackers. During the second dash forward, I myself was hit in the left thigh by a ricochet and thrown to the ground. Left and right of me were the heart rending screams of the seriously wounded, battling against death. Swiftly the assault stalled due to the heavy losses.

"It soon became clear that the enemy was firing mercilessly at anybody who showed any sign of life. As a result I stayed perfectly still. For the time being there could be no question of binding my wound and I felt rather weak from a serious loss of blood. The thought that I might never return caused me to break out in a cold sweat. The daylight had not quite faded when I eased off my knapsack and attempted to get up, but my wounded leg failed me. There was nothing else for it, but to attempt to crawl back. This was a very slow process. Finally I reached our badly shot up position and was pulled into the trench by comrades from 3rd Company. I then gasped a heartfelt, 'Thank God for that!'

"Numerous comrades had to spend many hours lying in water-filled shell holes and were only able to get back to our lines with extreme difficulty and the ever present risk of death. They arrived totally exhausted. It was only then that I discovered that my company commander, Leutnant Losshagen, platoon commanders Leutnant Semmler, and Feldwebels Dähne and Kühne, together with Unteroffiziers Baganz, Behnack, Machewitz, Welk and Zeyer and about ninety gefreiters and musketiers had found the deaths of heroes during this hellish assault. Only Feldwebel Huebsch and about twenty five men returned from this pointless attack. The only man of 2nd Company to reach the French trenches was Kriegfreiwilliger Mewes, but he died in French captivity as result of a bayonet wound."

The situation was no better for the men of Reserve Infantry Regiment 208. Although its 1st Battalion on the right succeeded in gaining the first line of enemy trenches, a series of counter-attacks and mounting losses drove it back to its start line that same evening, whilst the attack of its 3rd Battalion withered away just forward of its own wire obstacle in a hail of small arms fire. This dismal, pointless enterprise had cost the regiment no fewer than eighty five men killed in action, three hundred wounded and two hundred missing[63] – and, like that of Reserve Infantry Regiment 205, had achieved absolutely nothing.

By this time, with the positions solidifying once more, the battle was largely over as far as the German army was concerned. Its losses up until that point had exceeded 35,000; those of the British army were almost 60,000,[64] whilst the French lost 18,000 men on 22 April alone.[65] Nevertheless, progress having been made, there was one final attempt to storm the crest line from Wieltje, through Velorenhoek to Frezenberg. Reserve Infantry Regiment 236, of 51st Reserve Division, for example, moved forward on 12 May to relieve Marine Infantry Regiment 2 northeast of Wieltje just prior to an assault on 13 May.

Barely had they had time to organise themselves in the new position than there was a three hour bombardment of the enemy positions then, at about 8.00 am, the assault began. Success was extremely limited. Some parts of the enemy line had not been properly suppressed, machine guns were able to open fire from a flank, some sub units made a bare fifty metres before they were forced to dig in for cover and even the most successful advance moved the line forward a mere 150 metres. It hardly seemed worth the thirty two all ranks killed and fifty wounded that the day cost, though there was a useful surrender the following day of British troops which had been isolated by the advance at Chateau Wieltje.

Unteroffizier Brücken 4th Company Reserve Infantry Regiment 236[66] **14.**

> "The morning following the last assault of our regiment against the Chateau, we observed from our new trench British soldiers who were waving and trying to catch our attention. Apparently they were trying to make contact with us. Because I could speak English my comrades pressed me to go over and begin negotiations. I could not raise the slightest enthusiasm for the task. In answer to my question what would happen if the enemy did not allow me to return to my trench, Leutnant Ricken, supported by my comrades, promised, 'We shall attack and rescue you.'
>
> "At that I removed my equipment and, feeling rather tense, set off on my adventure across No Man's Land towards the British lines. To my relief, I was received in a friendly manner by the British. However, in order to ease observation from our own position, I remained standing forward of the British position and in full view. There I began to negotiate. During the conversation which followed, it became clear to me that the morale of these troops, their willingness to fight on, had evaporated. They only wished to know how they would be treated in German captivity and if they would be fed and given drinks. Having been given reassuring answers by me, they informed me that they would come over later. At that I returned to my own lines unscathed."

There was a swift follow up to this information and the regimental commander himself was soon on the scene.

Oberstleutnant Grimm Commander Reserve Infantry Regiment 236[67] **14.**

> "Once I received information concerning the intention of the garrison of Chateau Wieltje to surrender, I went forward to the front line trench, accompanied by the regimental adjutant. There we could see the British standing around in the open and waving to us. I went with Leutnant Lange over the bridge into the chateau. He then negotiated with them – apparently without success at first. However, no sooner had we returned to our own lines than [we

were] followed by about sixty British soldiers, three officers amongst them, who surrendered. Later we also brought in a machine gun."

Despite the heavy fighting and consequent severe losses on both sides, the German assault at Ypres never achieved very much beyond the initial success caused by the surprise use of poison gas. It had been hoped to eliminate the entire Ypres salient, but this was not achieved. Subsequent analysis suggested that this was because the late timing of the gas attack meant that there was insufficient time fully to exploit the consequent surprise before night fell. However, the general lack of faith in the effect of the gas amongst the German commanders and the failure to provide significant reserves ready to follow up the initial advance played at least large a part, as did the strong defence put up by certain front line troops, especially the Canadians near St Juliaan. Nevertheless, the withdrawal by the British to the Wieltje-Klein Zillebeke line in early May was clearly due to pressure exerted over a period of days by XXVI and XVII Reserve Corps and certainly the compression of the salient was very much to the disadvantage of the British army for the next thirty months, a period marked by stalemate and high casualties from the continual shelling of the area.

The British subsequently dignified the spring fighting with the title 'The Second Battle of Ypres'. Joffre dismissed it in a few lines as, 'an annoying incident without serious consequences'[68] and noted merely that it caused him hurriedly to set in place studies on how to create a gas warfare capability and the means of defence against it. From the German perspective, the final word concerning the events of late April and early May came from the Commander Fourth Army, in the shape of a special Order of the Day, couched in typically extravagant language and issued at the beginning of June.

Duke Albrecht of Württemberg[69]

> "His Majesty the King and Kaiser has graciously expressed to me his recognition of the activities of Fourth Army during the recent heavy fighting before Ypres. I am bringing this to the attention of the Army in the expectation that this recognition by the Supreme War Lord will spur each individual to continue to give of his utmost. I am well aware that the driving back of tough opponents during the course of heavy fighting which lasted for weeks was a hard task, which could only be realised through the most relentless commitment of commanders and the irresistible courage of the troops. The objective was achieved. We succeeded in dealing the enemy a serious blow. This was success to be placed alongside the greatest successes achieved on the Eastern Front.
>
> "Here, as there, it was the spirit displayed by the troops which led to victory. It was the spirit of courage; of the will to get forward; of the unshakeable determination to hold on, which motivated every single commander and man. It was the spirit of the God-fearing [individual], faithful to the Ruling House and the love of our wonderful Fatherland! I direct that it is the bounden duty of every superior officer to nurture further this true German spirit in every last

man. It must be maintained. Only then shall we be able one day, despite our many enemies, to return to our dear Fatherland, knowing that we have achieved peace through the application, not only of our blood and treasure, but through the devotion of our entire beings. Only then will we bring this monumental clash to a satisfactory ending."

Notes
1. Falkenhayn *Die Oberste Heeresleitung* p 56.
2. The title 'Second Battle of Ypres' is a British designation for the fighting of April/May 1915. The Germans refer to these events simply as 'The Spring Battles around Ypres' or, more succinctly, 'The Gas Attack at Ypres.'
3. Not mentioned here, but another factor was the prevailing wind direction.
4. *OHL Kriegsbericht (Heft 9 – Ypern)* quoted Baumgaten-Crusius *Sachsen in großer Zeit Band II* p 214. Interesting to note, the report contains no mention of the use of gas, merely that the enemy were 'totally surprised'.
5. BOH 1 p 169.
6. Baer *Der Völkerkrieg, Fünfter Band* p 145.
7. Kriegsarchiv Munich Bavarian Reserve Field Artillery Regiment 6 Bd. 23 *OHL An sämtl. A.O.K. 9.4.10.00 Vorm.*
8. *ibid.* p 157.
9. The lack of reserves is one of the clearest indicators that Supreme Army Headquarters had no great hopes for the new weapon. According to a statement lodged post war with the *Reichsarchiv* by General der Artillerie von Ilse, then a Generalmajor and chief of staff Fourth Army, in turning down a request by Fourth Army for the subordination of a single extra division, Falkenhayn stated that, not only could he spare no formation for the role, he had doubts about the likely effectiveness of the gas. See GOH 2 p 39.
10. Chlorine gas was selected, because it could be made available in quantity without affecting conventional munitions production in Germany. Its density meant that it could be assumed that it would arrive on the enemy position in sufficient strength to be effective, despite losses due to diffusion in the open air and, furthermore, the fact that it effectively dispersed, leaving virtually no traces behind it, meant that attacking troops could follow up close behind the cloud.
11. Hennig History Reserve Infantry Regiment 235 p 43. Other sources state that '222' meant 'All preparations for the attack complete' and that '777', issued at 11.40 pm on 21 April meant, 'Prepare to Attack'. See Mayer History Reserve Infantry Regiment 236 p 155. It is to be hoped that the situation at the time left no such room for doubt.
12. Tiessen History Reserve Infantry Regiment 213.
13. Lennartz History Reserve Infantry Regiment 240 pp 51-55.
14. *Ehrverlust* [Loss of the rights of a citizen] was a harshly applied punishment in Germany. It included denial of the right to vote, stand for or hold any public office, serve in the armed forces or wear medals. The trial was controversial. Newspaper editorials were written attacking it on the grounds that the war was long over and no actual harm was done as a result of the betrayal. Others felt that Jäger was unfortunate to have been named as the 'Traitor of Ypres' by General Ferry, former commander of the French 11th Division, in the July 1930 edition of the magazine *Revue des Vivants*. See the socialist *Die Funke*, Berlin 20 December 1932. However many former soldiers were not willing to forgive and forget and some thought the sentence too lenient. See Tiessen *op. cit.* p 189.

15. Belgian GQG *Bulletin d'Information 247* dated 16 April 1915 quoted FOH 2 p 699.
16. Letter Max Stober 10 Apr 1915. Lambrecht Collection.
17. Tiessen *op. cit.* pp 197-198.
18. Knieling History Reserve Infantry Regiment 234 pp 122-123.
19. No Indian troops were involved. Speer is clearly using the word as shorthand for a member of the French colonial forces.
20. Lennartz *op. cit.* pp 58-61.
21. FOH 2 p 699.
22. Mordacq *Le Drame de l'Yser* Quoted in Mayer History Reserve Infantry Regiment 236 pp 160-162.
23. Makoben History Reserve Infantry Regiment 212 p 135.
24. Mayer History Reserve Infantry Regiment 236 p 162.
25. Binding *Aus dem Kriege* p 89.
26. Makoben *op. cit.* p 79.
27. *ibid.* p 138.
28. Tiessen *op. cit.* p 199.
29. FOH2 p 700.
30. Schatz History Reserve Infantry Regiment 239 pp 40-42.
31. GOH 2 p 41.
32. GOH 2 p 43.
33. Mayer History Reserve Infantry Regiment 236 p 164.
34. German accounts often comment adversely on the products of combustion when lyddite filled shells exploded, effectively accusing the British of using gas against them.
35. See BOH 1 pp 185-186. However, note that according to FOH 2 p 703 a regiment under Colonel Mordacq had attacked on order of General Quiquandon a little earlier astride the Ypres – Pilkem road, though it does admit that this had not achieved anything significant by 8.00pm. It is probable, therefore, that the two attacks were effectively sequenced, rather than simultaneous.
36. Winzer History Reserve Infantry Regiment 243 p 43.
37. Baumgarten-Crusius *op. cit.* p 214.
38. See BOH 1 p 217.
39. Herkenrath History Reserve Infantry Regiment 247.
40. Binding *op. cit.* p 90.
41. German accounts claim that the remaining houses of the village had been evacuated the previous night. See Baer *op. cit.* p 146.
42. See BOH 1 pp 275-277.
43. GOH 2 p 46.
44. Compare FOH 2 p 716 and BOH 1 p 284.
45. Mayer *op. cit.* pp 169 - 170.
46. As a stopgap measure to help overcome the chronic shortage of artillery ammunition, the British Government placed orders for shells with a wide variety of American companies, many of whom had not been involved previously with arms manufacture. As a result of inexperience and poor quality control, especially of the fuze assemblies, a large percentage of these shells were duds.
47. 'Sulphur shells' is a common German designation for British shells filled with lyddite. They frequently claimed (wrongly) that they were, in fact, designed as gas shells.
48. Kriegsfreiwilliger Hermann Kleckers is buried in the German cemetery at Menen Block B Grave 1796.

49. Reinhardt History Reserve Infantry Regiment 248 p 21.
50. Kastner History Reserve Infantry Regiment 242 pp 215-217.
51. Orgeldinger History Reserve Infantry Regiment 246 pp 84-85.
52. This must be a reference to the Hanebeek.
53. Orgeldinger *op. cit.* pp 86-87.
54. Binding *Aus dem Kriege* pp 91-92.
55. Reinhardt History Reserve Infantry Regiment 248 p 22.
56. Krämer History Reserve Infantry Regiment 245 p 32.
57. Kastner *op. cit.* pp 218-220.
58. If this accurately reflects the plan, then the tactics employed were peculiar. Over broken ground the two waves would have merged rapidly into one. A sensible tactical bound would have seen the third platoon following up about one hundred metres in rear, ready to react if required and able to manoeuvre.
59. The body of Oberleutnant Theodor Dependorf, together with the remainder of the regimental fallen, was taken for burial to a cemetery near the station in Moorslede. Post war he was transferred to the German cemetery at Langemark. He is buried in Block B Grave 14947.
60. Reinhardt *op. cit.* p 22.
61. Appel History Reserve Infantry Regiment 205 p 53.
62. *ibid.* pp 53-54.
63. Haleck History Reserve Infantry Regiment 208 p 20.
64. Dixon *Magnificent But Not War* p 351.
65. GOH 2 p 49.
66. Mayer *op. cit.* p 174.
67. *ibid* p 174.
68. Joffre *Mémoires Tome II* p 72.
69. Fuhrmann History Reserve Infantry Regiment 211 p 84.

Chapter 4

The Spring Battles in Artois: Arras, Aubers Ridge and Festubert

This chapter is primarily concerned with the battles of Aubers Ridge and Festubert, two engagements which, to the German army, were of vanishingly small significance. Neither name would be familiar to a German audience, which dismisses them as nothing more than minor actions around La Bassée: *Sie behielten jedoch im Rahmen der Gesamthandlung ... nur den Charakter von Ablenkungsunternehmen* [However, in the context of the overall situation, they are to be characterised merely as diversionary operations].[1] Aubers Ridge receives twelve lines of description in the German Official History and Festubert twenty three.[2] The reason for this dismissive attitude is obvious. While the British army was enduring the disaster that was Aubers Ridge and being goaded by Joffre either to renew the offensive, or at least take over more of the front, so as to release French formations for service elsewhere, elements of the German Sixth Army, commanded by Generaloberst Crown Prince Rupprecht of Bavaria, were fighting for their very existence to counter a major offensive launched by the eighteen divisions of the reinforced French Tenth Army around Arras.

The consequent highly significant German defensive actions have been described in more detail elsewhere,[3] but this brief sketch of the main features of the fighting for the Lorette Spur and Vimy Ridge is intended as a reminder to the reader that it was the gigantic Franco-German clash of arms which dominated in Artois that spring. Aubers Ridge and Festubert may have represented the best efforts of the BEF at that time but, in the greater scheme of things, they were insignificant events, which failed completely in their aim of easing the task of the French army or forcing the German army to divert major resources to counter them.

When, on 9 May 1915, the clashes which had been simmering for months for possession of the Lorette Spur, west of Souchez and for tactical advantage around the fringes of Vimy Ridge, erupted in a massive assault by five corps of the French Tenth Army, commanded by General d'Urbal, the final serious attempt of the spring of 1915 began. Its aim was quite straightforward. It was to break through the German lines, eliminate the massive bulge of French territory they held and so force them to withdraw from occupied France. Operations began with high hopes of success, but were compromised from the outset by the fact that it had proved impossible to launch the attacks to coincide with the major Champagne battles earlier in the year. The consequent sequencing enabled the German defenders to concentrate first on the battles in Champagne east of Reims, then to switch their attention to events in Artois several weeks later. This ceding of the advantage to the defence was further compounded by the fact that it made it possible for Falkenhayn to rush his limited supplies of 210 mm heavy howitzers from one threatened part of the Western Front to the other. Their concentrated fire played a disproportionately large role on all these fronts, where it harassed and disrupted offensive preparations, then broke up attacks repeatedly.

The weather in early May favoured the French. It was mainly cloudy and overcast, which greatly restricted air reconnaissance and, in turn, masked much of the pre-offensive activity behind the French lines. Patrolling was also curtailed, which made it difficult for the German defenders to keep up to date with the move forward of reinforcements. It was not until 8 May, for example, when a letter was recovered from the body of a dead Frenchman, that the presence of the French XVII Corps was detected.[4] That said, the increasing weight of artillery fire coming down all along the front from the Lorette Spur to the south of Roclincourt made the limits of the attack frontage increasingly clear. 9 May dawned bright and clear, with the promise of sunshine to come. The artillery fire increased to a crashing crescendo and aircraft delivered bombing attacks on targets throughout the rear areas. The final drum fire came down from 4.00 am. Positions were smashed, communications wrecked and the remains of the wire obstacle were pounded into the ground. All the German defences had disappeared behind dense clouds of black smoke and dust when, suddenly, at 8.00 am, the fire lifted. Hurrying out of the remains of their dugouts, the men of I Bavarian Reserve Corps, supported by Landwehr men from the lower Rhine area, rushed to man their fire positions. Supports were summoned forward, reserves alerted and every German gun in range began to bring defensive fire down on enemy trenches and No Man's Land. But this was a trick. Minutes later fire, designed to catch the trench garrisons in the open, came down once more, shrouding the entire landscape in dust and smoke until, finally, at 9.00 am, the firing of several mines between Carency and La Targette indicated the start of the main attack.

Despite the weight of fire directed against the defence, the men of 1st Bavarian Reserve Division, manning the front from the River Scarpe north to Ecurie, succeeded in shooting the assault to a stand still in short order. Dead and wounded soldiers of the French X and XVII Corps lay scattered all over No Man's Land; one German regiment later counted more than 1,600 bodies forward of its positions. There was a minor incursion near Roclincourt, but Bavarian Reserve Infantry Regiment 2 soon dealt with it. It was a different story between Carency and La Targette, however. Here overwhelming force was brought to bear on the section of line held by Landwehr Regiment 39 and the French Moroccan Division broke straight through the smashed defences and weakly held lines and then made astonishingly swift progress up to the summit of Vimy Ridge. A few surviving Landwehr soldiers fought on for a while, but the regimental commander was severely wounded and captured.

Further north Zouaves and soldiers of the Foreign Legion surged forward over the Carency river and threatened the southern slopes of the Lorette Spur and the complete encirclement of Carency village itself. The situation appeared – and was – grave for the defence. At midday it seemed as though the feared breakthrough might become a reality. The Tenth Army had bitten a swathe out of the German defences on a four kilometre front to a depth of three kilometres in places whilst, south of Neuville St Vaast, dogged progress was also being made in the so-called Labyrinth. However, the German reaction

124 THE GERMAN ARMY ON THE WESTERN FRONT 1915

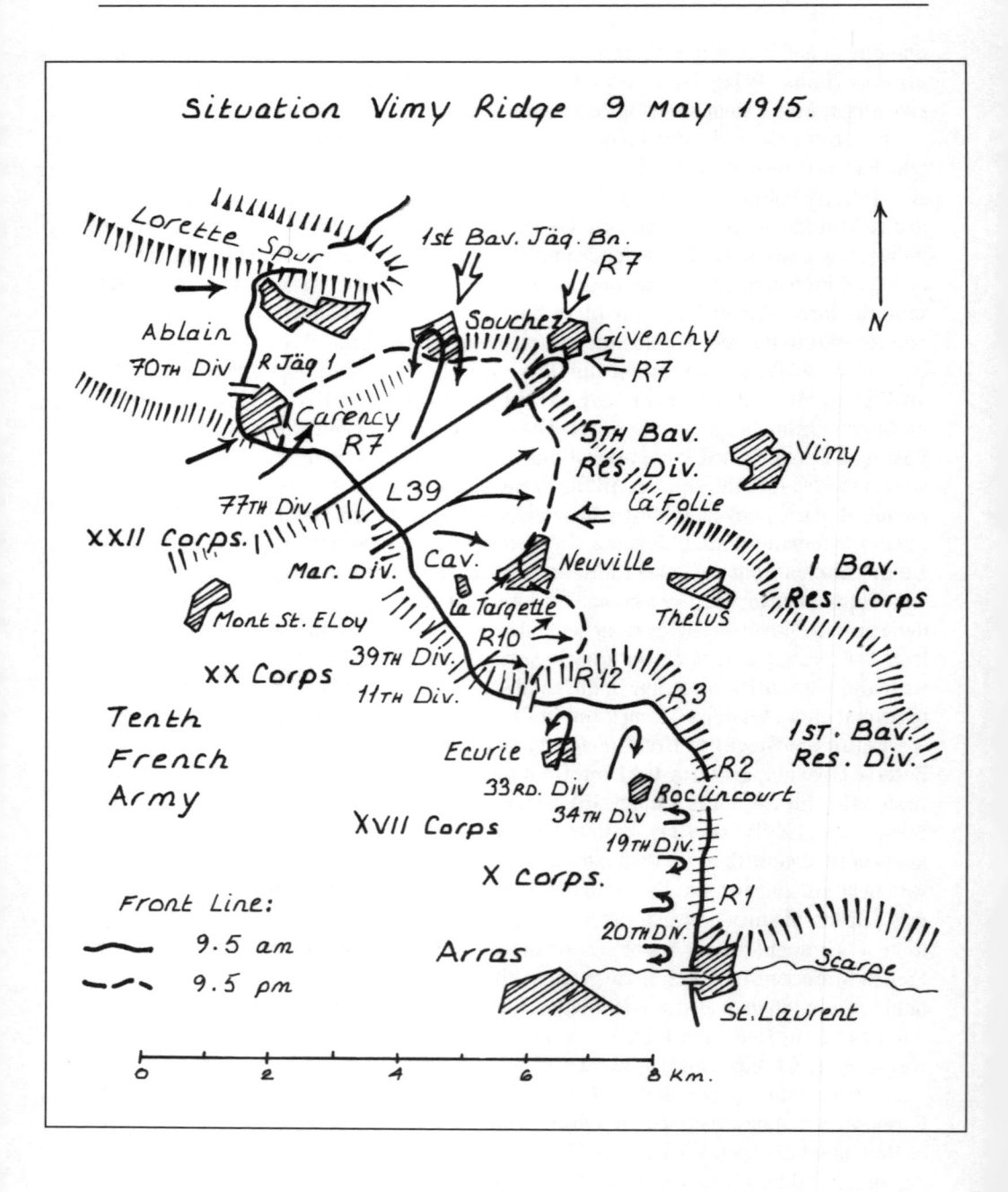

was swift and decisive. To the north of Ecurie the men of Bavarian Reserve Infantry Regiment 12 extended their frontage to cover to the north and held on, providing a firm shoulder against further French exploitation of the break in. In Neuville local counter-attacks pushed the French assault back and left the eastern half of the village firmly in German hands.

Along the road between Neuville and La Folie a rough firing line was established, which succeeded in bring the French forces under flanking fire, whilst hastily summoned reserves, primarily from Bavarian Reserve Infantry Regiment 7, stormed the Moroccans who had tried to establish a foothold on Hill 140 [modern 145] and the troops on the Pimple [Hill 119] and threw them back in the course of desperate hand to hand fighting. By 1.00 pm the immediate crisis had passed. French reserves were too far back to influence the battle and a German defence had been re-established along the vital ridge. To the west of Souchez an extremely hard battle was fought out on and around the Lorette Spur, where the Baden regiments of 28th Infantry Division defended with all their might against specially selected chasseur regiments drawn from the French XXI Corps. Despite all efforts, some ground was gained here and the men from Baden had to evacuate part of the First Position. On the second day of the battle General Barbot, the charismatic commander of the French 77th Division, was killed amongst the leading elements of his troops as he urged them forward.

Bearing in mind that this offensive was launched in overwhelming strength by the French Tenth Army, the results were rather meagre. Nevertheless, the fighting went on with undiminished intensity for another two weeks then, following an operational pause, there was a further sustained effort in mid June. In the wake of the dangerous developments of 9 May, there was an immediate reaction at the highest level of the German army; the local response has already been mentioned. By the late afternoon of 9 May, Sixth Army had already despatched forward every reserve which could be spared. Within twenty four hours, Crown Prince Rupprecht had the equivalent of an extra corps grouped behind the threatened sector, which was a great improvement but nothing to compare with the mass of French formations he was facing. Nevertheless, despite these limitations, it was possible to buttress the line wherever it was sagging.

Street fighting continued for days in Neuville and, initially, the situation on the Lorette Spur was a source of continuing concern; but two regiments from Württemberg and Saxony were thrown in to the battle, recaptured some lost ground and managed to hang on, despite suffering serious casualties in the process. The defence of Carency, which was virtually surrounded on 9 May, demanded desperate measures because, all the time it was held, it was impossible for the French to develop the left flank of their attack in any meaningful way. A composite force under Oberstleutnant Esche of Landwehr Infantry Regiment 39 was rushed forward on 11 May to try and hold the village but, despite considerable artillery support, it was lost after forty eight hours of ceaseless fighting, when it is presumed that the last of the defenders was overwhelmed – presumed, because not a trace of Esche or any of his men was ever found.

Down in the Labyrinth, a maze of interlinked trenches near Neuville of almost unbelievable complexity, the close quarter battle raged. Links to the rear were impassable or unusable in daylight. So for days only one single route could be used and that during the hours of darkness. The garrison, such as it was, was almost totally cut off from all the surrounding action. They had no idea what was happening in Neuville itself, or who controlled it. All they were aware of was the constant crash of shells exploding all around their precarious positions. Surrounded almost on three sides, they had to attempt to fend off French probing attacks from south, west and north simultaneously. Nevertheless they held on through 11 May and into the 12th. Aware by now that the hoped for breakthrough was proving to be elusive, the French restricted future operations to the Lorette Spur and the Neuville area. Nevertheless this reduction in geographical spread of the attacks did not mean that there was any diminution in their intensity where they were actually launched during the next two weeks.

After a few short days of the offensive the landscape was totally transformed. Up on the Lorette Spur the hedgerows which had greeted troops on their arrival the previous October had all disappeared, along with the grass, and the extensive wooded areas were reduced to a few dismal stumps in amongst one great boggy morass. Shells had ploughed down so deep that each successive explosion began to expose more and more of the chalky subsoil, which now coated everything a dirty off-white colour. The only safe route to the summit was via the so-called *Schlammulde* [Mud Hollow], which might have provided a covered approach, but was incredibly hard going for the heavily laden carrying parties, or those taking stretcher cases back down towards Souchez. Furthermore, the French gunners had its range to a metre, so it was under more or less continuous shell fire and the cemetery it contained was added to daily. Despite all the difficulties, as the *Mulde* came under attack from three sides, it was held firmly and the defenders even succeeded in launching local attacks from it most days and capturing French prisoners.

The fighting for Neuville was especially bitter and prolonged. The houses, which were fought over repeatedly, were of very solid construction and there were numerous cavities, cellars and passageways beneath them which had been created when the chalk was being mined in earlier times. As a result, many of them changed hands on numerous occasions and were still being defended effectively although they had been reduced to rubble. There was one day of especially high intensity battle. That occurred on 21 May when the German army planned a major blow designed to clear the French out of the territory they occupied between the Labyrinth and Neuville itself. Launched in the early evening, it was moderately successful. Some trenches were recovered, together with several groups of houses in the village. Two machine guns and one hundred prisoners were also captured.

Of more importance was the fact that, quite by chance, the operation had pre-empted a planned French one. The consequent disruption brought the defence a much needed breathing space in this critical sector of the battlefield. Pressure continued to be maintained during the following two weeks as Foch built up towards a massive renewal of the attack on 16 June. There was to be another comprehensive bombardment and this time reserves were to be held well forward so that they would be in position to exploit any penetrations which were made by the assaulting troops. The difficulty for the

French was that this time the attack would be going in against a fully reinforced defence which, though under pressure, was incomparably stronger, especially in heavy howitzers and other artillery, than had been the case prior to 9 May.

The other major problem was the fact that these preparations were impossible to disguise. As early as 10 June, Generalmajor Fritsch, commanding 15 Field Artillery Brigade, who was receiving streams of reports from his forward observers, reported up the chain of command, 'All the indications lead to the conclusion that the French are planning to try to break through in overwhelming strength from Neuville via the line Thélus – La Folie to Vimy ... '[5] The succeeding days were fully exploited by the defence, despite the fact that the French gunners fired twice the weight of heavy shells used in the May bombardment to prepare the German lines for attack. In consequence the defenders, both artillery and infantry, had access to large stockpiles of food, water and ammunition, which they used to provide, for example, a very hot reception for all French patrols and probing attacks. On 14 June, minor operations of this type were launched all along the front to be attacked and every single one was shot to a standstill by the alert defence.

That said, when the attack finally came in at about midday in bright sunshine on 16 June, the German obstacles and positions were all in a terrible state and casualties amongst the trench garrisons had been high. The French air force was present in great strength and the artillery defensive fire was not as effective as it ought to have been. As a result there were some French gains along the front. By that evening the situation was that up near Angres and Liévin, men of the French XXI Corps had a foothold in the sector of the German 7th Infantry Division. 8th Infantry Division had had to yield ground up on the Lorette Spur, whilst down below in Souchez, the French XXIII Corps had forced a way into the village and house to house fighting was taking place. South of there, the Moroccan Division, which had done so well on 9 May, had penetrated right into the rear area of 16th Infantry Division and was threatening the gun lines. If they had got further forward there would have been a breakthrough, but a scrambled defence just managed to hang on until reinforcements arrived.

Further south, the entire weight of the French IX Corps had hit the German 5th Infantry Division, which managed to hold its positions, though some of its forward companies had losses of seventy five percent. The 58th Infantry Division, still fighting heroically in the Labyrinth, and 1st Bavarian Reserve Division in the line to their left were engaged by elements of the French XX, X and XVII Corps simultaneously. There were several incursions and the fighting went on hand to hand deep into the night 16/17 June. To say the situation was precarious is barely to hint at the bad news which was arriving throughout the afternoon at Headquarters Sixth Army. The amazing thing, however, is that during the hours of darkness and in the early dawn on 17 June, a whole series of German counter-strokes and local counter attacks had restored much of the original line of defence.

Down in the Labyrinth and along the 1st Bavarian Reserve Division sector there were no French incursions left by 8.00 am and 700 prisoners had been taken. This was an astonishing performance in the circumstances and, although the situation was not so good around Souchez, where the Moroccans were still holding on to a wedge-shaped salient, a constant bombardment by the 210 mm heavy howitzers on the break in point prevented any further advance. In Souchez itself, only the church yard was still in French hands. Despite this the situation remained extremely difficult. Supreme Army Headquarters made VI Corps from Third Army available as an immediate reinforcement and VIII Corps was also moved and placed on standby in case the situation deteriorated further. Ironically, at the precise time when reinforcements were being rustled up from various sources and plugging the gaps in Artois, a directive from Falkenhayn arrived at all Army Headquarters along the Western Front:

> "According to reliable reports, the French and British will continue their offensive around Arras and also attack other points along the line. Some of these [attacks] will be serious attempts at breakthrough; others will simply be diversions. His Majesty expects that the armies, demonstrating the old proven qualities of courage and toughness, will hold their positions and destroy the attempts at breakthrough. In general the armies should not expect Supreme Army Headquarters to send forward their limited army reserves. These have to be saved for extremely serious situations. I wish you to bear this in mind before sending such requests to Supreme Army Headquarters. Not only that, the overall situation means that it is essential that the army reserves be released at the earliest possible moment, so that they can be at the disposal of Supreme Army Headquarters once more. Removal of forces from the Eastern Front to reinforce the Western Armies would only hobble the offensive in the east, which is making excellent progress. Every man on the Western Front must appreciate that by holding on obstinately he is making an essential contribution to the successes in the East."[6]

Clearly the crisis on the Sixth Army front counted as an 'extremely serious situation'. There were additional limited gains on 17 June. *Schlammulde*, manned by the forward companies of Infantry Regiment 26, had to be evacuated the following night, whilst both 58th and 16th Infantry Divisions were reported to be fought out and in need of immediate relief. Strenuous efforts were made to make troops available for this purpose. However the French chain of command was also engaged in urgent discussions about the future of their offensive. It was obvious that no dramatic breakthrough was going to occur and, even though the defence had clearly taken a severe beating, their own losses had also been high. The French artillery reported that their stocks of shells, particularly heavy calibres, were running critically low and, on 18 June, following a conference between General Foch and General d'Urbal, commanding Tenth Army, the decision was taken to call off the main offensive and scale all operations back drastically on the Artois front.

So, in the course of a sustained six week offensive, with several major battles, the French succeeded in advancing up to five kilometres in places, but at enormous cost. The French lost about 102,500 casualties, of whom 35,000 were killed in action,[7] the British 1,168 officers and 27,099 other ranks[8] and the German army 1,560 officers and 71,512 men.[9] The German casualties included Kriegsfreiwilliger Mauk of Infantry Regiment 113, who was mortally wounded on the Lorette Spur in early June. He was still fourteen, just short of his fifteenth birthday when he died, giving him the dubious distinction of being the youngest German fatal casualty of the entire war.[10] Most of the gains occurred early in the campaign; its continuation until late June simply increased the length of the casualty lists. At no point, despite all the pressure applied, were the German positions seriously threatened.

The British contribution to Allied operations in Artois was naturally timed to coincide with the major attack by the French Army. General Haig, commanding the British First Army, planned to attack with three corps leading – I and Indian Corps on a two kilometre frontage on the right flank and IV Corps on the left, opposite Fromelles. Thus the plan which, as for Neuve Chapelle, was very ambitious, involved two separate attacks on the German front line separated by a six kilometre gap. The declared objective was to smash straight through the German defences, advance some three kilometres onto Aubers Ridge and from there press on into the German rear area. It was felt that this offensive operation had a good chance of success. Analysis of mistakes made at Neuve Chapelle meant that there was to be careful control and use of reserves to maintain the momentum of the attack. Addressing his command team on 27 April, for example, Haig stated, 'All plans are to be made with the object of getting right on and continuing the advance ... Fresh troops are always to be at hand to fill up gaps and to push on the forward movement when troops in front are fatigued or held up.'[11]

Unfortunately for the troops committed to the operation, the analysis of Neuve Chapelle had not led to a thorough, or indeed any, consideration of how to deal either with unsuppressed machine gun strong points in depth or well placed and skilfully handled defensive artillery – despite the fact that the British were well aware that the Germans had been working hard to add both depth and complexity to their positions. What this meant was that the British, just as at Neuve Chapelle in March, were about to launch a mass attack against the weakly garrisoned German front line, confident that they could overwhelm the small numbers manning these trenches and then simply press on into the German rear areas. Once the attacks were launched, a high price was soon paid for this tactical naïveté.

Nevertheless, surprise was complete when the attacks began under a cloudless sky on 9 May, suggesting that, even if there were marked deficiencies in the overall British preparedness for offensive operations, poor operational security was not one of them. Located forward of Fromelles, Bavarian Reserve Infantry Regiment 16 of 6th Bavarian Reserve Division, reported later: **1.**

> "No changes to the enemy frontage, in particular nothing connected with the barbed wire obstacle, were detected. Not only that, but patrols reported later than 5.00 am that the barbed wire in front of both our positions, as well as those of the enemy, was undamaged."[12]

It was not only the forward units who were surprised. The Commander Sixth Army himself had a rude awakening as the attack began.

THE BATTLE OF AUBERS RIDGE.
9 MAY 1915.

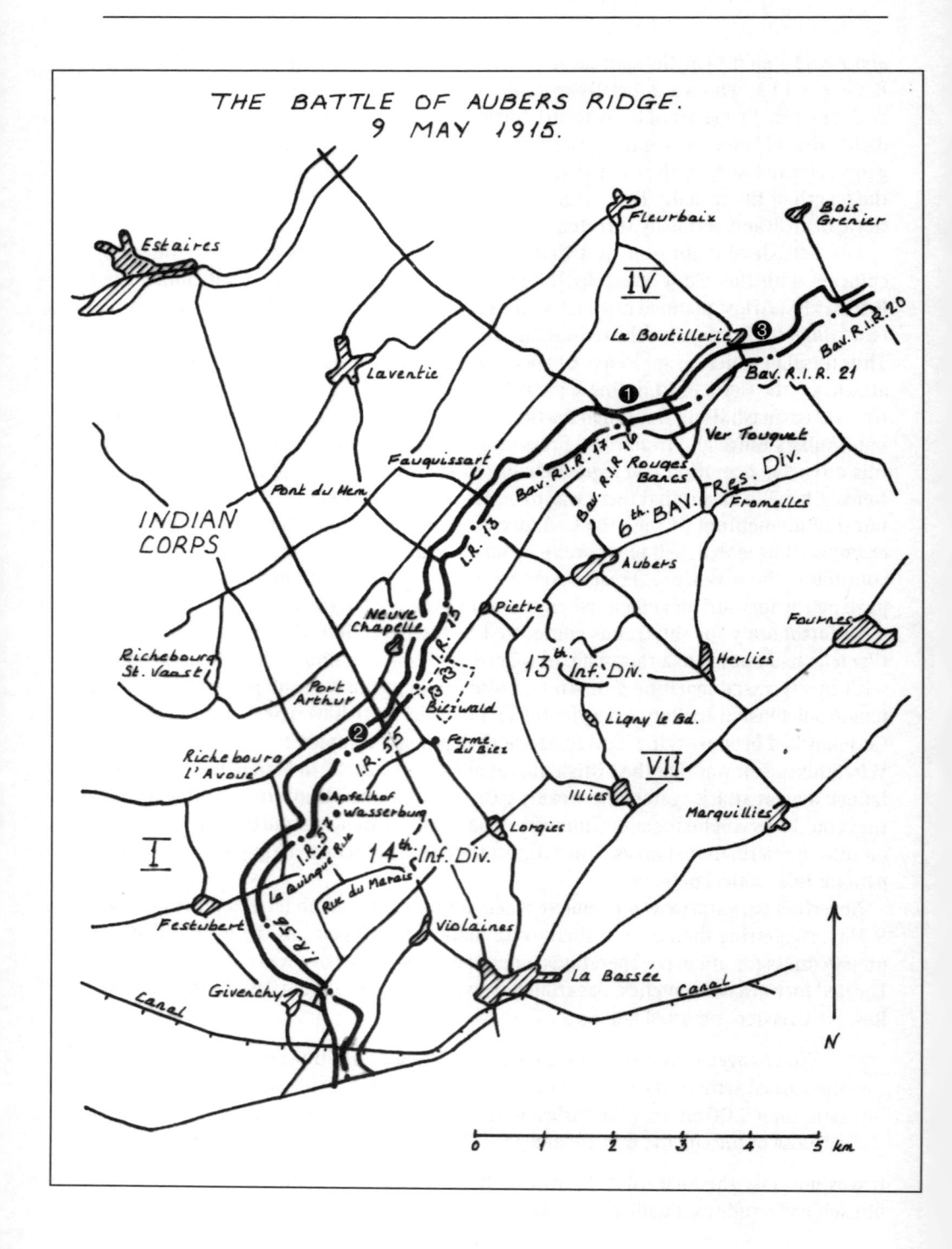

Generaloberst Crown Prince Rupprecht of Bavaria Diary Entry 9 May 1915[13]

"At 4.45 am I was awakened by the violent explosion of a falling bomb then, immediately afterwards, I heard the roar of an aircraft flying extremely low. An hour later I heard two more detonations which occurred rather further away. As I was dressing at about 7.00 am, it was explained to me that the first bomb had fallen right by the garden wall of a house which I had occupied earlier, but which I had vacated because it was far too easy to find. Its exact location had been published in a French newspaper. It is probable that this house was not the actual target; rather it was the adjacent [Sixth] Army headquarters building, where it caused the severance of every single telephone cable. The bombs dropped later were aimed at the station at La Madeleine Two others fell on the station at Don and another on a station east of Douai. This all indicated the imminence of a major offensive."

Just south of Neuve Chapelle, at Richbourg l'Avoue, some of the hardest fighting occurred in the so-called Sector C, manned by the Westphalian Infantry Regiment 55. During the night 8/9 May the normal reliefs took place along the front line and, as the morning of 9 May dawned, it was held by elements of 1st Battalion, commanded by Major Schulz right, with its left flank anchored on the La Bassée – Estaires road, and 3rd Battalion to the left of the road and commanded by Hauptmann von Rosenberg, standing in for Hauptmann Schmidt, who was on leave. With the night's work completed, the trench garrisons were relaxing, drinking coffee and enjoying the prospect of a warm and sunny day when, just before 5.00 am, a large cluster of British aircraft in several separate flights zoomed over the German lines. The sound of anti-aircraft fire could be heard coming from the rear area, interspersed by the dull thud of exploding bombs. At 5.20 am a salvo of shells landed. One hit the already heavily damaged Ferme de Biez, one a pumping station at Lorgies, a third the railway station at Marquillies and a fourth smashed an empty dugout belonging to 3rd Company.

It was not clear to the defenders what was happening, but later it was decided that these shells had been fired to check the ranging of some of the British heavy batteries. All was calm for a further thirty minutes then, suddenly, at 5.55 am, a positive hurricane of shells smashed down on the German lines and the battle, which was to last for several weeks, had begun. For the troops manning the front line, this was another example of drum fire, which appeared to be becoming more intense with each successive offensive. The forward positions were rapidly enveloped in clouds of smoke, dust and dirt and the regimental telephone switchboard came alive with reports that extremely heavy fire of all calibres was crashing down on the front line. Unfortunately, no sooner had the information started to arrive than all links with the forward trenches were abruptly cut off. Much was made subsequently about the inadequate nature of the British bombardment, but those on the receiving end were certainly impressed by its intensity while it lasted.

Just as rapidly runners began to be used in both directions, as the latest information flowed upwards and orders were passed down. It appeared that Indian troops were attempting with great difficulty to launch attacks; that these had been effectively nipped in the bud, but that German casualties were high and reinforcement was required. The sandbagged positions, so painfully developed during the past few weeks, were torn apart and the trenches themselves reduced to mere hollows in the ground, thus forcing the defenders to fall back on the support lines and communications trenches in many cases. Immediately, supports were rushed forward to the points under greatest threat. To begin with these comprised the reserve companies of the battalions, but the 2nd Battalion, which had only been relieved the previous night, was stood to and then ordered to move forward with all speed. The situation was especially critical in the 2nd Company sector but, luckily for the defence, Reserve Leutnant Bockhern, an experienced and cool officer, was still on his feet and able to direct the operations of his dwindling band of men until the first reinforcements - 3 Platoon of 3rd Company, commanded by Vizefeldwebel Steffen - arrived. His journey forward had been both eventful and hair-raising. Perceiving the need for speed, he had led his men across the open and a number of them had been killed or wounded in the process. Bowled over by a shell exploding next to him, he picked himself up and continued, despite the fact that tiny fragments of shattered stones and earth had been driven into his face and hands by the force of the explosion. Despite suffering from shock and wounds, he was roughly bandaged and was able to remain in command of his platoon throughout the day, by which time the remainder of his company had also made their way forward to assist.

Major Schulz Commanding Officer 2nd Battalion Infantry Regiment 55[14] *2.*

"For a full three hours the storm of fire continued, by which time the enemy believed that all life in the German trenches had been extinguished. The curtain of fire lifted from the trenches and began coming down so heavily on the rear areas that it was almost impenetrable. Great waves appeared from the trenches [opposite]. At long last the enemy began to close in to take up the honourable battle, man against man. From the British trenches emerged masses of khaki-clad figures, some with flat caps, others with turbans on their heads and threw themselves, several men deep, at the defenders of the portals to Flanders. The British I Corps and 3rd Lahore Division of the Indian Army Corps [*sic*.][15] launched their attack in six powerful waves.

"For the Westphalians and men from Lippe,[16] who had had to spend three terrible hours during the appalling drum fire, cowering defencelessly behind the ruins of their former breastworks, the battle at close quarters came almost as a relief. Every shot found a target as their fire tore great gaps in the ranks of the attackers. Could there possibly be a more straightforward target than this wall of men? In amongst the sound of rifle fire could be heard the chatter of machine guns. The cooling water turned to steam, the barrels became red hot. It was all the same [to us. We] would keep firing until they burst! Bodies piled up, whilst shell after shell exploded amidst all the turmoil, bringing the entire hellish experience up to concert pitch.

"On the gun lines around Halpegarbe, Lorgies, Illies and Gravelin the gunners worked as though their lives depended on it. The breeches could barely be worked fast enough and the sweat ran. The infantry and artillery commanders stood together in the observation posts but, in this crisis, there were few orders to be given. What was the point of giving minor sight corrections? The only feasible order was, 'Fire until the barrels burst!' Death reaped a dreadful harvest amongst the attackers, but fresh waves stormed forward over the corpses and the leading elements managed to penetrate as far forward as the wire obstacle in front of the German position, whose construction had come at the cost of endless determined work. Now it was reduced to a tangle of wire and posts, but the forward enemy troops were hung up within its remains and the remainder, with the exception of those who made it back to their own trenches, were all cut down.

"Only here and there were the enemy able to get into the German trenches and there a bloody struggle began. Most of this hand to hand fighting occurred on the left flank of the regiment. During the morning drum fire, 3 Platoon of 11th Company was destroyed almost to the last man and its gallant commander, Offizierstellvertreter Vesting, was mortally wounded by a shell splinter.[17] The first enemy assault at about 6.30 am was thrown back with bloody losses by two sections of 1 Platoon led by Gefreiter Prüßner, who had rushed to the endangered place. However, the overwhelming pressure brought to bear by the enemy enabled them to succeed in forcing their way into the trenches of Infantry Regiment 57 and from there to completely encircle 11th Company. About fifty British soldiers stormed the flank and rear of the company, but the men from Lippe, under their daring commander, Oberleutnant Herbert Reuter, were equal to the task.[18]

"Elsewhere Indian troops broke in and the Gurkhas and Sikhs [*sic*.] went for the weak trench garrison, kukris in hand.[19] But the Westphalians stood their ground and they beat back the coloured troops with bayonets and rifle butts. A short time later the hand to hand fighting was over. The British attack had collapsed."

Just to the south and in the direct line of the British 1st Division, men of 3rd Battalion Infantry Regiment 57 were manning positions to the north of *Apfelhof* [Apple Farm – known to the British as Ferme du Bois] and *Wasserburg* [Ferme Cour d'Avoué] on the day of the attack. Following earlier experiences at Neuve Chapelle, the regiment had given much though to the physical layout of the defensive positions, the placement and use of reserves and the methods and tactics which would be used to defeat any possible assault. There was an assumption that communications would fail swiftly in the event of an attack, so the intention was to ensure that all ranks would know their role sufficiently well in advance to be able to react automatically in an emergency. One consequence was that all artillery in range was to be used specifically to break up possible infantry forming up points and then to switch to domination of the relatively narrow strip of No Man's Land.

In the early morning of 9 May, 10th and 12th Companies 3rd Battalion, commanded by Leutnants Wartze and Ratte respectively, which were manning the forward positions, had to endure a solid hour of drum fire, which reached a peak of intensity at about 6.30 am. At that moment the destructive fire was lifted to the rear and the attack began. However, in accordance with the overall plan, its commanding officer, Major Wülfing, had already ordered his supports – 11th Company under Leutnant Marquis - to move forward and 9th Company, commanded by Leutnant Hüls, located back at La Bassée, began a forced march to the front. Similarly, the regimental commander immediately placed his reserve (5th Company, commanded by Leutnant Brauch) under command of 3rd Battalion and ordered 4th and 7th Companies to advance from La Bassée to Violaines, there to await further instructions.

Unfortunately for the attackers, who advanced in three waves at 6.30 am, the preliminary bombardment had been far less effective than had been hoped. The actual intensity was in many instances not even as heavy as had been the case at Neuve Chapelle. In addition, much of it was poorly delivered and inaccurate. A great many shells fell short, so that the remains of the German breastworks were being manned before the attack even began. So much for neutralisation and, much worse for British morale, was the fact that the leading British waves could see clearly before they set off that they would come under aimed fire the moment they broke cover. To make things worse for the attackers, almost all the machine guns in the front line were fully functional and over half of 11th Company was also already occupying its fire positions. The supporting field batteries opened up at the same time and the combined result was dreadful slaughter amongst the British regiments.

More or less as soon as the British fire lifted, the battlefield visibility improved and a warm sun was already shining in the faces of the assaulting infantry. The men of Infantry Regiment 57 could see three distinct lines of infantry forward of the British trenches, a fourth wave climbing out over the breastworks and two more waves closing up from the rear. Once the first wave was only fifty metres short of the 3rd Battalion trenches, it was met by an immense weight of small arms fire, which simply annihilated it. The few survivors got no further forward than the wire obstacle where they, too, were shot down. Pretty well simultaneously, the second wave was caught by enfilade fire from the German left flank. Vulnerable to raking machine gun fire, it was also shot to pieces. The tactics of the third wave were observed to be slightly different. Attempts were made to advance in small groups, but these were easily picked off in their turn.

Meanwhile the field batteries, firing in support, tackled the fourth and subsequent waves, which could make no progress whatsoever. Barely ten minutes had gone by and the British were already staring complete disaster in the face. Just as an indication of how one-sided the battle was, this determined attack was shot to a standstill by the relative handful of infantrymen manning the front line. By the time the reserves got forward the crisis was long since past. It is true that the German breastworks were penetrated in a few places. A party of about twenty all ranks from B Company 1st Northamptonshire

Regiment, under Captain Dickson, certainly entered the German position, but none lived to tell the tale. There were too few of them and they were completely unsupported.[20] As is often the case in battle, this piece of good news was relayed rapidly upwards.

Generaloberst Crown Prince Rupprecht of Bavaria Diary Entry 9 May 1915[21]

"The situation in front of 6th Bavarian Reserve Division caused me to alert the reserve of Jägers and, at about 11.30 am to order XIX Army Corps to transfer a field artillery battalion and a battery of heavy howitzers to 6th Bavarian Reserve Division. Meanwhile news had arrived that an enemy attack, launched from the direction of Richebourg L'Avoue had been beaten off by Infantry Regiment 57 of 13th Infantry Division. It was estimated that at least five hundred bodies were lying forward of one of the battalions of the regiment. The enemy attacked in six waves: the first two were British, the next two Indian and the last waves were once again composed of British troops, who shot down the Indians when they faltered."[22]

In support of 13th Infantry Division, just as it had been at Neuve Chapelle several weeks earlier, was Field Artillery Regiment 58. One of their battery commanders later recalled:

Reserve Hauptmann Karl Windhorst 5th Battery Field Artillery Regiment 58[23]

"In May the front became more active. Because in Russia the Germans were advancing from victory to victory and the Russians were severely pressed, the British launched a relief offensive in the west. It took place from Neuve Chapelle to Givenchy and included the left flank of 13th Infantry Division, i.e. Infantry Regiments 55 and 15. To the west of Fromelles, Infantry Regiment 16 was involved near to Rouges Bancs. 8 May was a clear day and the artillery fire increased noticeably in intensity. It covered the entire VII Army Corps frontage and also drew the batteries of Field Artillery Regiment 58 into the battle.

"Early on 9 May, just as at Neuve Chapelle, there was a marked increase in enemy air activity and numerous bombs were dropped – on Wicres and Don, for example. Extremely violent enemy destructive fire began to come down. Three times the enemy launched massed attacks and three times the gallant 55th threw them back, sometimes at the point of a bayonet. The batteries of Field Artillery Regiment 58, especially 5th Battery, that was located furthest to the left (southwest), were intimately involved in the battle and did their best to support the infantry. Because the weather was clear, observation was good. Even if the enemy assault waves could not be fired on directly, the batteries sent a hail of iron into the reserve positions and the strong points behind the front line trenches. This helped to hinder the activities and destroy the concentrations of enemy troops. Troops moving forward to relieve, ammunition columns, batteries closing up and even mounted cavalry were spotted by the observation posts and brought under immediate fire. In the gun lines, the reports of the observation officers were received with glee. 'Shells on target. The enemy is retreating with huge casualties!'"

Despite the failure of the initial attacks, the commanders of the British 2 and 3 Brigades, Brigadier-Generals Thesiger and Davies respectively, pressed Headquarters 1st Division for a resumption of the assault after further artillery preparation. Major-General RCB Haking, its commander, acceded to this request and there was a further bombardment from 7.15 – 8.00 am. A message was passed to the Meerut Division which agreed to conform to the renewed attack, but the gunnery was no better than it had been previously so that, when the fresh assault went in, the German defenders, now further reinforced as additional reserves arrived forward, simply shot the attackers to pieces, inflicting further heavy losses.[24] So complete was this second defeat that the German sources do not distinguish it in any detail from the 6.30 am assault.

There was now a pause on this part of the battlefield. The British artillery reduced its rate of firing dramatically so as to conserve stocks of shells while, on the German side of No Man's Land, frenzied activity was underway. The defending troops had to be reorganised, so as to compensate for losses and to accommodate new arrivals, ammunition (hand grenades in particular) had to be replenished, food and drink needed to be brought forward and, most important, the signallers had to attempt to restore telephone links as soon as possible. There was a general expectation that the assault would be renewed, so everything had to be ready to meet it. A certain number of wounded were evacuated at this point, but there was neither time nor medical capacity to complete this work. Nevertheless, the stretcher bearers and medical teams were kept extremely busy in the forward aid posts treating the most seriously wounded.

Despite the catastrophic outcome of the initial attacks, the British were all too well aware that the French Tenth Army attacking down to the south were relying on their allies to tie down German defenders to prevent them from intervening on the Arras front, so every effort was made to renew the assault later in the day. Word having arrived from French sources that excellent progress was being made on the Arras front, against Vimy Ridge in particular, the decision was made to reorganise the assault formations rapidly and attack again at 1.00 pm. It soon became clear, however, that losses in the Dehra Dun Brigade were such that it would be necessary to move the Bareilly Brigade into position to assume the responsibility for the afternoon attack.[25] A delay of H Hour to 3.40 pm was ordered, with artillery preparation beginning at 3.00 pm. In fact, on this sector, German sources report that drum fire did not come down until 3.15 pm and that a hail of iron continued for two hours, by which time there were unmistakable signs that another attack was about to start.

The German defenders could scarcely credit that the British were about to attempt a full scale repetition of a failed attack in broad daylight and they watched in total amazement as No Man's Land to their front was once more filled with lines of attacking infantry, who were being played forward by the pipers of the Black Watch.[26] Unfortunately for the attackers, this fresh attempt was greeted in the same manner as those launched previously and, which was worse, the defenders were in even greater strength than they had been in the morning. The result was further carnage. Wave after wave was destroyed and the number of dead and dying British soldiers mounted alarmingly, as they were cut down by a combination of rifle fire and well-controlled machine gun crews all along the threatened front. Metaphorically shaking their heads at this display of collective gallantry, the compilers of the history of Infantry Regiment 57 later expressly praised the 'extraordinary courage' of the British troops committed to action on this dreadfully sanguinary day.

Naturally the defenders did not have it all their own way; half an hour into this later action, many of the gun batteries, which had been in action for hours, were running critically short of ammunition. One report reached Headquarters Field Artillery Regiment 22 from the commander of 3rd Battery, Hauptmann Rohlfing, that he was down to his last forty shells. The 1st Battalion was ordered to expedite resupply, but was able to report that replenishment was on its way forward. In an extremely gallant action, a light ammunition column galloped forward in full view of the British attackers and straight through harassing fire falling on the La Bassée – Illies road to deliver the much needed shells. Despite the difficulties and losses on the way, the vital ammunition was successfully delivered to the gun lines and the batteries resumed their destructive work. Simultaneously, more infantry reinforcements were being fed forward. The various covered approaches were either shot up badly or filled with dead and wounded men, so Oberleutnant Kühn, living up to his name, which in German means bold, audacious or dashing, led the men of 10th Company forward in a wild rush across country and filled out the severely depleted ranks of 11th Company. Kühn received a painful wound to the arm during this movement and one of his platoon commanders, Leutnant Epmeyer, was killed instantly by a bullet which hit him in the mouth. However the majority of the company arrived unscathed and, with their assistance, the crisis was overcome.

Off to the north in accordance with the two-pronged nature of the plan, the British 7th and 8th Divisions of IV Corps launched simultaneous attacks directed towards Fromelles. This area was held by formations of Bavarian 6th Reserve Division, which had been heavily involved the previous March during the Battle of Neuve Chapelle. From north to south, this sector was held by Bavarian Reserve Infantry Regiments 17, 16, 21 and 20 in that order, with fire support provided primarily by Bavarian Reserve Field Artillery Regiment 6. There had been ample time for the regiments to be reconstituted and to absorb reinforcements to replace the battle casualties of Neuve Chapelle, but there were still numerous problems for the defence. Not only were the regiments still not back to full strength when the battle for Aubers Ridge began, the lie of the land and the front line trace meant that under strength battalions were forced to hold overextended frontages. The experience of Bavarian Reserve Infantry Regiment 16 was typical in this respect.

"With company strengths at about 150 riflemen and in view of the length of the frontage, the forward firing line was only weakly held. It is certain that when the enemy began to bring down heavy artillery fire at 5.45 am, every man was in the firing line."[27]

At this stage of the war and despite the frantic work which had been undertaken in the wake of Neuve Chapelle, the barbed wire obstacle was still not very well developed and it soon succumbed to the bombardment. Within minutes gaps had appeared, some of them as much as fifty metres wide. However that was not the only unpleasant surprise that morning for the regiment.

"About 6.30 am a mine exploded on the right flank of the position [which was being held by 10th Company]. This threw up a crater ten metres deep and forty metres in diameter at the lip. The explosion destroyed an eighty metre stretch of the firing line and buried six sections of the garrison [i.e. up to fifty men]. Simultaneously, thick yellowish-black smoke enveloped the area, stretching all the way back to the enemy position and blocking off all visibility. Under the protection of this smoke, a great mass of the enemy launched forward on about a thirty metres frontage and headed straight for the breach. The remainder of the company and a machine gun put down the heaviest possible fire once the assault column was within thirty metres of our trenches. Despite this, because the assault force was extraordinarily strong and was able to continue to storm forward despite heavy loses, it proved to be impossible to prevent the enemy from thrusting in the direction of *Türkenecke* [Turkish Corner] until they were more or less level with *Gehöft am toten Schwein* [Dead Pig Farm].

"Because the enemy bombed along and in front of the trench with hand grenade teams simultaneously, the garrison, which had suffered heavily from the artillery fire, could not prevent the enemy from making ground towards the west, until the sector commander, Leutnant Bachschneider, managed to barricade the trench and halt the enemy with hand grenades and flanking fire. Similar methods prevented the enemy from rolling up the trench in an easterly direction. In addition a further advance beyond the general line Dead Pig Farm – *Einsamer Giebel* [Lonely Fork (in road or track)] was prevented by the actions of the sector commander, Leutnant Schmitt, who was reinforced by individual platoons from [Bavarian] Reserve Infantry Regiment 21 and held a flanking position to the east of Dead Pig Farm."[28]

The assault led by 1/13th London (Kensington) battalion against the craters had been observed by both Bavarian Reserve Infantry Regiments 17 and 21, left and right hand neighbours respectively to Bavarian Reserve Infantry Regiment 16, which bore the brunt of the attack. In his report to Generalmajor Danner, commanding 14 Bavarian Reserve Infantry Brigade, the commander of Bavarian Reserve Infantry Regiment 21,

Oberst Julius Ritter von Braun, described the way events had unfolded during the morning from his perspective: 3.

"At 5.50 am the regiment came under heavy small arms fire and, a little later, by a great weight of artillery fire from the direction of the regimental left flank. I ordered a general stand to, but did not direct the harnessing up of the wagons. Even before I could go forward to the command post at Le Maisnil, however, important reports came in from 2nd Battalion (Hauptmann Schmitz) that Bavarian Reserve Infantry Regiment 16 was under attack and, a short time later that the enemy had broken into [its position]. Other reports followed swiftly: part of the front line in Sector IIIB had been blown up and the British had forced their way through the gap, thrusting forward towards Dead Pig Farm. Elements then turned against 12th Company Bavarian Reserve Infantry Regiment 16, some of whom pulled back towards the left flank of Bavarian Reserve Infantry Regiment 21, whilst others bent back their front towards Dead Pig Farm.

"All reports were passed on to 14 Reserve Infantry Brigade as they came in. At 9.40 am the Division ordered the divisional reserve to prepare to move. Hauptmann Schmitz, who had already taken action on his own initiative and reinforced 12th Company Bavarian Reserve Infantry Regiment 16, was directed to provide all possible support to this company and, to that end, two platoons of 3rd Company, on stand by in La Fresnoy, were sent forward to assist. One platoon was ordered to move to the strong point at Pont de Pierre and to remain there at my disposal ... [Bavarian] 12 [Reserve Infantry] Brigade made it known that they were taking no immediate action, except to bring down heavy artillery fire on the break in point. In the meantime the British attack had stalled completely. Those elements which had broken in attempted to dig in and also fired on our positions from the rear. The ever increasing fire of 8th and 10th Companies and the remnants of 12th Company Reserve Infantry Regiment 16, which was slowly, but steadily, pushing forward along the trench, in an action during which Offizierstellvertreter Keller distinguished himself, caused some of the troops who had forced their way in to try to withdraw towards the break in point. Those who attempted this during daylight were all killed."[29]

Whilst attempts continued to be made to pressurise the British attackers who had penetrated the lines by means of light mortars and showers of hand grenades, which had been brought forward in large quantities, the brigade reserve company was marched forward and placed under command of Bavarian Reserve Infantry Regiment 21. In the event it was not used, possibly because, as the regimental report later stated:

"About 2.30 pm the first report arrived from 2nd Battalion [Bavarian] Reserve Infantry Regiment 21 that the front line was once more completely in our hands and that the British who had broken in were completely cut off. As it later transpired, this report was not correct. In fact a gap created by the enemy near the craters was still open. When this became clear, the regiment placed a platoon, which had been held back near Pont St Pierre in reserve at the disposal of Hauptmann Schmitz and then ordered him to use it, plus [other troops drawn from the *Wasserburg* [Moated Grange] and Depot Farm] in an advance on Ver Touquet and Dead Pig Farm and so neutralise the British in that area before nightfall ... Despite all efforts, the attack did not begin to have a real effect until darkness was actually falling, so some of the British managed to escape ... During the night the enemy really were driven out of the entire forward position and work could begin to repair it ... With the exception of those enemy who had escaped just after it went dark, all the rest were killed or captured."[30]

Although most attention was paid to events on the inter-regimental boundary between Bavarian Reserve Infantry Regiments 16 and 21 in the wake of the mine explosion, there were problems elsewhere, as this description by a member of 8th Company Bavarian Reserve Infantry Regiment 16 shows

Infanterist Otto Bestle 8th Company Bavarian Reserve Infantry Regiment 16[31] **1.**

"We were manning the very front line as the left flank company of the regiment. The position comprised sandbagged breastworks. At 2.00 am comrade Huber and I left the dug out to relieve the listening post, which was located one hundred metres in front of the front line. The relief took place silently and, tensely, we strained our ears in the dark. From Arras, Givenchy, Souchez and the Lorette Spur could be heard the sound of explosions. Masses of white, green and red flares rose in the sky. There was one great sea of flames all the way to Carency and, with all the flashes which lit up the night sky, it was as though the heavens were one great fire eater. We watched this gruesome spectacle for more than two hours, feeling for all the poor soldiers, whose fate had already been sealed by this time.

"As dawn broke, we left the listening post and returned to the front line, where we found our company at a high state of alert. A light blanket of mist lay over No Man's Land, until the sun sent down its golden rays and treated us to a beautiful May morning. At about 6.35 am [*sic.*][32] three enemy aircraft appeared on the horizon and then overflew our positions. One of them began to orbit and fired a flare. A hurricane of drum fire began. Low trajectory shells, shrapnel and shells of the heaviest calibre crashed on and around our positions and everything began to tremble and heave under the force of the explosions. We rushed to man our weapons; every single one of us was well aware of the danger posed by the imminent attack. The fire rose in intensity, thick yellowish-black clouds hovered over our positions. The very air seemed literally to roar with the racket caused by the heavy shells. The dugouts barely protected us against the shrapnel balls, as we pressed ourselves against the parapet, taking a quick look towards the enemy every minute in case they were coming.

"The fire hammered down with undiminished force. It seemed as though the earth itself was on fire. Infanterist Meisl was hit in the midriff by a shell, which tore him in two. His upper and lower body lay separately on the duckboards of the trench. Infanterist Sweighofer's skull was smashed by a shell splinter and he fell back, dying, from the fire step. Immediately after this one of Gefreiter Muck's feet was crushed and my friend Huber was shot in the back of the head. He tumbled to the ground, but heaved himself back up. I bandaged him up and he managed to reach the aid post. There were only about fifty men of my company still unwounded when, suddenly, there was a dreadful explosion on the right flank of the regiment. The air trembled, the ground heaved and a pillar of fire rose flickering skywards. Fountains of earth were thrown up violently, as high as towers, then all was still. The fire was lifted to the rear. Our hour had come. We manned the fire step and stood to, ready to engage. However the British assault wave still surprised us.

"Making use of the cover of weeds which were almost head high between the lines, they had worked their way forward to our barbed wire obstacle, but we met them with a hail of small arms fire and hand grenades. About one hundred dead and dying men were already lying in front of our position when the second British wave broke cover from a line of trees about two hundred metres to our front. They ran into flanking fire from 7th Company to our right. 6th Battery Bavarian Reserve Field Artillery Regiment 6 began to bring down defensive fire in and around their ranks, which began to waver ... Gripped by fear, they flooded back in panic to their start line leaving their dead and wounded behind.

"However the British had already stormed forward into the sector of 1 Platoon which, unfortunately, was almost totally cleared at the start of the drum fire. Had our allocated machine gun commander returned, carrying the working parts which he had taken to a place of safety, it would have been a simple matter to have mown down the attackers. But lacking working parts and a crew, the only machine gun was in a firing position with 3 Platoon and we of that platoon, using our very best endeavours, could only just manage to neutralise the attack which was aimed directly at us. Infanterist Geiger, a tough Schwabian, climbed upon onto the parapet and brought one down with a mighty blow of his rifle butt. Mad with rage, he lunged at a second man, who fell to the ground, his skull smashed. The stock of his rifle came away, but as a third British soldier tried to get forward, he suffered the fate of the others as he was hit a terrible blow. A wounded man, armed with a pistol, pointed it at Geiger who clenched his fist and bawled at him. At that the man let his pistol drop and begged for mercy.

"Meanwhile, the thirty men who had broken in[33] began to roll up 3 Platoon. Heroically, comrade Neumeier from Freising threw one hand grenade after another at the enemy, who were barely visible. He had already dealt with five when he threw a grenade which landed at the feet of a British soldier. This man threw it back and Neumeier collapsed, fatally wounded. Sergeant Vilsmeier-Bilsbiburg then shot four charging enemy soldiers. Shouting, 'The British have broken in!', Signaller Simbeck abandoned his equipment and grabbed his carbine, which was hanging on the wall of the telephone dugout. Rushing over to me, he was brought down by British rifle fire. Comrade Greimel also launched his own attack. Hit by four bullets, he lay dying for over an hour by the British barricade. Nobody could rescue him.

"The remainder of 1 Platoon then joined the trench battle. Geiger threw grenades over a traverse, was slightly wounded and bandaged up. He then received a second cut, or a bullet through his outstretched right hand. Seized with fury, he grabbed a picket and charged at the amazed British shouting, *'Ihr Bazi, ihr elende!'* [You miserable bastards!] He was followed closely by Unteroffizier Kreß, and comrades Schaudek, Lorenz and Lesser-München. A blood bath ensued. In this heroic struggle, Schaudeck and Lorenz were killed and Kreß received a severe chest wound. Only then was it possible to recover Greimel, who had been lying wounded four times in front of the British barricade. He lay in front of me, this young comrade who had been so full of life, tears coursing down his white cheeks. He closed his eyes and I tried to comfort him, saying to the dying man a last, 'Farewell'.

"Suddenly, a British soldier sprang up from the 1 Platoon sector onto the parapet and disappeared in a flash down a shell hole. He was the sole survivor of those who had entered our company area. It was 6.00 pm and still broad daylight. Our company commander, Reserve Leutnant Gies, who was killed in 1916, then arrived unexpectedly. Together with comrade Inhofer, he had worked his way forward from the adjacent [Bavarian] Reserve Infantry Regiment 17 to his company. We took new courage from the sight of our tried and tested leader. He orientated himself quickly, allocated fire positions to each man, took the ten surviving members of 1 Platoon and stormed at their head against a British pocket of resistance in the platoon sector. There was the dull thud of hand grenades, pistol shots cracked out and, swiftly, the British were knocked out. An officer dashed into a dugout. His surrender was demanded in English by comrade Merkl, but he replied with his pistol. A hand grenade was thrown into the dugout and he was laid next to his comrades as the thirtieth corpse. The linkage to 7th Company was then re-established." [34]

One member of 3rd Battalion wrote home later, also describing the events of the day:

Reserve Leutnant Adolf Meyer 10th Company Bavarian Reserve Infantry Regiment 16[35]
1.

"9th May, the hardest day for our company, is over. It was bad enough: we lost eighty nine killed, fifteen wounded and three captured. The British achieved surprise and broke in unexpectedly left and right. Heavy drum fire and a successful mine blast – the first such enemy mine so far – directed against our right hand platoon made this possible. We survivors, one officer, one doctor and sixty four NCOs and men, were cut off for the entire day by the enemy. Our trenches to the left and right were occupied by the 13th London Regiment [*sic.* 1/13th London (Kensington)]. We only held 200–250 metres. The heavily manned enemy position was only seventy metres distant. A 400 metre section of communication trench to the rear was in British hands. Most of our ammunition was buried; the hand grenade throwers were either dead or wounded.

"Despite all that the enemy could advance no further. Towards 10.00 pm we were freed by our 1st Battalion. The morning of 10 May is quiet and we can look for our fallen. The majority are buried metres down. We have located about forty comrades; we have left the others buried in their first graves, they were too deep down. We have laid out the dead in an open space behind our trenches. We are able to risk it. Hardly a shot is being fired, the exhaustion is too great. So our faithful comrades are lying there. I must go and look each one in the face once more. There lies one who has been with us since October 1914. He was fated to die on a Sunday. Next to him is a man from the Landsturm. He moved into the field on 5 May, joined the company during the evening of 8 May and was killed on 9 May!

"Here there is a kriegsfreiwilliger, still a lad. He must have had a gentle death; a slight smile is still playing on his lips. Many are dreadfully crumpled, some have no wounds: suffocated! We were relieved this evening. The company, which only a few days and hours ago was such a fine body, could be accommodated in a single cellar in Fournes. Everyone slept the sleep of the dead; nobody noticed that Fournes was under fire from heavy calibre guns. Twelve comrades from another company were buried when a shell hit a neighbouring house. They escaped with shock, but a French family in an adjacent room suffered a direct hit: a babe in arms has departed this life almost before it began."

So, although the day ended with a total, bloody setback for the British army, the local German defence had suffered severely as well. In addition to heavy casualties, their trenches, breastworks and dugouts had been smashed beyond recognition. Order had been replaced by one gigantic crater field. Priority had to be given to rescue work in order to recover the many wounded who had been trapped or buried beneath collapsed overhead cover, but a frenzied effort also had to be made to restore the positions in case the attack was renewed the following morning. Covered by reinforced listening posts, there was no sleep for the exhausted survivors, who managed to restore some resemblance of order by dawn and, fortunately, carrying parties had managed to get forward with ammunition, water and rations. In the event and unsurprising to relate, 10 May was relatively quiet all along the front so recently attacked. The British had to come to terms with the fact that between them the 1st, 8th and Meerut Divisions had lost nearly 11,000 casualties for no gain whatsoever.[36] The French also had their problems, in that an initially very promising situation at Vimy Ridge had foundered in the face of skilfully conducted German counter-attacks and a poor performance by those controlling the movements of the French reserves. It was also very soon clear to the French commanders that the British had completely failed to fix any German reserves to their front; something which increased the tension between the Allies and caused the British to scramble to plan some sort of follow-up operations, so as to keep faith with the French. Whilst all this was happening, the German defenders made use of the pause to complete the evacuation of the wounded and transport the fallen, less those too deeply buried by the explosions, to the rear area for burial.

Throughout the following day, despite ammunition shortages on the British side, sporadic gunfire was maintained, probably to interfere with German repair efforts. 2nd Company Infantry Regiment 55 came in for particularly hard treatment and their trenches were completely destroyed once more. Even more problematic was the fact that a British heavy battery brought down fire on the Ferme du Biez in the mid morning. This building masked the sector command post, but such was the destruction that it had to be abandoned and the divisional engineer company had to labour long and hard to produce another temporary one to the rear of the farm. Battalion Headquarters Infantry Regiment 55 was relieved and was able to be back in Illies where the regimental band, which had been heavily involved in stretcher bearer duty, was on hand to play solemn music for the burial of no fewer than 230 members of the regiment.

Following the disaster for the BEF of 9 May there was, unsurprising to relate, an operational pause on this sector of the front though, further to the south, the great battle for the Lorette Spur and Vimy Ridge continued with undiminished ferocity. Clearly shaken by the failure of 9 May, which he had witnessed personally, standing in the tower of a ruined church as his lines of infantry were mown down by machine gun fire, the British Commander in Chief, Field Marshal Sir John French, wrote in his diary on 10 May that he wondered whether, 'we ought not to stand altogether on the defensive until an adequate supply of HE is available'.[37] He may have wondered that but there was no way that Joffre or Foch would permit such a thing to happen and huge pressure was put on French to fulfil his side of the bargain. Meeting on 12 May, Joffre expressed his extreme dissatisfaction that not only had no German reserves been moved away from the Tenth Army sector, the German 58th and 115th Infantry Divisions, previously located more or less opposite the British sector, had actually been moved south to counter the French offensive operations.[38]

Despite urging by Joffre, French did not commit himself until he had consulted the commander of First Army, General Haig, the following day. In the event, after further discussions and because it was obvious that something had to be done to demonstrate Allied solidarity, the British 1st Division relieved the French 58th Division in the line on the southern end of the British sector and Haig undertook to renew the attack with an assault in the Festubert sector, but only after a systematic preliminary bombardment had softened up the German positions. From that moment and through until the Battle

German trenches near Tahure early 1915.

German *Spanische Reiter* [knife rest] hasty barbed wire obstacles being prepared …

and in use on *Arbre-Höhe*. Champagne, March.

Men of Reserve Infantry Regiment 92 manning a forward trench north of Perthes. Champagne, March .

French soldiers observing through a trench periscope. Champagne, Spring

A German 210 mm heavy howitzer in action in Champagne, early 1915.

Ferme du Biez, Neuve Chapelle March.

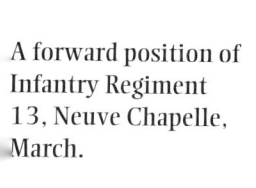

A forward position of Infantry Regiment 13, Neuve Chapelle, March.

German trench south of Neuve Chapelle, Spring.

A vertically mounted gas cylinder being prepared for discharge north of Langemark 22 April.

An artist's impression of a gas battery ready to be discharged north of Ypres 22 April

British soldiers embus for the Flanders front, April.

Captured French trenches south of Biskschote, April.
Lambrecht Collection.

A German trench near Polygon Wood. Ypres, May.

British casualties at Van Heule Farm near Ypres, May. *Lambrecht Collection.*

Captured British position south west of Poelkapelle, May. *Lambrecht Collection.*

A wrecked fortified farm near Zonnebeke, Spring. *Lambrecht Collection.*

Shell Trap Farm, May. *Lambrecht Collection.*

German soldier gathered around a huge shell hole near Pilkem, May. *Lambrecht Collection.*

Officers of Reserve Infantry Regiment 236 relaxing near St Juliaan, Spring. *Lambrecht Collection.*

A shell bursting forward of the positions of Reserve Infantry Regiment 236. Spring. *Lambrecht Collection.*

Zouaves in the assault. Arras front, May.

French positions in the wrecked village of Carency, May.

Mass attack by troops of the French Tenth Army, Artois, May.

Neuville St Vaast, May.

Street barricade Souchez, May.

Shrapnel bursting over a typical improvised position in French Flanders, Spring.

A depth machine gun position in French Flanders, Spring.

Part of the *Deckungsgraben* near the *Apfelhof*, northeast of Festubert, May.

Field tramway leading right up to the forward positions near Richebourg l'Avoué, Spring.

A French forward position smashed by shelling. Argonne, June. This photograph gives a good impression of the dense nature of the undergrowth at that time.

A German trench in the Argonne Forest, Summer.

The use of German infantry shields to provide additional cover during trench construction being demonstrated in a posed photograph Argonne, Summer.

A super-heavy 'Big Bertha' howitzer of the type used to shell Loos, September.

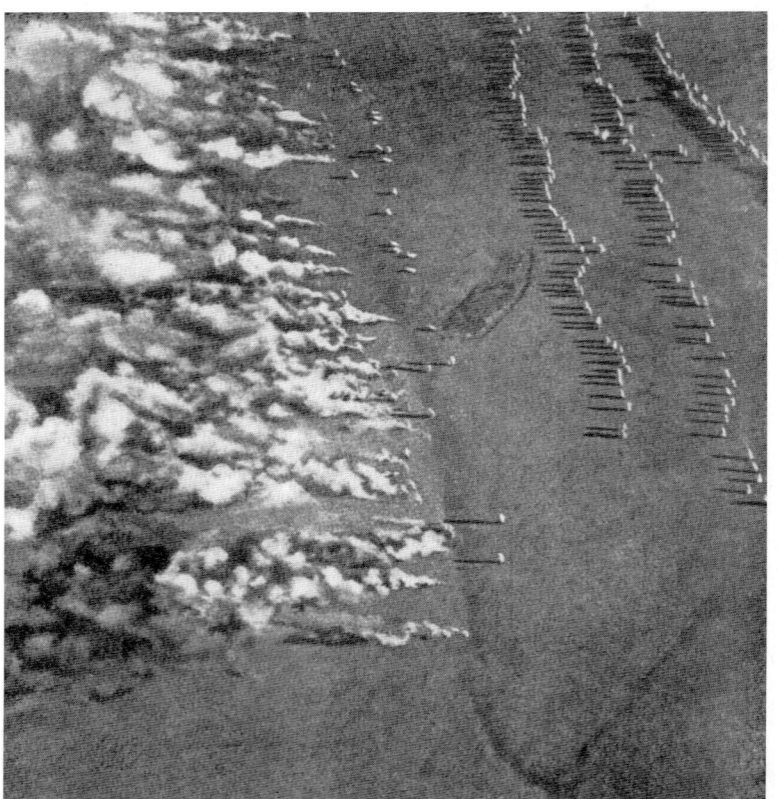

German forward position northwest of Loos, September.

A typical cylinder gas attack, with troops poised to follow the developing cloud.

Carnage alongside the Souain – Somme-Py road. 25 September.

German troops manning their stand-to positions. Champagne, September.

The chaotic battlefield round Navarin Farm, late September.

French prisoners being interrogated in the field. Champagne, late September.

A protected German forward holding area. Champagne, September.

of Cambrai in November 1917, lengthy, destructive bombardments were an integral part of all British offensive planning. Once again there were to be two separate thrusts, but this time the separation was a mere five hundred metres between the sectors of 7th Division attacking north of Festubert and 2nd Division attacking just to the west of the La Tourelle – La Bassée road.

According to the British account[39] the bombardment prior to the Battle of Festubert began on 13 May. Unfortunately, such was the shortage of ammunition that the fire plan, restricted to a front of only five kilometres from Port Arthur to Festubert, was not recognised by the Germans for what it was for forty eight hours. Until 15 May, the defenders thought that they were simply being subjected to harassing fire designed to interfere with the repairs to - and development of - their position. Even the Sixth Army Commander, Crown Prince Rupprecht, commented on its unusual pattern on 14 May. 'There was heavy fire on VII Army Corps at 4.00 pm, but it ceased completely at 6.00 pm.'[40] However, on 15 May, the defenders realised finally that the fire of hundreds of guns was being concentrated to drum fire, which was falling on selected parts of their front. This view was reinforced by the appearance of numerous British aircraft over their line during the afternoon. After it went dark, the infantry of the Lahore Division opened up with everything they had for several minutes. There was then a pause of an hour and the process was repeated. In fact, according to the British Official History[41] there were four repetitions: 9.45pm, 10.30 pm, 11.00 pm and 12.30 am (German time).

There could hardly have been a clearer warning of intent and, after the final fusillade had died away and the British guns had lifted their fire to the rear, all the forward troops of Infantry Regiment 55 and their supporting artillery were waiting for them. The British 5 Brigade and the Garwhal Brigade of the Meerut Division came under an appalling weight of fire as soon as the troops left their trenches just after 1.30 am. The guns of the support batteries were already laid on their defensive fire tasks, reacting instantly to the red signal flares and instruction of their forward observers.

Major Schulz Commanding Officer 2nd Battalion Infantry Regiment 55[42] **4.**

> "The front line troops of 2nd Battalion Infantry Regiment 55 fired red flares, which was the agreed signal for the start of the infantry attack. What then happened astride the Estaires – La Bassée road cannot be described in words. Every German battery, both those in direct support and those located in neighbouring sectors, concentrated their fire on this point. The earth heaved under the weight of this fire. The enemy attack of the Meerut and Lahore [*sic*] Divisions collapsed totally. At 3.00 am there were two more British attacks in strength directed against the regimental left flank, but these were beaten back by 2nd Battalion. However the enemy did succeed in breaking in, in the area of our left hand neighbours. From there they threatened the left flank of the regiment via the *Apfelhof.*
>
> "In order to counter this new danger, the 3rd Battalion, which had been

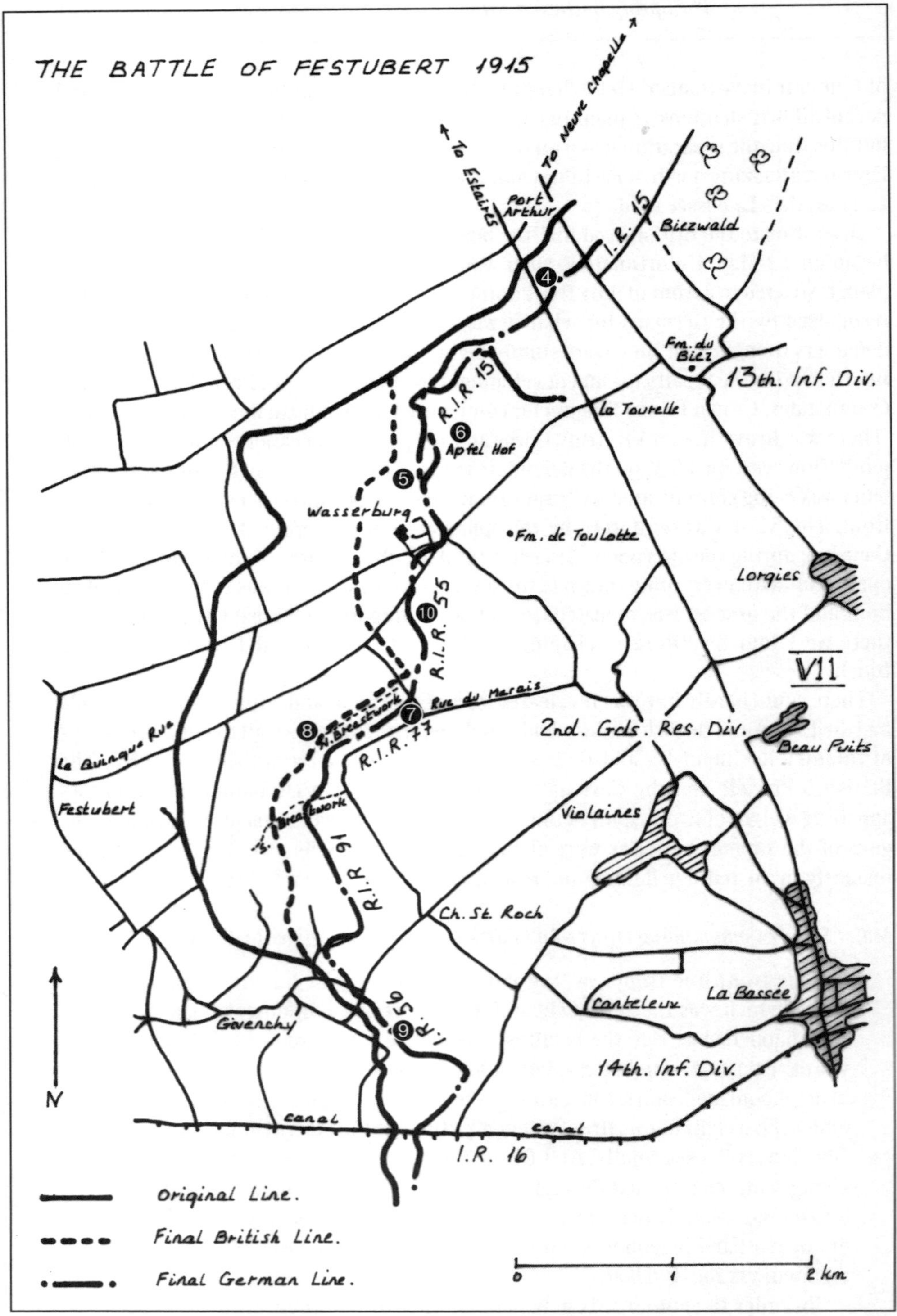
THE BATTLE OF FESTUBERT 1915
To Estaires
To Neuve Chapelle
Port Arthur
I.R. 15
Biezwald
Fm. du Biez
13th. Inf. Div.
R.I.R. 15
La Tourelle
Apfel Hof
Wasserburg
Fm. de Toulotte
Lorgies
R.I.R. 55
VII
Rue du Marais
N. Breastwork
R.I.R. 77
2nd. Gds. Res. Div.
Beau Puits
La Quinque Rue
Festubert
S. Breastwork
Violaines
R.I.R 91
Ch. St. Roch
La Bassée
Canteleux
Givenchy
I.R. 56
14th. Inf. Div.
N
canal
canal
I.R. 16
Original Line.
Final British Line.
Final German Line.
0
1
2 km

relieved the previous evening, was alerted and called forward to the battlefield. During the early morning of 16 May it arrived at the 2nd Battalion location, despite having to negotiate heavy shrapnel fire. 5th and 9th Companies then moved to the *Apfelhof* to close the dangerous gap ... Hauptmann Schmidt, who had assumed command of the left hand sector, reported during the afternoon of 16 May that the enemy were attacking Infantry Regiment 57 and that that regiment had evacuated its front line position. There was heavy, close-quarter fighting with bayonets and hand grenades that day and during subsequent days at the point where Infantry Regiment 57 had withdrawn and the British had occupied their positions.

"However, the enemy never succeeded in rolling up the Infantry Regiment 55 trenches. Oberleutnant Herbert Reuter was killed in heroic circumstances there on 17 May. Leutnants Büterowe, Waubke and König were killed the same day, whilst Leutnant Röwe had already been shot dead the previous day.[43] The British high command made a further attempt on 18 May [when] an overcast and rainy morning gave way to a bloody evening. The main effort that day was further to the west and did not affect the regiment ... On 18 May the regiment was relieved by Reserve Infantry Regiment 15 of 2nd Guards Reserve Division, the relief in the line being complete by 2.45 am. The news that the regiment was to be withdrawn to distant villages to recuperate had an electric effect. All the stress and misery were forgotten in one moment. Happy and singing, the much reduced companies marched back to Sainghin."

Just to the south, where Infantry Regiment 57 had experienced such hard fighting on 9 May, the artillery fire continued to be particularly heavy on 10 May, with a concentration on the routes leading back to La Bassée. Despite this, General der Infanterie von Claer, the Corps Commander, came forward that day to an artillery observation post forward of the Infantry Regiment 57 command post and received a full briefing on recent events from its commander, Major Castendyk. Concerned that there might be an early repetition of the previous day's attacks, priority was given to filling out the depleted ranks and 3rd Battalion, whose losses had been severe, was reinforced by the whole of 7th Company, which moved forward out of reserve. It was also considered essential to restore communications without delay, so the ruined telephone connections were replaced by a wireless station, which set up in an unobtrusive location near to the command post.

In the event these concerns were not realised, though there was considerable additional damage to buildings and infrastructure all the way back to La Bassée as a result of British harassing fire. Repair of the positions was also problematic and, even as late as 15 May, many of the breastworks were still in disrepair and the communication trenches mere crawl ways. As a result the regiment, despite allegedly being in good spirits, was ill-prepared to meet the resumption of the attacks, as its commander admitted to General von Claer during a telephone call late on the evening of 14 May. Unfortunately, the truth of this assessment was proved soon afterwards. The British attack came in under cover of darkness and, at around 4.00 am, the battalions of the British 6 Brigade partially drove in the right flank of 3rd Battalion, as noted by Major Schulz of Infantry Regiment 55 in his account. There were few casualties on the British side, though Major Shakerly, commanding 1st Battalion KRRC, was mortally wounded during the advance.[44]

This was a critical moment for the defence. Its forward troops had been forced back into the depth of the position and drum fire was coming down all over the sector. Even worse, Major von Stephani reported that, to the best of his knowledge, three companies of 2nd Battalion had been attacked in the flanks and rear and had either been destroyed or captured. This was contradicted by other accounts, including statements by wounded men making their way to the rear, that an enemy attack which followed a sharp artillery preparation had been halted. It was exceedingly difficult to establish the truth, because all the telephone lines, so painfully restored, had been destroyed once more. Gradually it became clear that the listening posts and engineer wiring parties working forward of the *Apfelhof* had been overrun and that the enemy had broken into the 11th Company sector, which was under the command of Leutnant Goetz.

The British account states that there was hardly any opposition and that the defenders turned tail and ran; Infantry Regiment 57, on the other hand, maintains that the company defended stubbornly until it ran out of hand grenades and had to pull back, being forced (with serious losses) to break through the so-called *Deckungsgraben* [Hidden Trench – protected by high screens] which was already occupied by British troops.[45] The truth probably lies somewhere in between. The survivors, having linked up with a half company of 12th Company, under Leutnant Ruppenthal, at the 3rd Battalion rallying point, began to dig in, so as to resist a further advance. This was made extremely difficult, because the entire area was still under heavy fire. Shell splinters and shrapnel balls took a heavy toll of the defenders throughout the remainder of the day.

Whilst the men of 11th and 12th Companies struggled to get under cover, it was effectively quite impossible for runners to move about and it is probable that observers from Infantry Regiment 55 knew sooner than any member of the command structure of Infantry Regiment 57 what had happened. Eventually, some three hours after the withdrawal, regimental headquarters discovered the truth and every available reserve and recently relieved working party was summoned forward once more to help plug the gaps. In the early dawn it was finally clear that the British were firmly established in the trenches that they had captured and that 7th, 9th and half of 12th Company were holding the remainder of the 3rd Battalion frontage. The remainder of the regiment was located either in the front line, or along the *Deckungsgraben*, or further in the rear, holding positions astride the *Rue de Marais*, which led back towards Violaines.

The units had been shaken, suffered casualties and were somewhat disorganised. Many of the battle positions were smashed or improvised and little was left of the wire obstacles. Nevertheless, a renewed British assault during the morning of 16 May stalled almost at once in places though, elsewhere, making use of abandoned trenches and covered approaches in the 1st Battalion area, the attackers managed to penetrate far enough into the depth of the position to get in behind much of 2nd Battalion and overwhelm several minor strong points. As soon as the regimental commander received news of this disaster, he ordered 4th Company to clear along the line of the 1st Battalion communications trenches. Ignoring heavy indirect fire, Leutnant Brüning and his men fought their way forward and pressed the British back through the use of large numbers of hand grenades. Eventually they got as far forward as the old front line and there, reinforced by two companies of Infantry Regiment 56 and a company of Jäger Battalion 11, they managed to reassert control of this part of the front.

Meanwhile a further Jäger company was sent to prop up 3rd Battalion and Hauptmann Kristen, of Infantry Regiment 56, who had force marched his way forward with two companies, was given the task of recapturing the 2nd Battalion sector. This was easier said than done. By midday it had still not been achieved and, furthermore, Hauptmann Giersberg and Hauptmann Renneburg of Infantry Regiment 56 had both been seriously wounded when a shell crashed through the overhead cover of a dugout they were sharing. Limited reinforcements continued to flow in. These included three companies of the Saxon 2nd Battalion Infantry Regiment 104 (which brought an entire wagon load of hand grenades with it) and a further company of Infantry Regiment 56, commanded by Hauptmann Dültgen, to reinforce Kristen; whilst another Saxon company went to buttress 3rd Battalion, which was still under great pressure.

Some Bavarian battalions were also sent south from the Messines area when the initial counter-strokes failed to dislodge the British penetrations, especially that in the Infantry Regiment 57 sector. However, these reinforcements were only deployed down at La Bassée for seventy two hours before being returned to their parent formations. The experience of 2nd Battalion Bavarian Infantry Regiment 5 is typical. Moving south under the command of Major Zobel, it reached La Bassée at 5.30 pm on 17 May. There it received orders from commander 14th Infantry Division to advance to contact, then throw the enemy out of the *Apfelhof – Quinque Rue* area. No sooner had it reached Violaines, having moved under constant artillery fire, than word arrived that the enemy attack had been halted and the battalion was to remain in Violaines. Only three hours later, at about 9.30 pm, however, orders arrived for it to move right up to the front line to relieve some sub-units of Infantry Regiment 57.

Despite unfamiliarity with the terrain, this was achieved and the new arrivals set to work to repair the wrecked defences. They then stayed in the line for forty eight hours, beating off a succession of relatively weak attacks, before returning to Messines on 20 May.[46] 2nd Battalion Bavarian Infantry Regiment 18 had a similar experience, having been also despatched forward by Headquarters 14th Infantry Division to help hold the line in the Infantry Regiment 57 sector until they could be relieved by 2nd Guards Reserve Division. They, too, did their best to strengthen the positions, despite the lack of trench stores. They also found it impossible to get rations forward to the front line, so their men were reduced to eating what they had originally brought forward in their bread pouches and their iron rations. Helping to beat off a succession of British attacks proved to be costly in terms of casualties, so they were far from sorry to leave the area on 20 May.[47]

It is, however, important to appreciate that this renewed attack, designed to draw

German attention and reserves away from the continuing battles near Arras, largely failed in that respect. A few composite units were organised and drafted in to go to the assistance of the hardest-pressed trench garrisons, but they were all minor reserves which could easily be spared elsewhere. In addition to the battalion from Infantry Regiment 104, the corps reserve of XIX Corps operating south of Ypres also released sufficient troops from 24th Infantry Division to form another. Under command of Major Demmering of Infantry Regiment 139, it actually comprised 1st Company Infantry Regiment 133,[48] 3rd and 12th Companies Infantry Regiment 139 and (allegedly) 1st Company Infantry Regiment 179.[49] However, it transpires that Reserve Hauptmann Künzel of Infantry Regiment 179 was simply told to assemble the fourth platoons of each of the companies of 2nd Battalion, who were back in billets resting and move to join Major Demmering.[50]

These minor reinforcements hardly justify suggestions that major diversions of effort were forced on the German defence by British offensive action, though it is fair to comment that their intervention was locally significant. Demmering's battalion may have been a scratch unit but, at considerable cost, it filled an important five hundred metre gap in the position of Infantry Regiment 57 for three critical days. It deployed with a total of sixteen officers and 843 other ranks. When it was transported out of the battle on 20 May, it was reduced to ten officers and 483 other ranks.[51] The battalion commanding officer wrote a detailed report concerning this difficult and costly three day deployment, which was forwarded to 24th Infantry Division once the survivors had been redeployed.

Major Demmering Infantry Regiment 139[52] **5.**

> "All the trenches which served as [covered] approaches forward were full of water and could not be compared with those to the north of Lille. 3rd Company Infantry Regiment 139 arrived in its appointed location and held it until the morning of 17 May. The orders which were despatched during the night to withdraw to the position newly dug by Landwehr Regiment 77 along the line *Apfelhof – Wasserburg* [known to the British as Ferme Cour d'Avoué] did not arrive in time in the front line – just as Infantry Regiment 57 feared. Not until it became light [on 17 May] could the attempt be made. The remnants of the right flank of Infantry Regiment 57, intermingled with 3rd Company, came under rifle and machine gun fire from the front and left rear from the trench running between *Heckenhof – Jägerhaus* and, in addition, there was drum fire on their trenches periodically.
>
> "During the course of the morning, the encircled elements of Infantry Regiment 57 and 3rd Company, having beaten off a fourth attack, were forced to surrender. 3rd Company was down to about fifteen men. Only a handful made it back. A mere five members of 3rd Company and an officer of Infantry Regiment 57 were the only ones to break through. I was in attendance as the officer of Infantry Regiment 57 made his report to the regimental commander

(Major Castendyk) and I give you my word of honour that the order to wave white cloths and surrender had been given by two feldwebels of Infantry Regiment 57. The five men of 3rd Company, whom I met during the evening of 17 May at the *Feldkuchenhof* [located by the road about 400 metres southeast of the *Wasserburg*], also confirmed this.

"All links between the forward and rear [areas] had been broken long before. Infantry Regiment 57 had been fighting continuously since 9 May. Because the artillery fire never stopped, not even during the night, it was impossible to distribute rations. The frequently contradictory reports from the front line did not permit a clear picture to be obtained, not even where the front line ran. Brigade had a more optimistic view of the situation and refused permission for the construction of a new continuous second line (which I feel would have been for the best), simply to facilitate reorganisation. Instead, repeated orders were issued to recapture at all costs the lost sections of trench, which were presumed to be in the possession of the enemy. This would have been possible had forces in sufficient strength to dominate the entire Infantry Regiment 57 sector been available. However, the deployment of individual companies to the different threatened sectors cannot be said to have been appropriate to the situation and had little prospect of achieving the desired aim."

There was in fact no further British advance in this area, but they were present in too great a strength to be thrown back by means of hasty counter-attacks, just as Major Demmering stated. Nevertheless, a final effort had been made by a composite battalion comprising two companies of Infantry Regiment 104 and two of Infantry Regiment 55, which were sent across in the early evening of 16 May to add their weight to the attacking force: but it was all to no avail.

Hauptmann Wolff Infantry Regiment 104[53] **6.**

"Hauptmann Eulitz of Infantry Regiment 104 was appointed commander of the composite battalion. 5th and 6th Companies Infantry Regiment 104, commanded by Reserve Oberleutnant Naumann and Reserve Leutnant Hanske respectively, were allocated to him ... At about 4.30 pm Battalion Eulitz, to which 5th and 11th Companies Infantry Regiment 55 had been subordinated, was assembled in the trenches at the *Lipperkreuz* [one kilometre west of Ferme de Biez] ... In the attack order, which was issued at 5.00 pm, 11th Company Infantry Regiment 55 was directed to advance, passing the northeast corner of the *Apfelhof*. 5th Company Infantry Regiment 55, maintaining contact, was to deploy on a 120 metre front. 5th Company Infantry Regiment 104 was directed to advance along the communication trench to the *Deckungsgraben* behind the left flank of Infantry Regiment 55, then to attempt to link with 5th Company Infantry Regiment 55 and push forward. 6th Company was to remain in reserve under command of the battalion at the track junction.

"It took only a few moments to issue the orders, but it took hours to carry them out. The deployment of the 55th was severely delayed by the need to cross a wide water-filled ditch without any equipment to assist them. Having finally negotiated that obstacle, they had to advance in absolutely open country devoid of any cover. There they came under such heavy artillery and machine gun fire that really serious casualties occurred and it was only possible to continue the advance very slowly in short dashes. Back at the *Lipperkreuz*, 5th Company Infantry Regiment 104 was also under fire from enemy artillery of all calibres. The communication trenches and the *Deckungsgraben* were so smashed by the constant shelling of the past few days that they no longer offered any protection to the advancing troops. It was not until 8.00 pm, when the 5th Company was finally at the appointed place and deployed ready for action, that the attack could begin. The neighbouring companies also renewed their attacks.

"However, the enemy fire had not let up. It swept the entire battlefield with undiminished strength. Fiery trails turned into discharges of shrapnel which spread deadly sprays in the form of hundreds of lead balls, which left long beaten zones in the soft ground of the meadowland. In between was the cracking and bursting of shells of all sizes, which ripped great holes in the surface of the earth. Iron splinters, some with low trajectory, others describing high arcs through the sky, rained down in appalling quantities. Bursts of machine gun fire added to the wild storm of fire, cutting many men down. The gaps in the ranks became greater. Already three platoon commanders of 5th Company Infantry Regiment 104 had been killed.

"Leutnant Mittmann, who had been wounded at the same time as Runner Seifert, was killed by a direct hit with a shell as he was being transported to the rear. As it went dark, the *Apfelhof* was reached and contact was made to the right with 3rd Battalion Infantry Regiment 55 and to the left with Infantry Regiment 57. During the late evening, two platoons of 6th Company Infantry Regiment 104 were called forward to the *Deckungsgraben* and the other two were held at readiness behind the left flank of the battalion. There was a strong British attack just before midnight, but it was beaten off easily. The enemy pulled back into their starting position and did not attempt to consolidate in No Man's Land."

It was not only the British who had temporarily shot their bolts. All the momentum had gone out of the German counter-attack as well and it was obvious that the troops of 7th, 9th and 12th Companies holding positions right forward were vulnerable to a renewed enemy assault so, with reluctance, permission had to be sought from corps headquarters to withdraw some eight hundred metres. This was achieved smoothly and, at around midnight, Landwehr Regiment 77 arrived to take over the critical central sector of the new line. The next day saw heavy shelling, but an attack launched during the afternoon was easily repulsed and that evening Bavarian troops arrived to relieve the exhausted remnants of Infantry Regiment 57. The confused days of fighting had seen them yielding some territory but, overall, its units had fought and defended well, though at the high price of more than 1,700 casualties.

That night Reserve Infantry Regiment 15 of 2nd Guards Infantry Division relieved Infantry Regiment 55, so Reserve Infantry Regiments 55 and 77 did the same service for Infantry Regiment 57. From north to south, during the final stages of what the British were to refer to as the Battle of Festubert, the German front line from Port Arthur crossroads to the La Bassée Canal was held by Reserve Infantry Regiment 15, Reserve Infantry Regiment 55, Reserve Infantry Regiment 77, Reserve Infantry Regiment 91 and, on the extreme southern flank, Infantry Regiment 56 of the original 14th Infantry Division. This meant that during the final days of battle the German defences were substantially stronger than they had been on 9 May.

The exhausted Westphalians, duty done, headed to the rear and the men of Infantry Regiments 104 and 139 departed too.[54] After their earlier efforts in the Argonne Forest and elsewhere, the Guards regiments had spent some time resting and retraining in Alsace when the call came to reinforce VII Corps. A lengthy train journey was followed by an equally tiring move forward to the front and by a difficult relief in the line.

Major Kiesel 2nd Battalion Reserve Infantry Regiment 15[55] **6.**

> "The relief turned out to be extremely awkward, because it was totally dark and the entire area was constantly under very heavy artillery fire. Some companies did not reach their allocated positions until dawn. All the routes were blocked with wounded and fallen being carried away. The position itself was as good as destroyed. Every single dugout and their entrances had fallen in. If the right flank was in a pitiful state, the remaining parts were so shot up that the rifle sections had to seek cover holes in the ground, where they were cut off and had to share them with the dead and wounded."

This view was echoed by another member of the regiment, who wrote home, describing the experience:

> "As soon as the barely distinguishable line had been indicated to them in the dark, our men threw themselves into the deepest craters, oblivious to the ground water which had seeped in. To begin with it appeared as though their first impressions had had a paralysing effect on them, but they soon pulled themselves together and began to work on the positions during the night. Wherever they cleared away rubble and began to dig, they came across things which had been scattered and buried. It was no longer a trench; rather it was a thirty metre wide stretch of huge craters, collapsed dugouts and trenches. In other words, it was an area of total, tangled, confusion and chaos. There they had to huddle down throughout the day, remaining motionless; whilst, at night, they suffered from machine gun and rifle fire as they attempted to restore order. There was no hot food. In any case most of them had lost interest in it.

"[However] the fighting spirit of our lads was beyond all praise. They kept egg-shaped hand grenades in both trouser pockets, with rifle grenades carefully stored in a dry covering. Their rifles were in their hands and a pick and sharpened spade were always to hand. In the sector of Reserve Infantry Regiment 91 [opposite Richebourg] Indian [troops] cruelly mutilated wounded men and similar things have happened to us.[56] There is no mercy any longer! Our only concern is that the British might not come and so we shall have to postpone our revenge for Ypres![57]

Whilst Reserve Infantry Regiment 77 was coming to terms with the problems of digging in the waterlogged ground of French Flanders, not to mention overcoming problems such as the fact that there were no maps to be had, nor any clear guidance concerning the tactical situation, the British artillery continued to harass their every attempt to strengthen their positions and to launch attacks from their newly won positions in the old German second line. One of the company commanders, whose sub-unit was deployed forward during the evening of 20 May, later reported a busy first night of occupation.

Reserve Leutnant Sauerbrey 4th Company Reserve Infantry Regiment 77[58] **7.**

"Yesterday and all through the night, the company sector was constantly under heavy enemy artillery fire. A high proportion of the shells contained evil-smelling yellowish-brown gas.[59] Having increased considerably in intensity towards 9.00 pm, the gun fire stopped abruptly and, simultaneously, the company detected an enemy infantry attack. An old communication trench ran from a farm building about one hundred metres forward of the trench forward to the old position held by Infantry Regiment 5. It was secured by a sentry position commanded by an unteroffizier. During the artillery bombardment the enemy crept along this and overran the unteroffizier sentry position. Once the artillery fire ceased they launched forward from the trench in tightly packed ranks, in order to shake out on a broad front in cover of the building and to launch an attack on our lines.

"Simultaneously, an enemy machine gun came into action from another trench. The enemy attack was nipped in the bud. In fact after only about fifteen minutes, it could be regarded as over. The enemy did not get closer than eighty metres. It is impossible to report on their losses because visibility was reduced due to a hedge near the building and also it went dark. About two British platoons[60] attacked the company sector, which must certainly have suffered heavy casualties as they pulled back.

The British attacks were not confined to the 4th Company frontage, as is clear from a further after action report provided by a sub-unit of 3rd Battalion on 21 May.

Reserve Leutnant Quittel 12th Company Reserve Infantry Regiment 77[61] **7.**

"During yesterday's attack, only 12th Company[62] was assaulted directly. Following considerable [enemy] artillery fire, which began at about 1.00 pm, serious artillery preparations, including fire from the heaviest calibre guns, began about 6.30 pm. The infantry attack came in at about 9.00 pm and it is to the credit of the company that we clearly spotted the enemy emerging from their trenches, which were between 600 and 900 metres away. In contrast to the weight of artillery fire, the infantry attack was weak and lacking in energy. It stalled some 300 – 400 metres short of our position and there was no need for reinforcement. 11th Company, which had been deployed as a precaution, was sent back as soon as it arrived. Our own artillery performed outstandingly as it contributed to the defence against this attack, despite the fact that there were no artillery observers forward. The attack was by about two companies and the enemy comprised exclusively British or Canadians."

It is in fact possible that what was interpreted as an attack was no more than a preliminary operation by the newly arrived Canadians of Alderson's Force[63] to move the British line forward. 3 Canadian Brigade, commanded by Brigadier-General REW Turner VC, was later reported to have closed up considerably during the period 19 – 22 May against the so-called North Breastwork, located about two kilometres east northeast of Violaines and defended at that time by Reserve Infantry Regiment 77. Additional force is given to this supposition by the fact that the experience of Reserve Infantry Regiment 77 was replicated all along the frontage as, the relief of the worn out British complete, preparations were made for a final effort at breakthrough on 25 May. These minor actions, heavily supported by the British artillery, took a considerable toll on the defenders, who were racing to complete work on their new line of defence, some 750 – 1,000 metres east of the original and to dispute some of the recent Allied gains of territory. On a number of occasions, clashes between the lines led to sharp small-scale actions and the capture, or release of prisoners. One such, which occurred west of the North Breastwork, saw eight men return to 1st Battalion Reserve Infantry Regiment 77.

Reserve Leutnant Sauerbrey 4th Company Reserve Infantry Regiment 77[64] **8.**

"The men who were cut off after the actions of 20 and 21 May, report the following information: Because of extremely heavy artillery fire during the evening of 20 May, we withdrew to our dugout, leaving only the double sentry post outside to block the communications trench. (These men were later found dead.) The very moment that the artillery fire lifted, the garden in front of our dugout was already teeming with British soldiers. Four men immediately occupied our entrance, so we could not get out. However the British seemed content to post a sentry to prevent us escaping and we were not captured directly. We spent twenty hours with our weapons at the ready, waiting in vain for enemy to attack us.

"When, during the evening of 21 May, a stack of straw very close to our position was set on fire by our artillery, it caused such confusion amongst the enemy that we were able to escape, aided by the fact that the small arms fire of our comrades also distracted the enemy. We estimate that there were about fifty British soldiers in and around the farm and that they were digging out a trench about the width of a company sector. According to the men who had been trapped, the enemy comprised youthful-looking clean shaven English and Scottish soldiers, accompanied by tough, older colonial soldiers. The enemy sentries seem not to have dared to touch the German knapsacks which had been deposited by the entrance to the dugout."

A member of Infantry Regiment 56, holding the line between the Givenchy – Violaines road and the La Bassée Canal, also later recalled the dangerous intensity of these days: 9.

"From 21 – 23 May preparations for the second major British attack were in full swing, whilst the 3rd Battalion was attempting in the *Talstellung* [Valley Position] to carry out the relief of 3rd Battalion Landwehr Regiment 78. It was a moment of weakness. The entire position between had been lost, with the exception of the flank between *Steilhang* [Steep Slope] and *Wasserloch* [Waterhole]. A counter-attack was planned for 22nd. It was carried out by 4th Company under Ziegler, together with volunteer grenade throwers from 1st Company, led by Vizefeldwebel Stürmer – his name alone [Stormer] inspired trust! Together, they crept like Indians through the high grass and the crater field, so as to be able to launch forward unexpectedly.

"The surprised enemy gave up ground considerably faster than they had won it. The greater part of the position, together with two built in revolver – cannons, were soon back in the hands of their rightful owners. Both Leutnant Ziegler and Vizefeldwebel Stürmer were wounded. Heavy mortar rounds rained down from the former trenches of Infantry Regiment 57, which the enemy had incorporated into their positions. There was one explosion after another and torrents of fire came from the area of a much-feared sunken road. 2nd and 7th Companies, commanded by Lütkenhaus and Theyson respectively, went forward the next night. Crossing a rise, they were illuminated by a flare and pinned down by machine gun fire. Elements of Reserve Infantry Regiment 91, part of 2nd Guards Reserve Division, which had been moved up from Alsace, were deployed and 9th and 11th Companies Infantry Regiment 56 pushed forward along the communications trenches.

"[As a result of this action] the enemy were pushed back everywhere, though the enemy hung on desperately to their remaining sections of trench. The casualties were high. Hauptmann Theyson was killed,[65] then the hurricane roared on into 23 May. During the early hours of 24 May, the enemy clashed once more with the relief of 2nd, 4th and 7th Companies by 7th and 8th Companies Reserve Infantry Regiment 91. 6th Company, manning a communications trench, had to withdraw one hundred metres and its commander, Leutnant Kurth, was killed."[66]

Reserve Infantry Regiment 55, deployed more or less opposite the centre of the new line established by the British, had an equally torrid time during these final days. Writing home on 27 May when the crisis of the battle was well past, one of its medical orderlies conveyed a vivid, if somewhat disjointed, picture of events, finishing by telling his parents not to worry about him which, given the picture he painted, cannot have been easy for them.

Sanitäts-Soldat Bernhard Holtmann 10th Company Reserve Infantry Regiment 55[67] **10.**

"The days of terror are over! It was our baptism of fire! I am once more on top form. You will have read in the newspapers of the British attempt to break through at La Bassée. This was the precise place where we of 10th Company Reserve Infantry Regiment 55 were deployed. We are always ready to move, held as close to the front as possible, so that we can intervene if required. We moved from Berclau, where the 11th Jägers were deployed, to La Bassée. When we arrived in Billy, we already had a bit of an idea about what lay ahead! The churchyard was full of new graves and, from time to time, a heavy shell would crash down. Our 210 mm howitzers were changing position and their plated wheels made an enormous noise. We found a place to sleep in the rough remnants of a school which had served as a stable for horses. We obtained some fresh straw and waited at immediate notice to move. Then the order arrived. '3rd Battalion Reserve Infantry Regiment 55 is to move today, Saturday 22 May, for a three day tour of duty in the line!' Through briefings and information from the wounded of 2nd Battalion we had heard so much that we knew that we had to be prepared for the worst.

"Moving silently through the night we zig-zagged our way forward carefully through meadows and fields, so as not to give ourselves away. Our position was bow-shaped. 10th Company was in the centre, closest to the enemy. We pushed on further forward, halting at a track junction. From that point we had to move across open ground. The order was, 'Load and make safe!' We each fed a round into the chamber, still not knowing what we faced. Then we heard 'Scht, scht, crack', followed by a howling sound. It was a shell! We were under fire. 'Quick, behind the wall!' One man threw himself to the ground here; another, there. But, until we had seen a dead or wounded man, we were not alert to danger.

"I felt completely overtired and almost fell asleep as I lay on the ground. Then there was another – a dud this time, which fell into a midden and sprayed me with liquid manure. Now that was a bit close! We lay there a while longer, while the first two platoons went forward, followed by some of 3 Platoon. The rest of us just lay there, not knowing what was happening. I was one of those. Luckily there was a vizefeldwebel with us so, led by him, we set off to try and find the others. Here and there we caught the smell of corpses and at the same time there was thunder and lightning and awful, driving, rain. Blue beans [bullets]. We could not find the others. Towards morning somebody came from the position to collect us, but it was already light. We certainly could not move across country to the position. There were still no communication trenches, because the enemy were occupying our former positions, so we had to pull back to the totally shot up village.

"Once there we occupied a cellar initially, because artillery fire was coming down all over the place. That evening, as dusk fell, we moved through the moonlight to the position, arriving safely, despite having to throw ourselves to the ground frequently because of the flares. We were next to the 15th [Reserve Infantry Regiment 15]. Everything was shot up and the trenches flattened. All the cover was destroyed. There were huge shell holes and everywhere there was the stink of corpses, with bodies lying everywhere. 'Don't tread on that corpse!' I looked around me and there was one which had been tossed to the rear of the trench and covered with a groundsheet. There was another just behind it. I found the whole thing gruesome and there – there was a group of men digging a dead man out from where he had been buried.

"It was like that all the way until we reached the 10th Company position and it was the same there. Silently the shapes of soldier could be seen digging – under cover as far as possible – so as to produce better cover for themselves during the hours of darkness. It was impossible to move about freely, without attracting artillery fire. I stayed with my comrade Franz, manning a place where two bodies had been dug out. We had to dig in to the best of our ability. Luckily, because one of our unteroffiziers fell ill, I was able to take over another spot and there I constructed a tiny little shelter ... Morning broke. Enemy aircraft appeared. They were French with national markings. They flew along our positions. Everything remained quiet. By midday and then throughout the rest of the day, we were under artillery fire, such as none of us who were there had ever previously experienced.

"Amongst them were heavy guns! One shell burst and produced a hole large enough for horses to stand in. Everything anywhere near it was destroyed, of course. Then we were fired at by shrapnel and low trajectory shells, which systematically raked the entire position. Then we came under fire from a flank. If they keep this up and do not stop, sooner or later there will be a direct hit. It was like this day after day. However our artillery has enough ammunition now and we have seen its effect during the past few days. I believe that it has been firing 200–300 shells every half hour into the British positions opposite. This evening we are going into our position once again, but it is not so bad. The British have clearly given up their attempt to break through. They are not moving anywhere and are working on their positions. At midday yesterday six duds slammed down just next to my position. I earnestly ask you not to be too worried!"

There are repeated remarks in the British accounts of the final stages of the Battle of Festubert that lack of ammunition compromised the preparations for the attacks launched on 25 May. Nevertheless, given the weakness of the hastily constructed German depth position, the casualties suffered by the regiments on the receiving end of what fire there was, were not light by any standard. Despite that fact, when the attack itself was launched, it was generally executed very weakly and easily dealt with.

Major Steuer 2nd Battalion Reserve Infantry Regiment 77[68] **7.**

"After the enemy artillery had begun bringing down extraordinarily heavy gun fire from the afternoon, the expected attack was launched at 10.00 pm yesterday. By means of the telephone and an outstandingly efficient relay chain of messengers, the battalion was already fully orientated when the leading enemy elements – in about battalion strength – shook out to our front for the attack. We informed the artillery and they were right on target very quickly. It was only on the 6th and 8th Company frontages that the attack actually developed and there the enemy managed to close right up to our barbed wire obstacle. Opposite 5th Company the enemy plan fell apart before it could even be launched.

"The companies had not suffered much as a result of the enemy preparatory bombardment and so were able to meet the enemy with calm and careful shooting. It seems as though our artillery was very effective against the enemy rear area. Because observation over the ground [to our front] is extremely difficult and because of the long grass, it is impossible even to hazard a guess concerning enemy losses. Because of the short range (the attackers deployed a mere two hundred metres to our front), the light night, our calm small arms fire and the well placed artillery fire, the enemy losses cannot have been inconsiderable. The action gave us the impression that the British had difficulty in organising their troops for an attack."

In view of the poor quality of many of the attacking formations, this feeble end to the Battle of Festubert is hardly surprising. The 51st (Highland) Division, for example, was, according to General Haig, 'practically untrained and very green in all field duties'. Furthermore, it had to rely on the loan from the Indian Corps of infantry and engineer officers and machine guns.[69] Leaving aside any issues about availability of shells or their effectiveness, it is small wonder that so little of substance was gained. Despite this, the last British official word on Festubert was that 'considerable success had been achieved'[70] and that, 'the operations at Festubert had brought to the battle every German who could be spared'.[71] If these thoughts were intended to comfort the relatives of those whose lives had been sacrificed for so little, then their appearance in the British official history is entirely understandable. If they represent a genuine British assessment, then the compiler was deluding himself.

Stripped of any post war gloss, the facts were these. The initial British attack made some gains and created a small gap in the German defences. There was a local crisis, which was countered much as it had been at Neuve Chapelle, by summoning minor reinforcements which could be easily spared – primarily by XIX and II Bavarian Corps - and deploying them to the threatened front for seventy two hours. By this time a new defensive line had been hastily prepared, largely by Landwehr Regiment 77, assisted by Bavarian troops and the leading brigade of 2nd Guards Reserve Infantry Division had arrived from Alsace and was able to relieve the battered Infantry Regiments 55 and 57. The prompt arrival of 38 Reserve Infantry Brigade, the second brigade of 2nd Guards Infantry Division and its insertion into the line to the north of Infantry Regiment 56, meant that the final British attacks were launched against experienced regiments, battle hardened in the Argonne Forest and around Vauquois, rested and at full strength.

2nd Guards Reserve Infantry Division then remained in the line in French Flanders for the next nine months, so in fact all that the BEF had managed to do, at the cost of many thousands of casualties, was to capture a worthless strip of ground of no tactical importance whatsoever and cause the German army to relieve one ground holding division with another: some success. If the German army was barely inconvenienced at Aubers Ridge and Festubert, what of the attitude of the French army, in support of whose major offensive these battles had been fought? Post-war, General Joffre, whilst acknowledging the bravery of the British troops at Aubers Ridge, devoted one single sentence of his memoirs to the failure there[72] then, damning the subsequent efforts at Festubert with faint praise, simply noted,

> "The British army launched a fresh attack on 16 May, on a frontage of three divisions. On the 18th our allies managed to force the German front line back 800 metres on a five kilometre front."[73]

General Foch, in seeking subsequently to explain the failure to exploit the success achieved by the Moroccan Division on Vimy Ridge on 9 May, could hardly have been more dismissive of the BEF.

> "The delayed arrival of the reserves was not the sole reason why we obtained only an incomplete result. The attack of the Tenth Army was supposed to benefit from an attack to the north carried out by the British First Army, but this operation, which was preceded by a completely inadequate artillery bombardment, stalled almost completely on the 9th, then petered out and was not resumed until the 16th. This failure, followed by inaction from the period 10th – 15th, allowed the Germans to concentrate against Tenth Army all the forces that had newly arrived in the area."[74]

It was a sorry time for British arms, revealing, as it did, the inability of the BEF at that period to operate effectively against a first class enemy. The sole redeeming feature was the great courage shown by the men who went forward against unsupressed machine guns and concentrated artillery fire in a hopeless cause; men whose bravery is repeatedly acknowledged in the German accounts of the desperate fighting; men whose gallantry deserved a better fate. The German army, aware that it had been severely pressed by the French, was altogether more content with the outcome of the battle, despite the fact that a certain amount of ground of tactical importance had been lost. The achievement was summed up on 28 June 1915 in a special Sixth Army Order of the Day, of which this is an extract.

Generaloberst Crown Prince Rupprecht of Bavaria[75]

> "Hard weeks lie behind us: by day, with our weapons; by night with our spades, as we maintained and defended our positions which we had built up with great care. Many a brave officer, many a courageous soldier gave his life for Kaiser and Empire. But the iron wall which we erected around Arras during the past few weeks, the wall which our enemies tried in vain to break down, always held . . . "

Notes
1. GOH 2 p 76.
2. *ibid.* pp 59 and 71-72.
3. Sheldon *The German Army on Vimy Ridge 1914 – 1917* pp 45-89.
4. Baer *Der Völkerkrieg: Siebenter Band* p 124.
5. Kriegsarchiv München HS 1992/5
6. GOH 2 p 89.
7. FOH 3 p 101.
8. BOH 2 pp 39 & 76.
9. GOH 2 p 93.
10. Beumelburg *Loretto* Ehrentafel p 11. Kriegsfreiwilliger Paul Mauk was born in Freiburg im Breisgau on 19 July 1900 and died of his wounds on 7 June 1915 having been mortally wounded by a shell splinter the previous evening, whilst serving with his brothers Walther (who was also underage), Karl and Fritz in 4th Company Infantry Regiment 113. He had received a slight head wound earlier on 9 May, but had secretly discharged himself a week later from a field hospital and rejoined his company. He is buried in the German cemetery at Lens-Sallaumines Block 11 Grave 268.
11. Notes on conference 30 Apr 1915, WO 158/183, quoted by Sheffield *The Chief* p 113.
12. Kriegsarchiv München Reserve Infantry Regiment 16 Bd 4 *Feindlicher Angriff am 9.5.1915, Fournes 15.5.1915.*
13. Rupprecht *Mein Kriegstagebuch: Erster Band* pp 336-337.
14. Müller-Loebnitz (1) *Das Ehrenbuch der Westfalen* p 169.
15. In fact the Indian formations involved were in the first instance from the Dehra Dun Brigade of the Meerut Division (BOH 2 pp 27-28). Later in the day the Bareilly Brigade was substituted. The Lahore Division, recently arrived from Ypres, was holding trenches slightly to the north.
16. The territory of the historic area of Lippe, which was formed in 1811 when the Grand Duchy of Berg was annexed by France, is now divided between Lower Saxony and North Rhine-Westphalia. Named after the River Lippe, it was centred on Münster. After the defeat of Napoleon, this former département was split between the kingdoms of Hannover and Prussia.
17. Offizierstellvertreter Karl Vesting is buried in the German cemetery at Illies Block 3 Grave 234.
18. This is almost certainly a reference to a fairly substantial break in by a group from 2nd Battalion Royal Munster Fusiliers, which caused some problems for the defence initially but

was eventually eliminated with few survivors; only about three of the Irishmen were taken prisoner. The remainder perished in confused close quarter fighting. See Bristow *A Serious Disappointment* pp 74-75.
19. Apart from the fact that only Gurkhas carried kukris, the only other Indian troops in the Dehra Dun Brigade were the 6th Jats. See BOH 2 p 419.
20. Hancock *Aubers Ridge* p 53.
21. Rupprecht *op.cit.* pp 336-337.
22. This story sounds improbable. It is certainly unverifiable.
23. Windhorst History Field Artillery Regiment 58 p 96.
24. BOH 2 pp 22-23.
25. *ibid.* pp 23-24.
26. *ibid.* 2 p 27.
27. Kriegsarchiv München Reserve Infantry Regiment 16 Bd 4 *Feindlicher Angriff am 9.5.1915 Fournes 15.5.1915.*
28. *ibid.*
29. Kriegsarchiv München Reserve Infantry Regiment 21 Bd 3 *Gefechtsbericht über den 9.5. und die folgenden Tage, le Maisnil 25.5.15.*
30. *ibid.*
31. Sollider *Vier Jahre Westfront* pp 145-148.
32. The timings given by Bestle are inaccurate but this is far from uncommon in these personal accounts. He may have been writing from memory and, even if he had had access to a watch, it may well not have been showing the correct time.
33. This was a party from 2nd Battalion Northamptonshire Regiment, who exploited a gap created by the fire of 104th Battery RA See BOH 2 p 34.
34. Almost all the fatal casualties mentioned in this report have known graves, suggesting that the positions were cleared carefully subsequently and the casualties buried in a temporary battlefield cemetery in the rear. The following men lie in the *Kamaradengrab* of the German cemetery at St Laurent-Blangy, presumably together with many other fatal casualties of 9 May from the Fromelles area: Kriegsfreiwilliger Ludwig Neumeier, Infanterist Joseph Maisl, Infanterist Theodor Simbeck, Gefreiter Bernhard Schweighofer and Gefreiter Adolf Schaudeck.
35. Sollider *op. cit.* pp 141-142.
36. BOH 2 p 39.
37. French Diary 10 May 1915 quoted by Holmes *The Little Field Marshal* p 293.
38. BOH 2 pp 46-47.
39. *ibid.* pp 52-55.
40. Rupprecht *op. cit.* p 357.
41. BOH 2 p 57.
42. Müller-Loebnitz *op. cit.* (1) p 171.
43. Four of these officers have known graves. Oberleutnant Herbert Reuter is buried in the German cemetery at Wicres Village Block 2 Grave 372; whilst Leutnants Röwe, Büterowe and Waubke are all buried in Block 3 of the cemetery at Illies in Graves 228, 231 and 226 and presumably are surrounded by many of the other fallen of Infantry Regiment 55.
44. BOH 2 p 57.
45. This trench was typical of many others in low-lying ground which were easily overlooked. It was equipped with high screens to provide cover from view.
46. Weniger History KB Infantry Regiment 5 pp 46-4.
47. Ritter History KB Infantry Regiment 18 pp 88-89.

48. Niemann History Infantry Regiment 133 p 37.
49. Baumgarten-Crusius (2) History Infantry Regiment 139 p 111.
50. Goldammer History Infantry Regiment 179 p 65.
51. Niemann *op. cit.* p 37.
52. Baumgarten-Crusius *op. cit.* (2) pp 114-116.
53. Wolff History Infantry Regiment 104 pp 152-153.
54. *ibid.* p 156.
55. Forstner History Reserve Infantry Regiment 15 pp191-192.
56. It should be noted that no such accusation appears in the History of Reserve Infantry Regiment 91, so this assertion can probably be dismissed as a trench rumour.
57. Forstner *op. cit.* pp 192-193.
58. Wohlenberg History Reserve Infantry Regiment 77 p 119.
59. Sauerbrey is in fact describing the products of combustion produced when shells employing lyddite bursting charges exploded. The British army had no gas shells at this time.
60. Given the size German platoons at that time, Sauerberg probably estimated that the attack was launched in a strength of between 120 and 140 men.
61. Wohlenberg *op. cit.* pp 119-120.
62. Presumably Quittel meant that of the companies of 3rd Battalion, only 12th Company was directly affected.
63. This was a combination of the 1st Canadian Division and 51st (Highland) Division, which replaced the fought-out British 2nd and 7th Divisions to the south of the Indian Corps on 18 May. It was commanded by Lieutnenant General EAH Alderson of the 1st Canadian Division. BOH pp 73-76.
64. Wohlenberg *op. cit.* pp 121-122.
65. Hauptmann Emil Theyson is buried in the German cemetery at Salomé Block 4 Grave 803.
66. Müller-Loebnitz *op. cit.* (1) p 175.
67. Wißmann History Reserve Infantry Regiment 55 pp 78-80.
68. Wohlenberg *op. cit.* p 124.
69. BOH 2 p 73.
70. *ibid.* p 78.
71. *ibid.* p 82.
72. Joffre *Mémoires: Tome Second* p 78.
73. *ibid.* p 79.
74. FOH 3 p105.
75. Baer *op. cit.* p 145

.Chapter 5

The Argonne Forest

From autumn 1914 the French army fought tenaciously to defend the Argonne Forest and the German army tried ceaselessly for a year to capture it for one crucial reason: the main east-west railway line serving Verdun ran through it from Saint Ménéhould in the west to Aubréville in the east via Les Islettes and Clermont. Control, or denial, of the use of this line was of fundamental importance if Verdun were ever to be attacked with a reasonable chance of success. So much for the strategic prize; the difficulty was in bringing decisive fighting power to bear in one of the most inhospitable sectors of the Western Front. The Argonne Forest, some forty kilometres in extent from north to south and fifteen from east to west, was deeply incised mountainous terrain, containing only isolated settlements or foresters' cabins connected by a very limited and poor network of roads and tracks.

In addition, for the Germans, used to well tended and managed woodland in their own country, the overgrown, tangled mass of vegetation came as something of a shock. Although there were a great many tall oak trees, these were hemmed in by undergrowth, beech, alder, elderberry and large areas of gorse. In the early days of the campaign, before shelling had had an effect, there were places where the woods resembled secondary jungle and it was barely possible for a man on foot to push his way through the tangle of saplings, briar and thorn bushes. Not only was coordinated movement almost impossible to organise, with visibility virtually non-existent, but also command and control was frequently more a matter of luck than judgement. Then, even when the effect of battle, with its mining and extensive bombardments, had begun to influence the local geography, movement was still rendered very difficult, due to the quantities of loose rock, general debris and twisted and smashed trees and branches.

As if this was not problem enough, the entire area was marked by steep sided ravines running in all directions, often marshy, or with streams at their bases and, furthermore, the mapping was so poor that many of these features did not appear on the topographical maps at all, or were wrongly placed, or were only partially correct. This meant that thrusts into the area almost always came up against unexpected obstacles. The one saving grace for the German army was that much of the French gun fire was directed speculatively against ravines and choke points selected from the map so that, with target acquisition a constant problem in the early stages of the campaign in 1914, many German artillery units were able to operate with relative impunity from unmarked hollows and folds in the ground. Improved French air reconnaissance began to overcome this and there was some regret on the German side that there had been a tendency at first to clear dense vegetation from around positions, routes and dumps – all of which tended to draw attention to such places. Later in the battle much more attention was paid to the need for camouflage, so as to avoid the unwelcome attention of French aircraft, particularly those carrying artillery observers.

Initially it was the French army which exploited the potential of the Argonne Forest when, at the end of September 1914, it inserted strong forces into the region, which acted like a wedge, driving apart the German forces engaged to the east and west of the wooded area. From the early autumn of 1914 XVI Corps, commanded by General der Infanterie von Mudra, had been heavily engaged in this area and the German army began to thrust into it from the east via Montblainville and Varennes and from the northwest via Binarville. For many weeks the main weight of the battle was borne by the 27th Infantry Division from Württemberg and the Prussian 33rd and 34th Infantry Divisions, whilst the flanks to the east were covered by 2nd Landwehr Division of VI Reserve Corps, with 9th Landwehr Division deployed just to the west. The most rapid progress was made from the east, where penetration along the axis Varennes – Le Four de Paris met relatively little resistance but, further west, a dogged and heavily disputed advance across the Moreau Valley and Bagatelle Pavillon towards St Hubert Pavillon was necessary. It took days of fighting to overcome the defence in both those places and with each bound forward the difficulties multiplied and progress was reduced to a snail's pace.

Once the two sides became locked in close combat, many of the operations were on a very small scale as the German troops mined and sapped their way forward into jumping off positions close to the French lines and fierce battles were fought for days or even weeks at a time over minor points of only local tactical significance. However, the German pressure never let up and barely a week went by without the capture of a particular trench, blockhouse or strong point. At times this was the work of small groups of infantry or engineers but, frequently, entire brigades or even divisions became involved. Some idea of the closeness of this fighting may be derived from the fact that the men of 27th Infantry Division, under its commander, the Prussian Generalleutnant Graf von Pfeil und Klein-Ellguth, had to overcome no fewer than fourteen lines of defence as they worked their way forward painfully a mere 1,200 metres in early 1915. Nevertheless, their progress was such that, by the end of January 1915, 27th Infantry Division had pushed the lines forward to a point roughly half way between the Moreau and Dieusson valleys, inflicting such heavy casualties on the formations of the French II Corps that the entire corps was withdrawn from the front and was replaced by the reinforced XXXII Corps, commanded by General Humbert, which was transported south from Flanders for the purpose.

One particularly important day of battle occurred on 29 January when, storming forward from the Moreau Valley, they overcame no fewer than three significant lines of resistance manned by the French 40th Division. Up until 22 January there had been a lengthy period of wet weather but, on that day, there was heavy persistent frost which froze the ground and improved the going for troops on foot considerably. So as to take advantage of this change in the weather, General von Pfeil directed his two brigade commanders, Generalleutnant von Wencher and Generalmajor Langer, of 53 and 54

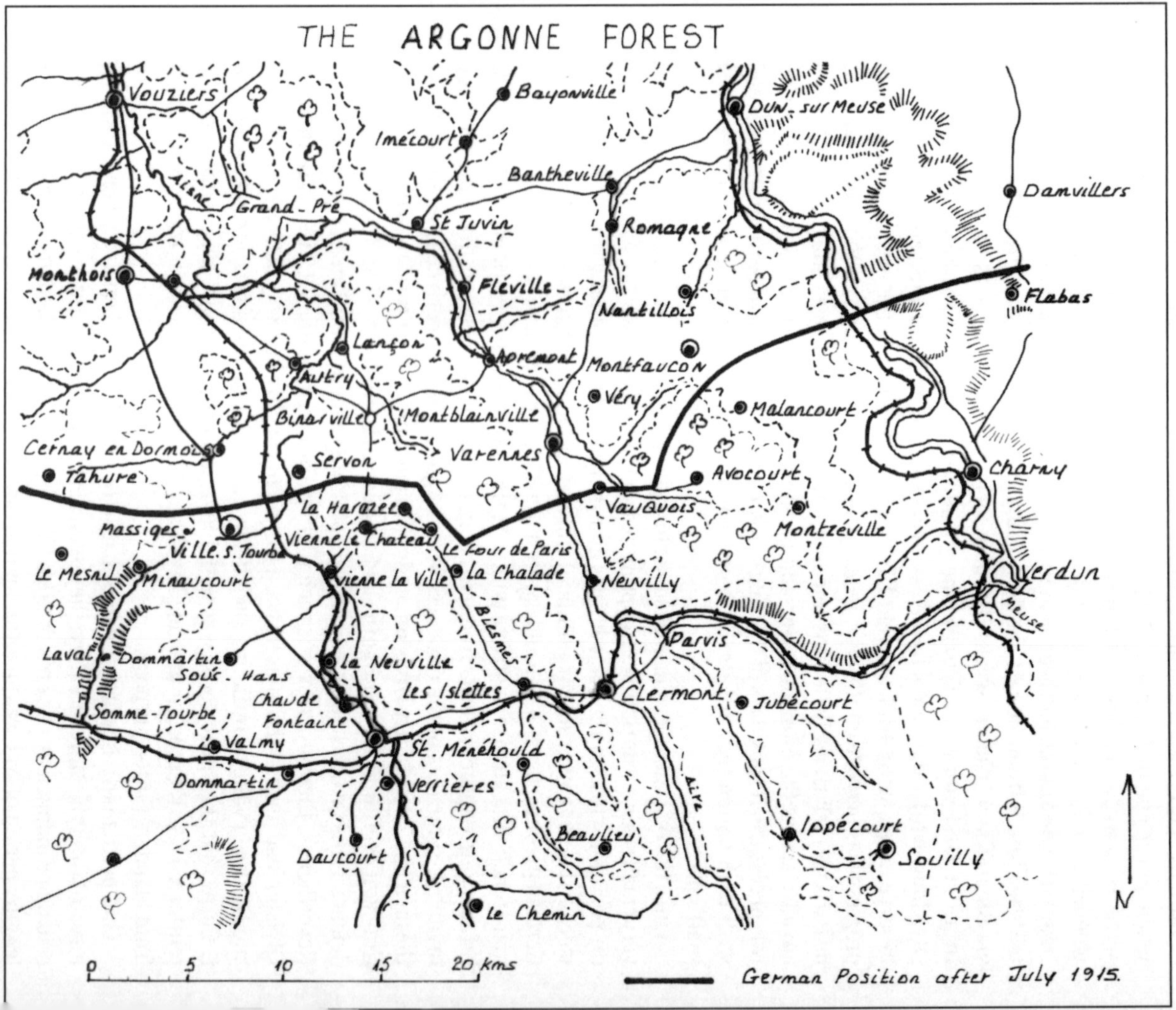
THE ARGONNE FOREST
Vouziers
Bayonville
Imécourt
Bantheville
Grand-Pré
St Juvin
Romagne
Aisne
DUN-sur Meuse
Damvillers
Monthois
Fléville
Nantillois
Flabas
Lançon
Apremont
Montfaucon
Autry
Véry
Binarville
Montblainville
Malancourt
Cernay en Dormois
Varennes
Servon
Tahure
Avocourt
Charny
La Harazée
Vauquois
Massiges
Vienne le Chateau
Montzéville
Ville. s. Tourbe
Le Four de Paris
Le Mesnil
Minaucourt
Vienne la Ville
La Chalade
Neuvilly
Verdun
Meuse
Biesmes
Parvis
Laval
Dommartin
Sous-Hans
La Neuville
Chaude Fontaine
Les Islettes
Clermont
Jubécourt
Somme-Tourbe
Valmy
St. Ménéhould
Dommartin
Verrières
Aire
Ippécourt
Beaulieu
Daucourt
Souilly
Le Chemin
N
0 5 10 15 20 kms
German Position after July 1915.

Infantry Brigades respectively, to prepare a general attack, with the aim of gaining control of the French positions to the north of the Dieusson valley.

Preceded by the explosion of four mines, the entire 27th Infantry Division was involved in this attack. An early decision had been taken not to organise a preliminary bombardment and to concentrate on achieving surprise instead. The use of the mines compensated for the lack of preliminary fire and certainly contributed to the necessary shock effect. Instead of providing close support for the infantry, the artillery commander, Oberst Freiherr von Watter, was directed to concentrate his efforts on counter-battery fire. In this he was largely successful, so the French artillery, both during and after the attack, only produced a feeble response. In the event tactical surprise was complete. In the early dawn of a cold winter morning the German assault forces, launching forward over their parapets, which were rimed with snow, as the echoes of the mine explosions died away, were able to overrun the French forward trenches almost without incurring casualties.

On the right flank of 27th Infantry Division, the men of Infantry Regiment 127 rushed across a wide clearing at H Hour, managing to overcome strong resistance in three successive lines of trenches and by 8.40 am were on their objective, the north edge of the Dieusson Ravine. On their right, however, Fusilier Regiment 38, also with three lines to attack, found that their attack stalled some three hundred metres in rear of that of Infantry Regiment 127 and there were some anxious moments until the Württembergers were able to bend their flank back and complete the linkage to 11th Infantry Division, thanks to the assistance of 6th Company Fusilier Regiment 38, which was subordinated to it for the purpose and, in particular, to the courage and initiative of Fusilier Rupprecht, who led a succession of contact patrols through unsecured woods until the line was complete. He was later awarded the Iron Cross Second Class for his work that day and the following night.[1]

To the left of Infantry Regiment 127, Infantry Regiment 120 also encountered problems. The French defenders of the second line trench were strongly dug in and offered determined and lengthy resistance, which was only gradually broken after a lengthy battle with hand grenades. Eventually, however, once there had been approximately fifty French casualties, about one hundred more surrendered, others fled to the rear and Infantry Regiment 120 reached the Dieusson Ravine at about 9.20 am. The Silesian Fusilier Regiment 38 had attacked with great dash, but had encountered unexpected problems on their way to their final objective. They had chosen to spearhead the attack of their 3rd Battalion with 9th and 12th Companies, both optimised for the assault and provided with specialist engineers to throw grenades and deal with obstacles. Organised into three waves, they, too, made swift initial progress but, on the 12th Company front, the defence was conducted with increasing obstinacy. One particular problem was that several of the 'dugouts' were in fact only set back into banks and it proved possible for the French defenders to carry on the fight from their shelter. Dealing with each of these pockets of resistance in turn was time consuming and costly. Nevertheless they were eventually reduced and digging in began immediately.

According to the regimental historian,[2] the greater problem occurred in the sector of

1st Battalion Fusilier Regiment 38, which was adjacent to that of Infantry Regiment 127. Here a mine had failed to explode and, although it was eventually blown, this occurred twenty minutes too late. Not only that, but the mine had not been driven forward sufficiently far and did not explode beneath the enemy trenches. The delay and consequent loss of surprise was fatal. All the noise and commotion had provided the defence with ample time to arrange for machine guns to cover this area so that every time that the assaulting troops tried to get forward, they were met by withering fire and quickly pinned down. Nevertheless, the day was almost completely successful, despite the fact that, gradually, the French artillery brought down increasingly heavy fire on the newly captured positions until late into the night, causing casualties and complicating the business of digging in and consolidating the gains.

Supported by the direct fire of a battery of light field howitzers, Infantry Regiment 124 launched a phased attack, beginning with an assault by its 2nd Battalion on the right [western] flank and followed closely by its 3rd Battalion in the centre. All went according to plan, with the exception of a pocket of resistance, comprising about sixty men commanded by a French lieutenant, which held out in an area of dense scrub and, despite being deeply outflanked on both sides, continued to resist courageously for several hours, until two platoons of 7th Company arrived to reinforce the men of 5th Company and succeeded in eliminating the defenders. Further east the left of Infantry Regiment 124 had an extremely trying day. Their advance was checked by a strongpoint and, although it was eventually reduced, the 3rd Battalion was the last to arrive on the northern edge of Dieusson Ravine.

Despite these various checks, by about mid-morning 1st and 2nd Battalion, together with elements of 3rd Battalion, had pushed forward, pressing the French defenders back to the southern edge of the valley. Some even reached the weakly held outer trenches of the *Central Redoubt* and a party, commanded by Leutnant Rommel of 9th Company, penetrated the entire defensive work, reaching the Servon – Bagatelle Pavillon road, before it was halted. The problem was that this thrust had exceeded the laid down limit of exploitation by a wide margin and was effectively isolated south of the Ravine. Galling though it was, the regimental commander, Oberstleutnant Bader, had no choice but to recall all his forward elements to the northern side of the ravine. It was to be many weeks and numerous hard fought engagements later before German troops reached the same point once more. However, the decision was absolutely correct. As Rommel's men were attempting to cross the Ravine, they were hit in the flank by an immediate French counter-attack, suffering severe casualties in the ensuing hand to hand fighting.

The situation on the 54 Infantry Brigade front was, however, rather different and its commander, Generalmajor Langer, ordered a limited further advance by Infantry Regiments 120 and 127, aimed at securing a line on the southern edge of the Ravine. In order to avoid subsequent confusion, he then informed 53 Infantry Brigade about what was happening. Infantry Regiment 120 was able to cross over without encountering any resistance, digging in on the southern side and the situation was the same for the left flank battalion of Infantry Regiment 127. However, as has already been noted, the problems that Fusilier Regiment 38 was having off to the right made it impractical for all three of the battalions of Infantry Regiment 127 to move south and the bulk of its units remained on the northern edge of the Ravine.

Unsurprising to note, there was a violent French reaction to the entire advance and, by 2.00 pm, attacks were building up against those elements of 54 Infantry Brigade forward of the ravine. Infantry Regiment 120 was soon in trouble, with a distinct threat building up against its open flank facing east. 5th and 6th Companies Infantry Regiment 124 hurried forward across the Ravine once more, but the remainder had to remain on the northern side, so as to counter French troops which were once more active there. Grenadier Regiment 123 on the German left had an altogether easier time of it. Its attack was directed against the upper reaches of the Dieusson Ravine which, with its gently sloping sides, resembled a shallow valley more than a ravine. As a result, progress was generally good and it reached most of its objectives easily.

The one exception was on its right where, close to the junction with Infantry Regiment 124, its 3rd Battalion was confronted by a well placed French strongpoint defended by about four machine guns. Furthermore, French counter attacks during the afternoon caused a temporary withdrawal of its right flank. There were several critical moments, but the two companies most affected, 9th and 11th, held their nerve and beat them all back. Displaying reckless courage during the first of these, one of the platoon commanders, Reserve Leutnant Vogt, stood up in full view of the enemy so as to have a clearer field of fire and fired bullet after bullet from a standing position. This inspired a number of his men to do the same and they held on until a machine gun could be brought hastily into action.[3] By the time the fighting finally died away, the situation had been restored and there was a firmly held junction point between the two regiments.

As a result of the successful, if costly, assault on 29 January, the Germans had worked their way forward about eight hundred metres to the close proximity of the main French line of resistance and had actually managed to reduce the overall length of the front, so it was possible to withdraw some formations, including Fusilier Regiment 38, from the front line and to redeploy them. The Württembergers, however, stayed put. Henceforth the division would be responsible for a sector approximately three and a half kilometres wide facing generally south. On both flanks the German font line was established on the southern side of Dieusson Ravine; in the centre it was to the north of it. From west to east each of its regiments in the order Infantry Regiments 127, 120, 124 and Grenadier Regiment 123 were responsible for a part of the front line. Out to the right of Infantry Regiment 127 was Landwehr Infantry Regiment 83 of 9th Landwehr Division, whilst Infantry Regiment 67 of 34th Infantry Division was located next to Grenadier Regiment 123.

Although the attackers had suffered heavy casualties – those of 27th Infantry Division alone amounting to six officers and 409 other ranks killed and even more wounded or missing, 29 January was a disaster for the defence. The French Infantry Regiments 94, 154, 155 and 161 lost between four and five hundred all ranks killed in action. Over 650 prisoners were taken, together with a large haul of arms and equipment, but the most important seizure was a diagram which showed the main French

WESTERN ARGONNE DEFENCE LINE

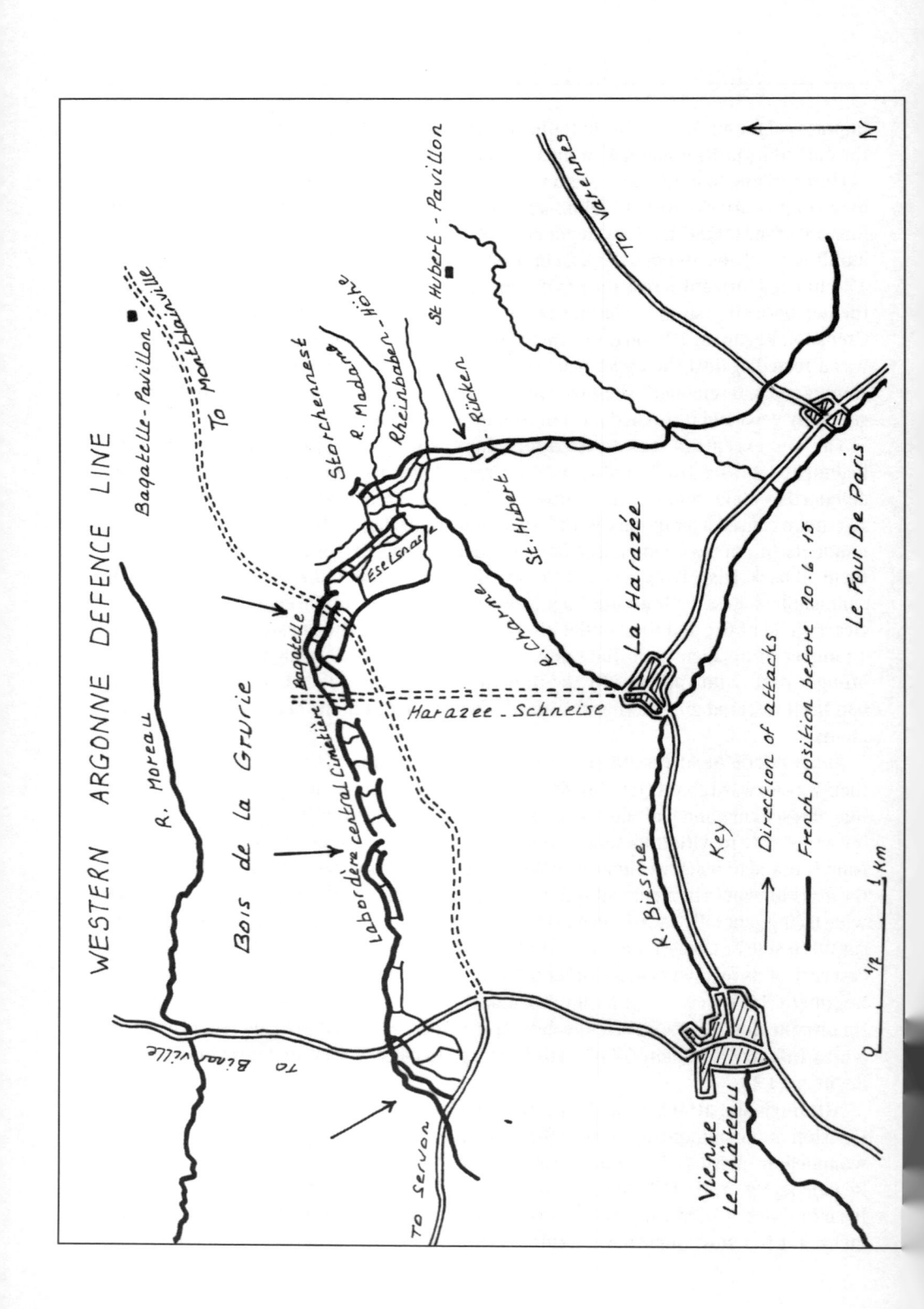

Map labels:
- Bagatelle-Pavillon
- To Montblainville
- R. Moreau
- Bois de la Grurie
- Storchennest
- R. Madame
- Rheinbaben-Höhe
- Rücken
- St. Hubert-Pavillon
- To Varennes
- Esel Lanas
- Bagatelle
- Labordère central Cimetière
- R. Chavane
- St. Hubert
- La Harazée
- Harazée-Schneise
- R. Biesme
- To Binarville
- To Servon
- Vienne Le Château
- Le Four De Paris

Key
- → Direction of attacks
- ▬ French position before 20.6.15

Scale: 0 — ½ — 1 Km

N ←

strong points in fullest detail. Up until that moment their extent, layout and armament had had to be guessed. Now even their French names were known and, from then on, these were also used by the German army. Furthest west, south of the Servon – Bagatelle-Pavillon road, came *Pavillon* then *Labordère/Martin* with *Central, Cimitière* and *Bagatelle Redoubts* stretching away to the east along a ridge.

Once this succesful phase of operations was over in the Argonne Forest, the battles for La Harazée and Vauquois also died away and the incessant small scale actions, primarily directed against the forces of the three divisions, that made up the French V Corps, were gradually replaced by carefully planned attacks on a rather larger scale. Naturally, whilst all this fighting was going on, the French did not stand idly by. To the rear the time so gained was exploited and lines of strong points were further developed until they became field fortifications of the highest quality and the subject of detailed enquiry whenever prisoners were captured and interrogated. It was at this point in early February that the decision was taken to reinforce the sector with formations of 2nd Guards Reserve Division, which had only just been relieved after an extended period of duty garrisoning the line near to Reims. They were swiftly plunged into the unique circumstances of the Argonne and found adjusting to the novel situation difficult.

Reserve Hauptmann A. Grave 3rd Battalion Reserve Infantry Regiment 91[4]

"In the Argonne Forest the companies had to adapt to a method of fighting which was completely new to them. Here what was needed above all was the ability to work away like a mole, because the development of saps – of which there were six in the battalion sector - and mine galleries was the method by which we closed in on the enemy. Although light and medium artillery played a far from minor role, essentially this was war fought at close quarters with grenade launchers, and hand grenades following the blowing of numerous mines. During this type of warfare, very little of the 'Forest' was to be seen. Both trees and undergrowth in No Man's Land were largely swept away, only isolated remnants remaining to bear witness to the earlier natural cover.

"Initially it was far from easy to navigate through the confusion of saps and trenches but, within a few days, we were so familiar with our surroundings that we knew every detail of them. Because of the difficult terrain and in view of the strength of the French positions opposite, it was quite obvious that a very slow advance was all that could be expected and that the battalion could be proud if it managed to maintain its positions and to achieve modest success by moving them forward slightly. The main burden of the battle was carried by the forward platoons in the front line whilst, in order to shield them from the worst of the fire, the remaining platoons were accommodated more to the rear in the old trenches and saps. This provided ample opportunity for some of our brave fighters to achieve distinction through their personal commitment when they beat off unexpected enemy attacks, or managed, through surprise, to wrest a section of trench away from the enemy.

"We were located so close to the enemy that it was almost impossible for the platoon commanders to summon timely assistance from the elements of the company stationed in rear; it was much more the case that they had to take decisions on their own responsibility. Here, pre-war training and practice in independent action proved itself brilliantly. In certain isolated spots we found ourselves occupying the same trench as the French; a situation which earlier we should have regarded as impossible. This often happened after we had attempted to roll up an enemy position and part of a trench remained in their hands. When this happened, both sides rushed to create a sandbag barricade, blocking the trench and leaving only a small aperture for observation. This sometimes meant that we spent days only two to three metres apart.

"In addition to capturing trenches during battles, the battalion gained ground through digging saps and pushing out advanced sapheads. In this way, after a few weeks we had established a new battalion position sixty metres in front of the [existing] front line. The 29th Pioniers, with whom we maintained close relations as brothers in arms, performed sterling service during this digging work. One of the engineer officer, Reserve Leutnant Konrad, enjoyed special popularity. We called him *Der forsche Konrad* [Konrad the thruster] for short."

The closeness of the positions was further underlined by the fact that, even on days when their was no aggressive action, soldiers on both sides kept boredom at bay by throwing stones, empty bottle and similar items at one another. On 17 February, for example, 12th Company Reserve Infantry Regiment 91 was on the receiving end of a stone, with the following note attached to it: *Vous ne baiserez pas les femmes de Paris, bande! Guillaume est une vache, un assassin, un bandit!* [Your gang will never screw the women in Paris! Wilhelm is a cow, an assassin, a brigand!][5] If nothing else, its arrival must have served to lighten the day. In the sector of Reserve Infantry Regiment 77 the separation varied between thirty and 200 metres.

Landwehr Leutnant Onken 1st Battalion Reserve Infantry Regiment 77[6]

"On the left flank of the company the enemy were located at a distance of about two hundred metres; on the right a mere thirty metres. That was the place where one day the trench was completely shot up, burying an unteroffizier and fifteen men who were sheltering in the only form of cover – a natural cavity on the rock. Together with Andreesen and Schönefeld I went across in order to release the men who had been trapped. Avoiding all noise, we crept across to the shelter in the darkness but, because the surface all looked the same, it took us some time to establish where the rock shelter was located. We were unable to call out because of the proximity of the enemy, so we had to make ourselves known by tapping. At long last we received a reply from below.

"Whilst the other two, working as carefully as possible, removed the loose rock, I lay with my rifle trained on the enemy, ready to fire, so as to prevent us from being surprised. I could clearly hear the French as they worked away quietly and whispered to one another. Despite all the care, clearance of the rocks caused a loud noise from time to time. The enemy must have been able to hear this, because they then suddenly went completely silent. Thanks to the inky blackness we could not be seen but, a few minutes later, about twenty shells landed close to us. Fortunately they were all duds, so all was well. We worked on feverishly, twice as hard as before and, after about one hour, all our comrades were safely back on the surface.

"We came across the sentry lying dead behind a spur of rock and elsewhere in the trench another man, his legs broken and one arm smashed, but still alive. The transportation to the rear of this seriously wounded man was indescribably problematic. We had to carry him through narrow places where each unavoidable knock caused him cry out in pain. We attempted to muffle these cries with a handkerchief, because each shriek brought a wild volley of French fire down on us. However we managed to complete the evacuation successfully and we heard later that he had escaped with his life. The dead man, like all the other fallen, was buried in an old dugout by being covered with rocks. We were not able to offer them a more worthy grave. It was almost impossible even to move the wounded to the rear.

"Having hung on in this terrible place for twenty four days, where we did not dare so much as to remove our boots because we had to assume that at any moment the enemy would attack, where we stood permanently soaked to the skin, we were finally relieved by 3rd Battalion and marched – or rather dragged – our greatly thinned ranks for four hours back to the bivouac sites, known as the *Römerlager* and *Hanauer Lager*, where the companies were accommodated separately."

By now the particular conditions of this theatre of operations were forcing both sides to learn and apply new lessons. It was soon found that it was a near impossibility to establish conventional gun lines, so individual gun positions almost became the norm. This was a challenge for the survey teams and put considerable demands on the signallers who had to maintain communications, and those responsible for resupply. Steep sided slopes made the use of standard field guns difficult, so both howitzers and mortars gained in relative importance. Both sides swiftly became extremely skilled in exploiting the geography of the area to dig and develop very strong positions. The French, in particular, concentrated on flanking positions, mutual support, concealed machine gun posts and the like so, although it was possible with care to destroy or neutralise potential objectives, time and again attacks would wither away under fire from unexpected directions, or carefully aimed gunfire directed by concealed and well placed observers.

Throughout the heaviest of the 1915 fighting, the main French positions were located in the Bois de la Grurie, just to the north of the Servon-Bagatelle-Pavillon road, to the west of the minor River Charme. For the most part they comprised individual, heavily fortified strong points, linked by well constructed and deep communications trenches. Along the crest line running west from the area of Bagatelle Pavillon to Servon beyond the outer edge of the wooded area were located four major works: *Bagatelle, Cimitière, Central* and *Labordère Redoubts*. Just south east of *Bagatelle*, from a point in rear of the *Eselsnase* [Donkey's Nose], known to the Germans as the *Storchennest* [Stork's Nest], the defensive line swung away to the south from the so-called *Rheinbaben-Höhe* [Rhinebaben Hill] two and a half kilometres to a point just north of Le Four de Paris, where it led east towards *La Fille Morte*/Hill 285. Behind the *Eselsnase*, the ground dropped away sharply east and southeast into the valley of the Charme, a tributary of the River Biesme, which it joined at La Harazée. There were clear and obvious advantages for the Germans if the French army could be dislodged from these dominating positions. Instead of the French being able to enjoy the benefits of holding reinforced positions on the high ground, they would be forced back onto the dip slopes leading down to the valley of the Biesme

At the western end of the line, where the Vienne-Le Chateau – Binarville road cut through the positions, visibility was quite reasonable. The tree cover was fairly light and had, in any case, been largely shot away, so the lines of French trenches, stepping upwards on natural terraces were clearly visible; the front lines were separated by no more than between fifty and one hundred metres. Further to the east, observation was a major problem. Dense thorny areas, coupled with tumbled trees and rank growth, produced areas which were effectively impenetrable and, according to some reports, reduced visibility to less than ten metres. To make matters worse, at the western end of the sector, the opposing positions were divided by a steep sided, narrow valley, the base of which could not be observed from any of the German positions. Patrols sent forward by the German regiments soon established that the French had created an obstacle belt thirty metres wide in the base of the valley. A high chicken wire fence was reinforced by a broad water filled ditch and an immense tangle of barbed wire. Hidden away behind this obstacle belt and camouflaged by dense undergrowth was a series of trenches, which were laid out in depth and reinforced by pill boxes and concreted machine gun posts. In order to thwart attempts at surprise, advance saps and posts were established in front of the German lines. Work on strengthening these positions and pushing forward tactical mines went on incessantly.

At the end of February a first serious attempt was made by 34th Infantry Division to mount an attack against the French 42nd Division, commanded by General Duchêne. The assault force was found by 68 Infantry Brigade, under Oberst von Sydow, and the objective was ambitious – no less than the capture of ground which would not actually fall into German hands until the end of June. During the planning process the map captured earlier by 27th Infantry Division proved to be extremely useful. In order to close up on the *Bagatelle Redoubt*, Infantry Regiment 67 had to conduct a preliminary operation designed to capture an outwork just to the north of it. The ground dropped away gently towards it, before rising again quite steeply towards *Bagatelle*. Over a period of several days siege warfare techniques were employed and Infantry Regiment 67 sapped down the slope towards their target then, on 28 February, 9th Company

Infantry Regiment 67, under Leutnant Eilers, carried out a smart coup de main strike, which captured a forward mortar baseplate position and a major dugout, some forty metres long.

This success was followed by a confused battle of great intensity which lasted no less than six weeks for the so-called *Hexenkessel* [Witches' Cauldron], a confused mass of trenches down in the valley bottom. The fighting inevitably sucked in reinforcements, including 3rd Battalion Reserve Infantry Regiment 91, whose 3rd Battalion, commanded by Major Lorenz, played a prominent part in the March battles below *Bagatelle Redoubt*. Between 10 and 15 March, 12th Company was deployed right forward and, although its losses were not particularly high by the standards of the Argonne, nevertheless the sheer intensity of the experience was exhausting and nerve wracking for all concerned.

Reserve Hauptmann A. Grave 3rd Battalion Reserve Infantry Regiment 91[7]

"Already during the very first afternoon the company [12th] had a hard time of it. Following a period when it was unnaturally quiet, about 5.00 pm a very heavy bombardment suddenly crashed down on the company position – on the battle trenches as well as the communications trenches and dugouts in rear. Enemy artillery fire came in from half left, half right and directly to the front and, in amongst it, came mortar bombs, grenades and the chatter of machine guns, all intended to knock over or destroy our parapets and our steel infantry shields which had been built in [to the defences]. When to this concert was added rifle fire (which did not cause any damage worth the name) the racket was so intense that we could only communicate by means of sign language.

"The bombs from grenades launchers – aside from the damage they caused to our positions – did not generally pose too many problems for us. The firing signature, which from a distance made a dull sound like a cork popping out of a bottle, was easy to spot. The sentry would shout, *Achtung, Mine!* and we could watch its trajectory as it climbed steeply, but not especially quickly. There was usually time before it impacted to take evasive action. It was rather different on 10 [March], however, because the company position came under fire from five launchers simultaneously, two of them heavy. If an attempt was made to avoid one round, the risk was of moving into the path of another.

"Once our position had been under fire for about an hour, the French infantry launched an attack from a sap. This was aimed at the section of trench between Saps IV and VI. The French came forward boldly but, due to the way some of them were lurching about, a number of our men were convinced that their attacking spirit has been boosted by plentiful supplies of alcohol.[8] There then followed a vicious battle with hand grenades, during which our men performed outstandingly. In view of this heroic defence which, following the earlier thorough preparation, was probably not anticipated by the attackers, not one single Frenchman penetrated our trenches. Instead, after taking a considerable number of casualties, the enemy had to pull back to their starting position.

"Our own casualties were painful: fifteen wounded, some of them seriously and three killed, including Offizierstellvertreter Gerlach. An entry was made in the company war diary, 'In Gerlach we lost a courageous platoon commander who was always faithful to his duty. He will live on in the thoughts of the company. Gerlach has been laid to rest in an honoured and worthy grave in the Argonne cemetery.'[9]"

Whilst this particular battle was being fought, Infantry Regiment 145, reinforced by engineers, sapped forward to *Bagatelle Redoubt* and, once it came so close to the strong point that it was impossible to continue on the surface, it began to mine forward instead. The French immediately spotted what was happening and a period of intense mining and counter-mining involving large explosions ensued at the end of February and into March. Sometimes the effects could be unpredictable, as on 8 March when, following a large French mine explosion next to the Servon – Bagatelle-Pavillon road, 6th Company Infantry Regiment 145, with Hauptmann Henoumont at its head, seized the moment when the French were still under cover, to rush and capture one of their trenches, with barely any casualties, though Henoumont was killed a few days later whilst manning a forward sap.

During a period of several weeks the fighting was particularly intense in the area of the *Storchennest*. This strongly built, square strong point was connected to the west bank of the River Charme by means of a tunnel. All attempts at reducing it having failed, the German sappers resorted to driving mine galleries towards it. Additionally, in preparation for a major attack, a great deal of artillery, including heavy howitzers, was assembled within range and furnished with plentiful supplies of ammunition. Naturally there was a French response and their artillery seemed to have an inexhaustible supply of shells, including high explosive and smoke. The gun fire throughout the remainder of March and into April was so heavy that many men of 68 Infantry Brigade were longing to attack, on the grounds that occurring casualties whilst waiting for the operation felt worse than anything which might happen when they finally went forward.

As the final days of April approached, the winter weather, which had included late frosts and even snow during the past few days, gave way to warmer spring conditions. Winds helped to dry out the ground and the trenches and leaves began to appear on the surviving trees. From 20 April final preparations began for an attack scheduled for 1 May. During an unfortunate incident on 29 April, the Brigade Commander, Oberst von Sydow, and his adjutant, Rittmeister von Beck, were wounded by mortar splinters and command had to revert to Oberst von Wahlen-Jürgas. Despite this setback, preparations continued. The drab greyness of the tortured ground and torn trees and undergrowth also began to sprout new green shoots and spring flowers emerged in all manner of unsuspected places, so softening the harsh outlines of the battlefield and boosting morale. The artillery reinforcements for the forthcoming attacks included the arrival in the forward areas of the entire artillery of 27th and 33rd Infantry Divisions. The object of thus concentrating the gun fire was to aid surprise. A particularly heavy bombardment in the last two days of the month was to increase sharply in intensity on 1 May and was then to reduce slowly from 5.00 pm. The assault was timed for 7.00 pm, but was not to be preceded by a further increase in fire. The underlying aim was to exhaust the defenders during the days leading up to the opening of the attack, then to lull them into a false sense of security on the day.

In addition, there were to be diversionary measures. Twenty minutes before the attack, the neighbouring 86 Infantry Brigade was to pretend to be launching an assault, so as to divert defensive artillery fire then, simultaneously with the main attack, Infantry Regiment 124 was to storm forward against an advanced sap in front of the *Central Redoubt* and Grenadier Regiment 123 was to provide every possible support for the attack of Infantry Regiment 67. 1 May 1915 was a fine spring day and the sun shone down on the battlefield. The clear skies also enabled German aircraft to operate over the sector to be attacked during the afternoon and early evening. This always tended to lead to a reduction in defensive fire as the batteries sought to conceal their exact locations. As the evening sun began to sink, the men of Infantry Regiment 67 and 3rd Battalion Infantry Regiment 145 made their final preparations and prepared to place their assault ladders in position then, at 6.40 pm precisely, in accordance with the plan, a great concentration of fire was brought down forward of the 86 Infantry Brigade front.

As anticipated, every French gun within range retaliated and brought down fire on the rear areas of 86 Brigade. Punctually, at 7.00 pm, 68 Infantry Brigade began its attack, whilst the German guns switched their fire suddenly to *Bagatelle*, *Central* and *Cimitière Redoubts*, as well as communication routes to the rear and known French battery locations, which were so disrupted and confused that it was a full thirty minutes before the actual sector under attack began to be engaged systematically. Infantry Regiment 67, attacking with six companies in the lead, swept through two French lines and even closed up on the third and fourth lines in places, though these had to be yielded once more later. Fighting continued at close quarters well into the night under a starry sky, then the Infantry Regiment 67 sub units dug in along a new line located between the French second and third lines.

Infantry Regiment 145 had a more difficult time of it. Their centre and right butted up against well dug in French troops who resisted fiercely. The assaulting forces were met by a 'hail of hand grenades' and one particular strong point, the so-called *Eiterbeule* [Abcess – clearly an unpleasant place] did not finally fall to Infantry Regiment 145 until 26 June.[10] As a result, when the fighting died away, its right flank was still somewhat in rear of the positions of Infantry Regiment 67, but these points were later connected by means of a trench, which crossed the exposed Servon road by means of a tunnel. The left hand companies, 9th and 10th were more fortunate, capturing two French trenches. At a cost of forty three men killed, two hundred and eleven wounded and twenty one missing, 68 Infantry Brigade inflicted heavy casualties on the French defence, captured over 150 prisoners and numerous machine guns and other weapons.

Because the mines pushed towards the *Storchennest* were not complete, the left forward battalion of Infantry Regiment 145 did not participate in the attack.

Nevertheless Grenadier Regiment 123 supported the attack with fire and one platoon also joined the assault of Infantry Regiment 67. At first glance it might appear that the results were somewhat meagre but the attack was, nevertheless, judged to have been a success. All French counter-attacks were beaten off and 68 Infantry Brigade had succeeded in driving the French defenders back off the crest line, thus denying them direct and easy observation over the German lines. Furthermore the trenches taken by Infantry Regiment 67 were an integral part of the *Bagatelle Redoubt*, so this attack provided a springboard for the later, decisive, attack on the line of redoubts.

While all this activity had been taking place on the western side of the forest, the remainder of the front was anything but quiet. Following unsuccessful attempts to gain ground on the so-called *St Hubert-Rücken* the previous December, during the early part of 1915, men of Infantry Regiment 173, with engineer support, began to sap towards a projecting salient, known as the *Kopf* [Head]. At divisional level, a conference was actually underway on 22 January for an assault the following day when the local engineer commander, Hauptmann Lutz of 2nd Company Pionier Battalion 16, realised that for some reason the French were holding their positions opposite 2nd Company Infantry Regiment 173 with only very weak forces. Quickly the two commanders agreed on a surprise attack.

Leading the way at 10.30 am, a mere five sections of engineers commanded by Hauptmann Lutz[11] and plentifully equipped with hand grenades, rushed the opposing trenches without any form of preparation, overwhelmed the weak resistance with their grenades and pushed on into the second position to the north of the La Harazée road. This courageous operation was witnessed by one of the infantry men waiting to go over the top in his turn.

Vizefeldwebel Wilkens 4th Company Infantry Regiment 173[12]

> "Whilst the divisional commander was at brigade headquarters conducting a conference concerning the operation with the subordinate commanders, the commander of 2nd Company Pionier Battalion 16, Hauptmann Lutz, whose company was deployed in the Infantry Regiment 173 sector, realised that the enemy position directly opposite our 2nd Company was only weakly held and he agreed a coup de main strike with the company commander. At 10.30 am the machine gun built in to the 2nd Company position fired a twenty five round burst then, in a flash, Hauptmann Lutz and five sections of his engineers were in the enemy front line trench. The enemy, who only put up slight resistance, were finished off rapidly with hand grenades. 2nd Company, then 4th and 1st Companies Infantry Regiment 173 followed immediately on their heels and were soon established in the enemy main position north of the La Harazée road."

Not simply content with the fact that 1st and 4th Companies had rolled up all the trenches and were occupying the complete position north of the road, 2nd Battalion Infantry Regiment 173, observing this easy success, also rushed the positions opposite on the *St Hubert* - Position, its 6th Company even getting as far forward as the fourth line of French trenches. 3rd Battalion Infantry Regiment 173 also profited from the confusion to move forward, but had only achieved a modest foothold on the far side of Harazée road before the French artillery began to respond with heavy concentrations of fire. Despite this reaction, at a cost of only nine men killed and about twenty five wounded, the German position was consolidated and held. Almost 250 prisoners, mostly from the French 94th and 162nd Regiments, were captured.

Vizefeldwebel Wilkens 4th Company Infantry Regiment 173[13]

"The attack caught the enemy completely unprepared. As soon as the first grenades exploded in the front line trench we could see that the Frenchmen in the trenches to the rear simply leapt up out of cover and ran away. Because of the weather, the trenches were full of mud, which was knee deep in places. It was completely impossible to make rapid progress along these trenches and for several of the fallen Frenchmen this sticky, clayey, morass became their grave. Our own losses were none killed and twenty four wounded. We captured three French officers and 245 Frenchmen from the 94th and 162nd Regiments of the Line and the 8th Chasseurs. The French had obviously just had a delivery of rations, because there was plenty of freshly sliced meat, white bread and wine on the positions.

"Unfortunately time was too short to enable us to profit fully from these delicious things, because we had to prepare the newly captured trenches for defence with all speed. We had to assume that the French would rally rapidly and launch a counter-attack, especially because shells were already roaring overhead to land in the area of our regimental command post. Here forward, company sub-sectors had already been allocated and our infantry shields which, in the meantime had been brought up, were installed as quickly as possible.[14] Once this was done, the enemy could have turned up at their convenience; they would have been given bloody noses. Immediately after [the shields were placed] the usual items also arrived: primarily digging equipment hand grenades. However, the expected counter-attack did not materialise and so we were able to go on preparing the position undisturbed.

"The first night in the enemy trenches was not exactly comfortable. It was very cold and the French dugouts were in a dreadful state. The few blankets we laid our hands on were crawling with lice. A sharp frost descended during the early morning of 23 January and soon the ground was as hard as iron. Because the attack shortened the line considerably, 4th Company was withdrawn on 23 January from the front line and placed in reserve in the La Mitte Ravine, which was now free of enemy. None of the members of 4th Company who climbed down heavy laden into the ravine that January morning had any idea that this part of the Argonne Forest would provide both home and protection for a long time to come."

As a result of the advance on 22 January, 1st Battalion Infantry Regiment 30, under Hauptmann Nerlich, found itself occupying positions which were at right angles to the remainder of the brigade front and, in turn, this had produced a pronounced French salient in the line between. In order to reduce this salient and to create a more or less straight German front line running away west along the *St Hubert - Rücken*, 34th Infantry Division planned an operation by Infantry Regiment 173 and elements of Infantry Regiment 30, all commanded by Oberstleutnant André, commanding Infantry Regiment 30. All went according to plan, Field Artillery Regiment 69 put down a very short hurricane bombardment and the French position was assaulted. Brief, but stiff opposition was overcome and with the survivors of the French garrison last seen disappearing at high speed into the dense woodland, all the German forward units advanced carefully into line and began to dig trenches which would remain essentially unchanged until the heavy battles of the following June.

Although Hauptmann Roller, commanding 4th Company Infantry Regiment 30, was killed and there were around ninety other German casualties, no fewer than two hundred French dead were recovered subsequently and well over three hundred more were captured. For once there were no French counter-attacks, but the lost positions were kept under heavy fire for days on end. German casualties from this soon exceeded the numbers lost during the actual engagement. Naturally the German artillery joined in these exchanges of fire and, in addition, there was a considerable amount of mining and counter-mining on this front throughout the spring. The very first mine explosions in the Argonne had occurred during the previous autumn, but it was the solidification of the front in early 1915 which gave it its main impetus in this area.

Many of the early mines were dug for defensive purposes, but it was not long before this policy was largely replaced by one of offensive mining, with the aim of unsettling the enemy and providing the shock needed to facilitate the storming of particular defended localities. The consequence was that mines tended to be driven longer and deeper and to be charged with increasing quantities of explosive so, by May, charges as large as 600 – 1,000 kilograms were being placed and detonated. German newspapers often published first hand accounts of action, printing letters written by soldiers at the front and, in June 1915, one such, by an Oberleutnant of Pionier Battalion 29 and concerning a minor, but dramatic, mining incident on the Argonne Front, appeared in the *Vossische Zeitung*, a well known liberal newspaper, published in Berlin from 1721 until it was suppressed by the Nazis in 1934.[15]

"For months an underground war has been conducted; the aim of both sides being to blow the other sky high. On 23 May 1915 our sappers were driving a gallery forward towards the enemy at a depth of fourteen metres when they detected the sound of enemy counter-mining. Unteroffizier Mettin directed that work was to continue in the direction of the enemy gallery. Pionier Entpohl of 4th Field Company of Pionier Battalion 29 from Posen had barely pushed the heading another metre forward when, suddenly, the face gave way and collapsed into the enemy mine gallery. The French gallery was illuminated and, in the light, Pionier Antpöhler spotted two enemy miners. He crawled back swiftly grabbed a gas grenade and threw it into the enemy gallery. It failed to explode, however, so Antpöhler, noting that the French were trying to place a counter-mine, then got an infantryman to give him a pistol. He returned rapidly and fired several shots at the Frenchmen. It was essential to pre-empt the French explosion so, without more ado, Unteroffiziers Mettin and Leshalm rushed back into the gallery, set off the gas grenade with pistol shots to prevent the enemy from doing further work and started placing a large charge in the enemy gallery. After that our own gallery was heavily tamped and the charge was fired. The effect was particularly good because, not only did it blow in the enemy gallery, the trench, which was only five metres from the seat of the explosion, was also wrecked. Whilst the engineers were hard at work underground there was a tense period of waiting above ground. Had the enemy pre-empted our explosion then, quite apart from the loss of our sappers, an important strong point would have been endangered."

All the mining did not lead to any fundamentally decisive results, but it was fought with a fierce intensity in the Argonne and, notably, at the nearby Butte de Vauquois for a lengthy period after the main fighting died away in late 1915, not being abandoned finally for almost two more years.

The eastern sector of the Argonne Forest was the operational responsibility of 33rd Infantry Division. It began the year snarled up in confusing ground on the northern side of the deeply incised Meurissons Ravine, but its task in early 1915 and the focus of all its subsequent activities was to drive southwards and consolidate the line *La Fille Morte* – Hill 285 on the high ground running east from Le Four de Paris. This objective was far from easy to achieve and, for months on end, troops of 67 Infantry Brigade, commanded by Oberst Bacmeister (especially the men of Infantry Regiments 135 and 144, holding the most exposed positions forward on the *Bolante* feature just east of Le Four de Paris) were subjected to torrents of morale sapping shelling, which caused high casualties and was extremely difficult to counter.

Despite constant efforts by all the heavy guns and howitzers of XVI Corps which were within range and the placement of increased numbers of observers on the prominent heights, shell shortages and major resupply difficulties meant that counter-battery fire was fairly ineffective. Infantry Regiment 144 alone had lost ninety nine men killed and more than 250 wounded to French shell fire by the middle of January 1915.[16] The French even had an advantage in trench mortars; the six medium mortars allocated to Infantry Regiment 135 were outranged by fourteen French weapons directly opposite their positions. In the early days of January 1915 all this French fire rose to new heights and, on 5 January, one of the heaviest attacks the French ever conducted in the Argonne, was launched against the southern and southwestern sectors of Infantry Regiments 144 and 135 respectively.

By dint of a desperate defence fought virtually hand to hand, the line held, though not before Infantry Regiment 135 had had to yield ground and then retake it by means of a hasty counter-attack organised with the assistance of Landwehr Regiments 27 and 83. The day ended with the regiment in possession of the *Brode Kuppe* at the southern tip of the *Bolante* feature, but seriously weakened and its companies had to be relieved shortly afterwards by Infantry Regiment 98.

After rest and reinforcement, Infantry Regiment 135 was soon back forward, this time on the *Schwarze Kuppe* in the left forward [eastern] sector of the divisional frontage and very close to *La Fille Morte* - Hill 285. A major attack, involving Infantry Regiments 98 and 135, together with Reserve Infantry Regiments 22 and 23 and Landwehr Regiments 27 and 124, which began on 16 February and aimed to capture the northern slopes of *La Fille Morte*, was repulsed bloodily. The French Colonial Regiments 4 and 5 were on full alert before the attack started and, although some advanced trenches were captured, not only was the objective not achieved, it was also clear to XVI Corps that there was no prospect of success here all the time that the French had superiority in artillery. Only a systematic German build up and a very carefully prepared offensive offered any prospect of success.

Despite these limitations, 33rd Infantry Division showed itself to be more than capable of holding on to its positions, despite numerous French attempts to dislodge it. As early as 17 February a counter-attack was beaten off, establishing a pattern which lasted for months, as winter turned to spring and then summer. 67 Infantry Brigade up on the *Barricade* and *Bolante* features bore the brunt of these assaults, coming under especially severe pressure from 14 – 16 March, when 1st Battalion Infantry Regiment 98 and 2nd Battalion Reserve Infantry Regiment 77, established on the slopes northeast of Le Four de Paris, were in action incessantly for sixty hours. That degree of pressure was never exerted on any future occasion, though there was almost incessant artillery fire which wrecked what was left of the tree cover and vegetation and gradually exposed the contours of the numerous hills and summits right across the Argonne Forest from west to east.

Ever offensively-minded, anxious to move his lines forward where they would be much less vulnerable to carefully directed French defensive fire, the Corps Commander, General der Infanterie von Mudra, continued to refine his plans and complete his operational and logistic build up for a renewed assault on *La Fille Morte* – Hill 285. This was scheduled for 10 May 1915, but the opening of the major offensive in Artois by the French Tenth Army on 9 May put a complete halt to it. All the heavy guns and howitzers which could be spared, together with all reserve stocks of ammunition, had to be transported north immediately to assist the hard pressed I Bavarian Reserve Corps north of Arras, so all non-essential operations the entire length of the Western Front were suspended immediately. By the evening of 9 May, with his forward troops already moving into position, Mudra had no alternative but to call off his attack, knowing full well that he was condemning his forward units to at least several more weeks of attritional gun fire in their exposed positions.

These prolonged periods that the troops spent manning forward positions took a considerable toll on their fighting strength and morale. Month by month in the Argonne Forest, an average of three thousand men were killed, wounded or evacuated sick and, although men returning from wounds or sickness were available to boost numbers, it proved necessary to establish three field recruit training depots at Nouart, Bayonville and Mouzon, which despatched 1,000 – 1,200 reinforcements forward each month to the regiments in the line. In the rear areas, the lack of villages and towns forced the logistic staffs to arrange for the construction of hutted camps, de-lousing stations and bathing facilities in large numbers, not to mention the need to establish a complete logistic infrastructure from scratch. In order to overcome transportation difficulties, an entire network of narrow gauge railways and field tramways was laid down right up to off-loading points behind the front by Reserve Railway Construction Company 7 under Hauptmann Starke. This *Argonnenbahn* was a triumph of improvisational skill and engineering expertise. By the time of the major attacks in the summer of 1915, steam engines were operating the section between Lançon and Charlepaux Mill and from there forward petrol driven locomotives or horses were used to deliver men and materials to the battle area. Without it the entire campaign would have faltered for lack of administrative support.

Despite the setback caused by the cancellation of the attack planned for 10 May, General von Mudra was determined to press ahead with his plans to advance the German positions. Given the pressure on resources, this was far from easy to arrange. Falkenhayn himself cast doubt on the viability of continuing to press in the Argonne Forest but, later that month, having cleared his concept with Crown Prince Wilhelm, Commander Fifth Army, Mudra and his chief of staff, Major Freiherr von Esebeck, travelled to Mezières to make his case in person. The XVI Corps view was that, because of incessant French gunfire, the suspension of offensive operations had not led to a diminution in casualties, that withdrawal was out of the question and that, therefore, the only way to move out of the unfavourably placed positions was to go on the offensive with adequate quantities of artillery and ammunition.

The argument was accepted but, such were the demands of the contact battle in Artois in particular, that even a limited attack in the west by 27th Infantry Division, scheduled for 23 May had to be postponed due to lack of ammunition. An additional plan to use 12,000 gas cylinders to compensate had to be abandoned because the wind direction was completely unfavourable. However, gradually, as the fighting in the north reduced in intensity, the reinforcement and supply position began to improve and, with the arrival on 9 June of a number of heavy howitzers able to fire tear gas shells, preparations for a general assault could begin in earnest. It was decided that the attack would begin on 20 June, with a preliminary attack by elements of 27th Infantry Division and 9th Landwehr Division against the *Labordère Redoubt*. Commander 54 Infantry Brigade, Generalmajor Langer, was placed in command, not only of his own Infantry Regiments 120 and 127, but also the assault force of 9th Landwehr Division and a battalion of Infantry Regiment 124 as a reserve.

Eight heavy, eight medium and four light trench mortars were also placed at his disposal, but the factor that was destined to make all the difference to his attack was the fact that sufficient artillery ammunition was finally going to be made available for the operation. Drawing on all the artillery of 27th, 33rd and 34th Infantry Divisions, together with other reinforcements, the artillery commander, Generalmajor von La Chevallerie, had at his disposal: seventy six field guns, twenty six light field howitzers, six 100 mm guns, nine 120 mm guns, two 150 mm guns and ten 210 mm heavy howitzers. The ten heavy howitzers intended to fire gas shoots were also available and all these weapons and their associated ammunition were hauled into position.

Naturally all these preparations did not escape the notice of the French army, which reacted by reinforcing the sector and packing in ever more troops, despite space limitations in the West Argonne. In addition to the men of the French XXXII Corps, located in the area since January 1915, the newly formed French 125th Infantry Division was redeployed there from a holding area northwest of Verdun, together with the French 150 Brigade, withdrawn from the French V Corps. By mid-June there was little more either side could do to prepare the battlefield and, in the wake of constant skirmishing on both sides, the major battle for this defended locality began in late June 1915. The first phase of the offensive was designed to open the way for the principle attack, which was to be directed against the *Central – Cimitière – Bagatelle – Eselsnase* sector and this demanded in turn, a preliminary operation to capture the *Labordère Redoubt* and the other subsidiary and equally well defended positions along the Binarville – Vienne-le-Chateau road.

The ground over which the attack would be launched could be overlooked clearly by both the artillery and the trench mortar observers and the relatively highly placed trenches of *Labordère Redoubt* could also be seen easily from the Infantry Regiment 120 sector. It was a rather different matter as far as the ground in front of Infantry Regiment 127 was concerned because, it will be recalled, the relative failure of the Fusilier Regiment 38 attack the previous January had left much of the German position stranded back on the northern side of the Dieusson Ravine, which was itself, with its natural and man made obstacles, a considerable check on forward movement. For the attack, Generalmajor Langer split his forces into three distinct assault groups, with the boundary between the right hand Group Stolz and the centre Group Jetter running along the Binarville – Vienne-le-Chateau road.

The aim was for these two groups to push along astride the road to a point where a barricade was in position about 300 metres north of where the Bagatelle Pavillon – Servon track crossed it. The left hand assault Group Breyer was tasked with the capture of *Labordère Redoubt* itself and definite instructions were given that neither *Pavillon*, nor *Martin* redoubt were to be attacked. By 3.30 am 20 June, Generalmajor Langer was in his command post in the Moreau Valley and the first of the German aircraft were already airborne, ready to correct the fire of the guns. Luckily for the German assaulting force, the opening bombardment, which began at 4.00 am with a gas shoot designed to hamper the French gunners and isolate the battlefield, came down on the French trenches just as a relief in the line was in progress. In the grey of dawn of what was to be a bright and sunny day, troops from both the French 55th and 255th Regiments thronged the trenches, so casualties amongst the defenders were correspondingly high, despite the fact that every dug out and natural piece of cover was soon crammed with men seeking cover from the appalling weight of fire.

By 4.30 am the heavy howitzers were pounding the redoubts and the heavy trench mortars joined in, putting down destructive fire. During the next four and a half hours, the gun and mortar fire increased in intensity. At 5.50 am all the remaining heavy and light howitzers, together with all the field guns, poured down fire on the infantry positions and final attack preparations were made. Hundreds of assault ladders were placed in position to aid the climb out of the trenches, bayonets were fixed, hand grenades primed and the engineers made ready to deal with any obstacles which might be encountered. At 8.30 am, the artillery fire increased even further in intensity, a proportion of it having been lifted so as to maintain a dense and almost impenetrable barrage on the rear areas then, at 8.50 am, men of 54 Infantry Brigade from Wuerttemberg stormed forward. Infantry Regiment 120 concentrated on *Labordère Redoubt* at the western end of the attack sector, whilst Infantry Regiment 127, at the cost of high casualties, assaulted the Dieusson Ravine.

The problem for Infantry Regiment 127 was the fact that the geography on their attacking sector was such that the preparatory fire had not been very effective, especially on its right flank. Most of the obstacles were either intact, or very nearly so. Its 1st and 2nd Battalions attacked with two companies leading, with two more from each plus the 3rd Battalion in reserve. Very quickly these leading elements found themselves under heavy and accurate machine gun fire as they struggled to get through the obstacle belt and the 6th Company suffered particularly badly. The situation was slightly easier for 2nd Company, part of the eastern assault group and gradually progress was made, leaving a group Frenchmen tenaciously guarding what became a salient in the German lines as the day wore on. Eventually, calls for surrender having been ignored, 9th Company Infantry Regiment 127, commanded by Reserve Leutnant Müller launched an all out attack on this pocket of resistance at 7.30 pm. Most of the defenders were killed or wounded and about one hundred of them were captured before the position was finally cleared in the late evening.[17]

There were numerous other tense moments elsewhere during the attack. Right at the start, despite the great weight of preparatory fire, there was a great deal of uncut wire protecting the forward French positions. The German assault troops, without waiting for the engineers, simply threw themselves at it. Some became completely entangled and fell victim to French fire, others forced their way through, clothing and equipment torn to shreds and fought their way into the forward French positions, where they were confronted by large numbers of pill boxes, blockhouse and other positions reinforced with concrete. With the artillery fire lifted to the rear, progress was most marked astride the road to Vienne-le-Chateau. Here the preliminary bombardment had been particularly effective and, in one great rush, two lines of French trenches and various barricades had been overcome and the attackers were soon established on the crest line beyond, having captured more than one hundred prisoners.

It was a rather different story in the more heavily wooded sectors, where there was hand to hand fighting for the French front line trenches. Here it was necessary to capture or destroy every single machine gun, pill box, trench barricade individually and sequentially. It was extremely difficult to maintain a cohesive front and the overall tempo of the attack, because the assaulting force was soon splintered into small groups forced to fight their way forward through a confusing maze of totally unfamiliar trenches and saps. The French defenders, operating in a familiar setting, were able to exploit every single tactical advantage that the positions offered and posed formidable problems to the attackers. Nevertheless, courage and determination enabled the Württembergers to make slow but steady progress. At one point a group commanded by Leutnant Sommer forced its way right on to the roof of a blockhouse where, despite being under fire from three sides, it succeeded in suppressing the fire of a machine gun operating within it and killing its crew by firing directly into the weapon slits with revolvers and posting grenades. Sommer was killed, however, at more or less the precise moment when the gun fell silent.

Other groups were less fortunate when, having penetrated deep into the French defensive system, they were isolated, cut off and killed or captured. Elsewhere on the *Labordère Redoubt*, where the defences were particularly strong, an extraordinarily determined attack led by Leutnant Walker succeeded in penetrating the enemy lines in almost company strength. There the thrust stalled, with the small band of men under observation and fire from three sides by the French defenders. Despite being isolated and effectively cut off from all assistance, Walker's men managed to hold out all day long. Finally, at about 8.00 pm, reinforcing companies managed to force their way through on either flank and relieve the intense pressure on the handful of men still on their feet. This type of bloody close quarter battle also occurred at the eastern end of the *Labordère Redoubt*, where two junior commanders from Infantry Regiment 120, Leutnant von Spindler and Fähnrich Kurz, succeeded in gaining the French front line trench, accompanied by a small number of men. They then proceeded to roll up the trench left and right and made significant progress during the day, though, by nightfall, both the leaders were dead, killed whilst encouraging their men to get forward.

As night fell, the cumulative effect of all these small scale actions meant that the greater part of the *Labordère Redoubt* and the entire French defences astride the road to Vienne-le-Chateau were in the hands of the Württembergers of 27th Infantry Division and the neighbouring Prussian Landwehr men. German casualties were not inconsiderable but, during the fighting that day when several French counter-attacks were also beaten off, six machine guns, fifteen trench mortars and grenade launchers, more than 1,000 rifles, together with masses of other trench stores and war materiel, fell into German hands. Seven officers and 627 men were also captured.[18] Some of the prisoners belonged to the relieving French regiment which had only been in the Argonne for a few days and a number were newly joined recruits, one of whom is reported to have remarked to his captors, 'I have only been in the field for three days and here I am a prisoner. Just my luck!'[19]

Because the loss of these key positions threatened the integrity of their entire defensive position, the French reaction was violent and prolonged. For over a week, from 21 – 29 June, the French artillery hammered the captured positions throughout the day and night with ceaseless concentrations of artillery and mortar fire. In addition, there were daily French attacks, supported towards the end of the period on 28 and 29 June by the use of flamethrowers, aimed at recapturing the lost positions, but it was all in vain. Despite the fact that they were under extreme pressure, it proved to be impossible to dislodge the Württembergers from their newly captured trenches. In the wake of the capture of the *Labordère Redoubt* the men of Infantry Regiment 120, having arranged an internal relief of the forward troops, were able to take a moment to pay their respects to those who had fallen in the operation and who were buried in the regimental cemetery.

Reserve Leutnant Wilhelm 5th Company Infantry Regiment 120[20]

"Our fallen had already been moved to the regimental cemetery and were at rest in a mass grave, to which I led the company. In silent prayer we thought about our courageous comrades who fell for the Fatherland."

Wilhelm, in his diary entry, went on to make special mention of some of his other men: Musketier Sieber, 'an excellent soldier', Offizierstellvertreter Mauser and Fähnrich Mauser, of whom he wrote, 'That was a dreadful blow. The brave young lad had held on and delivered even more than he had promised.'

On 30 June it was the turn of the Germans once more to resume their attacks. It was to be a major day of battle for 53 Infantry Brigade. The artillery bombardment began promptly at 5.15 am, achieving surprise, as evidenced by the relatively weak French response then, at 8.45 am, the assaulting troops of Grenadier Regiment 123 and Infantry Regiment 124 (which included one formed from dismounted elements of the divisional cavalry regiment, Uhlan Regiment 19) stormed forward. The front line was captured with barely a pause and almost without casualties. The divisional historian attributed this to especially outstanding work by Field Artillery Regiment 49 and the bold forward placement of two guns, commanded by Reserve Leutnant Beck. This had been achieved by dismantling them, manoeuvring them forward and reassembling them secretly only 150 metres from the *Cimetière Redoubt* [Cemetery Redoubt], from which point they were able to blast precisely predetermined gaps in the defences for the attacking troops.[21]

Another factor of decisive importance for this particular attack was the fact that the intensity of the battle and the enormous weight of artillery fire which had been directed against the positions during the past few weeks had almost totally cleared away the dense woodlands. As a result, for the first time, *Central* and *Bagatelle Redoubts*, the strong points on the *Eselsnase*, the *Storchennest* [Storks' Nest] and the *Rheinbaben-Höhe* were fully exposed to aimed fire. In consequence, the majority of the French trenches were levelled, the dugouts and pill boxes were full to overflowing with dead and wounded men and, in many cases, the entrances were blown in, burying their occupants alive. When the moment for the assault came, however, the French survivors rushed to ready their machine guns and take up fire positions. However, resistance was not maintained for long, once the main assault came in at 8.45 am.

In an early example of how tactics were beginning to be adapted to the current situation, many men of the assault force slung their rifles and moved forward with hands full of grenades and heavy infantry shields which were intended to provide cover whilst new trenches were dug and old ones turned round. There was a fear that the French might make use of their rudimentary chemical–filled hand grenades, so crude wadding masks were worn over mouths and noses. Progress was rapid. In less than thirty minutes the *Central* and *Cimitière Redoubts* were captured. Max Barthel, who subsequently became a well known German working class poet[22] and who served in the Argonne, was present during all the decisive fighting, later writing a very atmospheric memoir of his experiences. He was quick to pick up on the changed circumstances in the short time since the war began.

> "The war had long since altered its appearance. No longer were there mounted attacks, helmet plumes blowing, spear points and swords red with blood and gleaming in the sunlight. There were no colours or standards fluttering in the ranks. The colours of war were now grey, blue, red and black: grey and *bleu d'horizon* were the uniforms, blue-black the steel and the powder smoke and red for the gouts of flame and the blood. Instead of trumpeters, there was the howl of shells, with one single direct hit having greater power than an entire company storming forward in earlier times.
>
> "Rising out of the saps, the assault force stormed forward, racing towards the first position which was to be taken and had to be taken. The strong point, a reinforced field fortification, was completely smashed and ploughed up. Small mortar bombs were landing, there were bangs and crashes and the machine guns hammered away. Steel and fire smashed against the attackers, but the strong point was taken and two officers and 205 men were led off to the German lines as prisoners."[23]

Exploiting forward, Reserve Oberleutnant Bertsch, commanding elements of 2nd and 3rd Companies Infantry Regiment 124, even pursued retreating French soldiers over their Second Line and as far as the slopes leading down to the Biesme Valley. Not to be outdone, the dismounted cavalry assault troop, led by Leutnant Beißbarth, thrust forward beyond the Montblainville – Servon road.[24]

However, these groups were completely exposed to counter action and had to be ordered to fall back to the main position. This was a prudent move. Already as they pulled back they came under fire and a strong French counter-thrust from the direction of Houyette Ravine, when Reserve Oberleutnant Bertsch was shot through the head and killed, as were several of his men. Elsewhere along the line, the *Schwarze* [Black] and *Rote* [Red] Trenches, which made up the first and second lines of the *Bagatelle Redoubt*, were taken, as were the *Storchennest* and the position on the eastern slope of the *Eselsnase*, thanks to excellent fire support from the machine guns of Königs [King's] Infantry Regiment 145 off to one flank.

Once beyond the *Bagatelle Redoubt*, the assaulting troops paused in front of the so called *Grünengraben* [Green Trench], which was the next major French defensive line. During this brief halt, machine guns and a resupply of ammunition was brought forward. Whilst this was happening, German forces to the east on *Rheinbaben-Höhe* and *St Hubert-Rücken*, further south, launched attacks, in some cases on their own initiative. Similar attempts were made later in the day on the western flank, but the French responded vigorously, especially during the afternoon, by means of a series of hasty counter-attacks launched on the *St Hubert-Rücken* a few hundred metres south of *Rheinaben-Höhe*. As evening fell, the fighting died away, with the exception of the battle for *St Hubert-Rücken*, which continued into the night.

On the French side, the seriousness of the situation was all too clear and frenzied efforts went on throughout the night to rally the shattered remnants of their 42nd Infantry Division, to improve their positions and to ensure that the *Grünengraben* was in a fit state to withstand a renewed assault the following day. The German commanders were kept fully informed about these developments, because patrols were pushed forward through the night 30 June/1 July. For the first time the strength of the *Grünengraben* was established exactly and it was soon clear that, equipped at it was a with a belt of wire at least ten metres thick and mutually supporting pillboxes at regular intervals, it would be impossible to attempt to capture it without systematic artillery preparation. As a result, the attack planned for 1 July was postponed by twenty four hours and that day was simply punctuated by minor skirmishes as fighting flared up at places along the line.

Ammunition, rations and water having been transported forward, the morning of 2 July saw a resumption of massed German gunfire, this time directed against *Grünengraben* and the approaches to it from the rear. Fire continued throughout the day then, at about 5.00 pm, elements of Infantry Regiments 30 and 173 stormed forward against French strong points of *Rheinbaben-Höhe* and *St Hubert-Rücken* and threw the defenders out of all their forward trenches. For one eighteen year old member of Infantry Regiment 173, this attack was to be his baptism of fire.

Fahnenjuker Schemm 3rd Company Infantry Regiment 173[25]

"The 'Josephine' Sap acted as the assault trench for my section. Punctually to the second, the assaulting troops leapt up over the steps in the sap head and we doubled across the open ground to the enemy trench, which was about ten to fifteen metres away. Capturing it was not easy matter. The strong and fully alerted garrison reacted violently. The *Poilus* fought hard to save their skins. Hand grenades were flying in all directions, though many of them, being home-made and poor quality, did us no harm at all. Nevertheless, the hand to hand fight went on so long that it became doubtful if our attack would enjoy complete success. However, it had to; there was no going back. We threw even more hand grenades at the French to wear them down. Blood flowed – which it certainly had to. The French would not have given up otherwise. Not until the garrison had been knocked out or pushed back could we dare to take the decisive step of leaping down into the trench.

"'Into the trench', came the order, shouted above the racket and general confusion. There was a single rush and we were soon standing or lying in the trench. The enemy did not miss this moment and fired their 'blue beans' [bullets] at us. Mortally wounded crossing the barbed wire, Ersatzreservist Cornely tumbled headfirst into the trench. Step by step, the trench, which had been plunged into total disorder by the battle with hand grenades, had to be rolled up to the right. The first of the Frenchmen in their new blue-grey uniforms began to surrender. Streaming with blood they were despatched to the rear. The others withdrew to the second trench from which they continued to direct death and destruction [at us].

"An enemy machine gun opened up and our follow up forces would have had a hard time of it had a communication trench not been pushed forward from our previous position. Leutnant Kramer, who was prominently encouraging his men and, as a result was spotted by the enemy, fell but, in the meantime, the company commander, Hauptmann Gröning, had arrived in the captured trench. In order to orientate himself and to be able to give out further orders, he stuck his head up above the cover and this brief look cost him his life. Hardly had the movement caught the eye of a dangerous enemy sniper, than he fell back, hit in the head by a bullet. He died of his wound the following day at Chatel, having regained consciousness only once for sufficiently long to request that he be laid to rest amongst the heroes of his company and battalion in the woodland cemetery in La Mitte Ravine."

By 7.30 pm, though fighting continued until late into the evening, there were no more effective French defending forces on *Rheinbaben-Höhe*. In order to be able to reduce the defences of the infamous *Grünengraben* from the rear, at 5.30 pm a strong contingent, led by Major Freiherr von Lupin, attacked in the direction of the cross roads just to the south of *Bagatelle Redoubt*, whilst two Wuerttemberg battalions under the command of Hauptmann Hausser and Hauptmann Freiherr von Perfall, managed to press further forward to overrun a French dump along the forest ride leading towards La Harazée. The Württembergers finally managed to work their way in rear of the *Grünengraben* and then attacked in an easterly direction, rolling up *Grünengraben* as they went. Virtually surrounded, the French defence was thrown into total confusion, which was further compounded when men of Infantry Regiments 67 and 145 joined in, assaulting from the northeast and east. There could be only one outcome. Those French troops who did not surrender rapidly were shot down and the remainder, the greatest bulk of the defenders, was captured. Only in one small sector did the French, led by the gallant Major Remy, commanding officer 1st Battalion of the French Infantry Regiment 151, continue to resist. Impressed by the gallantry shown, the German attackers shouted offers of surrender for some time, but Remy refused to yield and was eventually killed in a hand to hand struggle against overwhelming odds.

By the end of the day, however, the attack had been successful all along the front line in the Bois de la Grurie. Once the *Grünengraben* and the last of the strong points were in German hands, there was no significant obstacle to a further advance. The whole line then moved forward, encountering no resistance and digging in began once more. The work went on at high pressure throughout the night, so as to be ready for the anticipated

French reaction the following day. However, day dawned with no French attack. For virtually the first time since the campaign in the Argonne Forest began, a success by one side did not generate an immediate response. For some days thereafter there was very little activity. No mines exploded and there was hardly any artillery or mortar fire or other activity from the French army. The experienced *Argonnenkämpfer* had not known anything like it for months, but they profited from the pause to recover from their earlier exertions and to improve their new positions. As the days went by, the front remained sufficiently quiet to permit the withdrawal of 2,000 all ranks from the line. These comprised detachments from all the regiments which had fought between 20 June and 2 July. They moved to a clearing southeast of Lançon on the western edge of the Argonne Forest where, in the presence of the German Crown Prince and a large gathering of senior officers, an outdoor service of thanksgiving, conducted by Pfarrer [Padre] Langhäuser of 27th Infantry Division, was held. This was followed by an address by the Crown Prince, the distribution of over six hundred Iron Crosses and other medals and a march past, during which the strains of the famous *Yorckscher Marsch* were punctuated by the far off roar of the guns.

The victors had certainly earned their day in the sun, because the three days from 30 June – 2 July had produced significant results. Thirty seven officers, including a major and four captains had been captured, together with 2,519 other ranks from three different French divisions. To this human tally must be added more than one hundred grenade launchers and mortars, almost 5,000 weapons of all types, 30,000 hand grenades, not to mention several engineer parks and dumps containing ammunition of all calibres. During the week that followed the bodies of more than 1,500 French soldiers were gathered in and buried. Given the numbers of missing and the likely total of wounded, French losses can hardly have been fewer than about 8,000 on this short length of front. Of considerably more importance, in view of likely French reactions, was the fact that the battle ended with the German attackers in possession of positions sited on high ground which overlooked any possible axis of advance against them. Prisoner interrogation also revealed that the German pressure had also succeeded in fixing French defensive forces in the Argonne even though they were urgently needed for service elsewhere along the front.

The loss of these important field fortifications caused the local French commander, General Serrail, to direct the preparation of a major attack. According to statements of prisoners captured later, this was to have taken place on 11 July to drive in the advanced German positions along the River Meurisson, which flowed into the Biesme northwest of Le Four de Paris. The French intended that the attack would be carried out by the entire V and XXXII Corps, together with other subordinated formations. In all, eight divisions were to have been launched across the full width of the Argonne Forest and the adjacent sectors east and west of the main wooded area. For reasons which are not entirely clear, the operation was postponed to 14 July but, prior to that date, the Germans having got wind of what was afoot, launched their own pre-emptive attack on 13 July. This was a high risk operation. The French positions were strongly held and their artillery, which had been reinforced for their own attack was plentifully supplied

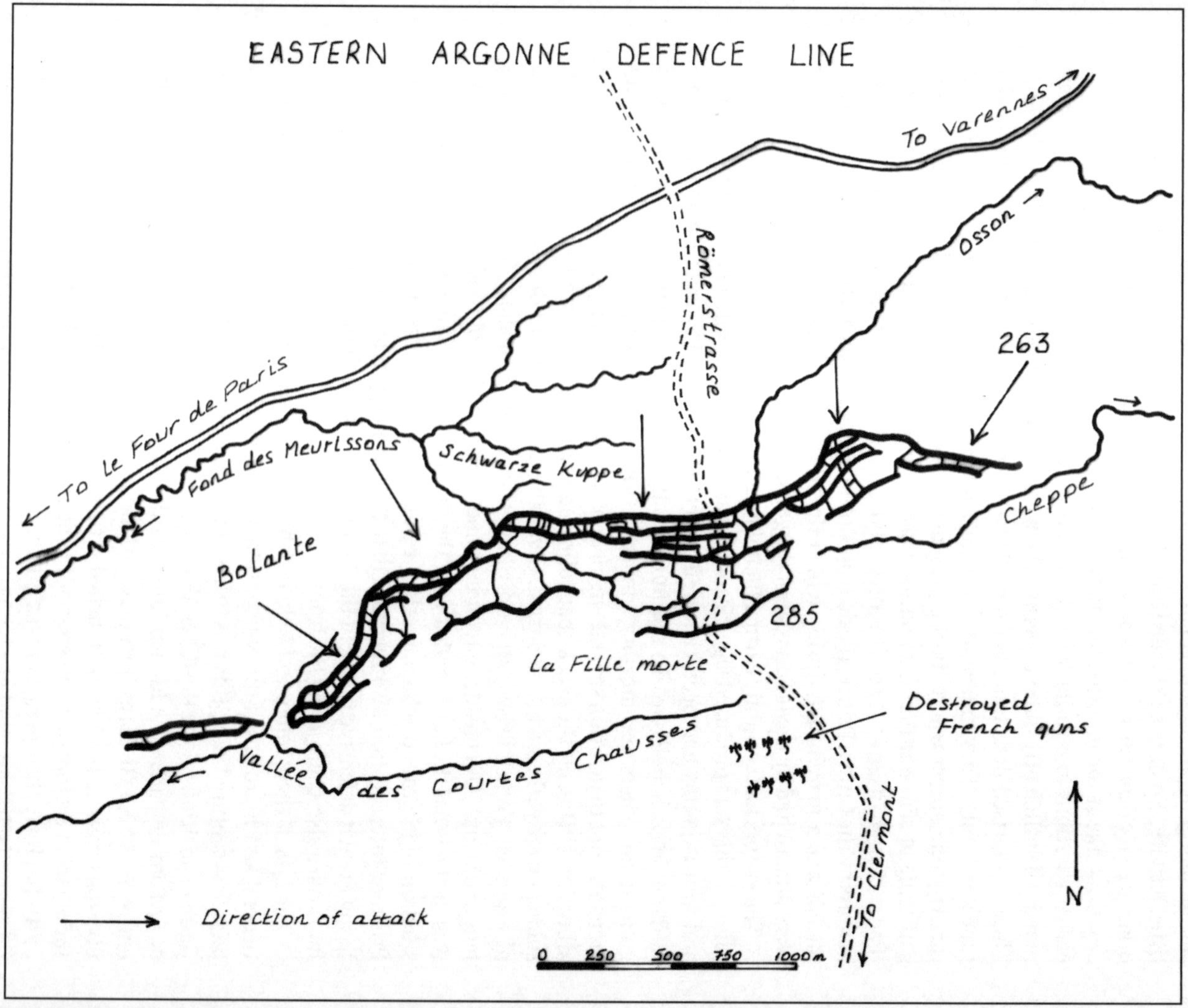
EASTERN ARGONNE DEFENCE LINE
To Varennes
Römerstrasse
Osson
263
To Le Four de Paris
Fond des Meurlssons
Schwarze Kuppe
Cheppe
Bolante
285
La Fille morte
Destroyed French guns
Vallée des Courtes Chausses
To Clermont
N
Direction of attack
0 250 500 750 1000m

with ammunition. There is also evidence that the increased activity of the German artillery and other minor operations meant that there was no tactical surprise and that the French were fully ready and prepared. However, German morale was extremely good following their recent successes, so the new attacks began with high expectations of a favourable outcome.

The main objective of this particular German thrust were the French positions located in an arc from northwest to northeast on the slopes of the dominating Hill 285 – and the adjacent *La Fille Morte*. In this sector the trenches were, on average, only about thirty metres apart and in places were very much closer. Here once more, due to the fact that the ground dropped away to the north from Hill 285, the French defenders had the advantage of height and, consequently, observation over their enemy. Furthermore, the compressed nature of the battlefield meant that their artillery could range in over very large sections of the German rear areas. Once more the vegetation was very dense in the valleys, gorges and the lower slopes of the hills, though shellfire had further thinned the less dense tree cover on the higher ground, which tended to be blanketed with ferns, bracken and tall grass. In an echo of the positions in the Bois de la Grurie, the French positions were based on several lines of trenches dug two to three metres deep in the hard, stony soil and connected by a complex web of communication trenches, which also led to the rear from Hill 285/*La Fille Morte*.

The Germans had managed to assemble well over 150 guns and howitzers to support the attack. A good proportion comprised heavy or super-heavy calibres and twelve of the heavy field howitzers were specifically tasked to fire gas shells. Some idea of the power of this concentration of guns may be derived from this account, written by an anonymous French officer and published in the *Geneva Journal*.[26]

> "During the night Saturday/Sunday the battalion had to occupy the trenches. Because I was suffering from a boil, for the time being I had to remain in the village. During the Sunday, the Germans brought down an appalling bombardment, the like of which I have never experienced. During the afternoon I could wait no longer and I rushed forward to join my company. On the way, I discovered from the flood of wounded men moving to the rear that a German attack was underway. I met up with the Brigade Commander, who ordered me to assume command of elements of another regiment and to go forward. Here and there I came across a few stragglers from my own company and added them to my small detachment. Shells smashed down with appalling crashes right next to us. Three men were killed at my side and eight more were wounded. Spattered with blood, I pushed on over them and went forward.
>
> "I was to retake a position on the left flank where a terrible gap had been punched in our lines and I was also directed to establish contact with a battalion, which was supposed to be located out to our left. I spent the entire night trying to link up, but without success. The battalion had simply disappeared. The following day I tried to collect together the remnants of my company then took command of them. With the aid of their dreadful artillery,

the Germans had succeeded in punching through one corner of our defences. That was the precise place where the battalion which had disappeared had been located, together with one of our own companies."

The plan for 13 July was to bombard for some three and a half hours from 4.30 am, then the left flank formation of 33rd Infantry Division, 66 Infantry Brigade, was to launch forward to take Hill 263, followed later by a more general advance across the entire attack frontage, whose objective was to carry out a wide encircling manoeuvre against *La Fille Morte*. It was a highly ambitious plan and its execution proved to be both difficult and testing for all involved. Day dawned on a cool and rather damp morning. In the German trenches some individuals risked being hit by their own stray shells or flying fragments to look out over the parapets and reassure themselves that the bombardment was having the desired effect.

One of the men present who witnessed the events of the day was Max Barthel.

"13 July', he wrote later, 'dawned cool and overcast. The sun broke through about midday and it rained in the evening. The attack was still being directed against Hill 285, which dominated the Forest. The aim was to push to line forward simultaneously over *La Fille Morte*, the *Bolante* and the Charmes Ravine, so as to make it more secure and shorten it. The upper Meurisson Valley, Hill 285, *La Fille Morte* and the *Bolante* feature were soon one great mass of crashes and smoke clouds, as the guns came into action with unparalleled violence. Gas shells fumed and, from Baulny, the heavy howitzers sent their roaring shells off on their long journey to the long suffering forest. The first guns opened up at in the early hours at 3.00 am then the heavy howitzers began to range in at 4.00 am. By 4.30 am every gun and mortar was firing and, at the same time, mines went off.

"The Frenchmen were on full alert, waiting for the attack. Their artillery had been reinforced and air reconnaissance had reported fresh troop movements from the camps at Clermont and St Ménéhould. The French were well aware what was at stake. Fire drummed down on their positions, came down on the little villages along the Aisne and the Aire and interdicted all the approach routes. Near Lançon in the valley of the Aisne, a huge captive balloon was aloft, swaying like a giant yellow sausage in the morning wind, but it was not in the air for long. Three French aircraft with growling engines approached from Clermont. They circled to gain height, then dived to attack the balloon with bombs and machine guns. The anti-aircraft guns barked and sent shrapnel up into the air, but the aircraft continued to close in through the defensive fire. The balloon had to be hauled down and was not launched again throughout the day."[27]

Shortly before 8.00 am gaps were blown in the French wire, but it still proved to be extremely awkward to negotiate. Nevertheless, within ten minutes of the start of the operation, the first three lines of trenches had been overrun. Intense local fighting by

Infantry Regiments 98 and 130, supported by Jäger Battalion 5 from Silesia, was widened when, at about 11.30 am, the artillery fire lifted to the rear a more general advance, supported by flamethrowers, was launched. Thanks to the preliminary operation the enemy were unable to threaten the flank of the main assault. From their start line hidden amongst shell craters and a maze of old trenches, the men of Infantry Regiments 135 and 144 charged forward, hand grenade teams to the front. It was extremely hard going, despite the fact that in one place two sappers, Vizefeldwebel Bansamier and Unteroffizier Tuttenuit, had managed to crawl forward and place a very large charge in close proximity to the French lines. In addition, throughout the day artillery observers made enormous efforts to get into positions where they could adjust fire in support of the hard pressed attackers and in three places, Leutnants Kayser and Fritsche, together with Offizerstellvertreter Bock, continued to man sap heads only a few metres from the enemy positions and calmly to adjust gun fire onto each succeeding threat.

Just to the west, forward troops of 86 Infantry Brigade of 34th Infantry Division were able to observe all the early heavy artillery fire as they waited for their own signal to attack.

Vizefeldwebel Wilkens 4th Company Infantry Regiment 173[28]

"Dawn had hardly broken – it must have been around 4.00 am – when, off to our left in the 33rd Infantry Division sector, in the direction of *Bolante* and Hill 285, the stillness of the forest was rudely broken. Heavy detonations shook the air and echoes rolled strongly through the woods. These were not mortars or mine explosions. In fact it was the sound of a battery of 305 mm coastal guns, located away to the rear of the forest in Baulny, ranging in. After about half an hour, extremely heavy mortar and artillery fire joined in all along the front. Soon the French artillery was responding and then the entire witches' sabbat was in full swing. In amongst all the spitting, crashing and roaring, the entire forest shook and boiled from end to end in every nook and cranny. The high pitched clang of exploding shells was mixed with the duller thuds as mortar bombs exploded. The storm lashed soil of the forest floor was thrown high into the air. Yellowish-grey clouds of fumes hung over all the positions and the ravines. There was no small arms fire whatsoever; at that moment the floor belonged to gun and mortar fire.

"The assault began at 8.00 am in our sector. Just before that the preparatory fire reached a peak of intensity. Immediately to our right two heavy trench mortars lobbed their barrel-like projectiles in high curving arcs into the enemy trenches, where they exploded with ear-splitting crashes. Flamethrowers had been readied in a number of the sap heads, ready to open up at the predetermined start time. As the minute hand moved ever closer to 8.00 am, the tension increased even more. Would it go well? Would I come through in one piece? Would the enemy trenches be heavily defended? These thoughts occupied all of us.

"Then came the destructive streams of fire from the flamethrowers and, under the cover of their black smoke, the first volunteers, amongst them Unteroffiziers Göring, Westermann and Wieger, together with Musketier Lukaschewski, rushed the enemy trenches opposite. There were dull thuds from the hand grenades, then all was quiet once more. Apparently the flamethrowers had done their work well ... we pushed on; there was no time to lose. Off to our right Infantry Regiment 30 was heavily engaged in a battle with hand grenades. To our front the sector was free of enemy and we succeeded in pushing on to where the wood became denser. Some time later, we managed to link up [with our neighbours] and the company commander, Leutnant Schweigert, came up to us and designated the line of the new trench."

Back on the 66 Infantry Brigade front, the improvised mine placed by Vizefeldwebel Bansamier and Unteroffizier Tuttenuit was exploded promptly at 11.30 and the shock it produced, coupled with extremely effective artillery fire from the guns in support of 67 Infantry Brigade, meant that once the remaining uncut wire had been dealt with by the German engineers, the first French trench was taken almost at a run, with very little resistance. Fire continued to be brought down close to the advancing infantry which helped to neutralise the defence further. One shell landed right in a large underground storage dump which was full of hand grenades. The resulting explosion could be heard all over the battlefield, despite the generally deafening sound of the fighting then, later, a second heavy shell pierced the overhead of a major French dugout. When it was examined the following day, it was found to contain the bodies of 105 French soldiers, all killed by the blast.

However, by the time the third and fourth lines were reached, French pillboxes had to be taken one by one which was no easy matter, given the mutual fire support they enjoyed. One particular difficulty was caused by the undetected presence of a French blockhouse, which featured a protected machine gun firing point and commanded a long, straight communication trench leading to it. The application of minor tactics overcame this obstacle eventually and 14th Company Infantry Regiment 130, together with two platoons of Infantry Regiment 135 under Reserve Leutnants Kummer and Hirche, neutralised the fire, but not before the brothers Schauß (both Leutnants and platoon commanders with 14th Company Infantry Regiment 130) had been killed and their company commander, Landwehr Rittmeister Thiele, had been wounded. So high were the losses that the length of trench was subsequently renamed *Totenallee* [Avenue of the Dead].

Even after this position was finally taken, it proved necessary to get close enough to each blockhouse in turn to be able to post hand grenades through the firing slits. This proved to be extremely problematical, because the whole position was a completely confusing maze of trenches and assorted obstacles. At one point, confronted by heavy fire from one particular blockhouse, one of the young Jäger officers, Leutnant Freiherr von Marschall, with complete disregard for his personnel safety, rushed forward and leapt over a low wire entanglement, said to be four paces wide. Suitably encouraged, his men followed him and in short order the blockhouse, which contained two firing machine guns was knocked out, together with all its occupants. Despite successes such as this, French resistance remained generally very obstinate and determined. German losses mounted and units and sub-units became increasingly intermingled but, finally, at the price of high casualties, significant progress was made and 3rd Coy Jäger Battalion 6, commanded by Reserve Leutnant Englisch, having managed to storm the heights and not realising that they had already gone beyond the summit of Hill 285, pushed further to capture one heavy and four light guns of the French artillery.

Despite the fact that French troops could be observed massing for an attempt to retake the hill, rapid attempts were made to move these weapons to the rear, but this proved to be impossible because they were too heavy and too well dug in, so the attackers set about the sights, breech mechanisms and other ancillary items with spades, picks, axes and hammers and so reduced them to unusable wrecks. Jäger Wistoba and Oberjäger Broll did further damage to them by placing hand grenades down the barrels, then Broll, throwing grenades into an ammunition dugout as a French counter-attack force closed in, set off an enormous explosion. The survivors of 3rd Company then raced to the rear to rejoin the remainder of their battalion, who were already digging in determinedly on the crest of Hill 285, escaping only moments before the French infantry arrived on their former position.[29] In another place, drawn to the point by the sound of a motor driven compressor, forcing air into underground workings, other Jägers smashed up the machinery, rendering it unusable and hampering further mining efforts for the foreseeable future.

Max Barthel, having changed the names of those responsible in his lightly fictionalised account, recorded:

> "He then took up a grenade, prepared it for throwing and rolled it in to the still hot barrel of the first gun. Graf grabbed his pick and smashed a sight mechanism. That was the signal to the tiny assault group to launch a lightning quick orgy of destruction. There they were, right next to the enemy, only it was the guns that were the enemy; the guns which, even on quiet days, made their life hell with their eternal concentrations of fire. They vented their spleen on the guns, just as the Silesian weavers in the Eulengebirge had reacted with violence against the first weaving machines. They rolled hand grenades down the glistening barrels, until the French began to bring down mortar fire in the hollow. The red-bearded Graf then blew up an ammunition dump before pulling back with his men. The smashed and useless guns remained where they were between the lines."[30]

Other attacking forces also enjoyed success that day. 1st Battalion Infantry Regiment 135, commanded by Hauptmann Wegener, did extremely well during the storming of *La Fille Morte*. Charging forward, the unit had to deal with an extremely strong position, the so-called *Stein-Festung* [Stone Fort]. Thanks to the initiative of the commander of its

2nd Company, Reserve Leutnant Breithaupt, who led his men around to a flank, making full use of the dead ground, and who assaulted it from the rear, this potentially major obstacle was dealt with most expeditiously and the advance continued, despite the desperate defence mounted at certain points by the French troops. In one particular instance, to which Infantry Regiment 135 later paid tribute, a single French officer - assisted by a French soldier who loaded rifles for him - manned the junction of two trenches and held up their advance for a considerable time by the simple expedient of shooting every single German soldier who came within range. Eventually a well directed grenade dealt with him and the battle along a maze of old trenches and shell holes could continue. By 3.00 pm 1st Battalion Infantry Regiment 135 had forced its way through the Meurisson Valley and, having overcome three more heavily defended localities, was digging in behind the northern slopes of *La Fille Morte* by 4.00 pm.

The subsidiary battle for the area round St Hubert-Pavillon was also hard fought, frequently at extremely close quarters, but it was ultimately reasonably successful, though at high cost.

Fahnenjunker Armin Fielder 8th Company Infantry Regiment 173[31]

"To leap out of trench, throw ourselves down and crawl as quickly as possible into the crater was the work of an instant. I could already hear the Tac! Tac! of the French machine gun. I leapt up once more and hurled myself down into the French trench, landing on my feet. Another man jumped in behind me – it was Fähnrich Kürsten, who also had no idea that this French ceremonial staircase would be quite so steep. Others began to arrive with, at their head, Unteroffizier Nöding, the best hand grenade thrower in the company. We then went through the French first position without a pause. Every shelter and dugout was peppered with hand grenades and we stormed on. Kürsten disposed of a sandbag barricade and on we went through the enemy trenches, rolling up traverse after traverse with hand grenades. We did not ignore the dugouts. [Under fire from another barricade], Nöding, the hand grenade unteroffizier, fired back and I emptied my magazine as well.

"An entire French section put their hands up and called out, 'Pardon, Camarades' [*sic*]. We ceased fire and closed up on the men, half hidden behind the sandbag barricade. Just then Nöding spotted a Frenchman bringing his rifle into the shoulder. Like a madman, Nöding rushed at this treacherous individual with huge strides and hit him so hard on the skull with a hand grenade that his left eye was knocked out of its socket and hung down his cheek. Jabbered, pleading apologies from the other Frenchmen dissuaded us from taking further action and, in this way, a well set up group of Frenchmen, an officer amongst them, laid down their weapons and headed off to captivity guarded by two or three German soldiers.

"As we advanced, we rounded up numerous other Frenchmen from their dugouts. We had to advance well beyond the line we had been ordered to reach, because we could get no reply from the right to our loud shouts of *Hurra!* Then, suddenly, we came under machine gun fire from a traverse. Ducked back in a recess in the trench wall, I shouted for sandbags to block the gap and these were thrown to me by a grenade team. Having built them up to half the height of a man, we topped this with a protective steel shield and left a sentry on guard. We then advanced to the side along the trench. At this point I met up with Offizierstellvertreter Werner and a few others who had broken through to link up with us. I briefed him on the current situation and requested his assistance to circumvent the problem.

"There could be no question of advancing along the blocked off sap because it was dominated by the French, who had installed a machine gun behind a sandbag barricade. Werner, however, would not listen. Shouting 'Follow me!' he leapt over the low barricade, followed by one other man and they went thus to their deaths. Caught between the German and French stops, they both fell to the ground, mortally wounded, within a few paces. A full blown duel with grenades then broke out between us and the French. Most of the French grenades landed on or around our daring comrades, where they exploded. We were filled with fury, but we could do nothing to alter what had happened, we were up against a solid blockage. In addition I realised that our casualties were gradually mounting. 'Where was Gonnermann?' I asked, but received no clear reply. I had seen him in a shell hole near the Nora [sap] as he urged on his men and threw hand grenades at the one French machine gun that was firing ..."

In fact Leutnant Gonnermann had been blown up and wounded by a shell, taking no further part in the attack after the first trench had been reached. It was left to the others of his platoon and company to consolidate their gains.

Off to the eastern flank of 33rd Infantry Division, where Infantry Regiment 130 were engaged, there was also hard fighting until, after a sustained assault, its 1st Company succeeded in making a breach in the line and then rolling up a series of pillboxes, capturing the occupants and making off with large quantities of arms and equipment. Finally, between 1.00 pm and 3.00 pm, the crest line was secured by men of 4th Battalion Infantry Regiment 98 and 1st, 2nd and 3rd Battalions Infantry Regiment 135. Throughout the afternoon, one counter-attack after another was launched against Hill 285, but all were beaten off by the combined efforts of Jäger Battalion 6 and Infantry Regiment 144. Following a hurricane bombardment by heavy guns firing large quantities of ammunition and a concentration of gas shells, at approximately 4.30 pm an entire French battalion of its 72nd Regiment hit the position of 8th Company Infantry Regiment 135 but this, too, was defeated with serious losses. To the east of the *Römerstrasse* [Roman Road] initial progress had been extremely slow but, seizing the initiative, Leutnant Johansen and a group of men from Jäger Battalion 6, launched a quick attack on the flank of the French position, which was being frontally assaulted from the west by Infantry Regiment 130. The defensive position crumbled quickly and, five hundred metres away, Leutnant Richterlein and 1st Company Infantry Regiment 130 managed to take advantage of the relative confusion to storm the French position and capture several blockhouses in quick succession. Although artillery and mortar fire continued into the night, by evening there was quiet satisfaction in the German ranks that the objectives of the day had all been achieved. The crest Hill 285 – *La Fille Morte* had been taken and was firmly under German control. Furthermore almost 3,500 prisoners had been captured, together with some small calibre artillery pieces, over thirty machine guns, fifty grenade launchers and countless quantities of ammunition. Infantry Regiment 135 alone buried 1,000 French corpses, though it had itself lost 200 all ranks killed or missing and well over 600 wounded.[32]

Altogether, by mid-July, the fighting of the past four weeks since 20 June had led to the capture of 116 French officers and more than 7,000 other ranks. 4,000 bodies were counted so, together with likely numbers of wounded, the French casualties must have approached 20,000, a very large number considering the compressed nature of the battlefield and the relatively small numbers of formations engaged. German survivors were united in their admiration for the performance put up by the French defenders in the period leading up to and including 13 July. In the context of the long drawn out slogging match which best describes operations in the Argonne Forest, they were quite certain in their own minds that they had achieved a clear cut victory that day. It came as a distinct surprise to General von Mudra and his men when it became known that the Parisian Press Agency had reported recent events as follows:[33]

> "The army of the Crown Prince has gone on to the offensive once more and has suffered a fresh setback. The enemy who gained a temporary lodgement in our front line trenches was ejected at once by means of our immediate counterattacks. In no case did the German advance exceed four hundred metres. Point 285, which the enemy held briefly, was recaptured at once by us."

In fact the French never retook any of the lost positions along the crest line and the advance had averaged seven to eight hundred metres. No wonder that some German wags joked, 'A few more setbacks like that and we shall soon be in Paris!' The King of Württemberg paid visit to the men of 27th Infantry Division a few days later to congratulate them on their performance and the Corps Commander, General von Mudra, published his own laudatory Order of the Day[34]

> "Wherever we needed to sweep the French away, there they were made to yield the field. That you all – like your comrades two weeks ago – proved once more on 13 July! I will not mention especially any particular formation, arm or service; my pride and satisfaction, for your energetic dash going forward; my thanks and recognition are due to all whom, wielding an iron brush, cleared out the trenches along the Cheppe river, on *La Fille Morte*, the *Bolante* and St Hubert-Rücken. You have blown the German Argonne March on an iron trumpet at the French. Above all, your victory on 13 July demonstrates your

superiority over the enemy. Wherever you press, breaches and gaps form! That is the way it is going to stay. I know my *Argonnenkämpfer*!"

The language may have been somewhat over the top, but Mudra was right about one thing. The recent battles had improved the German situation in the Argonne Forest enormously. His men may not have physically cut the railway line to Verdun, but they had denied the use of it to the French and they were holding crest line positions which, apart from degenerating into a moonscape of craters, were soon developed to the point of impregnability. The loss of the use of the railway line would be keenly felt the following year as the French army struggled to maintain and supply the defence of the symbolically vital town of Verdun. As the summer wore on and turned to autumn and then winter, the intensity of operations died away, but did not cease for many months to come, by which time most of the main participants, including the corps commander, appointed to command Eighth Army in November 1916, had been moved elsewhere. Thereafter, activity along the Argonne front was confined mainly to mining and counter-mining. This lengthy and unparalleled campaign, during which – and in contrast to the situation elsewhere on the Western Front at that time - the German army was permanently on the offensive, also produced one lasting reminder of the incessant fighting: *Argonnerwald um Mitternacht* [In the Argonne Forest at Midnight], became one of the most popular and widely sung German soldiers' songs of the war.

Notes
1. Burchardi: History Fusilier Regiment 38 p 435.
2. *ibid.* pp 77-78.
3. Bechtle: History Grenadier Regiment 123 p 39.
4. Kümmel: History Reserve Infantry Regiment 91 pp 132-133.
5. *ibid.* p 139.
6. Wohlenberg: *op. cit.* pp 87-88.
7. Kümmel: *op. cit.* pp 141-142.
8. Accusations that Allied troops advanced under the influence of alcohol appear constantly in the German literature. It is impossible, therefore, to judge how credible this statement is.
9. Offizierstellvertreter Rudolf Gerlach is buried in the German Cemetery at Consenvoye Block 3 Grave 1356.
10. Schmidt: *Argonnen* p 153.
11. Unfortunately Lutz, to whose initiative this success can be squarely attributed, was killed only ten days later by a stray shell splinter as he was supervising a routine task at an engineer dump.
12. Kalbe: History Infantry Regiment 173 pp 29-30.
13. *ibid.* pp 30-31.
14. These steel plates, which were equipped with a rifle slot, still turn up on the battlefields of the Western front and are usually (and erroneously) referred to as 'sniper shields', were standard issue in the trenches. Placed alongside fresh diggings they provided useful protection against direct fire, even when trenches were still only partially dug and parapets were incomplete.
15. Baer: *Der Völkerkrieg, Siebenter Band* p 192.
16. Schmidt: *op. cit.* p 160

17. Schwab History Infantry Regiment 127 p 46.
18. Baer: *op. cit.* p 177.
19. Schwab: *op. cit.* p 46.
20. Simon: History Infantry Regiment 120 p 23.
21. Deutelmoser: History 27th Infantry Division p 30.
22. Max Barthel (1893-1975) was born to humble parents in Dresden and lived in poverty once his father died when he was only eleven. He left school early and years of low grade, ill paid work and wandering followed, during which time he got to know a number of important social democrats. He was in Stuttgart when the war broke out, was called up and served as a soldier from 1915 – 1918. Having fought in the Argonne, he was seriously wounded in 1916 and the same year published his first book of poetry: *Versen aus den Argonnen*. After the war, he flirted briefly with communism in Stuttgart, but split from it in the early 1920s, remaining a life-long social democrat thereafter. Heinrich Lersch, Karl Bröger and he formed a trio of working class poets, well known for their strong views. In later life he became a prominent pacifist, a prolific writer, poet and playwright. Though he never joined the Nazi Party, his apparent links with organs of the Nazi state when he was working as a journalist, forced him to leave the Soviet Zone of Occupation after the Second World War and later defend his record in court. His contribution to Twentieth Century literature was recognised shortly before his death and he was awarded the *Bundesverdienstkreuz* by the Federal Government in 1974. His short book, *Sturm im Argonner Wald*, is a very lightly fictionalised and atmospheric account of his service on that front.
23. Barthel: *Sturm im Argonner Wald* pp 44-45.
24. Wolters: History Infantry Regiment 124 p 32.
25. Kalbe: *op. cit.* pp 60-61.
26. Baer: *op. cit.* p 192.
27. Barthel: *Sturm im Argonner Wald* pp 49-50.
28. Kalbe: *op. cit.* pp 71-72.
29. Schwarte: *Der Weltkampf um Ehre und Recht* p 252.
30. Barthel: *op. cit.* pp 58.
31. Kalbe: *op. cit.* pp 73-74.
32. Müller: History Infantry Regiment 135 p 40.
33. Baer: *op. cit.* p 188.
34. *ibid.* p 188.

CHAPTER 6

The Autumn Battles in Artois: Arras and Loos

From early September, there was no doubt in the minds of the German Supreme Army Command that the Allies were planning a major offensive on the Western Front. With each passing day the indicators increased in number. It had been clear weeks earlier that a large scale assault was being planned against Third Army in Champagne and, as the days passed, the intention to conduct operations simultaneously in Artois also became obvious. A gigantic pincer attack was to be conducted by sixty six divisions, supported by 5,000 guns, with a mass of cavalry poised to exploit any breakthroughs, aimed at excising the massive German salient in northeast France and bringing the war in the west to a decisive conclusion. Just as during the previous spring, the French army bore by far the greatest weight of the planned offensive. Events in Champagne will be considered separately in the next chapter and the French operations in Artois have been described elsewhere[1] so, whilst the brief description which follows is intended to remind the reader of the overwhelming importance of the French contribution in Artois in September and October, the primary focus of this chapter is the German perspective on what the British subsequently named the Battle of Loos.

A secret order signed by Joffre on 14 September, which was captured by a unit of Third Army down in Champagne and circulated in translation to all German higher headquarters, made clear what the aim of the offensive was and what was at stake for the Allies that autumn.[2]

> "To go over to the attack in the French theatre of operations is a necessity for us, in order to drive the Germans out of France. We shall not only be able to liberate our downtrodden fellow countrymen, but also deny the enemy his valuable possession of our occupied territory. In addition, a brilliant victory over the Germans is bound to convince neutral states to decide in our favour and force the enemy to slow their progress against the Russian army in order to counter our attacks ... Now is an especially favourable time for a general offensive. For one thing the Kitchener Armies have completed their arrival in France and, furthermore, during the past month, the Germans have withdrawn troops from our front in order to employ them on the Russian Front. The Germans have only meagre reserves behind their thinly held positions.
>
> "The offensive will be a general one. It will comprise several large-scale and simultaneous attacks on a very wide front. The British troops will participate with significant forces and the Belgians will also involve themselves in offensive operations. As soon as the enemy is shaken, forces on quiet parts of the

204 THE GERMAN ARMY ON THE WESTERN FRONT 1915

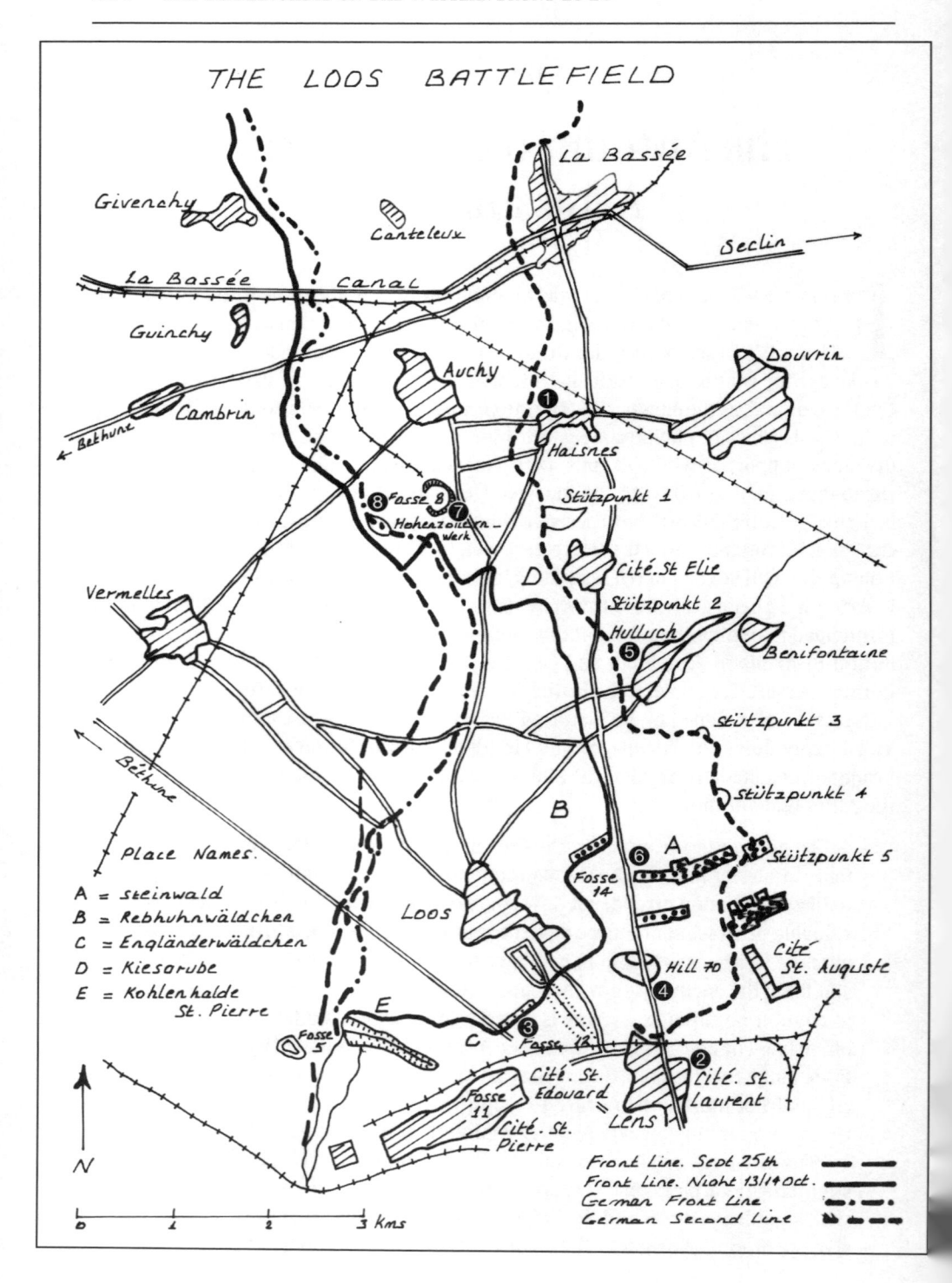

front will also attack in order to add to the confusion and then bring everything to a successful conclusion. For all attacking troops, it will not just be a matter of seizing the front line enemy trenches, but of thrusting forward without ceasing, day and night, to take the second and third lines and break out into open country. All the cavalry will participate well forward in these attacks in order to exploit the success of the infantry. The simultaneous nature of the attacks, their power and extent, will prevent the enemy from concentrating their infantry and artillery reserves in one place, as they were able to north of Arras.[3] These arrangements will guarantee success."

Although the attacks on the British part of the front began in the early morning, the French sector, despite the drum fire which was coming down, was giving no particular cause for alarm until the late morning of 25 September. This meant that, in view of the extremely threatening situation around Loos, the first of the reserves available to Sixth Army had already been directed to move in support of IV Corps. However, just as the situation was beginning to stabilise somewhat, reports began to arrive concerning a massive French attack on a fourteen kilometre front from Liévin to Roclincourt. Here there was no cloud gas attack, but a great many gas shells were fired in support of the infantry assault. At the southern end of the IV Corps sector 7th Infantry Division easily beat off an attack by the French 43rd Division, but the situation was more difficult for 123rd Infantry Division around Souchez, which was assaulted by both the 13th and 70th French Divisions.

The artillery fire had destroyed many of their positions, the area was swampy and difficult to defend and the division had already released its two reserve battalions to rush north to Loos. As a result the forward positions were overrun by dense masses of French infantry, who loomed up out of the cover provided by smoke. The attack was held, but not until ground had been lost between Angres and the *Gießler-Höhe* [just to the north of The Pimple]. To the south the French XXXIII, III and XII Corps launched a very heavy attack on VI Corps. Ground had to be given around Neuville St Vaast and the La Folie sector was disputed throughout the remainder of the day and into the following night. The French 24th Division thrust forward almost to Thélus, causing great concern to the chain of command. A hasty counter-attack did succeed in checking this and pushing the French troops back, but not all the way to the original German front line.

The situation was similar on the most southerly sector of the French offensive, held by I Bavarian Reserve Corps, but there decisive counter-action meant that the front had been restored by dark. This left the dent in the lines between Souchez and Neuville St Vaast as the greatest problem faced by the defence. Counter-attacks to be launched against the British around Loos had absorbed all the reserves immediately available, so all that could be done by Crown Prince Rupprecht, Commander Sixth Army, was to issue orders to defend the threatened sector at all costs until reinforcements could be brought forward. Fighting went on throughout the night 25/26 September but, as dawn broke on the second day of the offensive, superiority of forces meant that a significant amount of territory was still in French hands.

South of Arras the battle died away somewhat on 26 September. General Foch had decided the previous evening that the greatest chance of developing his attack was at its northern end, so offensive action further south was delegated mainly to the artillery. However, further north, heavy attacks were thrown in on the left flank of VI Corps and right flank of IV Corps and more ground was lost east of Souchez. That said, the French had been expecting far more impressive results from Tenth Army and, at a meeting with General Foch near Amiens during the afternoon of 26 September, Joffre decided on a partial operational pause to save on ammunition and to create a two division reserve for use elsewhere. The reason for this was that operations in Champagne seemed to be offering the best chance of success, so Joffre wanted to concentrate his efforts in that region. 'Unfortunately', he recalled later, 'the amount of manpower and equipment available did not permit me to maintain for long the assault in Artois, which in my view was of secondary importance, without compromising the success of the Battle of Champagne. I directed the cessation of the Tenth Army offensive.'[4]

Despite this decision it was important for the French to convey the impression that the Anglo-French offensive was actually continuing unchecked so, during the days that followed, there continued to be heavy fighting for the high ground from Souchez to Vimy. The Guard Corps was deployed with 2nd Guards Infantry Division, commanded by Generalleutnant Ritter von Hoehn, replacing the battered 123rd Infantry Division around Souchez and Oberst Prinz Eitel Friedrich's 1st Guards Infantry Division was involved in desperate fighting for the La Folie sector. The situation forward of Givenchy remained critical until 29 September. However, by that time, although VI Corps had suffered very heavy casualties and many of its formations were utterly exhausted, it had more than blunted the French attack. Over the next forty eight hours the entire corps was withdrawn and sent to recuperate around Cambrai.

All these changes imposed delay on the development of the attacks. There had been an intention to launch a fresh effort on 2 October but, after discussions between the Allies, it was agreed that the next major assault would be on 6 October and, in the meantime, bitter fighting continued on the heights west and south of Givenchy, where the entire German positions had been levelled and shell hole defence with extreme communications difficulties had to be conducted. On 3 October a thrust by elements of the French XXI Corps at *Fünfwegekreuz* up on The Pimple almost succeeded in reaching Givenchy before the Guards were able first to stop it and then to drive it back once more the following day. 6 October came and went without a major French assault. It transpired that preparations were still not complete within Tenth Army, so Joffre was forced, reluctantly, to delay until 10 October in Artois, which ruled out simultaneous action with operations in Champagne.

Before that date, German counter-actions had thrown the Allied timetable into confusion as they attacked on 8 October north and south of Loos. The attack failed, but the British were forced to delay yet again. German defences were being strengthened on a daily basis so, when the French artillery opened up drum fire on the Guard Corps and I Bavarian Reserve Corps during the morning of 11 October, then followed it at 5.30 pm with a massed infantry assault, the defenders were ready and waiting – and so was all its artillery. As flares went up the length of the front calling for defensive fire, the response was immediate and heavy. Elements of the French XXI and XXXIII Corps did manage to break into the positions of the Guards near Angres and on The Pimple but, to the south, the French XII Corps made barely any impression on the recently arrived Bavarian I Corps and none at all against Bavarian I Reserve Corps. That was enough for Joffre and he put an immediate end to further offensive action. 'A fresh attack took place on 11 October', he wrote in his memoirs. 'It was mounted by XXI, XXXIII and XII Corps. Launched at 4.15 pm [French time], it was more or less a complete failure. So, on 13th, I ordered that the offensive be halted and the captured positions consolidated.'[5]

The frontage attacked in September and October by the British army was approximately eleven kilometres as the crow flies, stretching from Givenchy-lez-la-Bassée in the north to a point about four kilometres due west of Lens. Lying within the sector of Sixth Army, it was the responsibility of 14th Infantry Division, commanded by Generalmajor von Altrock, in the north and 117th Infantry Division, which had only been formed the previous April, under General der Infanterie Kuntze, in the south. On 25 September, it was held from north to south by Infantry Regiments 57, 56 and 16, Jäger Battalion 11, Reserve Infantry Regiment 11, Infantry Regiment 157 and Reserve Infantry Regiment 22: little enough in the face of an attack preceded by a large scale release of gas, which was to be followed up by six divisions in the first wave.

A typical layout within each regimental sector is exemplified by that adopted by Infantry Regiment 16 near Auchy, once it became clear that battle was in the offing. The frontage was divided into two sub-sectors, each the responsibility of one battalion and manned with three companies in the front line with a fourth back in support. The third battalion was kept in reserve under the orders of its commander, Oberstleutnant von L'Estocq, who had taken over when his predecessor, Oberstleutnant von Hassel, was killed the previous March at Neuve Chapelle. Having been in the line there for months, the companies of Infantry Regiment 16 were fully familiar with the British positions opposite and, although they observed general offensive preparations, such as new batteries being ranged in and could hear increased train movements in rear when the wind was in the right direction, they later admitted that they lacked any detailed knowledge of what was happening immediately to their front. This meant that the installation of batteries of gas cylinders had been completely undetected.

On 19 September, a complete squadron of nine aircraft flew over their lines, which was regarded as unusual then, two days later, on 21 September, the preliminary bombardment began. From the start all the trenches, including the approach routes from the rear, came under heavy fire, as did the rear area right back to Douvrin. 3rd Battalion Infantry Regiment 16, which was in reserve east of Arras, resting and training, had a ringside seat and was able to watch, with detached interest, fire coming down all the way along the front to Arras. For 1st and 2nd Battalions in the front line, the bombardment was altogether a more unpleasant experience though, thanks to the extensive development work which had been done to the position throughout the past few months, well built dugouts shielded the trench garrison from serious casualties.

The actual date of the attack did not come as a surprise to the German army. It had, apparently, been indicated by prisoners of war and deserters.[6] However, its precise nature most certainly was. By 25 September in the sector of Infantry Regiment 16, the wire obstacle, like most of the others along the front, was badly damaged, as were the trench parapets. The intention was to relieve 1st Battalion with 3rd Battalion early that morning. In fact the 3rd Battalion was actually making its way forward when, at 6.45 am, a great cloud of heavy yellowish gas rolled forward and enveloped the entire area in a dense, impenetrable, mass of chlorine. The gas alarm was raised and all ranks rushed to don their 'Seclin' masks and to set fire to stacks of dry kindling wood placed on the parapets of the trenches to aid the dispersal of the gas. In no time at all flames were leaping up all along the regimental front. The artillery fire suddenly lifted to the rear and the front line troops rushed to get into position behind their wall of fire.

Despite subsequent British assertions that the gas was completely ineffective on this part of the front, it is clear from the German accounts that not only did gas drift over their positions, but also their gas protection was far from being fully effective. Some men were overcome by it and the company officers were in places hard put to it to maintain control and ensure that their men were ready to repel the attack. It was fully forty five minutes later before the assault waves of the British 2nd Division went over the top and were met by a hail of rifle and machine gun fire. No progress was made against this fire and most of the attackers withdrew rapidly back into their trenches. On the extreme right of the regimental sector, the so-called Prellbock Company, located just immediately south of the La Bassée Canal, became involved in a close quarter battle with hand grenades against 2nd Battalion South Staffordshire Regiment of 6 Brigade, but even this clash ended with the defenders being successful and no British troops got into their positions.

Every member of the regiment not already committed was alerted and sent forward to reinforce the forward companies. 3rd Battalion succeeded in advancing with great difficulty through the gas cloud and arrived at the front line in the 1st Battalion sector. There was, of course, no question of carrying out a relief so, for the time being, there was actually an undesirable massing of defenders in the forward area. One of the company commanders of 3rd Battalion who was involved with the move forward later described what happened:

> "According to plan, 3rd Battalion left Douvrin at 5.00 am to relieve 1st Battalion. When leading elements of the battalion had arrived in the forward positions, but others were still stalled along the approach routes, artillery fire suddenly began to fall. We thought at first that the enemy had spotted the relief then, suddenly, we became aware of a strange stink. Once the initial surprise had passed, we all realised that it was a gas attack. Thanks to good preparation, the issue of sufficient gas masks, suitable training and practise, we quickly recovered from the shock and reached for our gas masks. Where, however, was the protective [chemical] solution which was kept stored in niches in the trenches? Most of it had been buried by artillery fire, as were many of the boxes of inflammable material. Despite this we found supplies of the protective

liquid here and there and some fires were lit. We all lay in wait tensely because we knew that the gas would be followed by the enemy.[7]

"All of a sudden, though the misty gas clouds, we saw the evil enemy approaching us calmly, just as though they were out for walk. However, they had not reckoned with the *Hacketäuer*.[8] A torrent of rapid fire erupted all along the line and in a flash the enemy disappeared back into their trenches. One of their daring leaders, displaying exemplary courage and leading from the front, dashed into the *Monokel*.[9] He paid for his daring with his death. We had won! It was an uplifting moment. Even those suffering from the effects of the gas joined in the shouts of *Hurra!* yelled by the courageous *Hacketäuer*. The fact that we had sent the enemy packing in short order was the cause of much joy and jubilation.

"The main concern now was to reorganise the units on the left flank, because there were now two battalions in a sector meant only to hold one. We then ensured that we were prepared to repel a future attack. [Gas] protective liquid was brought up and wood was collected together. Many a smart dugout door or revetment plank was sacrificed in this way. There was one other major worry for the commanders. The gas had attacked the metalwork of the weapons to such an extent that the bolts could not be worked forwards and backwards. Copious quantities of lubricating oil which were stored in the battalion command posts solved the problem rapidly, however.

"With that we were all prepared, but the enemy opposite remained quiet. They had clearly had enough and were well aware that it would be no cakewalk against us. On the other hand, off to the left they had enjoyed much greater success. We frequently looked in that direction, greatly concerned, especially at night when enemy flares could be seen going skywards almost to our rear. During the coming days, the battle raged day and night off to our left, but it was a relief to see that the enemy was being forced back more and more towards their own lines."

From early on 25 September there was indeed great concern that the British thrust into the depth of the German positions off to the south would lead to a serious threat to the left flank and rear of Infantry Regiment 16. The commanding officer of 3rd Battalion, having gone right forward to assess the danger, lost no time in returning to the forward regimental command post in Auchy and reporting the facts to the regimental commander, Oberstleutnant von L'Estocq, who was located back in Douvrin. At that, immediate steps were taken to counter the threat and to seal the left flank against any British attempts to develop the attack to the north. Every single available man: runners, signallers, gunners and engineers, were pressed into service and sent to hold trenches south of the line Auchy – Haisnes front facing south against the enemy penetrations to Fosse 8 and the *Hohenzollernwerk* [Hohenzollern Redoubt], which had been captured by men of the British 9th Division and which they were holding in strength.

In this sector the news went on getting worse throughout the morning. By 10.15 am it was known that Fosse 13 on the Hulluch road had been captured and a mad scramble to rush reinforcements to the threatened area began. 2nd Battalion Reserve Infantry Regiment 77 and two companies of Infantry Regiment 57 were immediately subordinated to Infantry Regiment 16 and deployed to the threatened flank and by late afternoon these had been joined by four companies of Reserve Infantry Regiment 55, which were despatched to a holding area near Haisnes. Later two of these companies were to have relieved two of the Reserve Infantry Regiment 77 companies, but a torrent of British artillery fire prevented their movement forward. For similar reasons an attempt at around midnight by 117th Infantry Division to retake the line Fosse 8 – *Kiesgrube* [Gravel Pit = Quarries] failed.

Unteroffizier Schröder 3rd Company Pionier Battalion 7[10] **1.**

"During the night 24/25 September, 1 and 3 Platoons of the company had been forward working on obstacle and field tramway construction. Not until dawn had they marched back to Douvrin to rest. Barely had the exhausted sappers stretched out their limbs to go to sleep than they were stood to at 6.30 am. 'Get up and on parade as soon as possible. An enemy attack is expected in ten minutes' time.' Disbelievingly, we rubbed the sleep out of our eyes and then the seriousness of the situation hit us. Enemy small arms fire was rattling against the roofs of Douvrin and a greenish-yellow mist was swirling against the windows. It was chlorine gas, but was by now so diffused that it was scarcely a problem any more. The German artillery was firing defensive fire like men possessed. In a few moments the two platoons had fallen in in front of the company office, equipped to march and fight and the company echelon vehicles came rattling up behind, ready to move off in the direction of Bouvin – Provin.

"Hauptmann von Hanstein had already rushed on ahead with the two mining companies, the infantry pioneer company of Infantry Regiment 16 and the digging company of Infantry Regiment 57. Leutnant Wiebel followed with the two platoons, which had a combined strength of about one hundred men, and moved initially behind the stacks of tiles to the south of Douvrin. The heavy equipment was left there and, on order of the company commander, we doubled forward in the direction of Haisnes. Making use of the Douvrin-Haisnes road and then the communication trenches in the Second Position of the allotted sector, the so-called *Kaiser-Stellung* on the enemy side of Haisnes, we arrived without any casualties. Our right flank was on the Haisnes – Auchy railway then, to our left, was the 1st Mining Company.

"In the meantime the fog had dispersed, so we could see the battlefield and read the situation. After repeated heavy attacks, the enemy had broken in to the sector of our neighbouring division to the south of Auchy. To the left, in front of Haisnes, we could see widely spaced groups of British soldiers pressing forward. The machine gun which had been allocated to the engineers brought down heavy fire against them. On the left flank of 14th Infantry Division the enemy had penetrated as far as Haisnes and the Haisnes – Hulloch road. For the moment all that was known was that Hauptmann von Hanstein had thrown himself at the British south of Haisnes. There was a grave danger that the British who had broken in would expand their attack to the left over the Haisnes – Auchy road and fall on the rear of Infantry Regiment 16 and Jäger Battalion 11, who so far had heroically held their forward positions against every enemy assault.

"Individual British soldiers appeared at the southern exit of Auchy. Infantry Regiment 16 and Jäger Battalion 11 immediately pulled their left flanks back. The regimental staff of Infantry Regiment 16 in Auchy reacted to the crisis like lightning. Pulling together a company comprising spare detachments, clerks, cooks, grooms, batmen and telephonists, they had it occupy the *Schmandgraben* which ran parallel to the Haisnes – Auchy road. There it succeeded in halting the enemy advance. The engineers in the Haisnes Position were under constant small arms fire from the left as they awaited further orders. The artillery located at the Fosse near Haisnes brought down heavy concentrations of fire to the left, but it was subjected to intense counter-battery fire and there were numerous casualties. With engineer help, new guns were dug in along the railway embankment and then took up the task of destruction.

"In accordance with orders from the commander, an engineer unteroffizier[11] and his section were detailed to carry forward as much ammunition as possible to the troops fighting at Auchy cemetery and to inform their commander that the cemetery was to be held at all costs. Despite heavy fire, the engineers got forward, handing over part of the ammunition to the companies in *Schmandgraben* and then continuing in short dashes - mostly across open ground - to Auchy cemetery. There the enemy had been driven back already and were falling back in the direction of the line Haisnes–Fosse 9, there to link up with the British who had broken through near Hulluch. This freed up the German artillery which had been pushed forward to near Auchy cemetery.

"Two companies attacked forward to follow up the retreating enemy troop. It was astonishing how quickly the regiments of 14th Infantry Division, which had been involved in nothing but positional warfare for more than three quarters of a year, adapted to mobile operations once more and how well and appropriately the commanders of the endangered combat troops of 14th Infantry Division reacted. The way that they not only beat off all attacks launched in overwhelming strength against them, but also were in a position to react offensively against the break in on the sector of their neighbouring division will always be a glorious page in the history of the courageous *Hacketäuer* and the Kurhessisches Jäger Battalion 11.[12]

"Meanwhile the sad news of the death of their hauptmann had reached the engineers in their positions near Haisnes. Bravely leading his companies forward to the left of Haisnes on the road to Loos, he had launched his troops against the advancing British soldiers and fell at about 10.30 am[13]... His mining companies brought the British advance to a halt and steadied our somewhat shaky front. By this time the outcome of the breakthrough battle was more or less decided. Although the British, with their surprise attack, had succeeded in capturing a certain amount of ground, they had certainly not broken through. Within two to three hours, reserves released by the higher command headquarters were arriving on the spot and full scale German counter-measures could begin."

Whilst the regiments of 14th Infantry Division were putting up a spirited defence and checking the forward thrust of the British 7th, 9th and 2nd Divisions, the same could not be said of the 117th Infantry Division. Its one active regiment, Infantry Regiment 157, occupied the centre of the divisional frontage, being flanked to the north by Reserve Infantry Regiment 11 and to the south by Reserve Infantry Regiment 22. It had two battalions forward. 1st Battalion, right forward, had been in the line for several days but, on the eve of the battle, the 3rd Battalion nearest to Loos was relieved by 2nd Battalion, commanded by Major Guhr. During the previous few weeks the regiment had received several reinforcing drafts, so it entered the battle at near full strength, each of its battalions having about twenty five officers and around 900 men. The bombardment, which had been hammering the positions throughout 24 September, eased slightly during the evening, so there were few casualties during the relief in the line of 3rd by 2nd Battalion and, even though the British fire increased considerably in intensity overnight, the ready availability of dugouts and the relative lack of heavy calibre British guns meant that most companies were still well up to strength in the early hours of 25 September.

On this sector, the bombardment began once more in earnest at 4.00 am and increased to drum fire from 5.00 am to 6.45 am. The ground shook as it was repeatedly ploughed up by shells, the 2nd Battalion command post, located in a deep dugout in Loos, was said to have swayed under the impacts, whilst the over pressure of the heavy shells exploding all round threw the occupants in all directions. Suddenly, at 6.45 am, the fire was lifted and all was still and quiet. At 7.05 am, Reserve Leutnant Bargenda, adjutant, 2nd Battalion, stationed on top of the brewery as a lookout, sent an urgent report: '7.05 am. Gas attack along the entire line.'[14] All the telephone lines were cut, so Major Guhr personally alerted 7th and 8th Companies, which were in reserve and standby at the brewery, then despatched two messengers on bicycles to take the message to regimental headquarters.

In Corps reserve that morning was 3rd Battalion Infantry Regiment 178, part of the Saxon 123rd Infantry Division, which was responsible for the defence of the Angres-Souchez sector. However this particular battalion was detached and deployed on high ground near Lens from where its members looked on as the deadly gas attack was carried out against 117th Infantry Division.

Vizefeldwebel Giesecke 2nd Battalion Infantry Regiment 178[15] 2.

"From our elevated position we could see the west wind carry the greenish-yellow and black smoke clouds over the trenches of our neighbouring division. From many hundreds of pipes, set about one metre apart, streamed poisonous jets of gas which, after about fifty metres, combined into one great gas cloud. Gusts of wind caused ripples in the cloud, but it still held together, expanding and threatening as it flowed through the damp heavy atmosphere to where it would have an awful effect on the ranks of our comrades. We felt a little easier when our artillery began to bring down very heavy fire right into the cloud. Shot and shell of all calibres burst in the cloud, with the aim of halting it or at least reducing its effect. The gas did indeed swirl about when the shells exploded, but it still reached our trenches.

"The Tack! Tack! sound of British machine guns, which became evident at the same time, showed us that the gas attack was being followed up immediately by that of the infantry, with Indian troops in the lead. However this attack was beaten back, leaving the field covered in dead and wounded men. Once again, then for a third time, we saw clouds roll over the Indians. The fire of our own artillery slackened somewhat then English and Scottish troops stormed forward. The front line of our neighbouring division was overrun. Would the reserves manage to do their duty? Meanwhile the enemy artillery shifted the impact point of its rain of shot and shell further to the east, over Hill 70 and as far as Lens."

In and around Loos an extremely difficult period followed. It is impossible to reconstruct events along much of this sector of the front with complete accuracy, because neither Reserve Infantry Regiment 11 nor Reserve Infantry Regiment 22 produced a regimental history and their files were all destroyed in 1945 when the Prussian archives were bombed. However, it is possible to obtain a flavour of the way the day developed on the divisional left flank from information provided by Major Guhr, who personally commanded 2nd Battalion Infantry Regiment 157, survived the war and then became the regimental historian. From the observation post at the brewery in Loos, a dense grey coloured cloud was observed rolling forward on a gentle west wind. Quickly the forward positions were covered by it and for a considerable period no reports were received. Tension mounted as the uncertainty dragged on. Eventually an officer arrived at the command post. Almost overcome by gas, retching and in a state of near collapse, he described the effect of the chlorine gas, something of which none present had previously had any experience.

In the forward area, which was still largely obscured by gas and smoke, the sound of an intense battle with small arms was carried to the rear on the wind, but little could be deduced about the progress of the battle until some time between 7.30am and 8.00 am, when a group of gunners came rushing up to state that their battery positions had been overrun by British infantry, who had loomed up unseen out of the smoke and mist. Meanwhile 5th and 6th Companies, manning the forward positions, fought on, despite the fact that their ammunition was running short. Each man had been issued with 230 rounds prior to deployment, but such was the rate of fire poured into the attackers who followed the gas cloud that the situation soon became serious. Nevertheless, the survivors of Infantry Regiment 157 had imposed at least a temporary check on the assault in their sector, but all their efforts were undone because, immediately to their south, Reserve Infantry Regiment 22 had effectively broken. Panicked by the gas they gave ground rapidly.

Thrusting into the gap in strength, the British troops swung north to threaten the flank of 5th Company Infantry Regiment 157. Efforts were made to counter this, but all attempts failed as small groups of defenders were swiftly outflanked. The company commander, Reserve Hauptmann Sabaß, and other officers, who had gathered small groups of twenty to thirty rifle men around them tried to link up, but it was impossible in all the confusion and limited visibility. An attempt to make a stand in the so-called 1½ Position, where the supports were normally located, foundered at once because fighting was already taking place in Loos itself. Faced with a real crisis the cooks, runners, signallers, the staff of an engineer depot and the canteen, in fact every man in Loos who could carry a rifle, less Unterarzt Dr Kynast, who stayed with the wounded, turned out to do battle alongside 7th and 8th Companies, who fought almost to the last man in a vain attempt to stem the tide of attackers.

Despite the rapid progress made in the Reserve Infantry Regiment 22 sector, some German attempts were made to shore up the crumbling situation from about mid morning. 3rd Battalion Infantry Regiment 27 of 7th Infantry Division, back in reserve in Noyelles, was ordered forward at 9.00 am to the junction of the Lens–La Bassée / Lens–Béthune roads and there, amongst other tasks, to assume responsibility for the security of 1st Battalion Field Artillery Regiment 40, commanded by Hauptmann Groneweg, which was located on the outskirts of St Pierre and St Edouard.

Hauptmann Groneweg 1st Battalion Field Artillery Regiment 40[16]

"The neighbouring division had been overrun during a gas attack and most of the divisional batteries had fallen into enemy hands. All my links to the rear had been destroyed. On my right flank, as far away as Loos, there was not a single infantryman. With two guns in an open position, I spent the whole day protecting the right flank of the battery ... The entire crews of these guns, with the exception of me and a wachtmeister, were killed or wounded. I was filthy, hungry and filled with concern for my right flank, expecting the final enemy attack to come in at any moment.

"At that point [Hauptmann Lange] arrived, with a runner. He surveyed our situation then declared with a friendly beam on his face that he had come to place part of his battalion, so as to protect our right flank ... In response to my question how many companies of his battalion would arrive, he replied that he would certainly make available two or three platoons ... He spoke in praise of his men and stated that even though the gap to be filled was rather wide, his lads would manage it – and indeed they fulfilled their duty fully."

By this time Loos was well and truly lost, there was a broad gap in the front of 117th Infantry Division and the situation could hardly have been more dangerous. At 10.30 am the adjutant of 14 Infantry Brigade arrived with orders for Hauptmann Lange that the *Kohlenhalde St Pierre* (known to the British as the Double Crassier) was to be recaptured. This was a daunting prospect and the only saving grace was the fact that a swift reconnaissance showed that the British were only established on the northwest tip of this major slag heap. Before an attack could be carried out, however, Hauptmann Lange, returning to the road junction, met up with Oberstleutnant Grautoff of Infantry Regiment 26 who had a more modest, but still essential, mission to carry out. With two of his companies (4th and Assault Pioneer) and 3rd Battalion Infantry Regiment 27, which was now under his command, he was to move to the line Fosse 11 (by the eastern tip of the Double Crassier) – north tip of St Laurent and prevent the British from advancing further. Remnants of Reserve Infantry Regiment 22 under Hauptmann von Packisch were still deployed near Fosse 11, where 3rd Battalion Field Artillery Regiment 40 was still in action, so Grautoff's next priority was to secure a copse adjacent to the Lens-Béthune road west of Fosse 12 and near Point 69 (known to the British as Chalk Pit Copse and to the Germans as *Engländer Wäldchen* = British Copse).

Two platoons of 9th Company were rushed forward to link up with two platoons of Infantry Regiment 26 already in position. This was a most unenviable task.

Leutnant Vornkahl 1 Platoon 9th Company Infantry Regiment 27[17] 3.

"The position ran from the western end of the wood along its edge then suddenly bent at right angles and continued for some time straight through the wood. Because it comprised mainly thick undergrowth punctuated by mature trees, at this point there was effectively no visibility forward. This meant that it was not possible to guard against surprise and, furthermore, the right flank was not covered. The situation was made even more difficult due to the fact that this had been intended originally as a blocking position – a part of the Third Line connected by communications trenches, which the enemy were already occupying."

The commander 4th Company Infantry Regiment 26 greeted Vornkahl with the news that this really was the front line; that the British had already pushed into the wood, but had been driven out once more. This probing and skirmishing by 1/20th and 1/17th London Regiments of 141 Brigade continued throughout the day, with the British fighting their way forward to occupy most of the copse and German reinforcements being moved into position gradually until, by evening, the threatened sector was being held by elements of Reserve Infantry Regiment 22, 4th Company Infantry Regiment 26, then 9th, 10th and 11th Companies Infantry Regiment 27. A platoon of 12th Company completed the thin line of defenders and two platoons of 12th Company were held back in reserve.

Leutnant Vornkahl 1 Platoon 9th Company Infantry Regiment 27[18]

"British soldiers appeared individually in the undergrowth to the front of 9th Company, but were driven off with hand grenades. Immediately behind the German lines was a single 105 mm howitzer, manned by two gunners, apparently all that was left of the crew. Lacking shells, they kept up a rapid fire with cartridges every time the British entered the wood and shot at the advancing infantry with their pistols."

Already by mid morning, the sector commander in Loos village, Major Guhr, could not lay his hands on another single man. Acutely aware that only the prompt arrival of reinforcements could save the day, he hurried to the Loos artillery observation post, hoping that contact with the rear might be possible from there but, when he arrived, he discovered it wrecked and abandoned and the telephone out of order. He then raced back to his previous location, under heavy fire from British machine guns established on the slag heaps at the southern end of the village. Bullets were cracking along all the streets. Guhr's cap was shot off his head, Reserve Leutnant Bargenda, his adjutant, had a near miss when bullets struck his rolled up overcoat, whilst the artillery liaison officer with them was killed by a shot to the head.

It was clear to Guhr that the situation in Loos was hopeless. He had already despatched a howitzer battery to Hulluch and it remained only to gather together as many stragglers and isolated groups as possible and head back to the Second Position. Determined to make a stand, strenuous efforts were made to halt all survivors streaming towards the rear and Guhr, not noticing that he had already been wounded, placed Reserve Leutnant Klein of Reserve Infantry Regiment 22 in charge of rallying the troops as they arrived on the position. Taking up a prominent position on the parapet, Klein gave the necessary orders for some time in a loud clear voice but later the men near him noticed that he was increasingly unsteady on his feet and his voice was failing. At that point he called a nearby vizefeldwebel to him and, summoning his last reserves of strength, told him, 'I have been seriously wounded and can go on no longer. You are to assume command here'. He then collapsed. He had been, literally, dying on his feet all the time he had been on the position and his example made a deep impression on all who witnessed it.[19] Meanwhile Major Guhr was desperately trying to organise a coherent defensive line – above all he needed more manpower.

Leaving strict instructions that all men moving towards the rear were to be kept on the Second Position, he hurried some 400 metres south to St Auguste, hoping to find a working telephone. In his absence, Reserve Hauptmann Sabaß, together with the remnants of 5th Company, arrived on the Second Position and he assumed command. Amazing to relate, Major Guhr managed to locate the one surviving telephone line leading to the rear and was able to provide the first detailed briefing to divisional and regimental headquarters. On receipt of the news, the divisional general staff officer,

Hauptmann Beck, told Guhr to remain where he was; he would be arriving by car shortly in order to orientate himself personally. About the same time the reserve battalion of Reserve Infantry Regiment 11 arrived to occupy *Stützpunkt 5* of the Second Position. Gradually, having more or less absorbed the initial shock, the German defence was beginning to stabilise in this area and pose a threat to the continuation of the British advance.

That said, the successful forward thrust of 15th (Scottish) Division had led to the capture of Hill 70, which sat astride the Lens–Hulluch road by about 10.00 am. In fact there was effectively no opposition and the leading infantry, estimated at about 1,500 men, simply swarmed up the hill, taking a short breather on its crest. Unfortunately, by now the various units of 44 and 46 Brigades were intermingled and their blood was up so, aware of the need to press on forward and believing wrongly that they had observed British soldiers running into the two villages, an entirely disorganised band of Scottish soldiers, several hundred strong, rushed forward east of Hill 70, making for Cité St Auguste and Cité St Laurent. Unfortunately for them the movement out to the front was German and, by approximately 10.30 am, the advance stalled with no group closer than about seventy five metres from the German wire. A battalion of Reserve Infantry Regiment 22, having realised that it could get no further forward, dropped back to man trenches just in front of Cité St Auguste, whilst Cité St Laurent now contained numbers of stragglers, but also men of Infantry Regiment 178, which had been in reserve in Lens.

Vizefeldwebel Giesecke 2nd Battalion Infantry Regiment 178[20] 2.

> "Suddenly the runners sprang into action. The Brigade brought the battalion to immediate notice at 10.30 am. 'The companies are to move with all speed by the shortest route to the northern exits of [Cité] St. L[aurent]'. Messengers carried orders: 'All four companies are to ready to move in five minutes and are to assemble in fifteen minutes' time at the exit leading to St. Laurent.' Battle order was donned in no time flat, rifles were slung and the sections set off. Doubling forward through the streets, sometimes in single file, at other times formed into ranks because of the attentions of the constantly circling enemy aircraft, we followed our commanding officer, Major Gause, who had ridden on ahead so as to orientate himself on the situation.
>
> "Already British rounds were clattering against the walls of the houses of St Laurent and the British soldiers had just reached the first of the houses as our 3rd Battalion, moving like the wind, raced up to save Lens and prevent our comrades on the Lorette Spur from being cut off. By sections we advanced in dashes across the open ground which led right up to the outskirts of St Laurent. This was necessary, because accurate artillery fire was coming down on every significant point from Fosse 14 to Hill 70 and all along the road leading back to Lens. Whilst the shells began their work of destruction around the southern exit of St Laurent, the leading platoons entered the gardens of the first of the houses and so were able to make their way unnoticed up to Fosse 14 on

the northern edge of the built up area, where Major Gause, the Adjutant, Leutnant Ryssel, and the rest of the staff had set up their temporary headquarters. Major Gause deployed the 9th and 12th Companies to the right of the road, with the 10th and two platoons of the 11th to the left of the road, with orders that stressed the importance of launching a left flanking attack."

Whilst these critical scenes were being played and the German desperate, hasty defence was taking all the remaining impetus out of the overextended and disorganised 15th (Scottish) Division, 1st Battalion Infantry Regiment 157 was undergoing a severe trial, opposed by troops of both the British 15th and 1st Divisions. Its early experience was similar to that of its 2nd Battalion, already described. Its 3rd and 4th Companies were holding forward with 1st Company in support and 2nd Company back in reserve in Hulluch. Anticipating the forthcoming attack, the battalion commanding officer, Hauptmann Ritter, had caused all available ammunition in Hulluch to be carried forward during the night 24/25 September so, when the gas began to roll in just after 7.00 am, the forward companies had more than 400 rounds per man and very large stocks of hand grenades on their positions. With these quantities available, the first attack by the British 46 Brigade of 15th Division was stopped in its tracks, partly because so many of the British troops had been affected by the gas as they tried and failed to make their way forward masked up and had to roll up their gas helmets to be able to see and breathe at all.[21]

At 7.45 am there was a renewal of the British assault and this too was countered with heavy fire, which caused a great many casualties. A few British prisoners were taken, but the assault had gained a foothold in the forward trenches. Prompt work sealed the breach on three sides and a number of subsequent attacks, culminating in a major effort at 11.00 am, were all held by a genuinely heroic and epic defence, which was to have a serious effect on the entire British attack. Following the failure of the latest assault, the British began to dig in some thirty to forty metres short of the German wire and there was no further advance at that particular point all day. Unfortunately, the story was different to the north, where Reserve Infantry Regiment 11 held the line. Here the forward positions were broken through by 9.00 am and, despite their earlier losses, a mixed thrust of units of 44 and 46 Brigades were soon pressing forward towards Hulluch, where they were opposed by a platoon under command of Leutnant Jantzen of Infantry Regiment 157.

As the gas and smoke gradually cleared 3rd Company Infantry Regiment 157 could see British field guns being towed into position along the Vermelles – Hulluch road, so they engaged them effectively, their sights set on 1,200 metres, with volleys of rifle fire, but this could not be continued for long. Ammunition was running short and the deep break in on the Reserve Infantry Regiment 11 front meant that the danger to the right flank of Infantry Regiment 157 was becoming acute. The occasional message made Hauptmann Ritter aware of the severe problems down to the south, where the positions of Reserve Infantry Regiment 22 and 5th and 6th Companies Infantry Regiment 157 had been driven in and, furthermore, a patrol led by Fähnrich Stadthagen of 1st

Company had brought back a report about the chaotic situation at Loos. He could also see for himself, as the morning wore on, how British troops were swarming forward and onto Hill 70.

Increasingly desperate attempts were made to get messages through to the rear to request support, but every attempt failed and, little by little, the individual companies were surrounded and cut off. At 2.00 pm, Ritter summoned all his company commanders to brief them and discuss the situation. His two forward companies had completely run out of ammunition and, although 1st Company still had a few rounds available, effectively this meant that they would be defenceless against a renewed attack. Nevertheless, in hopes of relief, he decided to remain where he was. None had arrived by 4.00 pm when artillery fire began coming down on his sub-sector, followed by an infantry assault at 4.15 pm. He was surrounded and out of ammunition, so he had no hope of being able to break out. To have continued the fight would have meant needless sacrifice of his surviving men, so he ordered all weapons, equipment and documentation to be smashed or burnt then, at 5.00 pm, he despatched an emissary under a white flag, with a written surrender document.

Duty done to the limit of what was possible, the remnants of the battalion, numbering some 400 all ranks, surrendered to 1/9th Kings and the London Scottish of the so-called Green's Force of 1st Division and went into captivity. The British Official History fully acknowledged what Ritter's men had achieved.

> "The gallant defence they had put up against many times their number proved to be a decisive factor in the battle, for the delay caused to the centre of the British attack had arrested that initial momentum of the offensive, in the full weight of which had lain its principal chance of success."[22]

In what for a German regimental history is a fairly low key description of this desperate defensive action, their historian later quoted a British *Daily Chronicle* report about the battle that day.

> "The fact [is] that the tough defenders did not raise their hands until they saw that they were surrounded on all sides. They had done their work well. Their obstinate defence had effectively held up the advance of an entire British division and, [furthermore] the taking of these trenches had absorbed all the reserves which were could have been used urgently to exploit success [elsewhere] ... "[23]

One immediate outcome of this delaying action was that time was bought for reserves to be rushed forward. On this sub-sector, 3rd Battalion Infantry Regiment 157, commanded by Reserve Hauptmann Mende, was able to get into position around Hulluch and *Stützpunkt* [Strong Point] 5 by about midday. Linking up with Infantry Regiment 15, elements of Reserve Infantry Regiment 22 and Infantry Regiment 165 of 7th Infantry Division, the defences of Hulluch and *Stützpunkte* 3-5 presented a difficult obstacle to further British advances by early afternoon and from that baseline 8th

Infantry Division was able to prepare and launch an (admittedly unsuccessful) counterattack at midnight.

To the south, as has been mentioned, the Corps reserve, 3rd Battalion Infantry Regiment 178, had been stood to and despatched forward to Cité St Laurent prior to launching a counter-attack on Hill 70. By 11.15 am the companies had reached their assembly area, were placed under command of Reserve Infantry Regiment 22 and orders were given. 9th and 12th Companies were to attack to the right of the La Bassée – Lens Road, with 10th Company on the left and 11th Company initially in reserve.[24] Reserve Infantry Regiment 22 had managed to emplace one machine gun in a building where it had an uninterrupted field of fire against the men of 10th Battalion Gordon Highlanders and 7th Battalion Royal Scots Fusiliers who, commanded by Lieutenant Colonel Sandilands, were attempting to dig in just west of the original redoubt.[25] This weapon contributed considerably to the weakening of the Scottish hasty defence and helps to explain the success of the attack of Infantry Regiment 178, assisted by a few sections of Reserve Infantry Regiment 22, who struck the summit of Hill 70 at the precise moment the Scotsmen were beginning to waver.

Vizefeldwebel Giesecke 2nd Battalion Infantry Regiment 178[26] **4.**

"A short orders group with the company commanders sufficed to determine the deployment and method of attack. At about midday, the 10th, followed by two platoons of 11th Company, began to make their way forward using the cover afforded by the banks to the left and right of the road. Sometimes crawling, occasionally rushing forward, they reached the *Reservegraben* [Reserve Trench] to the north of St Laurent. The 11th Company platoons keeping left and, moving carefully along under cover of a huge railway embankment, ... arrived in position without casualties. The four to five metre height of the embankment meant that it offered good observation and they swiftly discovered that the Scots were already establishing themselves on the far side of the embankment, so we were only separated by the width of the embankment which, because it carried about six sets of tracks, meant that we were about twenty metres from the enemy.

"The elements of the 10th to the left of the road halted about 100-200 metres from the enemy, whilst those of 9th and 12th Companies deployed on the right hand side took some casualties ... as they closed up to the *Reservegraben*, about fifty metres behind the railway line. Having jumped down into the trench and after linking up with the remnants of the regiment which were located there, it could finally be said that the reinforcements meant that at long last there was a reasonably strong trench garrison in place. The Scots, who had closed up to about fifty metres distance, were held up by a strong wire obstacle and the size of the garrison and began to disappear into the ground like moles.

"While this weak skirmishing line called a halt to its victorious advance, the main force of the enemy was still on top of Hill 70, located about one kilometre from St Laurent and stretching out mainly to the east of the road. Because of the weight of enemy fire, it took some time before we were sufficiently well orientated about the strength and locations of the enemy but, covered by well aimed rifle fire, we began simultaneously to cut gaps in the barbed wire obstacle ... Machine gun fire from the left flank enfiladed the Scotsmen and, with Hauptmann Starke endlessly moving his forces from the right to the left flank, the enemy front could be seen to be crumbling gradually from about 1.30 pm. Individuals would disengage and crawl away so as to seek the cover of the reverse slope.

"With everyone eager to go into the attack and morale high, there was no holding us. Proceeding from left to right over the railway embankment, we pursued the Scots, noting that they had been in a majority of about two to one. Without further orders, as soon as the men of the battalion heard cries of *Hurra!* coming from the left, they leapt up and charged forward brilliantly. Over the newly begun trenches of the Scotsmen, past numerous wounded and dead men and all sorts of abandoned equipment we went, taking the first of our prisoners as we did so. For everybody who was there it was an unforgettable experience! For those observing from a distance it was a scene of war of the first rank as wide lines of the 178th, accompanied by a few reservists, swept forward in a wild charge onto the hill.

"Now and again we halted briefly to fire a shot from the standing position, to deal with one or two pockets of resistance or to take the weapons of the wounded from them. Meanwhile the Scottish and English soldiers ... closed up in superior numbers to the summit of the hill. In the clear weather we could see them occasionally silhouetted against the sky, but they disappeared behind the hill again quickly. By 2.00 pm the important task was done. This height, which dominated Lens, was once more in our hands. Now it was a matter of holding it without fail."

This, the battalion proceeded to do, with frequent forays to deal with threats around the hill, but all at high cost. Though he may have exaggerated somewhat for effect, according to Giesecke almost half of them became casualties, of whom sixty one were killed in action, or died of wounds. Amongst them Leutnants Richter, Ryssel, Strauß, Hagedorn and Gräber, as well as Unteroffizier Johann Vogel, Arthur Hatnick and Karl Göbecke, who were friends of Vizefeldwebel Gieseke.[27] Successful though this attack was, it only secured the southern part of Hill 70, so further development of the attack was a high priority as the day wore on. One of the few reserve formations on this part of the front was 8th Infantry Division back in and around Douai so, shortly after 1.00 pm on 25 September, orders arrived directing Infantry Regiments 93 and 153 to entrain and move forward with a view to launching a further assault on arrival at Hill 70. Infantry Regiment 153 was somewhat in advance of Infantry Regiment 93 and orders were issued at 7.00 pm for a night attack.

"1. General situation as previously briefed.
2. 1st Battalion Infantry Regiment 153 is to assault the two wooded areas from the east, starting from the area north of St Auguste.
3. 2nd Battalion Infantry Regiment 153 is to attack Hill 70 and the wooded area to the south from the south. Boundaries: left, the Lens-La Bassée road; right, the track running parallel 500 – 600 metres to the east. Once both objectives are secured, the battalions (2nd Battalion to the left of 1st Battalion) are to occupy the line of the road facing west.
4. 3rd Battalion Infantry Regiment 153 and the regimental Assault Pioneer Company are to assemble under command of the regiment at the northeast corner of St Auguste, north of the railway.
5. One machine gun platoon is allocated to each battalion.
6. Once everything has been completed, reports are to be sent to the regiment at the northern exit of St Auguste (by the eastern entrance to the wood)."[28]

To state that this mission was over-ambitious is barely to hint at the difficulties. The situation was largely unclear, the ground over which the attack was to take place was unknown close country, the passage of orders took hours, there was no artillery fire plan and there had been no time for reconnaissance or rehearsals. Only the extreme emergency could have justified it. The troops did their level best when the assault finally began at 11.00 pm, but the advance rapidly stalled with troops totally lost in the wooded areas, under heavy small arms fire and barely one hundred and fifty metres further on from the positions of Infantry Regiment 178. During a chaotic night the battalion and company commanders struggled to control the situation. In the early hours of 26 September 1st Battalion finally had to report that the more southerly of the two woods it had been ordered to attack did not even exist, its reported presence being no more than a trick of the light![29]

Infantry Regiment 93 had, if anything, an even harder time of it. It was not finally in a position to begin its attack until 4.30 am, having spent hours crashing about in the pitch black night under harassing fire to try to find its start line. To add to all the physical problems, its orders were totally unrealistic. They included the direction, 'Loos is to be back in our hands tonight.' To that end, 'The Regiment, with 2nd Battalion right and 1st Battalion left, is to attack from the Lens-Hulluch road with its right flank anchored on the track which runs from Point 70 to Loos and with its left flank on a track which initially runs parallel to the Lens – Hulluch road and later leads northwest to Loos'[30] It is obvious at a glance that these orders were worked up straight off a map. Even without any enemy interference, it would have been as good as impossible to give substance to them. The geographical features would have been unrecognisable in the dark and trying to maintain control of straggling lines of infantry quite impossible. Nevertheless, Infantry Regiment 93 did its best, came under immediate fire and did not even get as far forward as Infantry Regiment 153 before it was checked. However, despite this further setback, the move forward of these 8th Infantry Division regiments reinforced the survivors of Infantry Regiment 178 and the other formations engaged the previous day, which meant that the manning of this critical part of the battlefield and the strongly wired Second Position, with its numerous strong points, was now more than sufficient to cope with anything that the BEF was likely to be able to mount in the way of attacks during 26 September – and so it proved.

This was but one of the hasty counter-attacks launched that night. Formations of 2nd Guards Reserve Division which, until a few days earlier, had been located up near Ypres, found themselves hastily redeployed to General der Infanterie Sixt von Armin's IV Corps on 25 September and subordinated that afternoon to 117th Infantry Division, with the task of attempting to stabilise or improve the dangerous situation which had developed during the day. Whilst the newly arriving units assembled on the outskirts of Wingles, Oberstleutnant Schwartz, commander Reserve Infantry Regiment 15, went to Headquarters 117th Infantry Division to receive these orders, which were later confirmed in writing:

> "1. Infantry Regiment 157 is currently located in Sectors f & g. A battle for Fosse 8 is still going on. The *Kiesgrube*, *Stützpunkt III* and Loos have been lost temporarily.
>
> Tonight 117th Infantry Division will recapture the lost portions of trench.
>
> 26 [Reserve Infantry] Brigade [part of 2nd Guards Reserve Division] will prepare to attack the line Fosse 8 – *Stützpunkt III*, via Douvrin (one battalion Reserve Infantry Regiment 91) and Wingles (Reserve Infantry Regiment 15 less 3rd Battalion), from the reserve positions along the line Haisnes – Hulluch South held by Reserve Infantry Regiment 11. Two companies are to remain in Wingles in reserve.
>
> Using the fire of every battery located north of the line Alt-Vendin – *Stützpunkt V* and heavy howitzers of Kesselring's Battery, the artillery fire is to bring down in support of the attack the heaviest preparatory fire possible on trenches occupied by the enemy, on the *Kiesgrube* and *Stützpunkt III*. *T-Munition* [Tear gas shells] is only to be used against the former enemy lines.
>
> 14th Infantry Division is requested to provide fire support.
>
> Divisional Headquarters will be at Wingles."[31]

These somewhat sketchy orders were expanded by Reserve Infantry Regiment 15, then the companies struggled to get into position in pouring rain. They had only the vaguest idea about what they confronted and none at all about the dispositions or strength of the British forces they were about to attack. With immense difficulty and after a lengthy and slow approach march, the majority of the men of the battalions were finally on their start lines some four hours later, though the last of 1st Battalion did not arrive until shortly before midnight. The smell of chlorine was still strong and they were unsure how it would affect them. This forced them to don their unfamiliar masks, thus adding to the physical problems. The rain eased up and the moon came out, its light reflecting on their fixed bayonets. Of the expected artillery fire, next to nothing could be detected, but a short time later they set off and soon clashed with British troops, who were digging in – or with each other, as wild shooting led to misunderstandings.

There was some progress. A few British positions were overrun and their machine guns taken, but the racket alerted all the other British groups and the assault, which petered out, more or less along the line of the Lens – Violaines road, had come at a dreadful cost. British artillery and machine gun fire had cut great swathes in the ranks of Reserve Infantry Regiment 15. The battalions were splintered into small groups, taking cover as best they could. There was no continuity in the line finally reached and the surviving officers had to cast around in all directions in an attempt to link up with the neighbours. With the dawn came slightly greater clarity. Bit by bit the remnants of 1st, 2nd and 4th Companies made their way to the rear; their attack a complete fiasco. The 1st Battalion was down to 250 riflemen. Its commanding officer, Hauptmann Dombois, was missing, and a further eight out of eleven officers engaged were killed or missing. In 2nd Battalion the figures were eleven from fifteen. At the final roll call twenty out of twenty nine officers and 620 out of 1,750 men who took part in the attack failed to answer their names: seventy five percent of the officers were gone and more than thirty percent of the other ranks.[32]

In the wake of this disastrously costly operation one participant wrote home, justifiably bitter:

> "It does not require much imagination to visualise the situation. [We had] to advance in a pitch black night from the windings of a steep sided trench and pass through a thick and well constructed wire obstacle. There were no landmarks to head for, no clear task organisation, nor any recognisable objective ... That could not go well ... You simply cannot fight by night in any unfamiliar territory without several days of reconnaissance and, least of all, in a labyrinthine network of trenches: not with the best active troops, nor with the most experienced reserve forces."[33] Quite.

Throughout 25 September Generaloberst Crown Prince Rupprecht, Commander Sixth Army, found himself having to master the detail of a thoroughly confusing and dangerous situation and make a series of crucial decisions concerning the use of his meagre reserves. Concerned that the deep break in achieved against 117th Infantry Division represented the greatest immediate threat to his front, he released 8th Infantry Division to IV Corps to help stabilise the situation but, even as he was wrestling with the problems on his front, he still found a moment to voice his thoughts on gas to his diary at 1.30 pm.

Crown Prince Rupprecht of Bavaria Diary Entry 25 September 1915[34]

> "My greatest concern was the IV Corps situation. If they did not succeed in holding their positions, which were rather weak around the workers' villages northwest of Lens, and if Supreme Army Headquarters did not send sufficient reinforcements in time, there would be nothing for it but to withdraw to the

line Lens - Pont à Vendin – Deule Canal – Santhes. That which I had feared months ago has occurred. Through our premature use of the latest weapon of war, namely gas (which should not have been used until we launched a decisive attack), we had played right into the hands of our enemies. Because of the predominantly westerly winds in France they would be able to make use of gas far more often than we could."

Supreme Army Headquarters, whilst equally preoccupied with the serious problems facing Third Army down in Champagne and which are examined elsewhere, was concerned to rush reinforcements to Sixth Army as soon as possible. By 2.30 pm on 25 September orders had gone out to the Guard Corps in Belgium to entrain and move south with their 500 officers and 21,500 other ranks to the Lille – Douai area and come under the command of Crown Prince Rupprecht. The question of where best to deploy this valuable resource was one of the most important decisions he had to make during the battle – and one of the most difficult, as this brief description of the key parts of the second day of battle from his perspective shows.

Crown Prince Rupprecht of Bavaria Diary Entry 26 September 1915[35]

"It remained to be decided where the Guard Corps, which comprised eight regiments, should be deployed. Graf Lambsdorf [his chief of staff] proposed their insertion between 1st Bavarian Reserve Corps and VI Corps,[36] followed by the withdrawal of 11th Infantry Division. This would have involved a long drawn out sideways movement by 12th Infantry Division, which I considered to be inappropriate. I decided, therefore, to have fresh troops at the most endangered point and elected to place them between IV and VI Corps and to reduce the frontages of VI Corps and I Bavarian Reserve Corps at the same time …

"At about 11.00 am VI Corps reported that a [French] attack against the centre of 11th Infantry Division had been beaten off and that the enemy were massing in their trenches opposite the right flank of I Bavarian Reserve Corps and that an attack there was expected. At 5.00 pm IV Corps reported that 8th Infantry Division was attacking in the direction of Loos. We held Fosse 8. The attack against the right flank of I Bavarian Reserve Corps occurred at 2.30 pm and was beaten back and the same was achieved by 5th Bavarian Reserve Division and Landwehr Infantry Regiment 39 south of Beaurains.

"The apparently favourable situation of the battle on our French front meant that, for a while, I considered employing the mass of the Guard Corps against the British. Further consideration, however, indicated that the salient the enemy had created around Loos would later leave them in a most disagreeable situation. We should be able to make their life a complete misery with our artillery and, by means of sapping forward on both flanks, be able gradually to drive in their flanks without suffering particularly high casualties. Furthermore, the French had always been the more dangerous enemies and it was questionable if 13th Infantry Division and VI Corps could withstand a renewal of the assault. The original decision to place the Guards between IV and VI Corps stood, therefore."

While these considerations were dominating work at high level, the situation on the Loos battlefield remained critical. General Haig, commanding the British First Army, had decided during the night 25/26 September that the British 21st and 24th Divisions of Lieutenant General Haking's XI Corps, thrusting forward to the north of Loos, were to renew the attack on the German Second Position between Bois Hugo [= *Steinwald* (Stone Wood)] and Hulluch. The thinking was that if this move was successful, then Hill 70 could be easily isolated and the whole of this part of the front would fall into British hands. In any case, the intention was that Hill 70 would be assaulted once again and taken or neutralised during the morning by units of the British 45 Brigade. Unfortunately for the unlucky troops ordered to carry out the major attack, the strength of the Second Position was not known or, if known, seriously underestimated. With its various *Stützpunkte* [Strong Points] (III, IV and V on this part of the front) and a chain of concreted machine gun posts all protected by strong belts of wire, which had been rapidly strengthened the previous night, it was at least as strong as the original front line and also well manned by the morning of 26 September. One mixed reinforced battalion of Infantry Regiment 157 defended Hulluch itself and the sector immediately to the south, 1st Battalion Infantry Regiment 26 was in position between there and *Stützpunkt* IV with, on their left, a battalion of Infantry Regiment 27, together with all the surviving members of Infantry Regiment 153, and Reserve Infantry Regiment 22.

This represented a formidable challenge, one which would have required a full scale attack preceded by a lengthy bombardment, detailed reconnaissance and comprehensive orders and rehearsal. The BEF arranged for none of those things and the result was a full scale disaster for the attackers. The British artillery opened up with a feeble fire plan at 11.00 am, ceased fire about 11.30 am then, at about midday, the British, deeply echeloned, advanced north of Loos on a three kilometre frontage, with much of their field artillery galloping forward into open positions, where they could be observed clearly in the bright weather. These targets were then engaged by all the artillery of 117th and 8th Divisions, as well as that of the left flank of 14th Division and casualties began to mount immediately.[37] The batteries of Field Artillery Regiment 75 engaged them over open sights at 1,000 metres, causing huge gaps to be torn in their ranks.

Leutnant Rudolf Koch 1st Battalion Field Artillery Regiment 75[38]

"About 11.00 am [sic.] dense columns approached, led by mounted officers. They advanced on Hill 70 and, without any preparation at all, dashed towards our Third [sic.] Position, which described a wide salient towards the west here, so our men were in something of a sack. A combination of artillery and small arms fire ensured that they were almost entirely shot down. There were hundreds of men lying in front of the trenches. Towards evening, about 450 men and eight officers who had been pinned down in front of the wire, surrendered. It was a rare sight: our infantry stood up above the trenches waving them in, in a friendly manner, whilst the masses of British soldiers approached with their hands in the air."

Infantry Regiment 157 later noted that the first of the attacks went in against its 4th and 12th Companies south of Hulluch. The greater mass of the British infantry of 24th Division was described as advancing in columns when, at medium range, it was brought under accurate, aimed fire by the concealed machine guns and the riflemen of 2nd, 9th and 12th Companies Infantry Regiment 157, together with elements of Infantry Regiment 26.

This halted the advance in its tracks then to it was added flanking small arms fire from the remainder of 1st Battalion Infantry Regiment 26, together with that of 5th, 10th and 11th Companies Infantry Regiment 157. Leutnant Hentschel of 10th Company distinguished himself by calm, decisive leadership at this point. Climbing onto the parapet of his trench, where he was visible by everyone on both sides, he put a stop to wild firing, gave calm fire control orders and ensured that the successive enemy waves were allowed to approach to closer range where their destruction would be assured. On his sub-sector, the British troops were allowed to move right up to the wire obstacle, at which point he gave the order and the subsequent hail of fire simply wiped out the attackers. He later received the Iron Cross First Class for his work that day. From an observation post near Hulluch, one of the battalion commanders of Reserve Infantry Regiment 15 watched events unfold.

Major Kiesel 2nd Battalion Reserve Infantry Regiment 15[39] **5.**

"The British artillery was apparently badly ranged in, because our casualties were insignificant. At 1.00 pm the shelling ceased abruptly. Immediately after that, for a short while field artillery could be seen moving up. At 1.10 pm columns advancing on a broad front appeared from the same direction. I counted ten of them, alternately English and Scottish, each about 1,000 men strong. Some of the officers were mounted. As soon as the enemy approached to about 1,500 metres from the left flank of the battalion, two machine guns opened up, with the rifleman following suit a little later. Because the entire field of fire was covered with columns, the effect was excellent. Hundreds were sent to fall. However, undaunted, the columns continued their flanking march without ever turning to face the battalion.

"In order to halt any further advance, I ordered two platoons of 6th Company and one platoon of 8th Company to move forward from Communications Trench 4. Despite British fire against the right flank, they advanced about 200 metres. At that point some of the British swung round towards them, which threw nearby columns into confusion. The remainder, ignoring everything, continued on their way to a point south of Hulluch. At this time, the columns also came under flanking fire from Infantry Regiment

157. Casualties mounted into the thousands! The columns were increasingly mixed up. Nevertheless, the enemy succeeded in closing right up to the wire obstacles. Here they suffered further significant casualties. Then the survivors turned tail and flooded in the opposite direction to the rear. The masses shrank until only about a tenth of them succeeded in getting back into safety. Apparently large numbers had taken cover in the available trenches and dips in the ground, because the following day fifteen officers and 800 men were captured."

Further south, the men of 3rd Battalion Infantry Regiment 27 did not come under direct attack by the formations of the British 24th Division, but, from their positions between *Engländer Wäldchen* and St Laurent, they were able to observe and pour small arms fire into the advancing columns and their accompanying artillery.

Leutnant Vornkahl 1 Platoon 9th Company Infantry Regiment 27[40] **3.**

"On a hill, well to the rear, were the commander and his staff. I shall never, throughout my whole life, forget the scene which unfolded before me, as countless assault waves surged by; how the fixed bayonets and the drawn swords sparkled in the sunshine of this fine autumn day. It was like a scene from a peacetime manoeuvre, or such as is so often found in representations of battles long ago. No doubt about it, that was a serious assault, that was a major attempt at a breakthrough."

The same impression was gained by those elements of Reserve Infantry Regiment 106 who were still manning positions on Hill 70 following their intervention of the previous day, which had seen most of the feature retaken.

Hauptmann Peltz 11th Company Reserve Infantry Regiment 106[41] **4.**

"Masses of infantry advanced directly towards Hill 70 from the direction of Loos as well as north of the Lens-Hulluch road. Enemy columns moved until they reached approximately the line of the Lens-Hulluch road – *Rebhuhnwäldchen* [Partridge Copse = Chalk Pit Wood]. They then fanned out from there and in a southerly direction into dense attacking lines. I estimated the strength of the enemy, who were arranged into about twenty waves, as being at least a reinforced division. Simultaneously, the enemy dug in on the western end of Hill 70 began to bring down small arms fire on the *Stützpunkt*,[42] which was already under fire from shrapnel and heavy shells. The advancing masses of infantry were then brought under rifle and machine gun fire by the garrison of the *Stützpunkt*. By constantly varying the range and selecting only the most favourable targets out to 1,200 metres, we succeeded in causing the advancing enemy considerable casualties, despite the fact that our artillery did not come into action.

"We were able to observe the excellent success of our efforts. In places our machine gun fire mowed down entire rows. At the same time we fired to keep down the heads of those elements already dug in but, nevertheless, substantial enemy forces were able to close up into the dead ground to our front. About midday elements of Infantry Regiment 153 launched an attack from east of the Lens–Hulluch road in a westerly direction. This drove back the enemy advancing to the east of the road towards Hill 70 and reached the road between Fosse 14 and Hill 70, where they formed a front facing west. From there they were able to bring down enfilade fire against troops which had thrust past, or were approaching Hill 70. Under fire from two sides, the enemy lines fell back on Loos in total confusion. Our fire had a considerable effect on the fleeing multitude and this was reinforced by weak but well directed artillery fire."

The Infantry Regiment 153 attack, mounted hastily by the left flank of 1st Battalion and the right flank of 2nd Battalion and reinforced on the initiative of its commander by 10th Company Reserve Infantry Regiment 106, was an emergency measure intended to counter the threat of being outflanked. Launched unexpectedly, it was completely successful, though there were numerous German casualties.[43]

Leutnant Schmeil 10th Company Reserve Infantry Regiment 106[44] **6.**

"About midday, I noticed that 1st Battalion Infantry Regiment 153 was about to launch an attack. I decided to support it and inserted my company between 1st and 2nd Battalions Infantry Regiment 153. Our task was to clear the wood east of Fosse 14 (*Steinwald*) and the reach the line of the Lens – Hulluch road. It was all over in half an hour. It was a long and difficult afternoon for us, because the enemy brought down machine gun and artillery fire in support of attacks against the Fosse from the edge of the wood northeast of Loos (*Rebhuhnwäldchen*). We succeeded in bringing both offensive thrusts to a halt. Under fire from us, the enemy flooded back to the nearby wood.

"A renewed threat developed from a building about 800 metres north of Fosse 14. There I spotted numerous British soldiers firing into our flank from a trench. I requested the support of Infantry Regiment 153 and we were able to hold the British in check. Towards 5.00 pm their raising of white handkerchiefs gave us to understand that they had had enough of warlike activity. I ordered them to throw way their weapons and to head to the rear. One officer and about one hundred unwounded men rose out of the trench and I had them led away."

When the battle finally died away there was a scene of utter devastation in front of the German Second Position. The German infantry ceased fire, but the afternoon continued to be punctuated by artillery fire from both sides. British wounded were everywhere attempting either to make their way back to Loos, or to surrender. Infantry Regiment 157 noted corpses piled in heaps in front of their positions, amongst them, 'a white haired colonel', found amongst the leading row of fallen composed, 'without exception, of officers'.[45] The whole sorry tale of this misbegotten attack was later summed up by one commentator with these bleak words.

> "Twenty minutes of desultory shellfire, which appear to have caused the Germans no casualties, was followed by a pause of about half an hour. Then twelve battalions, 10,000 men, on a clear morning, in columns, advanced up a gentle slope towards the enemy's trenches. The wire behind which these lay was still unbroken. The British advance was met with a storm of machine gun fire. Incredulous, shouting in triumph, the Germans mowed the attackers down until three and a half hours later, the remnants staggered away from the *Leichenfield von Loos* [the field of corpses of Loos], having lost 385 officers and 7,861 men. The Germans, as they watched the survivors leave, stopped firing in compassion. Their casualties in the same time had been nil."[46]

It is improbable that German casualties were 'nil', but undoubtedly they were slight, especially around Hulluch and nothing to compare with those of the British. Compassion there certainly was in places, as attested by the British official historian: 'The retirement was carried out unmolested ... The Germans did not follow in pursuit, but from Hulluch, about 2.00 pm [3.00 pm German time], they sent out medical personnel and stretcher bearers who, regardless of the shelling, worked at binding up the British wounded, sending all who could walk or crawl back to the British lines.'[47] Once the majority of the survivors had departed the field, parties of men from the German Second Position went forward and cleared through the battlefield. This led to numerous minor actions as pockets of resistance were encountered by 3rd Battalion Infantry Regiment 157. Leutnants Werfft and Hentschel (once more) distinguished themselves in a series of incidents which led to the capture of one commanding officer, seventeen other officers and 500 other ranks.[48]

One of the commanding officers of Reserve Infantry Regiment 15 described the end of the action in a letter home once the regiment had been withdrawn. The way row after row had been mown down had made a dreadful impression on all concerned. Wounded men had crawled into his position on a daily basis – the last of them fifteen days later.

Major Kiesel 2nd Battalion Reserve Infantry Regiment 15[49]

> "The day before yesterday, on the 30th, I had another look at the *Leichenfeld von Loos* ... and movement could be detected clearly. That means that there must have been British still alive amongst the estimated three thousand lying out there! The area covered in khaki seemed to be endless ... and my heart was heavy with strange thoughts ... The following fact is an indicator of the knightly demeanour of our men. When the British 24th Division degenerated into a leaderless mass which did not know if it was coming or going, numerous men lay down and played dead. Because none of them moved, our men ceased fire. After a certain amount of time some of the heaps came back to life. Dozens started to stumble or crawl to the rear, others leapt from shell hole to shell hole.

Without doubt many were unwounded. From our side there was not another shot! [It was] German mercy and magnanimity in victory. We were not in the business of slaughtering the defenceless ... "

The final British foothold near Hill 70 was by now lost, as was Fosse 8. General Haig's orders for 27 September included orders for elements of the newly arrived British Guards Division to attack Hill 70 once more, but they were no more successful than 45 Brigade had been the previous day. Joffre insisted that the British continued to press in this sector, but Sir John French made it clear that he now lacked reserves and the French agreed to take over the Loos sector of the front line and replaced the British 47th Division by the 152nd Division of their IX Corps. However, despite this assistance, efforts by the released 2 Guards Brigade to renew the assault north of Loos, were shot to pieces on 28 September. Regardless of this and other setbacks, the fighting staggered on into October. The *Hohenzollernwerk* was recaptured from the British 28th Division on 3 October and IV Army Corps then set about planning for a more ambitious assault, designed to retake all the territory lost at the beginning of the battle.

As a result, on 8 October, 8th Infantry Division was given the task of attacking and recapturing Loos and the trenches north and south of it. Elements of Reserve Infantry Regiment 106 were subordinated to the division for the operation and it enjoyed considerable reinforcement in artillery, including the services of a pair of massive 420 mm super-heavy howitzers (the so-called *dicke-Berta* = Big Bertha – allegedly a tilt at the female head of the Krupp family of Essen). The boundaries of the attack were laid down as *Rebhuhnwäldchen* – Lens–Béthune road. Infantry Regiment 153 was deployed on the right flank, Reserve Infantry Regiment 106 centre, with Infantry Regiment 93 on the left. Infantry Regiment 72 and 7th Infantry Division formations were intended to broaden the attack to the left (south) depending on progress. All the necessary preparations were completed on 7 October and, at 8.00 am 8 October, the entire assault force was in position.

Unfortunately, it was a misty morning and it was not until about midday that the meteorological conditions favoured artillery observation. This cut both ways; there was little Allied gunfire during the morning either but, perhaps sensing that something was in the offing, Allied harassing fire gained in intensity from about midday onwards. The final orders, bringing the assault force to a high state of alert, were passed by telephone at 1.15 pm then, promptly at 1.30 pm, the preparatory bombardment began. The observers all felt that the fire was coming down accurately on the enemy positions near *Rebhuhnwäldchen*, the heights north of Loos, Fosse 15 and on various other points where enemy trenches and positions had been located previously. The 420 mm howitzer was observed to be having, apparently, a devastating effect on the ruins of Loos but, for some reason, no fire was falling on the trenches in the centre of the sector to be attacked. Initially the Allied artillery response was weak but, as the bombardment ground on, it grew heavier and fell with accuracy on the Germans' forward trenches and approach routes from the rear.

At 3.40 pm orders were received to attack on the stroke of 5.00 pm. However, it was clear at 4.00 pm that the enemy positions in front of Reserve Infantry Regiment 106 had still not been softened up sufficiently and this information was passed back by telephone at 4.30 pm. The fire continued but then, at about 4.50 pm, intense small arms fire could be heard coming from the sector of Infantry Regiment 153. It appeared as though the attack had been launched there prematurely. It was certainly the signal for large amounts of artillery defensive fire to be brought down all along the line. Eventually, despite all the difficulties, the general attack began at 5.00 pm and losses were incurred at once due to the heavy gun fire falling around Loos. The attackers from Reserve Infantry Regiment 106 encountered an intact wire obstacle and were only saved by the presence of an unknown trench, dating back to 25 or 26 September, which offered cover at a crucial moment. From this point they were able to return fire and, to begin with, the British withdrew from a section of their trenches.

This situation did not last long. The German attackers were somewhat isolated and subjected to heavy artillery and small arms fire from the forward battalions of the British 1st Division (from south to north: 2nd Royal Munster Fusiliers, 1st Gloucestershire and 1/9th Kings), especially from their left flank. Their numbers began to dwindle and, at the same time, the British began to reoccupy their forward positions and manoeuvre machine guns into positions from which they could engage the attackers almost from the rear. Eventually, having stuck it out near to the enemy wire until darkness fell, the survivors of this failed attack then made their way back to the rear. During the night all, or almost all, the wounded were conveyed back to the rear. Leutnant Seltmann of Reserve Infantry Regiment 106 ascribed his survival to the fact that he lay and sang the hymn *Eine feste Burg ist unser Gott*[50] repeatedly and loudly. He believed that, as a result, the British left him alone until two German stretcher bearers discovered him and carried him back.

The work of recovering the wounded continued during successive nights. Vizefeldwebel Wappler, Assault Pioneer Company, Infantry Regiment 153, lay seriously wounded in a shell hole which he shared with a wounded British soldier for three days until he was rescued.[51] The 8th Division casualties were extremely high that day. Infantry Regiment 93 suffered 142 killed and 401 wounded or missing,[52] Reserve Infantry Regiment 106, fifty six killed, 298 wounded and eighty four missing[53]; whilst for Infantry Regiment 153 the total was 534.[54] In other words, in achieving nothing, in excess of 1,500 men became casualties. The analysis of the failure was interesting. There were suggestions that British telephone intercepts may have played a part in revealing the plan, though this would appear to be most unlikely.

Far more significant was the role played by the short range 420 mm howitzer battery. Nobody in 7th or 8th Divisions had any experience of this weapon and they believed the battery commander when he told them that it would, 'pulverise everything within a 500 metre radius'.[55] Two linked conclusions were drawn from this. The first was that, with friendly trenches a mere three hundred metres from the British lines, it would be unsafe to use these weapons against the trenches forward of Loos and the second point was that that would not matter, because engagement of Loos village would simultaneously neutralise or destroy the forward British positions. However, not only did the heavy howitzers not, as promised, *Loos dem Erdboden gleich machen*[56] [raze Loos to the ground], their likely effect on trenches and field fortifications had been greatly exaggerated. In consequence, these places were insufficiently engaged by other guns and the attackers paid for it.

On the 7th Division front, their attack, launched out of Cité St. Pierre to the west of the Lens – Béthune road enjoyed slightly more, though equally costly, success. Astride the road itself, Infantry Regiment 72 on the extreme left flank of 8th Division failed to break clear of the northern edge of the *Engländer Wäldchen* [Chalk Pit Copse]; their attack withered away in a torrent of rifle and machine gun fire and 322 of its members became casualties. However, out to their left, Infantry Regiment 26, the only 7th Division regiment directly involved in the operation, managed to secure almost all of its objective, namely the *Kohlenhalde St Pierre* [Double Crassier], from elements of the French IX Corps which had been defending it. 1st Battalion Infantry Regiment 165 of 7th Division, which had suffered serious casualties earlier in the battle, was in support, but not called on to reinforce the advance of Infantry Regiment 26, though Leutnant Linde, sent to Infantry Regiment 26 for the operation, was killed during the fighting for the slag heap.[57]

In an operation typical of much of the low level skirmishing of the past few days, an attempt was made further north by 2nd Guards Infantry Division to divert the attention of the British and to seek some slight tactical advantage. The aim was to sally forward simultaneously from the *Kiesgrube* [Gravel Pit = Quarries] and the *Hohenzollernwerk* [Hohenzollern Redoubt] with the aim of driving the British back or cutting off groups of them. For this purpose, two companies of Reserve Infantry Regiment 77 were subordinated to Oberstleutnant Staubwasser, the local commander, and placed under command of 2nd Battalion Infantry Regiment 57. A bombardment throughout the morning was followed by more concentrated fire on the *Alte 11er Stellung* [The Old 11th (Regiment) Position = The Chord] from 1.30 pm to 4.30 pm. A rapid gain in territory by Infantry Regiment 57 came to an abrupt halt when the British blew prepared mines and, with them, the assault groups of Infantry Regiment 57. At this point elements of Bavarian Infantry Regiment 16 and the companies of Reserve Infantry Regiment 77, which had been following up the attack, took up the operation, which eventually petered out in stalemate, in a confusion of shell holes and damaged trenches and with little achieved.

Reserve Leutnant Steinmann 10th Company Reserve Infantry Regiment 77[58] **7.**

"From 2.30 pm until 4.50 pm, our artillery softened up the British trenches in front of the shaft with both light and heavy calibre fire. 10th Company advanced at 4.30 pm through a communication trench, the so-called *Fliegergraben* [Airman's Trench = Slag Alley], which ran along about fifty meters to one side of the slag heap [The Dump] to the forming up place. Leutnant Klußmann and his runner were at the head of 1 Platoon. Knowing the exact location of this trench, the British artillery brought down murderous artillery fire on it with pin point accuracy. Many a brave lad of the company met his end here, caught by a direct hit. Suddenly we were standing in a trench overflowing with British dead and wounded. In this sector at least it did not appear that the Tommies had avoided our fire.

"For a long time we fought our way forward with hand grenades from traverse to traverse. Suddenly a sharp increase in British resistance brought our rolling up operations to a halt. Darkness fell as we fought over possession of one single traverse. If it had been difficult to maintain our bearings by day in this maze of trenches, orientation effectively became impossible during close quarter fighting in the dark. A number of comrades were sure that they had been engaged by our own guns. The British pressure increased as they brought up ever more reinforcements. The company stood its ground. Because it was no longer sufficient to throw grenades into the traverses, a large number of men took up positions on the parapet instead – amongst them our revered company commander, Reserve Leutnant Lampe.

"One by one they were wounded. Ersatz Reservist Seeliger lost several fingers of both hands to a grenade. Between 10.00 pm and 10.30 pm. Leutnant Lampe also collapsed to the ground, severely wounded. Having had his thigh bandaged up in the trench by Sanitätsgefreiter Staats, he was carried back in a groundsheet. He had also received a serious stomach wound at the same time and, on the way to the rear, this extraordinarily brave, tried, tested, calm and highly admired commander died."

The next few days was marked by further minor attacks by both sides as attempts were made to straighten lines or gain a tactical advantage, but it was also the time when the final large-scale battles of the Allied offensive in Artois were played out. Down on the Vimy front, shortages of artillery ammunition, rising casualties and lack of significant success meant that Joffre called a halt to French operations there from 11 October, though the battle for minor positions continued for a further few days and the French IX Corps was ordered to provide artillery support for a British operation by IV and XI Corps timed for 13 October and intended, respectively, to secure the line between *Rebhahnwäldchen* [Chalk Pit Wood] and Fosse 8 on the Lens-La Bassée road and to capture the *Kiesgrube* [Gravel Pit = Quarries west of Cité St Elie] and Fosse 8. Smoke and gas were to feature once more for this attack. A total of 3,170 gas cylinders was brought forward, of which only 1,100 were used[59] and, as will be seen, the effect was negligible.

From midday to 2.00 pm, drum fire hammered the German positions from the La Bassée Canal to Hill 70. The gas attack was then launched, mainly from advanced saps and was interspersed with copious amounts of smoke, partly for purposes of obscuration, but also to disguise deficiencies in the quantity of gas available. This preparatory work continued for about two hours, but sunshine, strong winds and German counter measures all diminished its effectiveness, with much of the chlorine pillaring high over the German trenches.[60] The defenders counted seven separate discharges of one kind or another, then the British 46th, 12th and 1st Division followed up. Almost everywhere the attack failed, smashed by artillery fire and bought to a halt by intense small arms fire from the forward German trenches. The commander of an artillery battalion deployed near Hulluch witnessed what happened there.

Leutnant Klauenflügel 1st Battalion Field Artillery Regiment 75[61] 5.

"In revenge for what happened on 8 [October], the British had been hammered constantly and had achieved little. About midday their artillery preparation began, but it did not amount to much. About 1.30 pm, thick white gas clouds could be observed at several different points. These did not drift directly across, but were blown to the northeast towards Hulluch and partly over the British trenches. Because from our position I did not have good fields of fire to the right, I had one gun brought into action on the northern edge of our *Eschenwäldchen* [Ash Copse] facing Hulluch, where it could bring down direct enfilade fire at the old German, now British, Communication Trench 3. With my remaining three guns, I fired at the sources of the gas. As soon as one had finished discharging, another opened somewhere else and soon all visibility had gone. All that could be seen were the trees along the Lens – La Bassée road. Everything else had disappeared behind the grey-white clouds.

"The gas did not produce the desired effect. Instead of drifting according to plan, it blew diagonally and so became dispersed and rather thin. As a result, our simple protective masks, comprising woollen or cotton wadding soaked in sodium thiosulphate, proved to be effective. The technique of setting fire to rolls of cotton soaked in tar or oil worked well and none of our men was overcome. As soon as we heard the infantry open fire, we fired our Hulluch gun in the planned direction, though we could still see nothing. The British got as far as our trenches and there they were shot to pieces. It was said that there were many corpses lying in front of our positions. The gas cleared by about 4.00 pm and we could see Hill 70 once more. Some sort of smoke generator was in operation in Communication Trench 3. Its plume stretched as far as the *Kiesgrube*.

"I was just about to open fire on it when a line of infantry approached over a rise, coming from the left. There was no plan, no artillery preparation, no cover from a gas cloud – nothing. Our first shell landed at their right hand end and tore a hole in the ranks. Another battery joined in and they turned tail and raced for the cover of a communication trench. An hour later, it was the same thing all over again. Gradually the fire died away all along the front; the British had had enough. The only success was at the *Kiesgrube*, northwest of Hulluch. The British had by now located our batteries – it was a miracle that they had not done so earlier – so every time we fired, they replied, with a total of sixty heavy shells, but they did no damage ... an autumn mist rose. We could see nothing and fired very little.

"How different it was from when the French launched an offensive. They operated mostly with their outstanding heavy artillery, firing at both positions and approach routes for weeks in advance with their heavies then, two day before, with endless drum fire. They then charged the garrison and the wrecked positions under the cover of smoke, whilst unobtrusively lifting their artillery fire to the rear. It was as big a difference as day and night. [Just imagine] what damage the French would do to a battery deployed in the open behind the trenches. The British, not having been told [to engage us] did nothing. However, to be on the safe side, a new protected position was prepared for us."

The same action was also observed by a nearby battalion commander of 2nd Guards Infantry Division.

Hauptmann Freiherr Kurt von Forstner 1st Battalion Reserve Infantry Regiment 15[62] **5.**

" 'Opposite Hulluch the British launched a series of five attacks.' This was how the Supreme Army Headquarters communiqué described what happened. So what actually occurred? From the artillery observation post at 1.15 pm I witnessed a dreadful, yet deeply striking, scene. In the crater field north of the road [from Hulluch] to Vermelles, shells were crashing down, just like strong rain hitting a stony surface and splashing upwards. Huge fountains of earth and black smoke pillared up and, in between, were the greenish yellow clouds of heavy shrapnel rounds, interspersed with the white puffs signifying light shrapnel. The skies became ever more leaden, whilst the blanket of smoke which cloaked the earth thickened constantly. The company of the 233rd had the worst of it, huddled in a small section of the *Artilleriegraben* [Artillery Trench]. The only hope was that the beaten zone of the shells would allow a few survivors to counter the attack with an intact machine gun and so retain the *Artilleriegraben* because, there was no doubt about it, this was all about a breakthrough to La Bassée via Haisnes! [*sic.*].[63]

"They were about to make the attempt between Fosse 13 and Hulluch and we were extremely concerned about the two and a half companies which were manning the new trenches, which had hardly any protective wire and absolutely no mined dugouts. I toyed with withdrawing them immediately via the 8th Company positions and the central communications trench and placing them back in the old secure positions ... but that would have meant that those manning the *Artilleriegraben* would have been lost for certain. A runner arrived to tell me that I was wanted urgently on the telephone by Hauptmann von Briesen, the Brigade Adjutant, but I stared on over the sea of smoke and studied the situation of my battalion. It seemed possible that our new trench had not yet been identified by the enemy artillery and, as a result, would be spared the drum fire. So that is how I decided to leave the company forward in the new trench.

"Back! We raced as though the Devil was at our heels, for the shells and shrapnel rounds were pursuing us swiftly ... The telephone system was totally jammed as generals, general staff officers, adjutants, orderly officers, regimental and sector commanders made calls in all directions – at a time when the only conversations should have been between the artillery commander and the batteries, which had the best view of all with tripod binoculars in their observations posts. There was not much else to be done. The reserves could not move here and there through the hellish fire as though they were on exercise. It was all down to fate. The hammer was striking. The anvil had to resist it. Throughout the entire afternoon only a narrow strip of ground between Wingles and the 1st Battalion remained unengaged. That was lucky, but was also the reward of those who had placed themselves skilfully. 1st Battalion kept up a stream of reports to the rear.

"Towards 3.00 pm we smelled chlorine. It was a gas attack with a favourable wind. The overcast day was almost like night. 2nd Company reported, 'Gas attack!' We prepared to defend ourselves. It was the final report from the front. Thereafter all the telephone lines to the battalion command post were broken. The battalion reported to the rear, 'Situation of *Artilleriegraben* and 2nd Company serious. They will never take the Hulluch position. If Hulluch is surrounded the battalion will assume that a relief force will be sent'. We had to mask up and we prepared to greet the Tommies if they suddenly appeared in our cellar. I climbed up into the rafters. Above the cloud of smoke, which hung like fog in the mountains, shone a pale, watery sun.

"Down below Jakobsen opined, 'If this gas gets any thicker we shall have to pull out ... the air is totally poisoned, it is impossible to breathe.' Our masks were unequal to the task. Within minutes our hearts were pounding and every breath was a struggle ... fire was coming down round our cellar ... ten direct hits on the house ... now the enemy was attacking ... On orders from Brigade we had to send a patrol to establish contact with the *Hohenzollernwerk*. With a heavy heart, the battalion sent three trusted runners who had been carefully briefed. After three hours they returned with no positive information. They had not found the commander of the 233rd. However, three of our five lads who had been sent forward with essential supplies brought good news from the front (one of [the five] had been hit by a shell and one collapsed, overcome by gas. This man, written off as dead, regained consciousness after five hours, returned and was greeted with great jubilation). The three explained, 'The Tommies attacked 8th Company. They will not do so again. We should have gladly stayed forward. It would have been better than here. One expanded further, 'As the gas became thicker behind us, we legged it forward rapidly!'

"One telephone line to the old position was working. Leutnant Dücker reported a direct hit from a 380 mm shell in the trench. Two dugouts were crushed and six men were buried. After feverish work lasting for hours, only three men were rescued alive. Leutnant Dücker also reported that the situation was serious off to the right and that the *Artilleriegraben* had been lost. A second patrol returned and reported at 7.00 pm, 'Enemy in the *Artilleriegraben* and the *Kiesgrube* has been lost'. Unteroffizier Heine and Gefreiter Niemann, the bravest of the brave, had to go out once more to clarify the situation. They were expected back at 9.30 pm. It became later and we gave them up as lost. Then Heine arrived, carrying his groaning comrade on his back. He had been hit by a shell splinter in the small of his back ...

"However, already at 5.00 pm, the battalion could report back, 'Attack completely beaten off. A battle with hand grenades is continuing off to the right.' The gas clouds were dispersing and, with relief, we could unmask. Encouraging reports arrived from the front. 2nd Company had only suffered two casualties as result of the bombardment so, the moment the bombardment had ceased and the gas cloud had lifted, they were ready and prepared, manning the parapet ... the enemy was hidden by smoke, but this swirled away in the wind just in time. Immediately, three strong waves of attackers could be seen. Our close support guns and mortars ... destroyed section after section and the Tommies were soon attempting to deviate left and right. Our troops were grateful for the accuracy of our artillery fire and the mortar bombs had a murderous effect. Our small arms then took over and did their duty to the full. Very few British soldiers escaped to run to the rear or north towards the lost *Artilleriegraben*."

In fact, as was mentioned by Leutnant Klauenflügel, the only British progress that day was made in the area of the *Kiesgrube* and *Hohenzollernwerk*, where the gas had had more of an effect and the defence was particularly stretched. The full weight of the British 46th Division was launched against two German battalions: 1st Battalion Infantry Regiment 57 facing the British left and 1st Battalion Infantry Regiment 104 the British right and guarding *Poppgraben* [eastern end of the West Face] back to the *Schutthalde* [The Dump] via the *Südflankengraben* [South Face]. In a hard but brief battle, the British battalions suffered terribly against the Prussians and Saxons, who had been in this sector for over two weeks and were intimately acquainted with the ground.

Hauptmann Ludwig Wolff 1st Battalion Infantry Regiment 104[64] **8.**

"At 2.00 pm precisely, the enemy suddenly lifted their fire to the rear. Almost simultaneously the sentries reported that the enemy was releasing gas. From a southwesterly direction, the dense white clouds rolled threateningly along the ground towards us. We instantly took gas precautions. The simple masks, comprising a nose clip and wadding mask for the mouth soaked in a solution, were donned and the [anti-gas] ointment was smeared on the eyelids. Fires of wood and straw were lit on the parapets, so that the heat would drive the gas upwards. The enemy took similar precautions. We could see fires flickering their ghostly light through the gas cloud. Despite all these careful measures, the majority of the courageous fighters in the trenches suffered badly from the gas. Their faces turned blue and red as they almost suffocated and coughed incessantly and painfully. Their eyes swelled, turned bright red, burning, hurting and streaming with tears.

"Holding on was utter torment. It was only due to the fact that the concentration of gas was not lethal and the combination of October sunshine and wind drove it upwards, that the men were not rendered totally incapable of action. With amazing calmness and tough determination ammunition, hand grenades and spades were all made ready for close quarter battle ... Everyone kept a sharp look out forward, but the only thing to be seen was our defensive artillery fire, which was coming down with complete accuracy. Suddenly came the shout, 'The Tommies are through on the right!' Sure enough *Popp*-and *Kohlmüller-Graben* [western end of the West Face] had already been overrun.[65] Astride *Solmweg* [North Face] they were storming forward and were closing on the *11er Stellung* [Fosse Trench] in the direction of the *Häuserkolonie* [Houses between Corons Alley and The Dump]. Some elements had already swung left, occupied craters behind *Westgraben* [Little Willie] and were threatening the rear of 2nd and 3rd Companies.[66]

"Here the great danger was spotted immediately. The parados was manned and fire was opened. In order to improve aiming many men leapt up out of the trench and fired from a standing position. Leutnant Stöckhardt proved an excellent example, until he received a serious shoulder wound. One of the machine guns allocated to 2nd Company also fired from an open position until its crew was destroyed. The field was littered with a great many fallen and the living sought shelter in shell holes or *Solmsgraben*. More or less at the same time, the British launched a strong attack from the line 301 – 318 [i.e directly towards Little Willie, to the west of the main redoubt]. This collapsed completely through a combination of gun fire and small arms fire from 1st and 2nd Companies. 2nd Company had the worst of it, because they suffered grenade attacks from D8 and D9,[67] together with others from the direction of *Kohlmüllergraben*. The defence was made even more difficult here, because the sideways move on the left flank by the 55th [Reserve Infantry Regiment 55] caused overcrowding ... "

Wolff then proceeds to provide an extremely detailed account of the events of the remainder of the afternoon as attack and counter-attack settled possession of one part of the sector or another. The attack by the British 137 Brigade against the *Schutthalde* was a total and costly failure, ending with the few survivors clinging on precariously to positions along Big Willie trench. Various German hand grenade teams pressed forward about 300 metres south along *Solmsweg*, but were halted by lack of grenades and strong British defences near where the *11er Stellung* crosses it and had to set up a blocking position. As evening neared a further gas discharge was spotted, accompanied by a further attempt to attack forward, but nothing came of it; the battle was stalemated, with the British battered and bloodied, but still in possession of part of the original German positions. They were not destined to hold them for long. The next few days were to see the small British footholds in these two sectors wrested back from them. The recapture of the western section of *Hohenzollernwerk*, in particular, was seen as matter of honour and prestige by 2nd Guards Reserve Division and, furthermore, there seems to have been genuine concern on the German side about letting the British have any claim to possession of a place carrying the name *Hohenzollern*. The fact that it had been reduced to a tangle of smashed trenches and wrecked dugouts was irrelevant. They feared the propaganda value attached and the consequent risk that it could be trumpeted to the world as a significant victory.

So 3rd Battalion Reserve Infantry Regiment 15 was moved forward at about 6.00 pm on 14 October to relieve the battered 3rd Battalion Reserve Infantry Regiment 55, which had been fighting on and off for the redoubt since 8 October. Once established, the mission was to clear out the entire *Hohenzollernwerk* once and for all. By 10.00 pm its companies were picking their way forward very slowly and painfully through the narrow and damaged trenches. Once on the position, the relief also took hours and was not finally complete until 5.00 am on 15 October. The order was left 11th Company in the *Vordere 11er Stellung* [more or less the line of Big Willie] with, successively 12th and 9th Companies to its right. 10th Company was kept in reserve along The Chord.

Leutnant Hans Petersen 10th Company Reserve Infantry Regiment 15[68] **8.**

"We felt that we had been given the best place, but we were to be rudely disabused of that notion. The position had no right to be referred to in that way. Completely wrecked, it comprised nothing more than a roughly linked up succession of hollows of varying depth. We moved more across open country than through trenches and the enemy artillery fell with considerable weight on it. Our job was to repair this trench during the night! Apart from a dugout for the company commander, there were only two modest pieces of overhead cover. The others were buried or crushed. Extreme speed was essential; already we had suffered additional casualties. All we could hear was, 'Medical orderlies right!' 'Medical orderlies left!' We worked feverishly to get everyone under cover, but it was all in vain. The very next minute everything was shot up again.

"Our nerves, which were already in shreds, were soon even worse. The feeling that we were being displayed on a presentation platter, waiting our turn to die, was dreadful. It destroyed all resolve, all power of decision. Sooner or later everybody sank into a state of resigned indifference ... If only the order to occupy the front line would come! If only the excitement generated would give us a breathing space – but no. Leutnant Loof, [the company commander] was not unaware of the appalling nature of this position, but the request of the company to be withdrawn and redeployed elsewhere was not granted. So instead we had to spend an entire night of torture in this hellish trench, expecting to be killed at any moment.

"We envied the forward companies who were at close quarters with the Tommies. We could not help but hear the sharp crack of the bursting metal cases of our hand grenades as they exploded; the sound travelling to us through the drum fire, the tumult of the firing signatures and the impact of shells. During the morning of 15 [October], the fire increased in intensity. So far I had lost thirty men of my platoon! That could not continue if any of us were to escape with our lives. We had to do something; it was high time. On my own initiative I saved the remainder by moving them to the area of 11th Company. Its position was in better condition and was not under such heavy fire and at least there we had the feeling that we were tucked away. That evening I received a Battalion order, which directed me to prepare, together with four sections of 9th Company, to be available during an operation to recapture a stretch of trench … "

The forward troops had been better off because the risk to their own men meant that the British artillery did not fire as much at them. However, the heavy mortar fire made them suffer. At first light, profiting from the morning mist, they began the work of clearance. The trenches were full of dead and wounded of 3rd Battalion Reserve Infantry Regiment 55. Some of them had been hit up to three days earlier, but it had proved impossible to evacuate them. The wounded were all moved back to the dressing station in Haisnes and the fallen were buried that night. During that afternoon heavy gun fire rose to another crescendo, when the fire of four super heavies was added to the enemy fire plan. It appeared as though there would be an attack on 11th Company via an old communications trench. The trench was immediately blocked and a section was placed there to provide security. Casualties continued to mount. 3 Platoon 11th Company was hit by a heavy shell, which buried fourteen men. Six were killed and one unteroffizier and seven men were wounded.

Battles with hand grenades continued with great intensity. In a six day period, 3rd Battalion Reserve Infantry Regiment 15 threw 10,000 of them. During the evening of 16 October, 12th Company had thirty one men wounded in this way which, coming on top of constant artillery fire, took a severe toll on morale. Eventually it was decided that the only way to put a stop to this was to conduct a grenade attack intended to drive the remaining enemy clear out of *Poppgraben*.

Leutnant Hans Petersen 10th Company Reserve Infantry Regiment 15[69]

"It was 9.00 pm. At 11.00 pm our heavy mortars were to bombard *Poppgraben* then, at midnight, the attack would take place. Slowly the hour approached. We were ready and had placed a stock of one hundred hand grenades near the left hand sap. At precisely 11.00 pm the heavy mortars, together with light and heavy artillery, opened up, the artillery concentrating on cutting the communications trenches and approach routes. The fire came down accurately and the mortars threw out their heavy bombs. The first two actually came down in our trenches, the next three did find their way to the Tommies, but that was the end of it! All hell had broken loose on the British side. 340 or even 380 mm shells knocked out the mortars and flat trajectory guns made it very unpleasant for us to stay in the trench. Observing from the left hand sap, we spotted a British skirmishing line. The British soldiers occupying the trench waved hand grenades at us. In these circumstances, it would have been madness to have attacked. The company commander reported the facts and the attack was cancelled."

A repetition was ordered for the following night, but it was thwarted by an earlier British attack. A torrent of fire was directed at the German positions and casualties were high. 12th Company alone lost sixty eight men this way. Despite this, and with the assistance of a platoon of Infantry Regiment 104 rushed forward to reinforce, all British attempts to advance came to nothing and they were gradually driven out. The cost to Reserve Infantry Regiment 15 had, however, been high. When they were eventually relieved by Bavarian Infantry Regiment 23 during the night 18/19 October they had suffered during a running, but ultimately successful, six day battle in an area hardly 500 metres by 500 metres, casualties of three officers and 300 other ranks. Fifty three had been killed and 212 wounded or missing. Ninety two men, who had been buried alive or only lightly wounded, stayed with the battalion until it was withdrawn.

The relief of Reserve Infantry Regiment 15 effectively spelled the end to the battle, though minor skirmishes continued throughout the following weeks. Although the fighting around Loos had lasted for almost three weeks, British hopes of a significant victory were in fact extinguished as soon as the Germans managed to arrange for the scrambled defence of its Second Position by late morning on 25 September.

Hauptmann Willy Lange 1st Battalion Infantry Regiment 27[70]

"All in all, the Kitchener Army [sic.] gave a somewhat diletanttish impression. The first attack with gas was programmed to the last detail and was quite successful. But then, unguided, unsure and in dense columns, the British streamed forward in the next attack past Loos and, naturally this caused them very considerable casualties. The attack launched out of Loos itself went no better for them and they seemed to be beaten before they ever set out. The regiments which fought us were those we knew from August of the previous year: Black Watch, Gordon Highlanders, Camerons, Royal Scots, Seaforth etc. They were the same and yet not the same."

Loos, indeed the entire Artois autumn campaign, was a comprehensive example of hopes dashed and at dreadful human cost. The BEF was clearly still not equal to the challenge of offensive warfare against a first class, determined opponent. That realisation led to a great deal of British heart searching and wholesale changes in its approach to war fighting on the Western Front. However, it was not just the Allies who drew lessons from the battles of September and October. In its wake General von Kuhl, who was posted in to Sixth Army in December as Chief of Staff when Oberst Graf Lambsdorf was sent to a command appointment on the Eastern front, wrote a staff study on the subject of the breakthrough battle.[71] To add insult to injury had the British known about it, he analysed the Battle of Loos and cited it as an example of how not to achieve a breakthrough.

Kuhl made the point that, 'At Loos the British came close to breaking through our front, but the attack stalled before the Second Position'. He then listed the main points which had gone wrong. 'The commanders did not keep a firm grip of the troops after the First Position had been broken through ... the momentum of the attack was not maintained, nor were the troops correctly deployed to continue the offensive. At Loos the British held their reserves too far to the rear and they delayed too long before deploying them ... It would always be possible to put together a carefully supported attack which would capture the First Position, but that was where the main difficulties began ... ' The one hopeful note for the Allies was Kuhl's conclusion. 'A breakthrough', he wrote, 'is extremely difficult [to achieve] and dependent on many variables. For us it will be harder than it was for our enemies in September. Everywhere there are ample French and British reserves behind the front. This makes all the more important speed of preparation and conduct of the attack, together with deception measures. We cannot attempt to exceed the extensive nature of French preparations; we require a different approach. In favourable conditions at a suitable place, with overwhelming artillery and determined infantry it will, despite all the difficulties, be possible to achieve a breakthrough.'

It is ironic to think that the disaster of Loos sowed the seeds which eventually were to lead to the stormtroop tactics, which were premiered in the Cambrai counter-offensive two years later and employed on a grand scale in the great offensives which began in March 1918.

Notes
1. Sheldon *The German Army on Vimy Ridge* pp 90-133.
2. Kriegsarchiv München AOK 6 Bd 44 *N.O. B. No. 2908 Armee-Oberkommando 6. Armee. Übersetzung eines bei A.O.K. 3 gefundenen Joffre-Befehls* dated 28.9.1915
3. This is a reference to the defensive measures and move north of resources during the spring battles in Artois.
4. Joffre *Mémoires: Tome Deuxième* p 92.
5. *ibid.* p 93.
6. Baldenstein History Infantry Regiment 16 p 85.
7. *ibid.* pp 85-86.
8. An alternative, unofficial, title for the Westphalian Infantry Regiment 16 *Freiherr von Sparr* was Infantry Regiment 16 *Hacketau*; hence the plural nickname *Hacketäuer*.
9. Monokel = Monocle – the company sector astride the Noyelles – Annequin road, towards the left flank of the regimental sector.
10. Müller-Loebnitz *Das Ehrenbuch der Westfalen* pp 198-200.
11. In fact this was Unteroffizier Schröder himself. See Müller-Loebnitz *op. cit.* p 199.
12. The garrison town of Jäger Battalion 11, originally raised in 1813, was Marburg, hence its full title.
13. Hauptmann Bruno von Hanstein, who was born in Coburg, was thirty one when he died. He is buried in the German cemetery at Lens-Sallaumines Block 4 Grave 415.
14. Guhr History Infantry Regiment 157 p 70.
15. Hottenroth *Sachsen in großer Zeit Band I* p 195.

16. Lange *Hauptmann Willy Lange* pp 117-118.
17. Werner History Infantry Regiment 27 p 123.
18. *ibid.* p 124.
19. Guhr *op. cit.* p 71. Reserve Leutnant Roland Klein is buried in the German cemetery at Lens-Sallaumines Block 10 Grave 188.
20. Hottenroth *op. cit.* p 196.
21. BOH 2 p 195.
22. BOH 2 p 220.
23. Guhr *op. cit.* pp 73-74.
24. History Infantry Regiment 178 pp 58-59.
25. Rawson *Loos – Hill 70* pp 97-101.
26. Hottenroth *op. cit.* p 196-197.
27. Of these men, Leutnants Friedrich Ryssel and Kurt Gräber are buried in the German cemetery at Lens-Sallaumines in Block 9 Grave 161 and Block 10 Grave 190 respectively, as is Soldat Karl Göbecke in Block 9 Grave 67. Leutnant William Strauß, 12th Company, who died of his wounds on 29 September, is buried in the German cemetery at Dourges Block 1 Grave 420.
28. Schmidt-Oswald History Infantry Regiment 153 pp 181 & 183.
29. *ibid.* p 184.
30. Trützschler von Falkenstein History Infantry Regiment 93 p 101.
31. Forstner History Reserve Infantry Regiment 15 p 219.
32. As an indication of the confused nature of the fighting that day, of the twelve officers known later to have been killed in action or who were missing, declared dead, only two have known graves. Reserve Leutnant Karl Lütge is buried in the German cemetery at Lens-Sallaumines Block 2 Grave 741 and Offizierstellvertreter Heinrich Kastner in Annoeullin Block 1 Grave 33.
33. Forstner *op. cit.* p 223 & 225.
34. Rupprecht *In Treue fest Erster Band* p 384.
35. *ibid.* pp 386-387.
36. i.e. along the front just to the south of Vimy.
37. GOH 2 p 69.
38. Berr History Field Artillery Regiment 75 p 275.
39. Forstner *op. cit.* pp 229-230.
40. Werner *op. cit.* p 124.
41. Bamberg History Reserve Infantry Regiment 106 pp 39-40.
42. Presumably this refers to the actual summit of Hill 70.
43. Schmidt-Oswald *op. cit.* p 188.
44. Bamberg History *op. cit.* p 41.
45. Guhr *op. cit.* p 74. This was probably Colonel FC Romer, a militia officer in command of 8th Battalion The Buffs, who was killed that day, aged 61. See BOH 2 p 332. According to the records of the Commonwealth War Graves Commission he was actually 64 at the time of his death. He has no known grave and is commemorated on the Loos Memorial.
46. Hackett *The Profession of Arms* p 157.
47. BOH 2 pp 333-334.
48. Guhr *op. cit.* p 75.
49. Forstner *op. cit.* pp 229-230.
50. Bamberg *op. cit.* p 49. Seltmann was singing 'God is our Refuge and our Strength', a famous hymn by Martin Luther (1483 – 1546).
51. Schmidt-Oswald *op. cit.* pp 195-196.

The Autumn Battles in Artois: Arras and Loos 245

52. Trützschler von Falkenstein *op. cit.* p 106.
53. Bamberg *op. cit.* p 49.
54. Schmidt-Oswald *op. cit.* p 197.
55. *ibid.* p 196.
56. Gruson History Infantry Regiment 72 p 220.
57. Fließ History Infantry Regiment 165 p 90. Leutnant Martin Linde was killed two days short of his twenty first birthday. He is buried in the German cemetery at Lens-Sallaumines Block 10 Grave 217.
58. Wohlenberg History Reserve Infantry Regiment 77 pp 148-149.
59. BOH 2 p 380.
60. Baldenstein *op. cit.* p 88.
61. Berr History Field Artillery Regiment 75 pp 278-279.
62. Forstner *op. cit.* pp 250-252.
63. This is not correct. The mission of the British 1st Division of IV Corps was actually to secure the line of the Lens – La Bassée road between Chalk Pit Wood [*Engländer Wäldchen*] and the Vermelles – Hulluch road as a first step towards the renewal of the assault north and south of Hulluch, which of course never occurred. BOH 2 p 380.
64. Wolff History Infantry Regiment 104 pp 182-186.
65. It is extremely probable that this trench was named after Hauptmann Kohlmüller of Bavarian Infantry Regiment 17, suggesting that it was his battalion which originally dug and manned it.
66. This is clearly a description of the attack of the British 138 Brigade. See Rawson *Loos – Hohenzollern* pp 125-128.
67. This refers to the attacks with grenades launched by 1/7th Battalion Sherwood Foresters on the southern end of Little Willie.
68. Müller-Loebnitz *op. cit.* p 196.
69. *ibid.* p 197.
70. Lange *Hauptmann Willy Lange* p 119.
71. Kriegsarchiv München AOK 6 Bd 417 *Oberkommando 6. Armee: Der Durchbruch* dated 26 February 1916.

CHAPTER 7

The Autumn Battle in Champagne

Following detailed analysis of the battles in Artois of spring and early summer, the French high command decided that there would be another attempt during the autumn at a huge pincer movement to break through the German lines in Artois and Champagne. An all-out effort would be made to eject the German invaders from the territory of France before the onset of winter and priority would be given to a massive offensive in Champagne. French intelligence officers calculated, quite accurately, that the front from Aubérive in the west to Servon in the east was held by only five German divisions and that, although several points along the German front line were well developed or naturally strong, there were numerous points of weakness which could be exploited, especially if overwhelming resources in artillery and infantry could be brought to bear. Furthermore, if the front line could be pierced, there were few troops to man depth positions, which were, in any case, far less well developed than the First Position.

The German formations and units began picking up indicators for a renewal of the offensive quite early on and Third Army first made mention of it in a report to Supreme Army Headquarters on 12 August, when it was stated that an enemy attack was a distinct possibility somewhere along its front. Throughout the war it was almost impossible totally to disguise the preparations for a major operation and the German units duly detected the arrival of artillery reinforcements, some of which were already ranging in, together with the presence of many more enemy aircraft and observation balloons in the area. A great many additional train movements forward from the Chalons area were detected and much additional work on potential jumping off points was also noted. In particular, from about 25 August, the French began to undertake an enormous amount of fresh digging. In order to disguise the exact start lines, this work extended from the Moronvilliers Hills to the Aisne, with saps and trenches being pushed forward to reduce the assaulting distances and strenuous efforts being made to camouflage new spoil heaps by covering them with large pieces of dull coloured fabric. This effort was not especially successful. Gaps in the camouflage or the action of the wind betrayed all too obviously what was happening and simply drew the close attention of observers to signs of progress.

As the days went by, the lines could be seen being pushed forward, with new wire obstacles laid to protect them, whilst the German artillery did everything possible to hinder the actual work and damage or destroy the new positions. Machine guns firing on fixed lines at these places also contributed, but it proved to be impossible to counter the massive French effort effectively. Meanwhile, intelligence indicators of a forthcoming offensive began to multiply. On 31 August a French deserter, who crossed the lines near to Aubérive, reported that for the past three weeks there had been an incessant inflow of reinforcements and that a major assault could be expected in approximately two weeks' time. With many other calls on artillery and other assets along the Western Front, it was far from easy for the German chain of command to devise a suitable response, yet the matter was of the utmost urgency.

The lack of heavy guns was, as always, a particular problem. For the time being, strenuous attempts were made to concentrate the fire of those batteries which were deployed and available against the places which seemed to be potentially the most dangerous, or where enemy preparations appeared to be the furthest advanced. This was a reasonably successful policy, but it indicated to the gunners only too clearly how much more could be achieved if they had access to more guns and greater quantities of ammunition. The point was fully understood, but reinforcements were agonisingly slow in arriving. Nevertheless, as the weapons became available, the heavy howitzers began to search out enemy batteries, whilst the low trajectory 130 mm field guns were heavily employed engaging rear area targets with harassing fire.

That said, artillery commanders were strictly constrained in their ability to respond because of the need to conserve ammunition and to build up stocks of shells, so as to be able to respond vigorously when the major attacks began. As the opening day of the offensive drew closer and the German infantry had to endure large volumes of French shelling without witnessing any significant friendly response, these shortages were not good for morale. To make matters worse, although the German scout aircraft engaged the French airmen vigorously, they were heavily outnumbered; the consequent reduction on their defensive capability was not being adequately compensated for by the work of their anti-aircraft batteries and so the French artillery were able to benefit from the advantage of aerial observation of the fall of shot, as their artillery ranged in on the German positions and approach routes.

In addition to observers mounted in balloons and aircraft, a French airship even put in an appearance over the battlefield though, having dropped bombs on Vouziers on one occasion, it was quickly shot down near Rethel and the crew captured. This was a rare gleam of light for the German soldiers because not only did the artillery preparation cause a great deal of damage, the obvious enemy superiority was disconcerting for them. In parallel with all this activity, French infantry working parties continued to drive ahead by day and night to construct jumping off trenches and to advance saps and improve communications trenches. In an attempt to reduce the exposure of attacking troops, the front line was advanced everywhere where the width of No Man's Land exceeded 300 metres, with particular attention being paid to the so-called *Balkon-Stellung* [Balcony Position] astride the St Hilaire-le-Grand – St Souplet road, in the 'Cauldron' northeast of Souain and all along the slopes of the valley of the Etang near Massiges.

It was, of course, already completely impossible to keep these extensive and obvious preparations secret and so determined counter-measures were put in place by the German defence. The boundaries of the ground holding divisions were redrawn and the front line garrisons were strengthened. Reserves were moved further forward and all available additional troops were set to work improving the depth positions. Meanwhile,

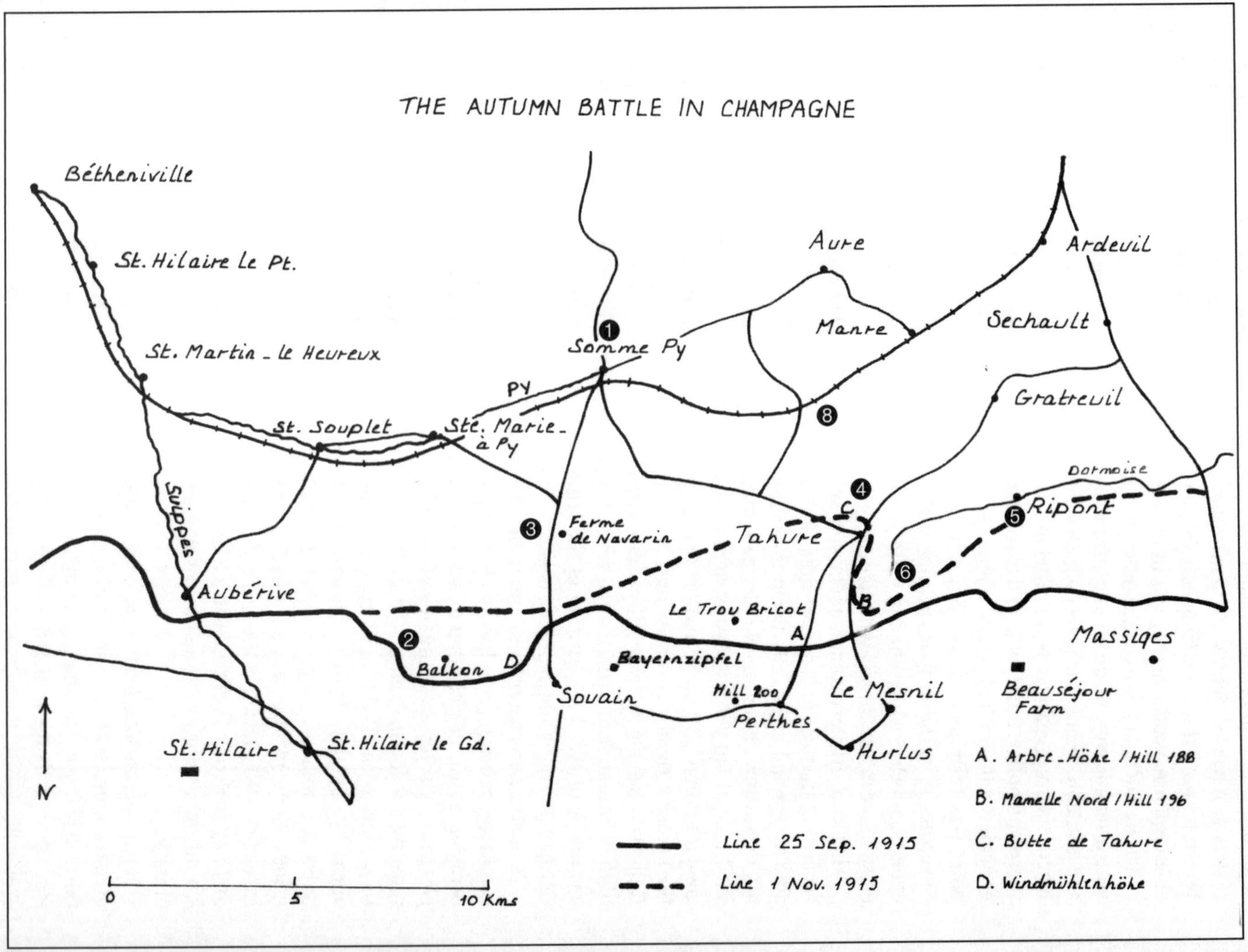
THE AUTUMN BATTLE IN CHAMPAGNE
Bétheniville
St. Hilaire Le Pt.
St. Martin _ le Heureux
St. Souplet
Ste. Marie _ à Py
Py
Somme Py
Aure
Manre
Ardeuil
Sechault
Gratreuil
Dormoise
Ripont
Suippes
Aubérive
Ferme de Navarin
Tahure
C
B
A
D
Le Trou Bricot
Bayernzipfel
Balkon
Souvain
Hill 200
Perthes
Le Mesnil
Hurlus
Massiges
Beauséjour Farm
St. Hilaire
St. Hilaire le Gd.
N
1
2
3
4
5
6
8
A. Arbre _ Höhe / Hill 188
B. Mamelle Nord / Hill 196
C. Butte de Tahure
D. Windmühlenhöhe
Line 25 Sep. 1915
Line 1 Nov. 1915
0
5
10 Kms

liaison between formations was intensified. Every detail of the defensive positions was checked, counter-attack plans were laid and all manner of emergency drills and procedures were rehearsed. Engineer units, which at that time were responsible for handling grenades, stockpiled huge numbers forward and the artillery, having ranged in on all its defensive fire missions, also verified that its batteries were completely surrounded by barbed wire and that its close-quarter actions were thoroughly tested.

All leave within Third Army was cancelled from 5 September, as it had become quite clear that the attacks would soon be launched, but there was still uncertainty about the date and, indeed, concerning the precise enemy organisation. The French Army, in a bid to confuse German intelligence officers, to familiarise large numbers of units and formations with the ground over which they would be attacking and also to prevent the soldiers from becoming exhausted in advance, arranged constant reliefs in the line and reduced the amount of patrolling. This made it difficult for the defenders to take prisoners or recover bodies for identification purposes. It was, nevertheless, clear that at least eight divisions would be involved in the first assaults, with numerous other formations available echeloned in rear of the planned attack frontage. Artillery fire intensified, damaging the forward trenches and forcing the defenders to expend considerable amounts of energy repairing them. This was, however, not just a one way street. Carefully controlled concentrations of defensive fire, directed against groups of French men digging their way forward caused numerous casualties.

Mid-September came and went with no sign of an assault. In many cases the French jumping off trenches had been pushed forward to an optimal 150 metres from the German front line, though there were still places where this had not proved to be possible. On 21 September, another French soldier deserted, bringing over tales of huge reserves of infantry, cavalry and guns and informing his interrogators that the offensive was just about to begin. Sure enough from about 7.00 am 22 September systematic fire began to come down. To begin with it was directed at particular points along the front but, in an attempt to bring about tactical surprise, concentrations were directed at various points from the hills around Moronvilliers to the high ground in the Argonne. Initially the greater weight of fire was aimed at key points in depth, but none of the defenders was in any doubt about the significance of what was happening.

Unteroffizier Haferkorn 4th Company Reserve Infantry Regiment 107[1] **1.**

> "22 September dawned fine and clear. At 7.00 am artillery fire was opened on a frontage of about two corps. This went on increasing in strength until its weight compared with that we had experienced during the winter battles at Ripont. It rumbled, roared and thundered all along the line. I was ordered to go and fetch more ammunition from Hauviné. From the hills to the north the clouds of dust and pillars of smoke caused by the explosion of the shells were clear to see. On the French side eleven observation balloons were up in the sky. I returned about 3.00 pm, but such was the weight of fire that I could not bring the wagon load of small arms ammunition right forward until the evening.

Everyone was on full alert. To our front in Somme-Py all was cracks and crashes, whilst reserves making their way forward were behind every bush and tree. The full length of the road and the terrain all around were under constant fire.

"The noisy racket reached an extraordinary crescendo. It bore heavy on our limbs and robbed us of all willpower. By the road to Aubérive there was a ceaseless crashing and banging of steel shells landing on the positions of the Mainz Artillery[2] and the 210 mm heavy howitzers. The station, the road leading to it and the village were being raked from end to end with 150 mm high explosive shells and shrapnel. The worst of all were the 280 mm heavy howitzers, which made the earth shake. Three to four metres from our dugout, a heavy shell ripped up the entire railway track. Our goose (which we really had with us) was thrown by the blast right across the dugout and we had to pick ourselves up off the floor. Fortunately everything was fine.

"We were sitting in absolute Hell, far worse than Ripont. All the roads, crossroads, level crossings, the entire rail network and the villages were being bombarded in accordance with a sophisticated plan, which covered the whole area and was directed from the air. It was impossible to bring up rations, though a very few men, braving the immense danger, managed to get through. This racket continued throughout the night; there could be no question of sleep or work. During the evenings the barrage fire increased even more so as to try to prevent the transportation of stores forward. Despite all this, ammunition columns pushed on with their loads right up to the battery position, though there were losses amongst the horses. Out in front everyone was pinned inside their dugouts. We spent the whole night expanding ours …"

Throughout the extended bombardment, the French gave priority to the engagement of command posts, artillery observation sites and key junctions in rear. At times the fire was so intense that all activity had to be suspended and from time to time lucky shell bursts caused a great deal of damage. One direct hit by a heavy shell, which landed right next to the main telephone exchange at St Souplet, for example, caused havoc when all the circuits and lines leading away were destroyed. It was a similar situation out towards the left [eastern] flank of Third Army, where towns and villages were singled out for exceedingly heavy gun fire. The railway stations at Challerange and Bazancourt were rendered unusable, whilst large calibre fire directed at the standard gauge railway running in rear of the front brought all traffic on it to a halt. The station located in a tunnel near Somme-Py had to cease operating and the narrow gauge lines and tramways running up to the front were also badly affected.

The fire plan had obviously been designed carefully and all manner of support units and accommodation from dressing stations to stables had to be packed up at high speed and the function dispersed into nearby woods, which were harder for the gunners to locate. Eventually it was established that, on average, between thirty and thirty five batteries were active on each divisional front and that gigantic stocks of ammunition were available. A survey conducted in the 24th Reserve Division area around Aubérive noted that in excess of 80,000 shells had landed in a single ten hour period of this, the first day of the bombardment. Nightfall brought no respite and a hurricane of French fire made repairing damage and routine replenishment extremely difficult, if not impossible, to organise.

23 September saw a repetition of the previous day's events. All the effort that had gone into restoring the trenches was in vain; very quickly they were reduced once more to their previous state. Even where dugouts survived the impact of shells, the resulting suffocating smoke and dust began to make their occupation virtually untenable and, all too frequently, they were crushed or collapsed, burying all those within. Always conscious of the need to preserve guns, so to be able to counter the anticipated infantry assaults, nevertheless the German guns did attempt a certain amount of counter-battery work, so as to ease the plight of the forward infantry. Furthermore, the obvious urgency of the situation had led to the redeployment of artillery assets from elsewhere. A battery of super-heavy howitzers arrived in the 15th Reserve Division area north of Souain and soon began to bring effective fire to bear to the south of that village whilst, elsewhere along the VIII Reserve Corps frontage, the two heavy howitzer batteries of 1st Battalion Foot Artillery Battalion 9 and three howitzer batteries of Foot Artillery Battalion 4 were also moved into position and began to contribute to the defence.

All these reinforcements were better than nothing, but they were too few and they arrived too late to make a substantial dent in the ability of the French guns to continue the softening up process. The second night of the bombardment was marked by a further intensification of the fire, with the flash of bursting shells filling the sky from horizon to horizon then, on the third day, the intensity reached drum fire proportions. The autumn weather, overcast and showery, did nothing to lift the spirits of the defenders, who had to endure watching their positions reduced to rubble filled crater fields cloaked with dense clouds of dust and powder smoke thrown up by the endless explosions, which also sent splintered wood and other materials spinning in all directions. For the surviving defenders, now experiencing a third day of the most intense fire, the situation was almost unendurable.

Their nerves on edge, they grimly stuck it out, emerging only to carry out sentry duty and responding by rushing to their alert positions every time there was a pause in the firing, just in case they were about to come under attack. Each time it turned out to be a false alarm, a tactic designed to catch them in the open and cause further casualties before they could get back under cover. Sometimes, as a variation and also to test the effect of the gun fire, lines of French infantrymen would appear in simulation of an attack but, such was the response of the defenders, these feints did not work and only very few reconnaissance patrols succeeded in closing up to the German positions. In the meantime, as 25 September dawned, there was no let up in the overall rate of French fire. There was no question of a shortage of ammunition affecting their ability to launch and support one of the greatest offensive efforts of the war.

Already, on 23 September, the French Commander in Chief had issued a rallying call to the men under his command.

Maréchal Joseph Joffre[3]

"Soldiers of the Republic,

"After several months of waiting, which have enabled us to reinforce our troops and build up our stocks, whilst the enemy has been depleting his, the hour has struck for us to launch an offensive to defeat them and to add fresh pages to the glory achieved on the Marne, in Flanders, the Vosges and around Arras.

"Behind the hurricane of fire, unleashed thanks to the labour of the factories of France, where your brothers have worked night and day on your behalf, you are going to launch a coordinated attack all along the front, in close harmony with the armies of our allies.

"Your *élan* will be irresistible. It will carry you forward in one initial effort right through the fortified lines which oppose you and up to the enemy battery positions. You will permit them neither rest nor repose until victory has been won.

"Let us go forward wholeheartedly for the deliverance of the soil of our home land and in order that justice and liberty may triumph."

The original intention had not been to attack on the morning of 25 September. Unfortunately the weather, which had been worsening, turned bad during the night 24/25 September. 'The rain began to fall', Joffre recalled later. 'There could be no question of delaying the offensive. Stocks of ammunition were already greatly reduced and were insufficient to permit a prolongation of the bombardment, possibly for days, until good weather returned. So, the offensive was launched at 9.15 am on 25 September. The rain, which had stopped at dawn, began once more and did not cease until 29 September.'[4]

On the face of it, the launch of the infantry assault at that time was fully justified. Apart from the severe softening up process, a great mass of troops had been assembled. General de Castelnau, in overall command of the main attacking force: Second Army under General Pétain and Fourth Army, commanded by General Langle de Cary, had no fewer than nineteen divisions available for the initial assault, with four more following up and additional formations in reserve. Profiting from reasonable weather early in the bombardment, which had facilitated aerial observation, the French commanders took comfort from the obvious extent of the damage and daily assured their troops that the task before them would be entirely straightforward. Nothing in the forward trenches could have survived the fire and all they had to do – as Joffre's message had spelt out – was to advance, occupy the remains of the defensive positions and turn a simple break in into a breakout into the open country beyond, where the cavalry would be unleashed to spread fear, alarm and destruction. One entry, taken from the diary of an anonymous French officer and found later by the Germans, read, 'The blow that we are about to strike will be final. All our strength, all our treasure, has been staked on it. If we succeed, our country will be free; if not Paris is lost. We all understand this and victory will be ours!'[5]

This optimism was not restricted to the army. The whole of France, buoyed up by optimistic press reporting, was convinced that its armies were on the threshold of a great victory which would end the war. Its cruel disabuse began almost at once. As the infantry moved into its starting positions, the bad weather grounded the supporting aircraft and blinded the balloon crews. Despite all efforts, rushed preparations meant that the jumping off trenches were often too shallow and restricted in size. This caused overcrowding, whilst dense lines of helmets and fixed bayonets sticking out above the parapets betrayed what was happening. The German artillery began to bring fire down as soon as it was light enough to see and the trench garrisons also joined in, bringing aimed small arms fire to bear. All of this caused confusion amongst the attacking infantry and rising casualties began to have a detrimental effect on the morale of the men about to go into the attack.

Nevertheless the die had been cast and, promptly at 9.15 am, masses of infantrymen in their distinctive blue uniforms rose out of their trenches and began to advance, led by their officers. Dense assault waves were followed by specialist engineers and machine gunners. It was an extraordinary sight. The German reaction was immediate. Showers of flares, replacing destroyed telephone lines, were fired to alert the guns. Clouds of shrapnel began to burst overhead and machine guns, hastily mounted, opened up on the advancing troops. Last minute reinforcements for the defence were still streaming towards the battlefield at this point but, with only five divisions in the front line when the battle began, the French enjoyed a very considerable numerical advantage. Nevertheless and despite the exhausting, nerve wracking seventy five hours the bombardment had lasted, the haggard defenders were swift to occupy their battle positions the moment shouts of 'Here they come!' were heard down in the dugouts.

Gefreiter Oswald Eichler 11th Company Reserve Infantry Regiment 133[6] *2.*

"At 7.00 am on 25 September we were already standing in threes in the horse dugout. Fearful drum fire, the worst of the entire bombardment, suddenly came crashing down on the trenches. A short time later the fire lifted onto our reserve positions. Then something suddenly exploded in the air and white clouds descended towards the ground. It was soon obvious that gas shells were exploding around us and we had to react at once. Ignoring the heavy small arms fire, we dashed across to the soldiers' dugout and grabbed for our gas masks: the dense gas clouds meant that we were not safe without them even there. The fact that we had not heard the planned horn signal warning us of a gas attack and because of the sharp increase in small arms fire, I decided to take five men and investigate along the communications trench.

"We did not get far. Men in blue helmets had closed right up to the dugout and were attacking with hand grenades. Swift action was called for. Shouting at my comrades to follow me, I dashed off to the cover of the aid post. It was soon clear to me that this was the correct choice because, benefiting from our covering fire, a machine gun came into action in the trench bringing down effective flanking fire to the right. Soon we heard the shout of 'stoppage', so we rushed forward out of the trench, shouting *Hurra!* To our front, a second machine gun opened up, doing good work in support of the attack which now began. Hauptmann Franke was at our head. Einjährig-Freiwilliger Fleischauer and I led a detachment and we succeeded in driving back the enemy, many of whom were Zouaves. Most of them were killed; very few escaped.

"As they pulled back, an enemy section attempted to bring a machine gun into action, but we soon captured it and pushed on. Reinforcements from Reserve Infantry Regiment 102 had joined us by now and Feldwebel H. took over command ... We brought fire down on the retreating enemy ... Soon we received the order to recapture the forward trenches. Under the command of a leutnant we stormed forward through machine gun fire but, because we lacked grenades or further reinforcements, we had to turn back just before the strong point where the enemy had established themselves in two shell holes."

Shocked by the violent reaction from the defenders, who were supposed to have been destroyed or at least subdued, the French troops pressed on forward wherever they could, suffering appalling casualties, which tore great gaps in the ranks. Nevertheless, such was the weight of numbers and so reduced were the defences, that it was inevitable that there would be break-ins all along the front under attack and close quarter fighting broke out everywhere. The thrusts were particularly deep along the line of the Souain – Somme-Py road defended by regiments of 15th Reserve Division (Division Liebert) of X Corps. Several of the battery positions of Reserve Field Artillery Regiment 15, located to the east and west of Ferme de Navarin, had remained largely silent during the bombardment, but poured fire at intense rates at the attackers until they were overrun.

Oberleutnant Stumme 5th Battery Reserve Field Artillery Regiment 15[7] **3.**

"In September 1915, 5th Battery, commanded by Oberleutnant Elten, was deployed south of Somme-Py, with four of its guns facing southwest and the other two pushed forward by the Souain-Tahure road. When, at about 9.30 am on 25 September, following drum fire which had lasted for three days, the assault began, the advanced section initially fired its defensive fire task as directed by the battery commander, Oberleutnant Elten. Once the telephone link was broken, the section shifted to fire over open sights instead, shooting directly at attacking columns of Zouaves which were directly threatening it. The section was assaulted at about 10.15 am. The crews, led by their courageous commander, Vizefeldwebel Müllenmeister, who had proved himself in many difficult situations, defended themselves manfully until, apart from three who were captured, every man had been killed by the guns.

"Once these two guns were lost, Oberleutnant Elten directed the fire of the other four guns at the captured section position, in order to prevent further advance by the constant stream of fresh attacking columns emerging out of the low ground. He was located in an elevated fire position, some three hundred metres from the gun line. The line was cut frequently, but always repaired by the skilful signallers: Zimmermann, Peters and Gerben. In the meantime, contact was maintained by runners led by Vizewachtmeister Zangerele. As the French began to push forward along the Souain – Somme-Py road via Hill 171 before advancing east, the battery fire was shifted from the southwest, more to the west. At about 11.00 am, Oberleutnant Elten ordered, 'Drop six hundred! At four hundred, rapid fire!' In so doing, he was directing the fire immediately in front of and on his own observation post. Then the connection was lost.

"Just after that the men on the gun line spotted that the black Frenchmen were forming up on the wood edge where the observation post stood, ready to launch a flanking attack on the battery position. On Leutnant Schreder's orders, the range was shortened somewhat and rapid fire was brought down on the wood edge. Oberleutnant Elten and all the men with him at the observation post – Einjährig Unteroffiziers Mecke and Schmidt,[8] together with Kanonier Heinrich, were overwhelmed and killed by Zoauves, furious at the losses inflicted on them by the battery. For about another hour, the four rearward guns, commanded by Leutnant Schreder kept the enemy at bay at about 250 metres, finally firing case shot to fend them off. On the right flank and half right to the rear, the enemy were also extremely close and attempting, with hand grenades, to force our men to abandon the guns, but they only succeeded in wounding one man. They must have assumed that we had substantial forces in our trench, otherwise it is inexplicable why they did not simply charge in against the very limited small arms fire we could bring to bear.

"After an hour of this, a powerful French thrust came in from the direction of the Souain – Tahure road and, simultaneously, the battery was assaulted from the left flank and also frontally. It was possible at the last minute to wreck three of the guns, but we did not manage this with the fourth. Fifteen men, whom the French had called upon to surrender, managed to save themselves by pulling back in a northeasterly direction through the only remaining gap. Two officers and about ten men, some of them severely wounded, went into French captivity, but more than thirty brave unteroffiziers and kanoniers, like their commander in his observation post, fell heroically by their guns."

One of the other batteries managed to withstand every attack, holding on, despite being surrounded at one point, until infantry reinforcements arrived and ammunition could be replenished.

Leutnant Vetter 3rd Battery Reserve Field Artillery Regiment 15[9] 3.

"From the early hours of 25 September, 3rd Battery, located to the west of the Souain – Somme-Py road, had been under heavy fire by enemy artillery of all calibres. The entire area was combed systematically by 280 mm shells, which knocked out one of the guns of the battery with a direct hit, causing heavy casualties. The battery observation post, about one hundred metres forward of the gun line, was manned that day by Leutnant Ludovici who, as well as directing fire, kept the battery commander, Oberleutnant Reinshagen, constantly informed about the enemy advance. Once the French had closed right up to the observation post, Leutnant Ludovici pulled back to the battery position. The guns were now manhandled about thirty metres right on top of the hill to prepared positions just immediately in front of the reserve infantry position, so as to be able to open fire at point blank range.

"By now the enemy were a mere one hundred metres from the guns and separated from them only by a clearing in the wood. Because of the previous rate of fire there were only about twenty rounds per gun left, most of them case shot, which could only be fired to counter large scale infantry attacks. Because there was no sign of any of our infantry – not until the afternoon did a recruit depot arrive to man the reserve infantry position – 3rd Battery Reserve Field Artillery Regiment 15 engaged the enemy with their carbines and deployed so as to provide flank and rear protection. By use of frequent salvos of carbine fire, we created the impression of a strong infantry defence and this stopped the battery from being stormed. Unfortunately, this infantry battle claimed the lives of Leutnant Ludovici[10] and several daring gunners.

"During the late afternoon and despite the proximity of the enemy, the battery echelon drove up boldly and resupplied the battery with ammunition, which was absolutely essential. Towards evening the teams came forward and moved the battery behind the rear reserve position, where it continued to support the battle for several more days, suffering further heavy casualties. The skilful and energetic resistance put up by 3rd Battery Reserve Field Artillery Regiment 15, during which every individual officer, gunner and driver was equally outstanding, was the sole reason why the enemy attack was brought to halt in this sector just short of the battery position and why, despite all efforts, was unable to get further forward. The entire battery had performed impeccably, earning the fullest recognition from its superiors."

Inevitably, damage to telephone cables meant that it was extremely difficult for the German chain of command to develop a clear picture of what was happening, though, naturally, it was obvious to Generaloberst von Einem, commanding Third Army, that his line was under extreme pressure. Appeals to General Falkenhayn at Supreme Army Headquarters for additional assistance could not be answered easily, because reports were also coming in from Sixth Army around Arras of a simultaneous opening of an offensive in the north, which also demanded attention and resources.

In the short term, the only hope was that the forward troops would be able to hold the constantly renewed attacks until the situation clarified itself and reinforcements could be rushed into position, though everything possible was done to feed formations forward as they became available. Already, at the height of the bombardment, the individual regiments of 192 Infantry Brigade were unloaded with the utmost difficulty and made their way forward to boost the sagging front line: Infantry Regiment 183 to 16th

Reserve Division, Infantry Regiment 184 and Reserve Infantry Regiment 122 to 15th Reserve Division, commanded by Generalleutnant von Liebert. Then, as battle was joined in earnest, Seventh Army released 185 Infantry Brigade and 4th Infantry Division arrived in Mezières from the Eastern Front. Over the next few days, they were joined by 22nd Reserve Division, also from the east, and 7th Division, both of which were committed, mostly on the VIII Reserve Corps front, which was under the greatest pressure.

With the situation on the Tahure sector, where 50th Infantry Division had suffered enormous losses on the first day of the attack, extremely precarious, Infantry Regiment 52 of 5th Infantry Division was rushed forward to bolster the front in rear of the hard pressed Fusilier Regiment 39 which, in addition to having confirmed one officer and twenty four men killed and one hundred wounded on 25 September, also had to report no fewer than twenty six officers and 1,667 other ranks missing that day.[11] It was to be the start of several days of confused and deadly defensive fighting for those involved.

Leutnant Neumann 1st Company Infantry Regiment 52[12] **4.**

> "... To our front, locked in a fierce defensive battle, was Fusilier Regiment 39. The gallant Rhinelanders had done their duty to the last. Only present as a few loosely organised groups, the companies manned their sub-sectors. There was no recognisable continuous position at all. The drum fire had done its work only too well. Some of the companies of the 39th were down to only twenty riflemen ... A mounted staff trotted by the Infantry Regiment 52 marching column. Even in the darkness we all recognised the outline of our brigade commander, Prince Oscar of Prussia. The word was quickly passed from company to company, 'The prince is leading us into battle!' Despite other ugly rumours, this inspired confidence in us all once more.
>
> "2nd and 3rd Battalions were to relieve Fusilier Regiment 39, while the 1st Battalion, acting as regimental reserve, was to dig in to the best of its ability in a small copse behind the two battalions ... In the early hours [of 27 September] an order arrived from regimental headquarters, stating that two companies were to be despatched to Massow's brigade, which was fighting to our left. 1st and 3rd Companies were nominated by the commanding officer and I, as the senior officer, took command of the two companies and sent for the commander of 3rd Company, Leutnant Junge, for a discussion. We decided to leave the position by half platoons because heavy artillery fire was already falling on the copse ... I had designated a gorge in rear of the copse as a rendezvous. It also housed regimental headquarters, so we were able to be given an explanatory briefing by the regimental commander, Oberst Fromme.
>
> "According to him the situation did not look good in the Brigade Massow area. Blacks had apparently forced their way into the trenches, but the enemy were said to have been ejected once more by a counter-stroke. As we left the commander shook us firmly by the hand, clearly concerned about his two

companies ... We set off east. An officer from Massow's brigade was to have met us at the regimental command post, but he completely failed to turn up. The bombardment had so smashed up the area that even someone with perfect local knowledge would have got lost. Our target was the Butte de Tahure. After we had only covered a short distance a French artillery spotter plane flew overhead and a little later our route was under fire.

"Advancing by half platoons, well spread out with two hundred metres between groups, we pressed on across the difficult terrain. To our front was the Butte de Tahure, at the base of which I had ordered the companies to assemble ... We received orders to act as Brigade reserve initially and then, the following night, to move to fill a two kilometre gap on the left flank of the brigade, which was a favourable break in point for the enemy. All we could do was to try to orientate ourselves, then, as dusk fell, I despatched two officers' patrols to the new sectors where we were to move. After two hours or so, both brought news that the village of Tahure, the sector and the butte itself were all free of enemy. About an hour later both companies were on the move and, by 1.00 am we were in position ...

"I sent patrols forward, which bumped into the enemy five hundred metres to the front, so we now knew where they were. Now I had to link up with the neighbouring formations. Leutnant Junge soon had contact on the right, but it was more awkward for 1st Company, because the right flank of Infantry Regiment 158 to our left was still forward of Tahure. However, I made contact that night with Major von Kitzling, commander of Infantry Regiment 158 ... In order not to have to pull back the well placed right flank of Infantry Regiment 158, or to have to give up the opportunity to defend the sunken road leading from Tahure, we decided to occupy the space with strong patrols that night and to deny it the following day by deploying two machine guns, which would be found initially by Infantry Regiment 158 ...

"At the crack of dawn, the whole area, especially the village, were brought under the heaviest artillery fire but [because of the placement of the machine guns] by around 11.00 am we were bringing effective enfilade fire down on the enemy columns advancing on the Butte de Tahure. That afternoon we even spotted enemy cavalry gathering in the area to our front. Unfortunately at that time we did not have access to one single gun which could bring down fire. However, because the enemy attack off to our left was not successful, the cavalry could not be used that day. We ourselves had very few casualties. The companies were not attacked but managed to bring down decisively effective flanking fire on the enemy attack to our right.

"Distribution of orders within the brigade was extremely difficult, so that night, when Leutnant Junge and I went to Major von Kitzling for briefing, I requested that we be subordinated to Infantry Regiment 158. Major von Kitzling, a first class man ... could not accede to this request. Apart from his own three battalions, he already had eight others under command. All he could promise was to supply me with three days of tinned rations. So we went off to our right and made the same request, but were refused there as well. The Saxon regiments had been locked into the most severe fighting throughout the day and were having the greatest difficulty commanding their own units. I then sent the gallant Leutnant Junge off to brigade headquarters and he returned at dawn to inform me that we would be under the direct command of brigade and that a battery, commanded by a young officer, which had driven into position behind us, would be under our command. Furthermore a machine gun company had been placed at our disposal.

"I caused four guns to be deployed within our positions and held two back in the sunken road in reserve. Finally, Junge brought the glad tidings that two field kitchens from our regiment had arrived at Brigade Massow, bringing not only food but also trench stores for our position. The next evening we had warm food once more. The second day did not pass as quietly as the first. The enemy had located our positions and launched an attack during the afternoon, having begun to engage us, unfortunately rather effectively, from 9.00 am. 3rd Company suffered from the artillery fire, whilst 1st Company in the sunken road, took numerous casualties from flanking machine gun fire. However the attack, conducted mostly by blacks from Senegal, withered away in our destructive fire.

"After the attack all was quiet along our front and eventually the artillery fire had died away. Unfortunately, the enemy launched a comprehensive air reconnaissance mission, so we had to expect the worst for the following day. We worked hard at our positions the following night, made contact with the battery to our rear and agreed a flare signal indicating when we needed defensive fire. I also took an artillery observer back with me to the sunken road. Only the following day would demonstrate the thoroughness of our preparations. Our own lines were distinctly porous, especially down by Tahure. As an example, a party of ours fetching water bumped into a French team carrying out the same function at the well in Tahure. Without showing any resistance, the twelve man French party, which included medical orderlies, surrendered.

"The next day we came under heavy enemy fire once more. This was followed by a strong assault on the Butte de Tahure, which affected 3rd Company in particular. The enemy broke into the trenches of our neighbouring battalion but Leutnant Junge, at the head of a half platoon, counter-attacked vigorously and cleared out the trenches of our neighbours, who were near to exhaustion. The 1st Company sector and Tahure itself were kept under very heavy fire and Major von Kitzling's men were attacked heavily. The battery in our sector was able to bring down very effective flanking fire following flare signals fired throughout the day. It demonstrated clearly how useful it can be when the infantry can fight in close association with its allocated artillery.

"The following day, the Saxons fighting to our right were relieved by Prussian regiments. Oberst von Ledebur took over the sector. Because the enemy attacks had tailed off, we could put all our effort into developing the positions and here our courageous musketiers really gave of their best, tackling the stone-hard chalk with the utmost energy ... On the eighth day orders for our relief arrived. That night we could link up once more with our beloved regiment in the *Kaisertreu* bivouac site north of Somme-Py. When we were relieved, Oberst von Ledebur handed me a sealed letter for my regimental commander. It concerned our performance in battle. When, after a successful relief and march to the rear, I reported to my regimental and brigade commanders and gave the letter to Oberst Fromme, he handed the open letter to my faithful fellow fighter, Leutnant Junge and to me, saying, 'You can read it as well. Both companies may be proud of its contents!"

One of the greatest difficulties for a proper organisation of the defence was that Falkenhayn, despite the reporting of all the indicators mentioned above, did not believe, right up until the last minute, that the French were intending to launch two major offensives.[13] He did not even change his mind about this on the morning of 25 September, when the assaults were about to begin. It came as something of a shock to him, therefore, when, having arrived at Headquarters Fifth Army at about midday for a conference, to see a signal which had just been despatched urgently by Third Army. This reported that the French had broken through on the right [western] flank of VIII Reserve Corps in the sector of 15th Reserve Division and were threatening the axis Souain – Somme-Py. Could Fifth Army spare some reinforcements?

In view of the fact that the right flank of Fifth Army was also under attack and that it needed to deploy its own reserves there, the signal was shown to Falkenhayn and a decision was sought. Before this could be done, another immediate signal arrived from Sixth Army, stating that another enemy attack had been launched in French Flanders at the junction between VII and IV Corps. At that, Falkenhayn telephoned General von Einem at Third Army, who immediately requested the support of several divisions with all speed. The Kaiser, who had been provided with optimistic briefings by Falkenhayn earlier, arrived himself at headquarters Third Army where, having been briefed on the situation by the commander, completely failed to grasp its seriousness. 'Tell the men to fix bayonets and drive these people out again', he told an amazed General von Einem.

The time for any such thing was long past. Returning to Mezières, Falkenhayn was briefed in detail about the situation both around Arras and in Champagne by Oberst von Loßberg. There were problems in the XII Corps area, where 24th Reserve Division had suffered a break-in one kilometre wide on its right [western] flank and three and a half kilometres on its left flank, though this thrust was of no great depth. Of far greater significance was the very serious situation affecting VIII Reserve Corps. There, 15th Reserve Division and the adjacent 50th Infantry Division had lost their entire First Positions on a twelve kilometre front and had been pushed back up to three and a half kilometres to the Second Positions, north of Souain and Perthes. These positions were located on reverse slopes, but very little work had been done on them. In many places they only existed as markings on the ground. The only slight gleams of light were the facts that the extreme left flank of 50th Division was still holding firm, as was the right half of 15th Reserve Division.

Both armies threw everything into the battle; Third Army even deploying all the troops of its field recruit depots into the Second Position. In addition, Falkenhayn had already ordered 56th Infantry Division to move to Third Army. Now, following suggestions by Loßberg, 192 Infantry Brigade was directed to Champagne, together with two *Musketen* battalions from Seventh Army.[14] Having studied the problems, Loßberg then suggested that the inner flanks of Third and Fifth Army needed unity of command and proposed that Third Army be subordinated to an 'Army Group German Crown Prince', stressing that this would enable entire formations to be transferred from unengaged fronts and that the redeployment of artillery in particular would be simplified.

While all these plans were being discussed at Supreme Army Headquarters, the chief of staff Third Army, Generalleutnant von Höhn, telephoned Falkenhayn and, in the course of a lengthy conversation, proposed straightening the line by pulling back in two large steps during the nights 26/27 and 27/28 September. Falkenhayn briefed Loßberg about the proposal whilst they were on the way to brief the Kaiser during the afternoon of 26 September. Loßberg spoke out vigorously against the proposal, but had no time to develop his ideas, but later did so, when called upon (most exceptionally) to brief the Kaiser on the overall situation.

Oberst Fritz Loßberg Deputy Head of Operations Supreme Army Headquarters[15]

"I described the situation confronting Third Army as very serious, because of the great numerical superiority in infantry and artillery of the powerful and deeply echeloned French attackers. I stressed in this respect that Headquarters Third Army would have to display a will of iron if the situation was to be mastered. There should be absolutely no question of ground being yielded voluntarily. Rather, Third Army would have to hold on and fight for every piece of ground in order to prevent a breakthrough. The troops of Third Army had fought heroically and would continue to do so in association with the reserves which were being moved forward, provided that there was unity of command and that [operations] were conducted with vigour. It was clear that my presentation had visibly made a strong impression on the Kaiser.

"At General von Falkenhayn's indication, I withdrew from the briefing room. A little later General Falkenhayn also returned from the Kaiser. As soon as the car set off, General von Falkenhayn turned to me and said, 'Well, my dear Loßberg. We shall have to part. His Majesty has nominated you as chief of staff of Third Army. I was deeply happy at this announcement which came as a complete surprise to me. For months I had wished silently to be returned to the front and, as had been the case earlier, to be able to carry a large burden of responsibility."

So for the first time, Loßberg, still only a newly appointed oberst, was despatched to solve a major crisis at the front, a role he was to fulfil for the remainder of the war in various critical times and places. No sooner had he arrived in the headquarters in Vouziers, than the telephone rang. On the other end was the commander of VIII Reserve Corps, Generalleutnant Fleck, who asked if the corps was to begin its planned withdrawal during the night. Orders were being prepared and would have to be issued shortly. Although he had had no opportunity for discussions with the army commander or briefings from the staff, Loßberg came straight to the point. 'There will be no withdrawal. VIII Reserve Corps is to stand and, if need be, die, in its current positions.'[16] Fleck recognised that the voice giving the orders was not that of Generalleutnant von Höhn and asked who was speaking. 'The new chief of staff of Third Army, Oberst Loßberg', came the reply and responding further to the question as to whether the commander in chief knew about this, Loßberg replied, 'I accept full responsibility and will be speaking to the commander very shortly.'

Further east, south of Ripont and equally pressed, the regiments of 16th Reserve Division had suffered badly during the bombardment and even worse during the initial shock of the assault on 25 September.

Oberst Müller Commander Reserve Infantry Regiment 29[17] **5.**

"The days of drum fire (22 - 24 September) tested the nerves of officers and men to the limit. This was the first time fire of this intensity was used and then it seemed as though further increases were impossible. However, this was achieved later in the war. During those days, rest was only possible for [the reserves] in the tunnel. The remaining trench garrisons were so exhausted by 24 September that they fell asleep at their posts along the parapet, despite the proximity of the enemy. Officers had to move up and down the trenches keeping the men awake and alert. On 24 September the companies worst affected, the 5th and 6th, were relieved after brigade had released two companies held at their disposal. This was, in fact, disadvantageous for 5th and 6th Companies. After a long hard march through the night under enemy fire, they reached the bivouac, which was also under fire, then, during the morning of 25 September, they had to rush to the aid of Reserve Infantry Regiment 25 [15th Reserve Division] at Maison de Champagne Ferme [located to the south of Ripont and just east of Hill 185], where they suffered such severe casualties that they had to be reconstituted subsequently.

"25 September was a critical day for Third Army. After three days of drum fire of previously unimaginable strength, the French attacked in overwhelming strength on a broad front from Aubérive to a point to the east of Massiges. Regimentally, we were of the opinion that we were outnumbered four to one. Reserve Infantry Regiment 29 and our right hand neighbours, Reserve Infantry Regiment 65, managed to hold the front line in its entirety but to the west and east ground was lost. The regiment next to Reserve Infantry Regiment 65 succeeded in holding the company sub-sectors on its left flank, but the remainder was driven back a considerable distance, as was the regiment further to the west. Where the front had been driven sharply back to the north, it formed a hook shape running right up to the Butte de Tahure, where the French continued to press their attacks.

"If this had been successful the situation would have been critical for the regiments holding Hill 196. The same would have been true on the eastern flank, where Reserve Infantry Regiment 68 held the heights. During the early afternoon, patrols sent out reported that they had made contact with the forward battalion of this regiment. However, on 26 September, the reports turned out to have been false, because the French, having crossed the boggy low lying area, had succeeded in gaining the heights, occupying Maison de Champagne and Massiges and bringing forward artillery. This meant that Reserve Infantry Regiments 29, 68, and 65 were threatened with being surrounded on both flanks and cut off. In turn, this meant that retention of Hill 196 was of decisive importance, because it dominated the rear areas as far as the Vouziers heights. Headquarters VIII Reserve Corps had contemplated withdrawal, but the cancellation of this order prevented the total destruction of 29 Reserve Brigade.[18] The loss of the dominating heights would have badly affected the entire situation of both Third and Fourth Armies."

Although Loßberg's courageous decision had staved off an immediate crisis, there was a desperate need for reinforcements to bolster this sagging sector of the front and the regiments of 56th Infantry Division, despite not being well placed, were rushed forward. When the call came, the commander of Infantry Regiment 88, Oberstleutnant Rogge, was actually on leave in Wiesbaden. It took hours to make contact with him and he was then faced with a hectic journey to reach Vouziers and report into Headquarters 56th Infantry Division there.

Oberstleutnant Rogge Commander Infantry Regiment 88[19] 6.

"Excellency Sontag briefed me on the situation. We had been allocated to the Crown Prince and were directed to hold Hill 199. This was one of the French objectives, because 199 dominated the surrounding area for a considerable distance. I travelled in a small vehicle to the command post of 112 Infantry Brigade and met up with members of my staff there. The regiment had been despatched forward in small groups and subordinated to other commanders... Starting out on the evening of 25 September, the regiment was transported forward by train from Lützelburg. 1st Battalion was unloaded in Attigny, the remainder in Brizy. From there they were rushed forward, some in cars, some in trucks and sent straight into action. Some of these convoys had to pass places which were under fire and there were casualties. Out in front and fighting desperately were Reserve Infantry Regiments 25 and 30, both decimated. The old trenches north of the line Massiges – Le Mesnil had been lost.

"5th Infantry Division, which was to have been transported away, was instead deployed forward and so it was possible to hold Hill 199, the

Kanonenberg and the heights north of Maison de Champagne, until Infantry Regiment 88, with Fusilier Regiment 35 on its left, could be deployed. The situation was utterly desperate, but the arrival of fresh troops caused the French to pause [fortunately], because Reserve Infantry Regiments 25 and 30 had almost ceased to exist, though Leib-Grenadier Regiment 8, Infantry Regiments 50, 79 and 88 suffered heavy casualties. To our right was the position on Hill 196, which we had constructed with huge, sacrificial effort the previous April. It was still in our possession, though Liebert's Divison [15th Reserve Division] had been forced back to a line south of Tahure. We still held Somme-Py and Infantry Regiment 118 was deployed down near Tahure.

"This meant that the defence continued to hold off the attacks. The rear areas were under heavy fire and Vouziers suffered greatly from the attention of aircraft, especially the station. The stations at Ardeuil and Challerange were virtually destroyed. It all demonstrated the immense French preparatory efforts and the surprise they had achieved."

As part of the emergency reinforcement programme, Fusilier Regiment 35, which had been in reserve near Saarburg, was moved forward by train to points in and around Attigny on the banks of the Aisne; then confirmatory orders arrived.

Reserve Leutnant Kriege 3rd Battalion Fusilier Regiment 35[20]

"The commanding officer 3rd Battalion, Major Hellwig, called the officers together and briefed us as follows: 'Gentlemen, to our front the French have broken through. It is our job to go and assist. I know you and you know me; we trust one another. The troops are rested, so we shall manage it. We are now going to march, with one short halt, about thirty kilometres, until we are right up behind the front line. What cannot be carried stays where it is. We shall sort ourselves out, then it will be, 'into battle'. Gentlemen, fall your men in, please."

Having arrived in their forward assembly areas, where they were met by representatives from the staff of 16th Reserve Division, the regiment was informed about the confused and critical situation to the front, where the defending regiments had withered away during the bombardment and subsequent fighting. In an attempt to prop up the crumbling front and to add weight to the defence where it was weak, the regiment found itself being deployed forward by companies, or even platoons, in order to bolster the defence. The experience of the 1st Battalion was typical.

Reserve Oberleutnant Erich Müller 2nd Company Fusilier Regiment 35[21] **5.**

"During the night 26/27 September, I went forward initially with two platoons into the position. Because there was no sign of any trench, other than one at right angles to the front line leading to Maison de Champagne, the two platoons took cover as best they could behind the stone walls surrounding a small field of cherry trees. Making my way along the battle front during the night, I came across the company commander of the troops who had been defending the line. He was there with the remnants of his men, about ten to twelve of them, taking cover in a shell hole. Neither the commander nor any of his men had noticed our arrival. They were completely worn down and listless as a result of the dreadful effect of the days of drum fire and were a sorry sight. I instructed them to leave and they made their way to the rear and a well earned rest.

Whilst these initial deployments were actually taking place, Loßberg was working at high pressure to take a firm grip on the defensive situation. For the first of several occasions during the war, he had been placed right at the centre of a major crisis and he began systematically to acquaint himself with the situation and to exert his personality and authority on events, which appeared to be in danger of spiralling out of control. To begin with he closeted himself with Major von der Hagen, the General Staff Officer Ia, in charge of operations, learning in detail about events since the opening of the bombardment and receiving the depressing news that average losses amongst the defending divisions were already approaching five thousand. Armed then with a marked situation map and ideas already crystallising in his head, Loßberg went next to see the army commander, Generaloberst von Einem. After a brief introductory discussion, Loßberg explained what he had directed Commander VIII Reserve Corps to do, persuaded von Einem that there was no alternative, then requested and received permission to tour all the major headquarters under command, armed with full powers to issue whatever orders he felt necessary to stabilise the situation.

Although he had had no sleep since 25 September and would not see his bed until almost midnight on 28 September, Loßberg set off at once for a comprehensive tour of the threatened front. Assessing its physical strengths and weaknesses as he was driven around from place to place, he spoke personally to all subordinate commanders and chiefs of staff, leaving them with clear instructions which allowed for no misinterpretation or dissent. They were to hold on where they were. Reinforcements of all types would arrive and would be fed into the battle in strict order of priority to be determined by Loßberg. Meanwhile, there were to be no more easy advances for the French. They were to be fought to a standstill where the lines now ran and their morale was to be shaken by denying them the satisfaction of making any progress against an increasingly solid front.

His will thus imposed on all concerned, Loßberg returned to his headquarters, where he carried out the same exercise on the staff. All the key posts – quartermaster general and the generals of engineers and artillery – were held by officers considerably senior to Loßberg, but they all agreed readily to follow, to the letter, both the words and the spirit of his direction. Doubtless his dynamic personality played a role here but the arrangement was far from unusual in an army where a man's appointment, rather than his rank, gave him his authority and, in any case, there is little doubt that Loßberg would have arranged for the removal of any member of the staff who would not cooperate. He swiftly exercised a grip of iron on the staff work, made himself available to all heads of department twenty four hours a day and, holding all the reins of power in his hand, gave out rapid decisions whenever they were needed. The desperate situation demanded such a centralised approach and events were to prove that his methods were effective.

Despite these organisational matters, for the time being everything depended on the courage and determination of the newly arrived reliefs who, despite the terrible mixing of formations and tangled chains of command, had to hold on to their positions regardless of cost. A typical example of this policy occurred south of Rouvroy, on what was to be the start of the second major attempt by the French to get their offensive back on track and break through the German defences once and for all.

Reserve Oberleutnant Erich Müller 2nd Company Fusilier Regiment 35[22] **5.**

"In the early morning of 27 September heavy artillery fire of all calibres started to come down. This was all the more intolerable for us because there was not the slightest sign of any activity by our own guns. There was also intensive use of enemy aircraft. For the first time we were targeted by gas shells, whilst the entire position was machine gunned from the air. Because the gas shells produced tears and a burning sensation, everyone was calling out for gas masks which, unfortunately, were stored with the medical company in rear. Such had been the need for haste that there had been no time to issue them. At about 7.00 am the fire lifted to the rear of our positions and the first attack by a mixture of French and coloured troops was launched. This attack was beaten off easily. Once more the enemy heavy batteries engaged us with gas shells from behind the Maison de Champagne Ferme [where they were shielded by the bulk of Hill 185].

"The second French attack came in about midday. Those attacking frontally were beaten off at once, but it was not possible to prevent about thirty to thirty five Frenchmen from advancing along the old communication trench which led forward at ninety degrees to the front from Maison de Champagne. 1 Platoon, led by Offizierstellvertreter Brümmel, was soon involved in a desperate hand to hand battle and it was only thanks to the intervention of a section of experienced soldiers of 2 Platoon under Offizierstellvertreter Bethmann, who leapt up out of their holes and rushed to assist Brümmel's platoon, that the entire French party was overwhelmed. The courage and comradely spirit displayed by our men was beyond all praise. Because our losses were so heavy, it was necessary that same afternoon to deploy 3 Platoon under Reserve Leutnant Albrecht and, with its assistance, we also defeated the third enemy attack."

A short distance to the west, around Tahure, the situation that day was so critical that individual companies of 1st Battalion Infantry Regiment 118 were thrown straight into the maelstrom of battle on arrival in the forward area. The after action reports of the various companies, produced in note form immediately after relief, provide a vivid description of the confused and costly close quarter battle during the next few days, as they attempted to cling on to advanced and highly vulnerable small salients in the French lines.

Leib [1st] Company Infantry Regiment 118 (Reserve Leutnant Baas)[23] 4.

"At 11.00 am 27 September, the company relieved a company of Infantry Regiment 158 at Tahure. Two platoons were deployed in the front line. The third, reserve, platoon was accommodated in a barn that had been used for stabling horses. There were no dugouts or other shelter for the forward troops, so they were constantly under the heaviest artillery fire imaginable and, in consequence, their ranks were thinned constantly and seriously. The heroic trench garrison was shot to pieces without being able to defend itself. Day after day passed like this! The enemy also used gas shells, then huge howitzers of massive calibre on 4 October. There are no nerves strong enough to withstand a thing like that! On 6 October there was an enemy attack which thrust forward as far as the stable. 1 and 2 Platoons were captured, but some members of the reserve platoon just managed to escape. Reserve Leutnant Baas was killed[24] and, with him, the majority of his company."

Reserve Leutnant Kratz 2nd Company Infantry Regiment 118[25] 4.

"On 27 September the company advanced ... to Tahure-East, came under command of Infantry Regiment 158 and was deployed at once to the front line. The trenches just looked like depressions in the ground. All day long there was heavy artillery and mortar fire. We fought here for the possession of a water point in the *Pionierschlucht* [Engineer's Ravine]. Every attack directed at the company on 29 September and 1 October was beaten off. The enemy had established themselves in the *La Goutte-Schlucht* [Droplet Ravine – presumably due to the presence of a water source], so the company was almost completely surrounded. The mortar fire was so intense that the position sometimes had to be abandoned for hours at a time. Then the French would attempt to roll up the position, the attack would be beaten back, the French would flee to the rear and the battle front would be re-occupied.

"There was a further attack on 6 October, which was successfully defeated, but some sections of trench were lost and had to be recaptured. It was an heroic battle by day and night. During all this time the field kitchen could only bring food forward twice. The company went for five days without rations or water. On the orders of higher authority the position was abandoned on 7 October. The company had performed in an exemplary manner: desperate attacks had been successfully defeated and had thereby made a considerable contribution to the failure of the great enemy offensive."

Leutnant Stein 3rd Company Infantry Regiment 118 [26] *4.*

"On 28 September, 3rd Company was deployed into the *La Goutte-Schlucht*. To our front, left, right and rear French flares shot up in the air. There were enemy in all directions! The absolute silence at night tortured our strained nerves. We were severely worn down due to lack of food or water and exhausted to the point of collapse because of the sleepless nights. On 29 September we launched a counter-attack in response to an enemy assault and took a number of prisoners. The attackers were drunk![27] During the night we laid barbed wire and dug out fox holes. We managed also to maintain contact [presumably with troops left and right]. On one occasion elements of the company were completely surrounded by the enemy and were about to surrender, but there was always a courageous individual who refused and called out to the remainder to defend themselves. No one ever surrendered voluntarily.

"Off to the right were troops who waved shirts and underwear at the French They could hold out no longer! They were men who had borne the bitter cost of all the terror of the past few days as long as they could, but now their morale had collapsed. Extremely heavy enemy artillery fire came down on the right flank of the company. One day, during the late afternoon, we spotted enemy cavalry riding behind a hill to our rear. Fresh replacement troops (Magdeburgers) arrived and were sent forward. Thirty percent at the most were all who arrived at the front. The rest of them crouched pale and silent, in the trenches and ravines of Tahure-East. The relay posts which we established [for the purpose of passing flare signals to the artillery] were shot at constantly, either with machine guns or, failing that, artillery.

"It was completely impossible to fetch rations. For a six day period each man in the company received only eighteen and half hard tack biscuits and half a glass of cider! The entire company command structure was either killed, wounded or fell ill. At long last, on 9 October, orders arrived directing the abandonment of the position, but this did not reach everybody. The withdrawal took place as quickly as possible. The wounded were left at the water point with rations which had just arrived, as were two wounded Frenchmen. Only by moving to the rear with all speed did some of the company succeed in avoiding being cut off. They had carried out to the letter their orders to defend this place to the end. About twenty men lost their way, were engaged with machine gun fire by the French and captured."

Oberleutnant Daub 4th Company Infantry Regiment 118[28] *4.*

"Just like 2nd Company, the company moved forward under intense artillery fire into the *La Goutte-Schlucht* (reserve position of Hauptmann Fither, Infantry Regiment 158). Three sections were deployed to block off the ravine in the evening. From 28 September to 5 October fire came down ceaselessly day and night. On 4 October most of 2 Platoon were knocked out by mortar fire. Constant defensive artillery fire prevented the move forward of rations or water. On 6 October the enemy blew a mine and launched an attack in the evening. This was totally defeated and sixty prisoners were captured. On 7 October we were ordered to leave the position and occupy the *Pionierschlucht*. On 8 October, we were relieved by Infantry Regiment 47. The march to the rear to a bivouac site near Ardeuil was accompanied by enemy artillery fire all the way."

Typical of the first of several days of heavy fighting for 56th Infantry Division, the first twenty four hour period had cost Fusilier Regiment 35 no fewer than 122 men killed, 252 wounded and forty four missing. The desperate defensive battle sucked in huge numbers of additional forces, resources and combat supplies of all kinds, but fortunately sufficient of them had arrived to blunt these attacks, which represented a serious attempt to bring fresh impetus to the attacks. In the event, the lines held more or less intact, the newly arrived *Musketen* teams being particularly useful in support of the hard pressed Infantry Regiment 158. It had been a hard fight, but it could certainly not be compared with 25 September and the defence was already stiffening.

Meeting in Savigny, at Headquarters VIII Reserve Corps, Loßberg, Generalleutnant Schmidt von Knobelsdorff, chief of staff of the army group and Oberst Freiherr von Oldershausen, chief of staff VIII Reserve Corps, had already agreed a common line for the conduct of the battle; and also, as a defence against a possible breakthrough, to arrange for a new position to be prepared as a matter of urgency, north of the River Py.[29] To this end seven engineer companies and twenty three and a half labour companies were to be deployed forthwith. It was also necessary, as reinforcements flowed in, to reorganise the front. X Corps with 19th and 20th Infantry Divisions and commanded by Generalleutnant von Lüttwitz, was to be inserted between XII and VIII Reserve Corps, responsible for the vital Ste Marie-à-Py – Somme-Py area, whilst the other corps sectors were to be reduced in width and reinforced further.

Although the battles after 27 September were not as broad in scope as those which had gone before, locally they were still significant and extremely hard fought. The defending infantry units were frequently in less than ideal positions and suffered particularly heavily from the French artillery because of the lack of overhead cover. However, this was the period when the German artillery began to play a more significant role as more heavy guns arrived, together with comparatively generous allocations of ammunition. The saw tooth nature of the front line following the early French successes was helpful in this regard. Guns located northeast of Perthes and southeast of Tahure in the 16th Reserve Division forward area, for example, were able to do great damage with flanking fire directed due west at French troops operating against the 50th Infantry Division sector. The sheer weight of fire involved brought its own problems, however, as guns failed and barrels wore out through overuse. A high priority had to be given at all times to servicing, repair and replacement of the guns upon which the defence relied very heavily.

At one place to the west of the Souain – Somme-Py road Infantry Regiment 184 was holding a section of the reserve position which was on a forward slope. This meant that it drew an immense amount of French artillery fire and was adjudged to be a place where a determined thrust might achieve good results. An attempt was made on 28 September to exploit this, but was defeated largely by the small arms fire of 2nd Battalion, commanded by Hauptmann von Gaza. Numerous prisoners were taken, but French hand grenade teams succeeded during the hours of darkness in penetrating on the flanks of the position. Fortunately, elements of Infantry Regiment 192 rushed over to assist and succeeded in establishing a blocking position.

The French, however, believing that they had located a vulnerable point, renewed the attack on 29 September. It was one of the hardest fought infantry actions of the entire battle. The regimental historian noted later:

> "As dawn broke the French Infantry Regiment 402 attempted to push on through the gap created the previous day. This was shot to a standstill due to the calm counter-measures ordered by the commanding officer of 2nd Battalion. The regiment was wiped out and 1,200 men were captured. The follow up in strength (seven battalions!) was shot to pieces. Opposite 3rd Battalion, there was a heavy preliminary bombardment, but it was not followed by an infantry attack."[30]

The rifles of the defenders had been fired red hot. Some riflemen fired as many as 1,000 rounds at the massed attackers and the machine guns poured out fire until the water boiled in their cooling jackets and all sorts of desperate measures had to be taken to replace it. Drinking water, coffee and urine were all pressed into service and, at the end of a desperate battle, which left the entire battlefield strewn with piles of dead and dying French *chasseurs*, the defence held. The battle had also cost Infantry Regiment 184 dear. They held on until nightfall, but were then relieved by Infantry Regiment 91. Such reliefs were vitally necessary because, even where the defence was still holding on grimly, the toll on the individual was by now almost intolerable.

oldat Hoffmann 2nd Company Reserve Infantry Regiment 107[31] **3.**

> "As dusk began to fall, it was necessary to man a double sentry post at the corner of the wood. Leutnant Pfeiffer gave us a handful of cigars to help us overcome the leaden tiredness we felt. We had to summon up every ounce of determination to remain awake. Three days of drum fire had been followed by three days without sleep, food, or anything to drink. It was an utterly wearying, exhausting battle that went on for hours at a time. Could it be assumed that the human frame could take any more testing punishment? In our situation it just had to. The responsibility of ensuring that we were not ambushed in the night spurred us on and we staggered out into the darkness. One quarter of an hour followed another. There was meant to be relief forward

in two hours. This time had long passed. Had we been forgotten? When would we eventually be overcome with exhaustion?

"I sent my mate back with a report. He found the trench deserted. What the Devil? That was an unpleasant surprise. We had to find Leutnant Pfeiffer, who said that he would be at the battalion command post. My mate made it clear that he would not be able to find his way there through the confusion of charred stumps, upended tree trunks and shot up trenches. 'You stay here, until I return!' Fortunately, as a runner, I was familiar with every fold in the ground. One minute later I was shaking awake our leader, who was sleeping the sleep of the dead and, fifteen minutes later the trench had been reoccupied, but the double sentry post had soon been forgotten once more ..."

29 September was, however, not a purely defensive day. Although in many cases small additional losses of territory had to be accepted, because there were insufficient forces available to launch more than local counter-attacks, on that day formations of 15th Reserve Division, operating to the south of Ste Marie-à- Py, managed to launch a sharp counter-attack towards evening. Assaulting forward from reverse slope positions, they achieved surprise, restored their former lines and captured more than 1,000 prisoners from the French 157th Infantry Division. Furthermore, concentrated German artillery fire broke up every French attempt to storm forward in this sector. It was a great effort, but almost the final contribution of Generalleutnant von Liebert's men before they were relieved by 20th Infantry Division, commanded by Generalmajor Freiherr von Lüttwitz.

Mention has already been made of the heavy rain which fell the night before the offensive opened. This continued throughout the early fighting and although it soaked everything and everybody, it was very much to the advantage of the defence, which needed every bit of assistance it could obtain in order to hold firm. The entire battle area comprised hard chalk covered in a layer of clay-like soil. Although the digging of trenches inevitably meant that the locations of defensive positions were easy to spot, disturbance of the chalk due to digging and shelling meant that the rain quickly turned the surface into a filthy grey, clinging mass of sticky mud, which made all movement extremely difficult. Furthermore the entire area over which the French forces had advanced had become one muddy morass of linked shell craters across which every man, piece of equipment and item of supply had to be moved.

At the beginning of October Third Army, working mainly from the interrogation of prisoners, calculated that from Aubérive in the west to Servon in the east the forces ratios were as follows: 24th Reserve Division, 6:1; 20th Infantry Division, 5:1; 5th Infantry Division 5:1; 50th Infantry Division 4:1; 16th Reserve Division, 3:1; 56th Infantry Division, 3:1 and 21st Reserve Division, 3:1.[32] There could only be one deduction from this assessment; the French were massing for a further major assault. Nevertheless, not content with passively awaiting this major renewal of the offensive, the operational planners under Loßberg at Third Army spent some considerable time planning a comprehensive counter-attack designed to eliminate the salients in the defensive line and to restore it along the line Hill 185 to the west of Navarin Ferme – Navarin Ferme – Hill 190 (Baraque) – Hill 185 (north of Le Trou Bricot Maison) – *Arbre-Höhe*/Hill 188 (two kilometres north of Perthes).

The intention, as briefed to Falkenhayn, was to parry the forthcoming French blow, then launch this counter-attack all along the line. Its feasibility, however, depended on reinforcement by additional divisions and more artillery. Supreme Army Headquarters, however, still under pressure to respond to events north of Arras, declined to make the forces available, sending only two regiments of gas troops, which were too few to make any difference. In the meantime, on 4 October, a fresh massive French bombardment began and continued for two full days, being coupled with local attacks from time to time, which sucked in forces and led to high casualties. By the end of the battle, no fewer than seven divisions and two independent brigades had served with VIII Reserve Corps alone. In addition a number of regiments from different divisions, such as Infantry Regiment 53 and Reserve Infantry Regiments 65 and 243 were sent into action in whole or part to prop up the line wherever it sagged along the corps frontage.

Just as in the battles of the previous winter, this major French operation had become an attritional slog for possession of the dominating high ground. The experience of the regiments of 56th Infantry Division had already demonstrated the lengths both sides were prepared to go in order not to yield any advantage to the other side and the situation was little changed when the Saxon 53rd Reserve Division began to be deployed. The bulk of this formation came under command of XVIII Reserve Corps of Fifth Army but such was the vital necessity of holding on near Tahure that Reserve Infantry Regiment 243 found itself detached, together with elements of Reserve Infantry Regiment 241, to this sector.

Having sent companies forward to relieve the trench garrisons, which were in dire straits after days of shelling and hard fighting, it was decided that, in order to forestall possible further French ambitions near Tahure, Reserve Infantry Regiment 243 was to attempt a surprise night attack to dislodge them from their newly gained positions. The task fell to 2nd Battalion, which was moved forward for the purpose to *Lager Neu-Paderborn* [New Paderborn Camp], a holding area a couple of thousand metres north of the Butte de Tahure. Casualties were high and little was achieved apart from some unquantifiable disruption of French plans.

Leutnant Richard Winzer 6th Company Reserve Infantry Regiment 243[33] **4.**

> "Orders arrived about 5.00 pm that this same day – it was 6 October – that we were to launch an attack. We were ordered to move to *Lager Neu Paderborn* and the foot of a hill, where we should receive more detailed instructions and also meet up with a guide who was said to have had a good knowledge of the ground. By now it was 6.00 pm and the attack was meant to begin at 6.30 pm as it started to go dark. The assault was intended to be a surprise, so no artillery preparation had been planned. The order of march was 7th Company, then 5th

Company and finally 8th Company. 6th Company remained in reserve under the battalion commander, Major von Lüder.

"Once Oberleutnant Stever, commander 7th Company, had spoken to his men, he set off over the hill past our artillery, which had just opened a series of concentrations of fire intended to neutralise the enemy. The guide led the battalion, with Major von Lüder and his adjutant Leutnant Häusler at the head, as far as a reserve trench, which was the last remaining one in our hands. There was a gap in the wire here. Our guide explained that we had to pass through it, shake out and advance, front half right, so as to overrun the enemy who had pushed forward into No Man's Land. 7th Company deployed – Oberleutnant Stever, his sword drawn, in the van – then, with bayonets fixed, the company doubled forward behind him.

"5th Company was meant to follow up a long tactical bound in rear, whilst 8th and 6th Companies were to await further orders. Nothing much was ever seen of 7th Company again. Oberleutnant Stever was mortally wounded and Leutnant Schneider, his leg smashed to pieces, was carried back. 5th Company, following up, found only dead and wounded comrades. The 7th Company had bumped into an unknown group of enemy lying in wait and had been wiped out. The battalion commander had advanced with 8th Company, behind 5th Company, leaving 6th Company behind. Left and right French flares went up. We had no idea where we were and no idea where the enemy who had clashed with 7th Company were located.

"Soon the enemy artillery began to open fire in response to the flares, so as to nip our attack in the bud. The various sections had split up and were now lying in the open in No Man's Land, or had taken emergency cover in one of the countless shell holes, where they had to remain and let the torrent of enemy defensive fire wash over them. Even though we had sacrificed one company, we had achieved something. The enemy knew that their forward movement had been checked – and by fresh troops about whose strength they knew nothing for the time being. We had found ourselves in extreme danger. The following day the enemy would have attacked in mass and would probably have broken through our lines.

"Tired out battle orderlies and runners picked their way around, gradually establishing contact with nearby companies, but unable to link up with neighbouring formations. Some of these brave men were never seen again. They were either victims of enemy shelling or fell into enemy hands in the dark. Top priority now was to obtain cover from view and fire, so shell holes were deepened, widened and linked together, so as to provide protection from small arms fire before dawn broke. 6th Company was called forward by Major von Lüder, so as to dig in and place its machine guns in position, ready to fire. The aim was to establish ourselves here, hold the line and await further orders from the regiment.

"Volunteer runners then attempted to find their way back along the dangerous, unfamiliar route back to *Lager Neu-Paderborn*. [Their route] was signalled by the rotting corpses of horses in No Man's Land, which we had passed the other way, and they were guided on their way by for the flash of the guns which marked the site of the *Lager*. Long after midnight our runners returned with regimental orders that the bulk of the battalion was to pull back to the reserve position, leaving only individual sections forward in No Man's Land, because there was no contact with the neighbouring troops."

Elsewhere along the front on 6 October the priority was the parrying of the renewed French assault. The artillery concentrated its fire primarily against French forming up places and start lines then, as soon as it became clear that attacks were imminent, defensive fire was brought down in No Man's Land, covering all approaches, Thanks to the recent arrival of considerable quantities of artillery, this tactic was enormously successful. The assaulting infantry suffered stupendous losses and only a relatively small proportion closed with and entered the German trenches. When this happened, vigorous counter-strokes, often lasting until well into the evening, succeeded almost everywhere in restoring the original positions.

Deployed around Aubérive, 24th Reserve Division, whose formations, it will be recalled, were outnumbered six to one, were subject to no fewer than six separate assaults that day, with pauses in between for additional artillery preparation. Despite this they held their positions, beating off each attack as it developed. Its regiments had fought heroically. Their best had been sufficient to make a great contribution to the foundering of the final major French offensive effort, but the cost overall since the battle began had been enormous. Withdrawn from the battle, Reserve Infantry Regiment 107 recorded the fact that it had lost twenty two officers and 151 other ranks killed, ten officers and 150 other ranks wounded and that no fewer than seventeen officers and 1,237 other ranks were captured or missing.[34] The situation of Reserve Infantry Regiment 133 was even worse, with thirty six officers and 495 other ranks killed, thirty three officers and 1,198 other ranks wounded, nineteen officers and 1,170 other ranks missing and thirty officers and 1,714 other ranks captured. Although massive reinforcements of twenty six officers, 232 NCOs and 3,056 other ranks arrived in early October, it was months before the regiment could be regarded as in any way comparable to that of the same name which had fought so hard in the Champagne region throughout 1915.[35]

Had the German chain of command but known it, there were no French plans for a further development of the offensive. The battles of the previous two weeks had torn the heart out of all the divisions involved. Furthermore, stocks of artillery ammunition, especially large calibres, were dangerously low. Despite this development, demands on the German logisticians were and remained immense.[36] Luckily the *Oberquartiermeister* at Headquarters Third Army, the Saxon Generalmajor Löffler, was not only highly experienced and efficient, but was willing to cooperate fully with and support Loßberg, who was considerably junior to him. As always during the First World War, the use of the railways was the key factor in determining how well the operations would be supported. For this battle, the vital railway junction was that at Amagne-Lucquy, some six kilometres east northeast of Rethel. Every man and every ton of supplies had to pass this point.

Fortunately, its importance had been underlined as a result of the battles the previous winter and the head of railway construction based in Sedan had caused loop lines to be constructed to the east of the station, which permitted trains to proceed directly between Charleville and Vouziers, which dramatically improved the carrying capacity. The train crews, too, performed exceptionally well. Day and night heavily laden trains rolled into the area and no sooner were they unloaded than their crews turned them round and went to bring forward a further load. At the height of the battle, some of the footplatemen and guards were working non-stop shifts of twenty four hours or more at one stint, but somehow they managed to keep going. There were no major accidents and, in general, traffic moved freely.

Further forward, the fact that the line between St Hilaire-le-Petit and Manre was within range of the French guns meant that movement along it had to be abandoned, but maximum use was made of branch lines and spurs to get material as close to the front as possible and so reduce the strain on horse drawn logistics. The stations and unloading ramps at Bazancourt, Bétheniville, Manre, Ardeuil and Challerange were shelled on a daily basis, causing a steady stream of casualties and damaging both tracks and infrastructure at times. However, despite all efforts by the French artillerymen, who were well aware of the importance of the track layouts and water towers, they never succeeded in bringing work to a halt for any significant length of time, because repair crews and heavy equipment were kept close at hand, ready to carry out essential repairs and maintenance day or night.

Generalmajor Löffler, gravely concerned at the loss of the use of the railway line Bazancourt – Challerange, assembled a special working group which managed to devise methods of compensating for it and, although this stretched carrying capacity to the limit, clearly laid down and enforced priorities ensured that the logistic troops were able to cope with a doubling of the local ration strength and demands for all types of ammunition, which almost spiralled out of control. Here, comprehensive oversight of stocks and their location, coupled with rigid control over supply, meant that, though severely tested, the system never collapsed. Somehow the necessary support for the planned operations was always on hand, despite the fact that French aircraft, roaming widely over the battle space, were constantly on the look out for stockpiles, which they either bombed or reported to the guns.

The fact that the unloading points were necessarily as much as twenty five kilometres behind the front posed enormous difficulties. Losses were heavy amongst the horses, due to enemy fire or simply through being overworked in appalling conditions. Whenever possible, Supreme Army Headquarters allocated trucks and other motor vehicles, but the already precarious road network was soon in a shocking state, due to the incessant passage of heavy loads and the effect of heavy autumn rains. In many places conditions were so bad that only the light weight *Panje* waggons, designed to cope with the notorious mud in eastern Europe, which the divisions arriving from the Eastern Front had brought with them, could be used. Despite all these difficulties, the troops were fed more or less regularly, the post arrived and the guns were kept supplied. It was a major organisational feat and a triumph of improvisation, which was fundamental to the ultimate defensive success.

Once the attacks of 6 October failed in their purpose, for the remainder of the first half of October the French attacks reduced in intensity, but there were still days when certain parts of the defensive front were subject to very heavy shell and mortar fire. A check kept by a battalion of 5th Bavarian Infantry Division revealed that in the twenty four hours to 10 October it had been on the receiving end of 2,600 shells, 800 heavy and 1000 light mortar bombs. Despite the overall slackening of the attacks, casualties went on mounting. The French army had thrown everything at this final attempt to break through and end the war in 1915. The Germans estimated French losses between 25 September and 7 October as 3,750 officers and 140,000 other ranks.[37] Their own casualties from 22 September to 14 October were calculated to be 1,700 officers and 80,000 other ranks.[38]

An enormous price was being paid in these hard fought battles and, despite the worsening weather, the German defenders, not knowing for certain what the French planned to do, felt that were still indications that they intended to keep up the pressure or further develop some of the isolated pockets of resistance they had established at the height of the close quarter fighting. In order to ensure that the lines were more easily defensible through the coming winter and to reduce the risk posed by the presence right forward of groups of French soldiers, General von Einem decided to make use of the increasing numbers of reinforcements which had reached Third Army and he set about reducing some of them by means of local attacks with strictly limited objectives.

One example occurred on 15 October in the 24th Reserve Division sector just to the east of Aubérive, when the Saxon 3rd Battalion Reserve Grenadier Regiment 100 and Reserve Jäger Battalion 12 launched a violent attack which led to the capture of a strongpoint, which had been held by the French army ever since 25 September, together with more than 600 prisoners, eight machine guns and eight grenade launchers.[39] However, any elation which might have been felt as a result of this success, which had been witnessed by the Kaiser, who was at Headquarters Third Army throughout the action, was immediately dampened when news began to filter in about one of the most shocking accidents ever to befall the German army on the Western Front. The precise circumstances were never established, but in the 7th Reserve Division rear area, north of Tahure, thousands of men, primarily from 1st Battalion Infantry Regiment 72 and Reserve Infantry Regiment 36, were sheltering in a railway tunnel when, at about 7.00 am, there was an enormous explosion amongst large stocks of hand grenades and flares at the eastern end. A minimum of 850 men were killed and a huge number wounded or badly burnt.

Vizefeldwebel Gerhard Krüger 4th Company Infantry Regiment 52[40] **8.**

"At 1.00 am we arrived at the tunnel. This was partly fitted out with planks and straw to lie on. It was absolutely full to capacity, so our company could hardly find any room at all in it. About 3,000 men were accommodated there. Our company feldwebel and the unteroffiziers found some space in a waggon. The batmen went and fetched some water so that we could make coffee. There were mail and gifts from home. At 3.00 am we lay down to go to sleep. At about 6.30 am I woke to an ear splitting noise. It was just as though all Hell had broken loose; all was crashing and cracking and there was smoke and the stink of sulphur. It was pitch black. People asked others frantically what was happening. From outside came the shout, 'Fire!' Unfortunately the door of our railway waggon was so solidly shut, that we could not open it. With the speed and agility of monkeys, we climbed out of a small hatch in the side and so reached the open air – or, rather, the tunnel, which was full of agitated men running hither and thither.

"What could have happened? Had a direct hit from a 280 mm shell burst in the tunnel? But, if so, what was the source of the dense smoke and all the flames. Everyone rushed for the left hand [eastern] entrance. Suddenly the fleeing mob was confronted by a sea of flames which was engulfing helpless wounded men, condemning them to an appalling death. The screams of a thousand men maddened with fear filled the air. Pressure from the rear forced men towards the flames and they fought back to try and avoid their fate. Desperate cries could be heard above the racket. Anybody who fell to the ground was beyond saving; trampled to a pulp beneath those pushing madly from behind. Deafening screams and yells reached a crescendo, interspersed with one explosion after another.

"Countless hundreds of fearful men stared death in the face. The smoke grew ever denser, threatening to suffocate us all. Finally, from somewhere, came the bellowed command, 'About turn!' Everyone rushed for the other exit, trampling underfoot those who collapsed from smoke inhalation. Thank heavens, we could see a glimmer of light up ahead. We reached the crater at the end of the tunnel and could smell a draught of fresh air. It was not before time and everyone scrambled towards it. Thick smoke clouds billowed out of the tunnel; it was impossible to see through them. Two medical orderlies attempted desperately to evacuate a wounded man. There was a further explosion and, hit by splinters, the two orderlies collapsed, together with their load. All three of them had been killed outright.

"One explosion followed another. Hand grenades, stored in huge quantities, blew up and rifle bullets, which had 'cooked off' in the heat, whizzed in all directions inside the tunnel. Wounded men, mostly suffering head wounds, staggered to the medical orderlies. Several men, driven insane by the shock, were shrieking and rolling over and over on the ground. The seriously wounded and men with extensive burns were taken away in large numbers. Pillars of smoke rose in to the sky. Luckily there was dense, impenetrable fog which clung to the ground; otherwise the French would certainly have brought fire down on this appalling scene. It was absolutely out of the question to rescue the men trapped in the tunnel. A few courageous individuals equipped with oxygen masks did try to enter this living Hell, but their efforts were in vain. They too were beaten back within a very few minutes, almost overcome themselves.

"The only thought was escape from this death-dealing underworld. Our poor comrades below had to be abandoned to their fate. Within, the work of destruction continued on to its bitter end. Outside, soldiers from all manner of diverse units stumbled around, their faces contorted in confusion. Here there were men of the 52nd, 72nd and 36th all hopelessly intermingled. Of course materiel worth thousands of marks had gone up in smoke. Expensive optical equipment and huge quantities of personal equipment had been consumed by the fire, but worse was the loss of irreplaceable human life. Some companies had suffered especially badly – 1st Company Infantry Regiment 72, for example. Those who remained were eventually rallied and despatched to the rear in one truly dismal column. They almost looked like a gaggle of prisoners of war as they stumbled to the rear, hatless and without weapons."

Infantry Regiment 72 felt that the catastrophe had probably been caused by an inexperienced soldier leaving a primed grenade loose near the main dump. This was then dropped or knocked over and set the remainder off. The subsequent explosion and flash was so violent that the tunnel was almost instantly set ablaze from end to end. A final casualty list was never established and Reserve Infantry Regiment 36, which suffered the worst of all, could only record that the outcome was 'so appalling that it is beyond description'.[41]

Despite this dreadful incident, operations had to continue without a break. South of Somme-Py and down around Ferme de Navarin, the fighting had been so hard that the decision had been taken to withdraw X Corps back into Supreme Army Headquarters reserve, replacing it with IX Corps under General der Infanterie von Quast. Immediately, formations of 17th and 18th Infantry Divisions began to move forward to relieve the worn out regiments of 19th and 20th Divisions, still located forward. One of the critical reliefs was that of Infantry Regiment 74 by Infantry Regiment 75, south of Somme-Py. One its members, H. Ludwig, later wrote of his experiences in the April 1926 edition of the regimental journal:[42]

"All along the main road from Semide to Somme-Py, there was an extraordinary amount of traffic. Horse drawn and motorised convoys, ammunition transports and infantry all vied for road space, so that our march only went forward at a snail's pace and frequently came to a complete halt. Already after a very short time our appearance blended with the background, as our shiny new *Feldgrau* uniforms acquired a layer of grey-white chalk dust, so, had we not been carrying weapons, we should have looked like a group of millers making our way forward. Our packs, which were already rather full after our period of static warfare in Bailly, became even heavier at Médéah Farm. Here each man was issued with iron rations. In the Champagne, because of the extreme difficulty due to artillery fire of preparing and transporting rations forward, each man had to have three iron rations on his person. We also found the issue of large quantities of digging materials an unpleasant burden. Everyone forced to carry a large pick wore a look of weary resignation.

"We advanced via *Lager Kaisertreu* to the positions we were to take over. Along the railway embankment between Somme-Py and Ste Marie-à-Py, the enemy sent us the usual 'welcome greetings'. We had not expected that our arrival would provoke such interest on the part of the Frenchies, so we were amazed to be greeted so 'warmly'. There was no trace of 'live and let live' between the gunners; there was constant wild howling of shells backwards and forwards. The closer we got to the front, the worse it got and soon rifle and machine gun fire was also very noticeable. We, who had just come from a relatively quiet spot, felt as though we had landed in a witches' kettle and we thought longingly of our comrades back in Bailly."

In this sector, as was the case for much of the Champagne front, the positions had not been selected for any tactical reasons. They were simply located where the initial French thrusts had been held. Around Ferme de Navarin the front line amounted to nothing more than a rough fire trench. There was an almost complete lack of obstacles, dugouts or communications trenches, which explains why the positions were so precarious, the troops so vulnerable to artillery fire and resupply frequently almost impossible. Attempts were being made to dig a second line of defence and everywhere countless corpses and heaps of discarded weapons, ammunition and equipment bore witness to days of bitter fighting. Ludwig's account continues,

"For many of the men who had joined us just before we changed locations, Champagne exposed them for the first time to the most appalling aspects of war. The impact on them was clear to see. The countless corpses and the sight of the plateau ploughed up by shells of all calibres could not fail to have an effect on the spirit and morale of our new comrades."[43]

One of the company commanders present, Leutnant Schneider, noted in his diary, 'Before, within and behind the positions lay corpses in greater numbers than we had ever seen during the war up to this point and more than we were ever to see again. The French attacking troops must have charged right up to the German machine guns in dense masses.' Commenting on the state of the trenches, Ludwig added,[44]

"When I have used the used 'Position', I only did this because that was the word we used to describe the place occupied by troops. To be precise, in the strict sense of the word, there was no position here at all and, indeed, it would have been impossible to hope for one because, right up until shortly before we arrived, heavy fighting had been taking place. We quickly had to forget about dugouts and other such comforts that we had become attached to in the trenches at Bailly and Tracy and get used to the sparse cover on offer here. Tiny holes hacked in the chalk, covered by groundsheets and camouflaged against aerial observation with fir twigs, had to serve as protection for the rain and the already noticeable chill of the nights. There was as good as no protection against enemy shell fire, so we went to work frenziedly to try and make up for this deficiency as we developed the position. Now everybody wished that he had received one of the cursed picks at Médéah Ferme, because the chalk was so hard that neither the large nor the small spades could make any impression on it."

These administrative concerns were typical of the situation on the western sector of the front, where the lines were beginning to stabilise slightly and normal routine in defence was increasingly being established.

Vizefeldwebel Voß Chief Clerk Grenadier Regiment 89[45]

"On 17 October, I received orders to move the regimental orderly room forward to *Kaisertreu*. The remainder of the rear echelon stayed behind in Leffincourt, whilst the forward echelon took up position in woods next to Médéah Ferme. However I did not spent long in *Kaisertreu*. Having been shelled out, I returned to the forward echelon. My two assistant clerks, Gefreiters Lübbe and Träbert – who stayed with me right until the end of the war – and I went to work with a will. We built a hut to serve as an office, just as the other companies had done. By 21 October our 'Villa Elisabeth' was so far advanced as to have a roof. This was where I spent the period of positional warfare in Champagne. This was also the place where we constructed a second regimental office, equipped with a small typewriter, which accompanied the adjutant wherever he went ... It was there to help produce tactical work quickly whenever it was needed ...

"The work of this team of orderlies was far from easy. They were often under fire as they maintained contact forward and I must record that the runners and cyclists under my command throughout the war never failed in their duty ... regardless of the severity of the battle, they were always at their posts and I must also pay tribute to the work of the regimental signallers: their duties were far from easy."

If, with the exception of continuing heavy shelling, there was a marked reduction in offensive operations on the western sector of the front, a much greater problem was posed by the fact that the French were still in possession of the dominating Butte de Tahure, the site of their greatest penetration. There were signs, especially on 12 and 13 October, that the French were planning to exploit their possession of this feature further. It was also obvious that it would have to be recaptured if there was to be any hope of creating a defensible line. A period of intensive planning at Headquarters Third Army then followed. The counter-attack force was to be based on 7th Reserve Division and 5th Bavarian Infantry Division, which were already located in the sector, whilst the

The Autumn Battle in Champagne 281

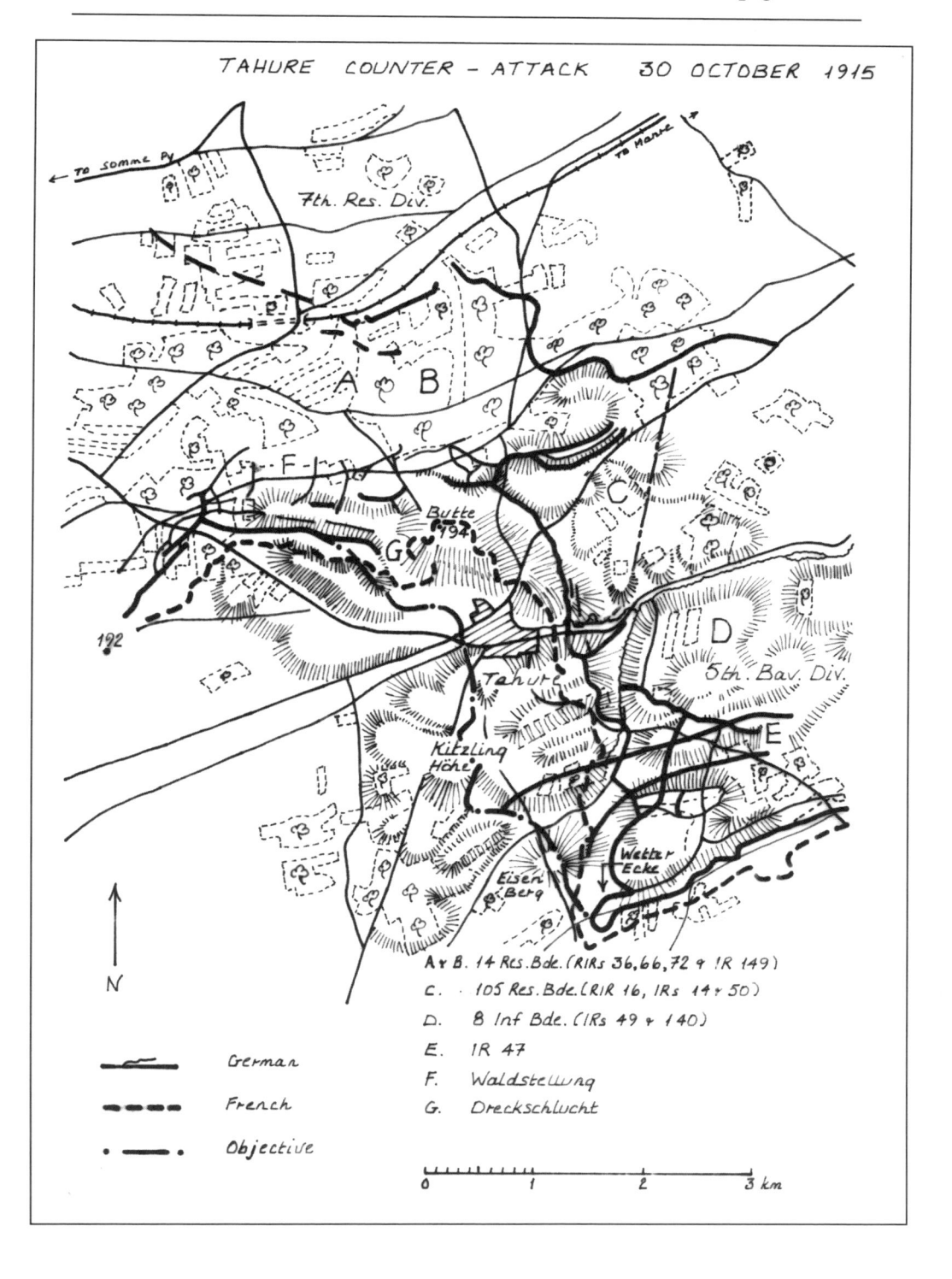

Pomeranian 4th Infantry Division, recently arrived from the Eastern Front, could also be made available.

It was decided that the key to success would be a significant build up in heavy artillery, equipped with copious amounts of ammunition, so all efforts were bent to achieving this and, after an almost superhuman effort by the logisticians, the number of heavy guns and howitzers in range was doubled and large stockpiles of shells were placed in position. It was impossible to disguise the preparations from the French, who also noted the digging of advanced saps and trenches by the infantry so, in addition to all the preparations, on numerous occasions work had to be suspended whilst minor French attacks aimed at disruption were dealt with. 5th Bavarian Infantry Division was most involved with this aspect of the preparatory period, which saw several see-saw actions, when isolated German garrisons were cut off by French thrusts and had to be released by means of local counter-strokes. It was exhausting, nerve wracking and caused a large number of casualties. A less auspicious way to prepare for a major attack can barely be imagined

On 25 October, a full month after the offensive had begun, during an operation to relieve 5th Company Bavarian Infantry Regiment 19, which had been cut off near the so-called *Wetterecke* [Weather Corner] Position, a French major, two captains and 140 other ranks were captured. Then, four days later and with the day of the attack looming, a French thrust against 3rd Battalion Bavarian Infantry Regiment 14 broke into the German lines, occupied them and scattered 11th and 12th Companies.

Leutnant Fürst Adjutant 3rd Battalion Bavarian Infantry Regiment 14[46] **4.**

"When the report concerning the disaster which had struck 11th and 12th Companies arrived at battalion headquarters, Hauptmann von Haas, displaying the clear determination he always showed in difficult situations, set in train immediate counter-measures. An order went out at once to 10th Company, deployed in support in the *Altrockstellung* [Altrock Position]. 'Distribute hand grenades and prepare to move!' Placing himself at the head of the company, Hauptmann von Haas led them through the dark night to the 9th Company sector, which was located to the left of that of 12th Company and which had not been attacked. Having patrolled forward to reconnoitre the situation, the counter-attack was launched.

"A half platoon was sent along the *Längsgraben* with orders to attack the front line directly. With the remainder of 10th Company, a number of hand grenade men, led by Hauptmann von Haas to the fore, we then began to roll up the front line. Initially the enemy was surprised and yielded ground. We progressed some two hundred metres then we called a halt. At a point where a trench branched off, the French had mounted two machine guns, sited so as to cover the trench from a flank and the crater field to the front respectively. Having thrown a few volleys of grenades, we attempted to charge forward, to shouts of *Hurra!* We were met by a dense hail of bullets, which slammed into our ranks and wounded the men in the lead.

"We tried another five or six times to assault the machine gun nests but, in the meantime, the enemy had brought up reinforcements and also obtained support from their artillery, so we, with our rifles and grenades, were strictly limited in what we could achieve. We lay there, locked in heavy fighting, for several hours. Our own artillery joined in, but we were so close to the enemy that many of our own shells hit our section of trench. All around us were crashes, roars and the drone [of shells] as though all Hell had broken loose. More and more gaps appeared in our ranks. Because it appeared to be impossible to roll up the trench any further and because there was no sign of our half platoon, I took two sections and attempted to work my way round in the crater field outside the trench.

"We had made a certain amount of progress when, suddenly, to our rear we heard shouts of *Hurra!* It was our long lost half platoon which had taken us for Frenchmen and launched an attack on us. The mistake was soon sorted out, but it also alerted the French to us and a curtain of machine gun bullets pinned us down, while grenades landed all round us. Our attempt to work our way along the enemy trenches was thwarted once more and our casualties mounted further."

All that remained was for a sandbag barrier to be built and manned in order to prevent further progress by the French. The stand off continued right through the remainder of 29 October, leaving 3rd Battalion with forty percent casualties and in no fit state to contribute to the forthcoming assault on Tahure. Despite all the interruptions, however, everything was ready and the artillery bombardment by about sixty batteries began on 30 October. An intense German fire plan, supplemented by gas shoots to neutralise the French batteries, which began at 11.00 am, was followed by an infantry assault launched at 4.00pm. On the right 7th Reserve Division, reinforced by elements of Infantry Regiments 14, 50 and 149, went forward, with 5th Bavarian Infantry Division to its left, reinforced by Infantry Regiment 49, 140 and 47 in that order. This deeply echeloned attacking force enjoyed almost immediate success. The butte itself was stormed and taken by the first wave of attackers from 7th Reserve Division, which captured twenty three officers and 1,215 other ranks;[47] but elsewhere the assault ran into trouble. It quickly stalled in the village of Tahure and on the slopes of *Kitzlinghöhe* and *Eisenberg/ Mamelle Nord* [Hill 196], which dominated the Goutte Ravine which ran between them.

Leutnant Gerlach 4th Company Reserve Infantry Regiment 66[48] **4.**

"The attack was prepared by pushing forward saps from the *Waldstellung* [Wood Position], which 1st Battalion Reserve Infantry Regiment 66 was occupying, with Reserve Infantry Regiment 72 to the right and our 2nd Battalion, commanded by Major Peiper, to the left. Assisting us in the work were 2nd and 3rd Battalions Infantry Regiment 149, which had returned from Russia. At 11.00 am on 30 October, the artillery preparation began, supported by mortars. For the first time *Bromgranaten* [a type of gas shell] were used, causing huge difficulties for the French. Large numbers of deserters came over. The response of the French artillery was weak, then the attack began at 4.00 pm. 4th Company, under Leutnant Gerlach, remained on stand by in the forming up place and one and a half platoons were retained as a carrying party.

"At about 6.00 pm Leutnant Gerlach received orders from Major von Pressenthin, commanding 1st Battalion, '1st Company under Leutnant Hugo has come under heavy machine gun fire in the wood on the southwest side of the Butte de Tahure and has been forced to pull back. Take 4th Company round to the rear of the Butte de Tahure and roll up the enemy position.' Gerlach left at once at the head of one hundred men, moving around the butte to the wood on the south west side. There was no French resistance and no machine guns could be located. The woods were clear of the enemy; there was only intermittent weak, unaimed, small arms fire and hardly any shelling. Although night was falling, visibility was good because the moon was shining. Leutnant Gerlach patrolled out to the right and there, on the western slopes of the butte, beyond the *Dreckschlucht* [Muck Ravine], found the stragglers from 1st Battalion Reserve Infantry Regiment 66. There were no enemy to be seen at all.

"After that we pressed on to Reserve Infantry Regiment 72 on the far side of the *Dreckschlucht*, where we heard from the commander of its left flank company that the attack had gone well and had continued a further five hundred metres as far as a French machine gun nest. Unfortunately there had been no hand grenades left to smoke it out. Men who had been despatched to the rear to report returned with orders to withdraw to the positions they were currently holding because Reserve Infantry Regiment 66 out on the left had withdrawn and the left flank of Reserve Infantry Regiment 72 was hanging in the air."

Gerlach had linked up with men of 3rd Battalion Reserve Infantry Regiment 72, which had indeed made rapid progress during the assault, but at high cost, especially to its 10th Company. Stalled as a result near the *Dreckschlucht*, 12th Company, which had been following up in support, was sent forward to renew the attack.

Reserve Leutnant Kettmann 12th Company Reserve Infantry Regiment 72[49] **4.**

"At the time I was commander of 3 Platoon 12th Company. My platoon was in reserve and at the direct disposal of the commanding officer. Due to robust enemy counter-action the assaulting companies – 9th and 10th – could not get forward any further, so the whole of 12th Company was soon deployed, attacking forward from *Jägerwäldchen* [Hunter's Copse]. Once we had negotiated with care our own near-intact barbed wire obstacle, all the time under heavy enemy machine gun fire, which caused us a number of casualties, we worked out way forward individually to the foot of the *Dreckschlucht*. Our progress was slowed by heavy enemy enfilading fire. Then something came to our rescue. One of our heavy mortars dropped a round short, just in front of our assault line. A thick black cloud of smoke drifted along the *Dreckschlucht*.

"Seizing the favourable opportunity and in one great rush, I led 1 and 3 Platoons of 12th Company right through the *Dreckschlucht* and on to the lower slopes of the Butte de Tahure. At that point we were in dead ground. The French machine guns could not bring their fire to bear and so we were able to work our way forward into a final assault position. By almost 6.30 pm we were in position about one hundred metres from the enemy trenches. It had taken us about two hours to get to that point. Following a quick discussion and agreement with Reserve Leutnant Müller, commanding 1 Platoon, we charged forward at 6.30 pm. Unfortunately Leutnant Müller was killed, shot through the heart, as he waited to lunge upwards and rush forward. To beating drums and with shouts of *Hurra!* we went forward unstoppably.

"As soon as the French saw how determined we were, they came running towards us with their hands up. Unfortunately, the attack of the Pomeranian Infantry Regiment 149 to our right could not get forward. As a result, we came under constant heavy enemy machine gun fire from the right flank as we charged forward. I was advancing on the extreme right flank of the line of attackers and, once I was right up against the French barbed wire obstacle and the French immediately to our front had already surrendered, I spotted an enemy machine gun nearby to our right. I had just gathered together a few men and was about to launch an attack with hand grenades on the enemy machine gun, when I was hit on the left temple by a machine gun bullet. Thank heavens it was only a slight wound. However it hit a minor branch of my temporal artery, I lost a great deal of blood and I was forced to go to the aid post and have it bandaged."

To be fair to the men of Infantry Regiment 149, their attack had got off to a very bad start. During the later stages of the bombardment the roar of the guns was suddenly drowned out by a very loud explosion. One of the heavy mortars, co-located with its 1st Battalion, had suffered a burst barrel when a bomb burst prematurely, with appalling effect. The entire crew was gruesomely wiped out and there were heavy casualties amongst the two adjacent infantry sections from 3rd Company.[50] To make matters worse, although the French artillery fire was generally weak that day, it was brought down with considerable effect on this regiment, which suffered a succession of casualties before the men ever had the chance to launch forward in the attack. Despite these problems a promising start was made, but casualties mounted, especially amongst the junior commanders then, just as the regiment was approaching its final objective, the fork in the road to the west of Tahure, it was hit by a concentration of heavy German artillery and was engaged simultaneously by French machine guns located in elevated positions to the south west. Casualties mounted swiftly and alarmingly. The attack stalled in its tracks and there was no alternative but to withdraw and consolidate.

Only Infantry Regiment 49 had closed right up to the French trenches but, enfiladed by heavy rifle and machine gun fire, had to pull back. That same night, 5th Bavarian Infantry Division repeatedly renewed the attack on Tahure, but could make no impression on the defences. VIII Reserve Corps planned to launch a fresh assault during 31 October, but this was forestalled by a violent French reaction to events of the previous day as they attempted to retake the butte. French drum fire hammered down throughout the day on the battered defenders of the butte then, at about 5.00 pm, large elements of the French XI and XVI Corps thrust hard against the butte, pressing in the centre of 7th Reserve Division. By 6.15 pm, the situation was critical. General der Infanterie Graf von Schwerin, commanding 7th Reserve Division, reported that the French had broken through and were thrusting north in considerable strength.

VIII Reserve Corps immediately released Infantry Regiment 147 to go under the command of 7th Reserve Division and, as soon as the message had been passed further up the chain of command, Third Army despatched its remaining reserves: Infantry Regiment 158, together with elements of Leib-Grenadier Regiment 8 and Infantry Regiment 52, to the threatened sector. In the event only Leib-Grenadier Regiment 8 went into action. To general relief it soon transpired that the original message had exaggerated the problem. There had been no breakthrough and 7th Reserve Division was still securely in possession of the butte. Nevertheless, casualties had been rising, ammunition stocks were running low and the weather was poor, so Third Army ordered a suspension of operations. Because the regimental commander of Leib-Grenadier Regiment 8 was ill, Hauptmann Reschke, commanding officer of the 2nd Battalion, assumed command of the whole of the defence of this vital sector.

Unaware of the true situation, Reschke's men rushed had forward, being met by the Orderly Officer of 7th Reserve Division, who passed them an order to recapture the Butte de Tahure the following morning. Detailed orders were issued and the troops moved forward to an assembly area north and northwest of Hill 192, ready to launch the assault after dawn on 31 October. However, moving forward on a personal reconnaissance, Hauptmann Reschke met up with a group from Infantry Regiment 149 on the summit of Hill 192. During an extraordinary conversation, a platoon commander of Infantry Regiment 149 explained how his men were deployed and stated that the forward line of defence was several hundred metres further on. It was then obvious that all but an insignificant part of the area due for attack was already in German hands, so the attack was cancelled, most of the troops were released and Leib-Grenadier Regiment 8 was directed to take over part of the front line and hold it.[51] During the next few days, despite heavy bombardments and prolonged periods of hand-to-hand fighting, the German defenders remained in possession of this key feature as the battle died away. Elsewhere, to the east, 56th Infantry Division managed to take several hundreds of metres of trench on Hill 199 near Ripont and, more to the west, IX Corps, commanded by General der Infanterie von Quast, so improved the defensive positions around Ferme de Navarin that the line was never again seriously challenged during the two and a half years of positional warfare still to come in this area.

It is impossible to overstate the significance of the autumn battles in Champagne. No matter what gloss the French attempted to put on the outcome, their offensive completely failed in its aim. Launched with the highest expectations of success, the inability of the French army to overwhelm the German defences, break though to open country and so end the war, the failure of this massive autumn offensive was a savage blow to French morale. Joffre's summary of events in his memoirs,[52] where he was reduced to commenting that the expenditure of four million 75 mm shells and almost one million heavier calibre rounds, demonstrated what progress had been made that year in increasing war time production, simply underlines what a massive disappointment this damp squib of a battle was to the Allies. For them 1915 had been a year to remember, but for all the wrong reasons.

Notes
1. Anspach History Reserve Infantry Regiment 107 pp 324-325.
2. This is probably a reference to Foot Artillery Regiment 3, which was garrisoned in Mainz before the war.
3. Joffre *Mémoires* Tome II p 88.
4. *ibid.* p 89.
5. AOK 3 *Die Champagne-Herbstschlacht* p 48.
6. Heintz History Reserve Infantry Regiment 133 pp 282-283
7. Noldt History Reserve Field Artillery Regiment 15 pp 70-71.
8. These men were high quality volunteers and potential officers.
9. Noldt *op. cit.* 65-66.
10. Ludovici was killed, shot straight through the forehead, as he helped beat off one French assault which closed right up to one of the guns. Jumping up on the trails, he fired his pistol until he fell.
11. Rudorff History Fusilier Regiment 39 p 79.
12. Reymann History Infantry Regiment 52 pp 72-75.
13. See Loßberg *Meine Tätigkeit* pp 164-168. Loßberg criticises Falkenhayn for having been absent from his headquarters during the final days before these attacks, which meant that he lacked the appropriate oversight of the developing situation.
14. *Musketen* units were equipped with the Madsen light machine gun, operated by four man teams.
15. Loßberg *op. cit.* pp 166-167.
16. *ibid.* p 168.
17. Rücker History Reserve Infantry Regiment 29 pp 70-71.
18. Müller attributed the change to the fact that the German Crown Prince, commanding Fifth Army, objected but of course Müller was a Prussian. In fact the decision was made by Oberst Loßberg, who had just taken over as chief of staff Third Army
19. Rogge History Infantry Regiment 88 pp 209-210.
20. History Fusilier Regiment 35 p 118.
21. *ibid.* p 120.
22. *ibid.* pp 122-123.
23. Freund History Infantry Regiment 118 p 91.

24. Reserve Leutnant Hermann Baas, who was killed on 6 October 1915, is buried in the German cemetery at Souain Block 2 Grave 603.
25. Freund *op. cit.* pp 91-92.
26. *ibid.* p 92.
27. It is impossible to verify this statement, but it is typical of many such accusations which appear throughout the German literature.
28. Freund *op. cit.* pp 92-93.
29. Kirchbach *Kämpfe in der Champagne* pp 102 - 103.
30. Soldan History Infantry Regiment 184 pp 17-18.
31. Anspach *op. cit.* p 320.
32. Loßberg *op. cit.* p 178.
33. Winzer History Reserve Infantry Regiment 243 pp 82-84.
34. Anspach *op. cit.* p 98.
35. Heintz History Reserve Infantry Regiment 133 p 92.
36. See Kirchbach *op. cit.* pp 110-112.
37. This assessment was remarkably accurate. The French reckoned the offensive to have lasted from 25 September until its suspension on 7 October. During that time its total casualties were: Officers 3,743, Other Ranks 143,567. See FOH 3 p 539.
38. Loßberg *op. cit.* p 185.
39. Kirchbach *op. cit.* p 115.
40. Reymann History Infantry Regiment 52 pp 78-79.
41. *Gedenkblatt* des Reserve Infantry Regiment 36 p 28.
42. Ludwig quoted in Zipfel und Albrecht History Infantry Regiment 75 p 159.
43. *ibid.* p 160.
44. *ibid.* p 160.
45. Zipfel History Grenadier Regiment 89 pp 198-199.
46. History Bavarian Infantry Regiment 14 pp 131-132.
47. Loßberg *op. cit.* p 193.
48. Wunderlich History Reserve Infantry Regiment 66 pp 390-391.
49. Hünicken History Reserve Infantry Regiment 72 pp 230-231.
50. Selle History Infantry Regiment 149 p 184.
51. Schöning History Leib-Grenadier Regiment 8 p 151.
52. Joffre *op. cit.* p 94.

Appendix I

German – British Comparison of Ranks

Generalfeldmarschall	Field Marshal
Generaloberst	Colonel General
	N.B. The holder of this rank was at least an army Commander.
General der Infanterie	General of Infantry}General
General der Kavallerie	General of Cavalry} General
	N.B. The holder of any of these last two ranks was at least a corps commander and might have been an army commander.
Generalleutnant	Lieutenant General.
	N.B. The holder of this rank could be the commander of a formation ranging in size from a brigade to a corps. From 1732 onwards Prussian officers of the rank of Generalleutnant or higher, who had sufficient seniority, were referred to as '*Exzellenz*' [Excellency].
Generalmajor	Major General
Oberst	Colonel
Oberstleutnant	Lieutenant Colonel
Major	Major
Hauptmann	Captain
Rittmeister	Captain (mounted unit such as cavalry, horse artillery or transport). It was also retained by officers of this senority serving with the German Flying Corps
Oberleutnant	Lieutenant
Leutnant	Second Lieutenant
Feldwebelleutnant	Sergeant Major Lieutenant
Offizierstellvertreter	Officer Deputy
	N.B. This was an appointment, rather than a substantive rank.
Feldwebel	Sergeant Major
Wachtmeister	Sergeant Major (mounted unit)
Vizefeldwebel	Staff Sergeant
Vizewachtmeister	Staff Sergeant (mounted unit)
Sergeant	Sergeant

Unteroffizier	Corporal
Korporal	Corporal (Bavarian units)
Gefreiter	Lance Corporal

Musketier	}
Grenadier	}
Garde-Füsilier	}
Füsilier	}
Schütze	} N.B. These ranks all equate to Private Soldier
Infanterist	} (infantry). The differences in nomenclature are due to
Jäger	} tradition, the type of unit involved, or the class of
Wehrmann	} conscript to which the individual belonged.
Landsturmmann	}
Soldat	}
Ersatz-Reservist	}

Kriegsfreiwilliger	Wartime Volunteer. This equates to Private Soldier.

Kanonier	Gunner }
Pionier	Sapper }
Fahrer	Driver } N.B. These ranks all equate to Private Soldier.
Hornist	Trumpeter }
Tambour	Drummer }

Medical Personnel

Oberstabsarzt	Major (or higher)
Stabsarzt	Captain
Oberarzt	Lieutenant
Assistenzarzt	Second Lieutenant

N.B. These individuals were also referred to by their appointments; for example, *Bataillonsarzt* or *Regimentsarzt* [Battalion or Regimental Medical Officer]. Such usage, which varied in the different contingents which made up the German army, is no indicator of rank.

Sanitäter	Medical Assistant } N.B. These two ranks both equate to
Krankenträger	Stretcherbearer } Private Soldier.

Frequently the prefix *'Sanitäts-'* appears in front of a normal NCO rank, such as Gefreiter or Unteroffizier. This simply indicates that a man of that particular seniority was part of the medical services.

APPENDIX II

1915: An Outline Chronology

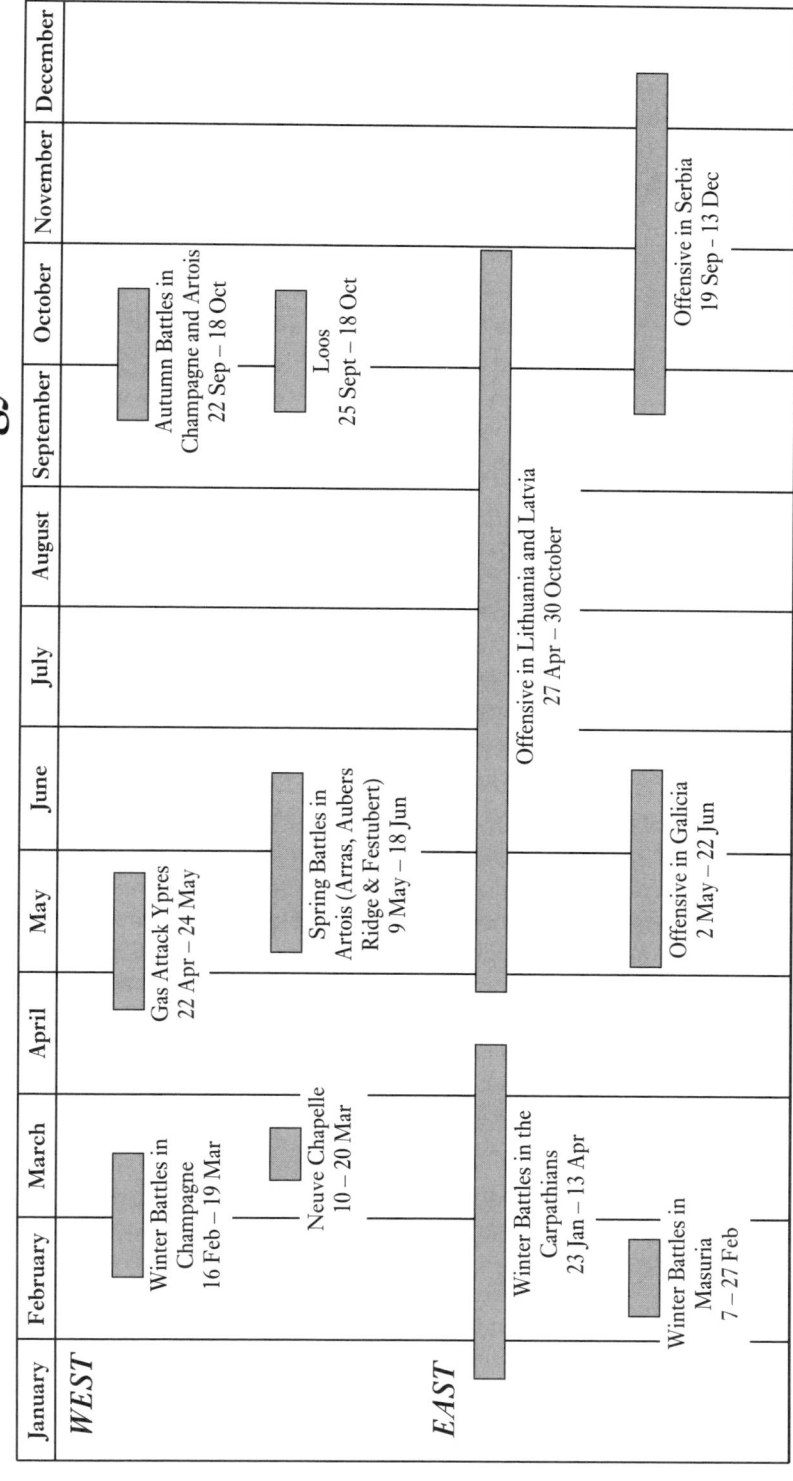

	January	February	March	April	May	June	July	August	September	October	November	December
WEST		Winter Battles in Champagne 16 Feb – 19 Mar	Neuve Chapelle 10 – 20 Mar	Gas Attack Ypres 22 Apr – 24 May	Spring Battles in Artois (Arras, Aubers Ridge & Festubert) 9 May – 18 Jun				Autumn Battles in Champagne and Artois 22 Sep – 18 Oct / Loos 25 Sept – 18 Oct			
EAST	Winter Battles in the Carpathians 23 Jan – 13 Apr	Winter Battles in Masuria 7 – 27 Feb		Offensive in Lithuania and Latvia 27 Apr – 30 October	Offensive in Galicia 2 May – 22 Jun				Offensive in Serbia 19 Sep – 13 Dec			

Appendix III
Selective Biographical Notes

The battles of 1915 involved a great many commanders and other personalities who may not be immediately familiar to the reader. Some of those who appear in the text are:

French
Barbot General Ernest Jacques (1855 – 1915) commander French 77th Division. Born in Toulouse, General Barbot was commissioned as thirty fourth from a class of seventy four in 1877. He spent most of his career serving with troops, commanding a battalion from 1898, being promoted colonel in 1912 and brigadier general in 1914. Appointed to command 77th Division, he led it with dash and élan, being mentioned in despatches on 2 October 1914. He died on 10 May 1915 of wounds received while advancing with the leading elements of his division near Souchez. General Barbot has always been regarded as an heroic figure in France. He was posthumously made Commander of the *Légion d'honneur* and a school was named after him in Metz. In May 1937 more than 50,000 old comrades and admirers attended the unveiling of the statue to him in Souchez, which was erected very close to where he fell.

Cary General Fernand de Langle de (1849 – 1927), commander of the French Fourth Army. General de Langle de Cary joined the French army in 1869, just in time to participate in the Franco-Prussian War, when he was wounded while serving with the Chasseurs d'Afrique. He was staff trained and was for a time a professor at the French military academy. Promoted to general rank in 1900, he was given command of a brigade in Algeria. He was appointed commander Fourth Army in 1914. He survived being heavily defeated in the Battle of the Frontiers, commanded the failed Champagne offensives, then replaced General de Castelnau as Commander Central Army Group. Scapegoated for the failure to foresee and prepare for the battle of Verdun the following year, he was removed from command and retired on the grounds of age.

Castelnau General Edouard Vicomte Curières de (1851 – 1944) was in overall command of the main attacking force in Champagne in autumn 1915. General de Castelnau was descended from an ancient noble family with a long tradition of military service. He passed out of St Cyr in 1869 and participated in the Franco-Prussian War as a member of the 31st Infantry Regiment. He became a brigadier general in 1906 and commanded successively 24 Brigade at Sedan and 7 Brigade at Soissons. He was made a major-general and commander of 13th Infantry Division in 1909 but, after only eighteen months at Chaumont and at Joffre's insistence, he was posted to the latter's staff, where he was heavily involved in the development of Plan XVII. After three years (1911 – 1914) as Joffre's chief of staff, he was appointed Commander Second Army on the outbreak of war. Despite his forces being handled roughly in its opening stages, he was sent north to command the attempt to turn the German right flank during the so-called Race to the Sea, but responsibility passed to Foch when the fighting reached Amiens. From June 1915 he commanded the Central Army Group and directed the autumn offensive in Champagne. He was chief of staff once more under Joffre in 1916, but was temporarily retired when Joffre was replaced by Nivelle. When Foch in turn assumed command, de Castelnau was recalled and placed in charge of Army Group East in Lorraine. He ended the war loaded with honours from France and Allied countries, but the personal cost had been high; three of his sons had been killed in action. His Catholic religion and controversial political views brought him enemies and probably account for the fact that he never became a field marshal.

Duchêne General Denis Auguste (1862 – 1950) commander French 42nd Division. General Duchêne entered St Cyr in 1881, passing out two years later. In an early career typical of officers of his generation, he alternated between periods of duty at home and abroad, most notably in the expedition to Tonkin in 1886 – 1887. After qualifying as a staff officer in 1893, he had a series of staff and command appointments of increasing importance until, in 1912, he was given command of Infantry Regiment 69 and followed this in early 1914 with the appointment of chief of staff XX Corps, which at that time was commanded by General Ferdinand Foch. This was a sure sign that he had been earmarked for future significant advancement, because that was the élite corps of the French army, charged with guarding the frontier of Lorraine. Despite the disastrous defeat at Morhange in autumn 1914, the then Colonel Duchêne distinguished himself at the defence of Grand-Couronné and was promoted brigadier general and made an Officer of the *Légion d'honneur*. His progress thereafter was rapid. After a brief period in command of 42nd Division, he was progressively commander of XXXII Corps and II Corps during the Battle of the Somme in October 1916. By December 1916 he was commanding Tenth Army then, a year later, having returned from Italy, he commanded Sixth Army along the Chemin des Dames during the very difficult months of 1917. Many of his best formations were stripped from this front and, in addition, General Duchêne refused for some reason to obey Pétain's clear instructions on the subject, or in any way to countenance the construction of strong depth positions. As a result, when Ludendorff unleashed a major offensive against the line in late May 1918, Sixth Army suffered a crushing defeat and was driven backwards. Its commander paid the price, being replaced in mid June 1918. He was thus unable to participate in the subsequent advance to victory. His conduct was the subject of a Board of Inquiry, but he served on after the war and was appointed commander 19th Division in 1920 (the year he was made a Grand Officer of the *Légion d'honneur*) and also commanded successively XIII and III Corps prior to his retirement in 1924.

Dumas General Noël Jean-Baptiste (1854 – 1943) commander of the French IV and XVII Corps. General Dumas was commissioned in 1876 and rose to become commander of a cavalry brigade in 1911, then 28 Infantry Brigade in 1913. He was given command of 17th Infantry Division on mobilisation and then was made commander XVII Corps, remaining in that appointment until May 1917. He was the holder of numerous honours and awards including that of Grand Officer of the *Légion d'honneur* and finished the war as Commandant of the French Northern Region.

Gérard General Augustin Grégoire (1857 – 1926) commander of the French I and II Corps. General Gérard was a distinguished French officer, who became a brigadier general in 1909 and was chief of staff to General Gallieni in Madagascar, before returning to assume command of the 41st Division in May 1912. In 1914 he was a commander of I Corps in Lorraine then, in early 1915, commanded two corps as Detachment Gérard. During 1916 he commanded the French First Army, then returned to Lorraine in 1917, where his detachment was renamed the Eighth Army. Amongst his many honours was the Grand Cross of the *Légion d'honneur*. The British awarded him an honorary KCB and the United States the Army Distinguished Service Medal.

Grossetti General Paul François (1861 – 1918) commander 60th Division. General Grossetti was born in Paris of Corsican parents. He joined the army in 1881 and saw a great deal of foreign duty, including tours of active service during the expeditions to Tonkin and Cambodia from 1885 – 1887. He was an outstanding student at the French staff college from 1890 – 1893 and rose through the ranks until he became commander of the 42nd Infantry Division on the outbreak of war. He is best remembered for his vital role in the defence of the Yser/Ijzer during the Battle of Flanders in 1914. Following that and his role in the Battles of Champagne and Verdun, he followed a short senior staff appointment with command of the *Armée d'Orient* in Salonika where, shortly after being awarded the Grand Cross of the *Légion d'honneur*, he contracted dysentery and died of it in Paris in early 1918. A statue to him in Ajaccio, Corsica, was donated by King Albert I of Belgium in recognition of his service to that country in 1914.

Humbert General Georges Louis (1861 – 1922) commander French XXXII Corps. As a junior officer General Humbert, having begun his career modestly as a member of the 20th Regiment of Chasseurs, saw much overseas service, participating amongst others in the expeditions to Tonkin from 1885 – 1887 and Madagascar 1895 – 1896. He was appointed commander of the 96th Infantry Regiment in 1907 and was chief of staff III Corps for nearly three years from September 1909 until he was given command of 56 Brigade in March 1912. His various command appointments during the war included the Morrocan Division in 1914 and later Eighth then Third Armies. Amongst his many honours, he was a Grand Officer of the *Légion d'honneur*. Two of his sons became generals later and a street in Paris is named after him.

Urbal General Victor (Louis Lucien) Baron d' (1858 – 1943) commander French Tenth Army. General d'Urbal was commissioned from St Cyr in 1878 and became a cavalry man, seeing action in Algeria from January 1889 – December 1890. Having commanded a cavalry regiment, he was given command of 4 Dragoon Brigade in 1911, in which capacity he began the war. His progress was then meteoric. He became Commander 7th Cavalry Division on 22 August 1914, XXXIII Corps on 20 September and Commander French Army Detachment in Belgium on 20 October. By 16 November this had become Eighth Army, which he commanded, until he was given command of Tenth Army on 2 April 1915. Here his luck ran out. Bested by the German defence during both the Spring and Autumn Battles of Artois, he was *limogé* [removed from command] in early April 1916. Thereafter, he was Inspector General of Cavalry and Cavalry Training until he retired in June 1919. He was a member of the *Légion d'honneur* from 1898, finally being awarded the Grand Cross in 1935.

German

Albrecht Generaloberst Duke of Württemberg (1865 – 1939) commander Fourth Army. Duke Albrecht was born in Vienna in 1865. Of royal descent and expected to succeed to the throne of Württemberg in due course, he numbered Frederick the Great amongst his ancestors. He was a professional soldier from the day he left Eberhard-Karl's University in Tübingen, being commissioned into *Ulanen-Regiment König Karl (1 Württembergisches) Nr. 19*, the élite cavalry regiment of the army of Württemberg. As a serious and highly competent soldier, he rose through the command ranks of that army, with only one appointment elsewhere, when he was commander of 4 Guards Cavalry Brigade. Prior to the Great War, he commanded successively 51 Infantry Brigade and 26th Infantry Division, then spent five years as commander of XIII (Royal Württemberg) Corps. Having commanded the original Fourth Army during the invasion of France, he then assumed command of the new Fourth Army for the Battle of Flanders in autumn 1914, remaining there until the Western Front was reorganised in February 1917. He then moved to command Army Group Duke of Württemberg, with responsibility for the front from Thionville to the Swiss border. He was held in the highest regard by both superiors and subordinates as a professional soldier of great competence and integrity. Ludendorff rated him more highly than either of the other two army group commanders. Amongst his many honours was the *Pour le Mérite* and he was created field marshal by both Prussia and Württemberg.

Bahrfeldt General der Infanterie Professor Max Ferdinand von (1856 – 1936) commander 19th Reserve Division. General von Bahrfeldt was a Prussian, who was ennobled in 1913 and who commanded 19th Reserve Division from mobilisation onwards. He was later accused of war crimes and condemned to death post war *in absentia* by a court in Namur, as result of events in Charleroi, Belgium on 22 August 1914, when wild shooting led to the deaths of numerous civilians, not all of whom appear to have been actively engaged in firing at the German troops. Bahrfeldt flatly denied that he had either ordered civilians to be shot out of hand or buildings to be set on fire. Bahrfeldt was an efficient soldier and commander and a brilliant numismatist of world renown; possibly the greatest expert on Roman coinage ever. He published his first articles and books on the subject while still a regimental officer in the 1870s and became Professor of Numismatics at the University of Halle-Wittenberg from 1921.

Barthel Max (1893 – 1975) poet and writer. Together with Heinrich Lersch and Karl Bröger, Max Barthel, who was born in Dresden, formed one third of a well-known triumvirate of working class social-democratic poets. He spent years before the First World War drifting in and out of unskilled jobs, found himself in the army in 1914, and fought in the Argonne, where he was wounded. This experience was the inspiration for his first published work *Versen aus den Argonnen* (1916). This made him a household name and he followed this with many other volumes of poetry as well as reportage and novels, for he was a prolific writer. Due to dubious links with the Nazis and the SS before and during the Second World War, he was threatened with arrest subsequently and had to flee the Soviet Zone of Occupation. His later writings were completely apolitical and he was honoured by the Federal Government shortly before his death at the age of eighty one.

Binding Leutnant Rudolf (1867 – 1938). Rudolf Binding was born in Basel, Switzerland, of well-to-do parents, who brought him up in Leipzig. His father was a distinguished academic lawyer and he himself studied law and medicine. He was, however, more interested in writing and horse racing and his time prior to the war was spent in horse breeding and race riding. He had a reserve commission in a cavalry regiment and rose during the war to become a rittmeister and a staff officer. Post war he turned more strongly towards writing. *Aus dem Kriege*, a published version of his highly praised war diaries, appeared in 1925, but he published numerous other titles of both fiction and non-fiction. His close association with the aims and aspirations of National Socialism up until his death from TB led to his books being banned in post war East Germany, but *Aus dem Kriege* remains a valuable contribution to the literature of the war.

Claer General der Infanterie Eberhard von (1856 – 1945) commander VII Corps. General von Clear began his army career as a sekondleutnant in the élite Fusilier Guard Regiment. He was selected for staff training in 1882 and thereafter he alternated between staff and command appointments. He served in two of the Hanseatic infantry regiments, before being selected to command, successively, Jäger Battalion 9 and Grenadier Guard Regiment 5, in which appointment he was promoted oberst in 1902. He went on to command 11 Infantry Brigade, 22nd and 11th Infantry Divisions, before being made Inspector of Engineers and Fortresses in 1913. On the outbreak of war, he was promoted general der infanterie and was briefly appointed commander of the newly raised XXIV Reserve Corps, before taking over as Commander VII Corps in September 1914. He was awarded the *Pour le Mérite* for his performance during the spring battles in Artois in 1915. For reasons which are obscure, he was posted from command of his corps to Supreme Army Headquarters to resume his former engineer staff appointment in June 1915. Presumably nettled by this action, he tendered his resignation and was permitted to retire in July 1916.

Dellmensingen Generalleutnant Konrad Kraft von (1862 – 1953) chief of staff Sixth Army. General von Dellmensingen began his career as a fähnrich in an artillery regiment. His intellectual ability was recognised early and he spent the greater part of his pre-war career in various staff appointments. He was commander of Bavarian Field Artillery Brigade 4 briefly from 1911 – 1912, but was then promoted generalmajor and became Chief of the Bavarian General Staff and Inspector of Training until war broke out. He was then appointed chief of staff of Sixth Army, which was commanded by Generaloberst Crown Prince Rupprecht, but was promoted general der artillerie and given command of the Alpenkorps in 1915. Thereafter he commanded troops on the Italian Front, at Verdun and in Romania. At the 12th Battle of Isonzo, in late October 1917, his troops broke through to the River Tagliamento, for which feat he was awarded the Grand Cross of the Bavarian Military Max-Josef Order. He then returned to staff appointments, being successively chief of staff of Army Group Duke of Württemberg, 14th (where he received the *Pour le Mérite*) and 17th Armies, before ending the war in command of the Bavarian II Corps. In the early post war period he became involved in anti-monarchist plots in Bavaria, but nothing came of the plans and he was thereafter noted mainly for his military and historical writing.

Einem-Rothmaler Generaloberst Karl Wilhelm von (1853 – 1934) commander Third Army. General von Einem was a veteran of the Franco-Prussian War, during which as a Leutnant in *2. Hannoversches Ulanen-Regiment 14*, he was awarded the Iron Cross. From 1880, when he became a member of the General Staff, he alternated between staff and command appointments, rising to become the Prussian Minister of War in 1903 and moving to be Inspector of Cavalry in 1907 and Commander VII Corps in 1909, a role he fulfilled until September 1914 when he was appointed Commander Third Army. He was awarded the *Pour le Mérite* for his conduct of the defensive Winter Battle in Champagne and Oak Leaves to it the following year. He carried on in the same appointment to the end of the war.

Fleck Generalleutnant Paul (1859 – 1921) commander VIII Reserve Corps. General Fleck was commissioned into Infantry Regiment 18 in 1876. A career mainly devoted to regimental duty and command appointments saw him in command of Infantry Regiment 42 in 1908. He was promoted generalmajor and commanded 27 Infantry Brigade in Düsseldorf from March 1912. On the outbreak of war, he was appointed to command 14th Infantry Division. He distinguished himself greatly at Liège and during the battles around St Quentin and the Marne, becoming a generalleutnant and commander VIII Reserve Corps in January. After outstanding service in Champagne, he was given command of the active XVII Corps on the Somme in September 1916. He was posted to Macedonia in January 1918, where he remained until he was involved in the withdrawal of the remaining German troops in early 1919. He was awarded Oak Leaves to his March 1915 *Pour le Mérite* before the end of the war, but never received them because of the turmoil in early post war Germany. He was, however, promoted to the honorary rank of general der infanterie prior to his death.

Hügel General der Infanterie Freiherr Eugen Otto von (1853 – 1928) commander XXVI Reserve Corps. General von Hügel was born in Stuttgart and served primarily in the army of Württemberg. He was commissioned into Infantry Regiment 122 in 1870, was later a major and battalion commander in Infantry Regiment 125 before promotion to oberst in 1901, when he was appointed to command Infantry Regiment 121. He commanded 54 Infantry Brigade in Ulm from 1905 to 1908 then served for four years as commander 2nd Infantry Division, before being placed on the reserve of officers in April 1912. Recalled to active duty on the outbreak of war, he was briefly deputy to General der Infanterie von Fabeck of XIII Corps, before being appointed commander of the newly raised XXVI Reserve Corps. He commanded the corps until he was retired once more in March 1918. He was awarded the *Pour le Mérite* in August 1916 and, on retirement, the high distinction of the *Kommenteurkreuz* of the Royal Württemberg Military Service Order.

Kathen General der Infanterie Hugo Karl Gottlieb von (1855 – 1932) commander XXIII Reserve Corps. General von Kathen was born in Pomerania and commissioned into Grenadier Guard Regiment 2 'Kaiser Franz' in 1873. He made steady progress up the ranks, seeing regimental service with various Guards regiments and commanding Infantry Regiment 74 in 1904, 83 Infantry Brigade in Erfurt from 1907 – 1910, followed immediately by command of 9th Infantry Division. Promoted generalleutnant in 1912, he then became general der infanterie in 1914. At the outbreak of war, he was Military Governor of Mainz, but by December 1914, after a brief period in command of 39th Infantry Division, was given command of XXXIII Reserve Corps, a position he held with distinction until he was appointed Commander Eighth Army in July 1918. During the winter of 1918 – 1919 he was in command of all German troops in Lithuania and Estonia. Amongst his numerous honours was the *Pour le Mérite* (August 1916) with Oak Leaves (August 1918).

Knobelsdorff Generalleutnant Konstantin Heinrich Schmidt von (1860 – 1936) chief of staff to the German Crown Prince. Generalleutnant von Knobelsdorff entered the Prussian army in 1878. A talented regimental and General Staff officer, he was a battalion commander by 1901, served as chief of staff of X Corps in 1904 and became commander of Footguard Regiment 4 in 1908. He was promoted generalmajor in 1911, when he became chief of staff of the Guard Corps and generalleutnant in 1914, by which time he was Deputy Chief of the General Staff. At the outbreak of war, he was chief of staff Fifth Army, which was commanded by the German Crown Prince and he served there with distinction to the end of the Battle of Verdun, though he clashed on numerous occasions with the Crown Prince during that battle when the latter disagreed with some of his decisions. Nevertheless, in August 1916 he received the Oak Leaves to his *Pour le Mérite*, which he had been awarded the previous October. General von Knobelsdorff was then given command of X Corps in Alsace, an appointment he retained until the end of the war. He was placed on the retired list in September 1919.

Lichtenfels Generalleutnant Gustav Scanzoni von (1855 – 1924) commander 6th Bavarian Reserve Division. General Scanzoni was an artilleryman who had a steady, if unspectacular, career in the Bavarian Army. His final peacetime appointment was command of 6 Bavarian Field Artillery Brigade in Nuremberg from 1906 – 1911. Thereafter he was placed on the reserve of officers. He was called out of retirement to succeed General der Infanterie Graf von Bothmer as the fourth commander of Bavarian 6th Reserve Division in December 1914, remaining in that position until January 1917.

Loßberg Oberst Fritz von (1868 – 1942) Oberst von Loßberg was a key figure in the German army throughout the First World War, rising from the rank of oberstleutnant to generalleutnant and finally becoming a general der infanterie in the Reichswehr after the war. His exceptional talents were first recognised whilst he was serving at Supreme Army Headquarters in 1915, when he briefed the Kaiser in person about the crisis in Third Army at the beginning of the Autumn Battle in Champagne. That same day he found himself posted with immediate effect as chief of staff to that army. This was a considerable honour for a newly promoted oberst and, for the next three years, he was despatched from army to army to handle one crisis after another. Possessed of the ability to reduce major operational problems to their essentials, he repeatedly brought to bear clarity of thought, dynamism and bold decision making. Although nominally working as the adviser to a series of senior field commanders, in fact, armed with the full power of command he always demanded (and was granted) by his superiors he *de facto* assumed command positions. It was, for example, Loßberg, personally, who directed the defensive battles against the British army on the Somme, at Arras and Passchendaele. He had a very strong constitution and an extraordinary capacity for hard work and long hours. He caught up with sleep by dozing in chairs at odd moments or during his daily car journeys to the front and, at times of crisis, never spent more than four hours per day in bed. He received numerous honours and awards, including the *Pour le Mérite* and Oak Leaves to it, from all the contingents of the German army.

Lüttwitz Generalleutnant Freiherr von (1859 – 1942) commander 20th Infantry Division. General von Lüttwitz, who was commissioned into Fusilier Regiment 38 of the Prussian army in 1878 is best known for his military and political activities after the war ended when he was responsible as Reichswehr commander in Berlin for putting down the *Spartakus* uprising and later took a prominent part in the failed putsch of March 1920. During the war he held a number of key appointments, including chief of staff to Fourth Army, Fifth Army and Army Group German Crown Prince. Following the end of the Autumn Battle of Champagne, he was given command of X Corps and, from November 1916 until the end of the war, he commanded III Corps. Having won the Iron Cross Second and First Class in 1914, he was awarded the *Pour le Mérite* in August 1916 and Oak Leaves to it in March 1918. General von Lüttwitz, like many other senior officers, did not attempt to disguise his opposition to the terms of the Treaty of Versailles and was dismissed from his appointment by Reichswehrminister Gustav Noske on 11 March 1920. Thirty six hours later he marched on the centre of Berlin at the head of a brigade of marines and appropriated Noske's position. The putsch attracted no significant support and Lüttwitz had to escape a few days later to Hungary, not returning to Germany until an amnesty was declared in 1925. He then lived quietly in Breslau until his death.

Mudra General der Infanterie Karl Bruno Julius von (1851 – 1931) commander XVI Corps. General von Mudra was commissioned into the Guards Engineer Battalion in 1870 and spent most of his career as a military engineer. In 1886 he became a member of the General Staff, specialising in engineer matters, but the bulk of his career was spent in command appointments. From 1893 – 1898 he commanded Pionier Battalion 7 in Cologne and was then appointed director of the Artillery and Engineer School in Berlin. In 1903 he was promoted generalmajor and became a generalleutnant in 1907 when he moved to Colmar as commander 39th Infantry Division. He was Governor General of Metz in 1910 and promoted to general der infanterie the following year, when he became Inspector General of Fortresses. In 1913 he assumed command of XVI Corps and took it to war as part of Fifth Army under the German Crown Prince. Following his forceful and highly effective leadership in the Argonne he became commander Eighth Army in late 1916 and had brief periods as commander First and Seventeenth Armies in 1918 in succession to Generals Fritz and Otto von Below respectively. He was awarded the *Pour le Mérite* in January 1915 and Oak Leaves in October 1916 as he handed over command of XVI Corps.

Pfeil und Klein-Ellguth Generalleutnant Graf von (1855 – 1937) commander 27th Infantry Division. Born in Silesia, General von Pfeil began his career in Grenadier Guard Regiment 3, but spent most of his pre-war career in a variety of artillery appointments, serving with artillery regiments in Karlsruhe, Kassel, Berlin, Breslau, Schweidnitz and Frankfurt an der Oder. In 1907 he commanded 28 Field Artillery Brigade in Karlsruhe, and was promoted generalmajor and then generalleutnant. Although he was a Prussian, he was given command of the 27th (Württemberg) Infantry Division in 1912, an appointment he held until June 1916. He was a successful commander in the Argonne and in Flanders, enjoying excellent relations with all members of his division. His final appointment from 1916 until his retirement in 1921 was commander of the Prussian Landgendarmerie. He was awarded the Knight's Cross of the Royal Württemberg Military Service Order in November 1914.

Quast General der Infanterie Ferdinand von (1850 – 1939) commander IX Corps. General von Quast fought in the Franco-Prussian War with Grenadier Guard Regiment 2 'Kaiser Franz', in which he served as a sekondleutnant and was awarded the Iron Cross Second Class. All his regimental service was with the Guards and he eventually commanded Grenadier Guard Regiment 2 himself when he was promoted oberst in 1903. By 1907 he was a generalmajor and commander of 39 Infantry Brigade in Hanover, though he returned to Berlin the following year to command, successively, 3rd and 2nd Guards Infantry Brigades. He served briefly in Danzig [Gdansk] as commander 36th Infantry Division, but returned to command 6th Infantry Division in Brandenburg, before being given command of IX Corps in Hamburg Altona in 1913. He was promoted general der infanterie in 1914. Having directed his forces with distinction in Champagne and elsewhere, he played a prominent role in the Battle of the Somme 1916 when he was awarded the *Pour le Mérite*. In January 1917 he was appointed commander of the Guard Corps and, in September 1917, commander Sixth Army. He received the Oak Leaves to his *Pour le Mérite* in April 1918 to go with his many other honours and awards. He ended the war in command of the *Hermannstellung* in the northern sector of the Western Front. He undertook a brief period of command in East Prussia after the war, but resigned once the Treaty of Versailles was signed.

Riemann General der Infanterie Julius Friedrich (1855 – 1935) commander VIII Corps. Having been a student of philosophy at the University of Berlin, General Riemann entered the army in 1878 as a one-year volunteer in Footguard Regiment 2. Instead of then following the usual route to a reserve commission, he managed to convert this into a regular commission in Infantry Regiment 83 and, by 1890, was a captain in the General Staff. His career progressed so well that in 1912 he was promoted to generalleutnant and command of 15th Infantry Division, with which he mobilised in 1914. Performing with great skill in the early battles, he was given command of VIII Corps in October 1914 and promoted to general der infanterie the following January. He continued in command of VIII Corps throughout the Champagne battles, being awarded the *Pour le Mérite* in March 1915. In 1916, he commanded VI Corps until he reached retirement age in December of that year.

Bibliography

Unpublished Sources: Kriegsarchiv München

AOK 6 Bd 44	N.O. B. No. 2908 Armee-Oberkommando 6. Armee Übersetzung eines bei A.O.K.3 gefundenen Joffre-Befehls 28.9.1915
AOK 6 Bd 417	Oberkommando 6. Armee A.H.Qu., den 26.Febr.1916 Der Durchbruch
K.B. RIR 16 Bd 4	Feindlicher Angriff am 9.5.1915. Fournes 15.5.1915
K.B. RIR 21 Bd 3	Gefechtsbericht über den 9.5.15 und die folgenden Tage, le Maisnil 25.5.15
K.B. RFAR 6 Bd. 23	OHL An sämtl. A.O.K.19.4.10.00 Vorm.
HS 1992/5	Das VIII (Rheinische) Armeekorps auf der Vimyhöhe vom 15. Mai bis 15./19. Juni 1915

Unpublished Source: Lambrecht Collection
Stober Leutnant Max. Letter dated 10 April 1915

Published Works (German: author known)

Anspach Hauptmann a.D. Siegfried *Das Kgl. Sächs. Reserve-Infanterie-Regiment Nr. 107* Dresden 1927

Appel Dr. Friedrich *Das Reserve-Infanterie-Regt. Nr. 205 im Weltkrieg* Berlin 1937

Baer CH *Der Völkerkrieg: Eine Chronik der Ereignisse seit dem 1. Juli 1914. Fünfter Band & Siebenter Band* Stuttgart N.D.

Baldenstein Freiherr Rinck von *Das Infanterie-Regiment Freiherr von Sparr (3. Westfälisches) Nr. 16 im Weltkrieg 1914-1918* Oldenburg 1927

Bamburg Hauptmann Georg *Das Kgl. Sächs. Res.-Inf.-Regiment Nr 106* Dresden 1925

Barthel Max *Sturm im Argonner Wald* Leipzig 1941

Baumgarten-Crusius Generalmajor a.D. Artur *Sachsen in großer Zeit: Geschichte der Sachsen im Weltkrieg Band II* Leipzig 1919

Baumgarten-Crusius Generalmajor a.D. Artur *Das Kgl. Sächs. 11. Infanterie-Regiment Nr. 139* Dresden 1927

Bauer Georg *Reserve-Infanterie-Regiment Nr. 74: Die Geschichte von Leben und Kämpfen eines deutschen Westfront-Regiments im Weltkriege 1914-1918* Oldenburg 1933

Baumgarten-Crusius Generalmajor a.D. *Das Kgl. Sächs. 11. Infanterie-Regiment Nr. 139* Dresden 1927

Bechtle Hauptmann d.R. Richard *Die Ulmer Grenadiere an der Westfront: Geschichte des Grenadier-Regiments König Karl (5. Württ.) Nr. 123 im Weltkrieg 1914-1918* Stuttgart 1920

Beumelberg Werner *Loretto* Oldenburg 1927

Binding Rudolf G *Aus dem Kriege: Weg einer Wandlung* Frankfurt am Main 1929

Blankenstein Oberleutnant a.D. Archivrat Dr. *Geschichte des Reserve-Infanterie-Regiments Nr. 92 im Weltkriege 1914-1918* Osnabrück 1934

Bolze Generalmajor a.D. Walther *Das Kgl. Sächs. 7. Feldartillerie-Regiment Nr. 77* Dresden 1924

Bibliography 303

Braun Generalmajor a.D. Julius Ritter von *Das K.B. Reserve-Infanterie-Regiment Nr. 21* Munich 1923
Burchardi Oberst a.D. Karl *Das Füsilier-Regiment Generalfeldmarschall Graf Moltke (Schlesisches) Nr 38* Oldenburg 1928
Deutelmoser Major a.D. Adolf *Die 27. Infanterie-Division im Weltkrieg 1914-18* Stuttgart 1925
Dellmensingen Königl. Bayer. General der Artillerie z.D. Konrad Krafft von & Feeser Generalmajor a.D. Friedrichfranz *Das Bayernbuch vom Weltkriege 1914-1918 II. Band* Stuttgart 1930
Falkenhayn General Erich von *Die Oberste Heeresleitung 1914-1916* Berlin 1920
Fließ Major a.D. Otto & Dittmar Hauptmann Kurt *5. Hannoversches Infanterie-Regiment Nr. 165 im Weltkriege* Oldenburg 1927
Forstner Major a.D. Kurt Freiherrn von *Das Königlich Preußische Reserve-Infanterie-Regiment Nr. 15* Oldenburg 1929
Freund Leutnant d.R. a.D. Hans *Geschichte des Infanterie-Regiments Prinz Carl (4. Großh.Hess.) Nr. 118 im Weltkrieg* Groß-Gerau 1930
Fuhrmann Major d.R. a.D. Hans, Pfoertner Leutnant d.R. a.D. Otto & Fries Leutnant d.R. a.D. *Königlich Preußisches Reserve Infanterie-Rgt. Nr. 211 im Weltkriege 1914-1918* Berlin 1933
Funcke Oberstleutnant a.D. von *F.A.R. 78 Unser tapferes Regiment: Das Königl. Sächs. 8. Feldartillerie-Regiment. Nr. 78 im Großen Kriege* – Berlin 1937
Goldammer Lt. d.R. a.D. Arthur *Das Kgl. Sächs. 14. Infanterie-Regt.179* – Leipzig 1931
Groos Generalmajor a.D. Carl & Rudloff Hauptmann Werner v. *Infanterie-Regiment Herwath von Bittenfeld (1. Westfälisches) Nr. 13 im Weltkriege 1914-1918* Oldenburg 1927
Großmann Generalleutnant a.D. August *Das K.B. Reserve-Infanterie-Regiment Nr. 17* Munich 1923
Gruson Oberst a.D. Ernst *Das Königlich Preußische 4. Thür. Infanterie-Regiment Nr. 72 im Weltkriege* Oldenburg 1930
Guhr Generalmajor a.D *Das 4. Schlesische Infanterie-Regiment Nr. 157 im Frieden und im Kriege 1897 – 1919* Zeulenroda 1934
Haleck Oberleutnant Fritz *Das Reserve-Infanterie-Regiment Nr. 208* Oldenburg 1922
Heintz Oblt. d.R. a.D. Dr. jur. Hans *Das Kgl. Sächs. Reserve-Infanterie-Regiment Nr. 133* Dresden 1933
Henke Oberstleutnant a.D. Carl *Das 1. Westfälische Feldartillerie-Regiment Nr. 7 1816 – 1919* Berlin 1928
Hennig Leutnant d. Res. Otto *Das Reserve-Infanterie-Regiment Nr. 235 im Weltkriege* Oldenburg 1931
Herkenrath Oberleutnant d.Res. a.D. Dr. August *Das Württembergische Reserve-Inf.-Regiment Nr. 247 im Weltkrieg 1914-1918* Stuttgart 1923
Hillebrand Leutnant d.Res. & Krauß Leutnant d. Res. *Königlich Preußisches Reserve-Infanterie-Rgt. Nr. 29 im Weltkriege 1914/1918* Berlin 1933
Hottenroth Oberst a.D. Johann Edmund *Sachsen in großer Zeit: Band I* Leipzig 1920
Kalbe Kgl Preuß. Hauptmann a.D. Richard *Das 9. Lothringische Infanterie-Regiment Nr. 173 im Weltkriege: Teil II* Zeulenroda 1938
Kastner Oberleutnant d.R. *Geschichte des Königlich Sächsischen Reserve-Infanterie-Regiments 242* Zittau 1924
Kellinghusen Hauptmann d. Res. Wilhelm *Kriegserinnerungen* Bergedorf 1933

Kirchbach Hauptmann i.G. Arndt von *Kämpfe in der Champagne (Winter 1914 – Herbst 1915)* Oldenburg 1919

Knieling Lutz & Bölsche Arnold *R.I.R. 234: Ein Querschnitt durch Deutschlands Schicksalringen* Zeulenroda 1932

Krall Oberstleutnant a.D. Paul *Geschichte des 5. Rheinischen Infanterie-Regiments Nr. 65 während des Weltkrieges 1914 – 1918* Oldenburg 1927

Krämer Max *Geschichte des Reserve-Infanterie-Regiments 245 im Weltkriege 1914/1918* Leipzig

Kümmel Leutnant d. Res. Adolf *Res.Inf.Regt. Nr. 91 im Weltkriege 1914-1918* Oldenburg 1926

Lange Ernst *Hauptmann Willy Lange* Diesdorf bei Gäbersdorf 1936

Lennartz Oberstleutnant d.Sch. a.D. J. & Nagel Postrat a.D. *Geschichte des badischen (später rheinischen) Reserve-Infanterie-Regiment 240* Zeulenroda 1938

Loßberg General der Infanterie Fritz von *Meine Tätigkeit im Weltkriege 1914-1918* Berlin 1939

Makoben Leutnant der Reserve Ernst *Geschichte des Reserve-Infanterie-Regiments Nr. 212 im Weltkriege 1914-1918* Oldenburg 1933

Mayer Landwehr Hauptmann Arthur & Görtz Kriegsfreiwilliger Joseph *Das Reserve-Infanterie-Regiment Nr. 236 im Weltkriege* Zeulenroda 1939

Möller Hanns *Königlich Preußisches Reserve-Infanterie-Regiment Nr. 78 im Weltkrieg 1914/1918* Berlin 1937

Müller Oberstleutnant a.D. Rudolf *Das 3. Lothringische Infanterie-Regiment Nr. 135* Oldenburg 1922

Müller-Loebnitz Oberstleutnant a.D. Wilhelm *Das Ehrenbuch der Westfalen* Stuttgart

Niemann Oberstlt. a.D. Johannes *Das 9. Königlich-Sächsische Infanterie-Regiment Nr. 133 im Weltkrieg 1914-18* Hamburg 1969

Noldt Oberstleutnant a.D. *Das Reserve-Feldartillerie-Regiment Nr. 15 1914 – 1918* Zeulenroda 1931

Orgeldinger Leutnant der Reserve Louis *Das Württembergische Reserve-Infanterie-Regiment Nr. 246* Stuttgart 1931

Pafferath Leutnant der Reserve a.D. Fritz *Die Geschichte des 6. Rheinischen Infanterie-Regiments Nr. 68 im Weltkriege 1914 – 1918* Berlin 1930

Poetter Hauptmann *Infanterie-Regiment Nr. 55* Oldenburg 1922

Reinhard Königl.Preuß. Oberst a.D. *Das 4. Garde-Regiment zu Fuß* Berlin 1924

Reinhardt Generalleutnant a.D. Ernst *Das Württembergische Reserve-Inf.-Regiment Nr. 248 im Weltkrieg 1914-1918* Stuttgart 1924

Reymannn Major a.D. *Das Infanterie-Regiment von Alvensleben (6. Brandenbg.) Nr. 52 im Weltkriege 1914/1918* Oldenburg 1923

Riebensahm Generalleutnant a.D. Gustav *Infanterie-Regiment Prinz Friedrich der Niederlande (2. Westfälisches) Nr. 15 im Weltkriege 1914-18* Minden 1931

Ritter Major a.D. Dr. phil. Albrecht *Das K.B.18. Infanterie-Regiment Prinz Ludwig Ferdinand* München 1926

Rogge Oberst a.D. Walter *Das Königl. Preuß. 2. Nassauisches Infanterie-Regiment Nr. 88* Berlin 1936

Rücker Generalmajor a.D, Toepfer Generalmajor a.D. Kuhn Oberstleutnant a.D & Peters Leutnant d.R. *Königlich Preußisches Reserve-Infanterie-Rgt. Nr. 29 im Weltkriege 1914/1918* Berlin 1933

Rudorff Oberstleutnant a.D. Franz v. *Das Füsilier-Regiment General Ludendorff (Niederrheinisches) Nr. 39 im Weltkriege 1914 – 1918* Berlin 1925

Rupprecht Kronprinz von Bayern *In Treue Fest: Mein Kriegstagebuch, Erster Band* München 1929
Schatz Leutnant d.R. Josef *Geschichte des badischen (rheinischen) Reserve-Infanterie-Regiments 239* Stuttgart 1927
Schmidt Major a.D. Ernst *Argonnen* Oldenburg 1927
Schmidt-Oswald Kgl. Preuß. Major a.D. Ernst *Das Altenburger Regiment (8. Thüringisches Infanterie Regiment Nr. 153) im Weltkriege* Oldenburg 1927
Schöning Königlich Preuß. Major a.D. Hans *Leib-Grenadier-Regiment König Friedrich Wilhelm III. (1. Brandenburgisches) Nr. 8 im Weltkriege* Oldenburg 1924
Schwab Oberstleutnant A & Schreyer Hauptmann A *Das neunte württembergische Infanterie-Regiment Nr. 127 im Weltkrieg 1914-1918* Stuttgart 1920
Schwarte Generalleutnant Max *Der Weltkrieg um Ehre und Recht: Der Deutsche Landkrieg, Zweiter Teil* Leipzig 1921-1933
Schwedt Major d.R. *Das Reserve-Infanterie-Regiment Nr. 204* Zeulenroda 1929
Selle Oberst a.D Hans von & Gründel Oberstleutnant a.D. Walter *Das 6. Westpreußische Infanterie-Regiment Nr. 149 im Weltkriege* Berlin 1929
Simon Oberst a.D. *Das Infanterie-Regiment 'Kaiser Wilhelm, König von Preußen' (2. Wüttemb.) Nr. 120 im Weltkrieg 1914-1918* Stuttgart 1922
Soldan George *Das Infanterie-Regiment Nr. 184* Oldenburg 1920
Solleder Dr. Fridolin *Vier Jahre Westfront: Geschichte des Regiments List R.I.R. 16* München 1932
Tiessen Leutnant d.R. Max *Königlich Preußisches Reserve-Infanterie-Regiment 213: Geschichte eines Flandernregiments* Glückstadt 1937
Trützschler von Falkenstein Major a.D. Hans *Das Anhaltische Infanterie-Regiment Nr. 93 im Weltkriege* Oldenburg 1929
Voigt Oblt. d.Res. *Geschichte des Füsilier-Regiments Generalfeldmarschall Prinz Albrecht von Preußen (Hann.) Nr. 73* Berlin, 1938
Wellman Generalleutnant a.D. *Das Infanterie-Regiment von Horn (3. Rheinisches) Nr. 29: Heft 2* Zeulenroda 1938
Weniger Generalmajor a.D. Heinrich, Zobel Oberst a.D. Artur & Fels Oberst a.D. Maximilian *Das K.B. 5. Infanterie-Regiment Großherzog Ernst Ludwig von Hessen* München 1929
Werner Lt. d. Res. Dr. Bernhard *Das Königlich Preußische Inf.-Rgt. Prinz Louis Ferdinand von Preußen (2. Magdeb.) Nr. 27 im Weltkriege 1914-1918* Berlin 1933
Windhorst Major d.R. a.D. Karl *Das Mindensche Feldartillerie-Regiment Nr. 58 im Weltkriege 1914-1918* Dortmund 1930
Winzer Lt. d.R. Richard *Das Kgl. Sächs. Res.-Infanterie-Regiment Nr 243 im Weltkriege 1914-1918* Dresden 1927
Wißmannoberst von *Das Reserve-Infanterie-Regiment Nr. 55 im Weltkrieg* Berlin N.D.
Wohlenberg Oberleutnant d.R. a.D. Alfred *Das Res.-Inf.-Regt. Nr. 77 im Weltkriege 1914-18* Hildesheim 1931
Wolff Hauptmann Ludwig *Das Kgl. Sächs. 5. Inf-Regiment 'Kronprinz' Nr. 104: Erster Band* Dresden 1925
Wolters Hauptmann G *Das Infanterie-Regiment König Wilhelm I. (6. Württ.) Nr. 124 im Weltkrieg 1914-1918* Stuttgart 1921
Wunderlich Leutnant d.R. Curt *Fünfzig Monate Wehr im Westen: Geschichte des Reserve-Infanterie-Regiments Nr. 66* Eisleben 1939

Zipfel und Albrecht Archivrat Dr. *Geschichte des Infanterie-Regiments Bremen (1. Hanseatisches) Nr. 75* Bremen 1934
Zipfel Archivrat Dr. Ernst *Geschichte des Großherzoglich Mecklenburgischen Grenadier-Regiments Nr. 89* Schwerin 1932

Published Works (German: author unknown)

Der Weltkrieg 1914 bis 1918 Siebenter Band: Die Operationen des Jahres 1915. Die Ereignisse im Winter und Frühjahr [GOH 1] Berlin, 1931
Der Weltkrieg 1914 bis 1918 Achter Band: Die Operationen des Jahres 1915, Die Ereignisse im Westen im Frühjahr und Sommer, im Osten vom Frühjahr bis zum Jahresschluß. [GOH 2] Berlin 1932
Die Funke Berlin 20 December 1932
Das K.B. 14. Infanterie-Regiment Hartmann Munich 1931
Geschichte des Feldartillerie-Regiments von Peucker (1.Schles.) Nr 6 1914 – 1918 Breslau 1932
Das Füsilier-Regiment Prinz Heinrich von Preußen (Brandenburgisches) Nr. 35 im Weltkriege Berlin 1929
Geschichte des 9. Rhein. Infanterie-Regiments Nr. 160 im Weltkriege 1914-1918 Zeulenroda 1931
Das Königlich Sächsische 13. Infanterie-Regiment Nr. 178 Kamenz 1935
Gedenkblatt des Reserve –Infanterie-Regiments Nr. 36 Halle 1925

Published Works (French)

Les Armées Françaises dans la Grande Guerre: Tome II: La Stabilisation du Front – Les Attaques Locales (14 Novembre 1914 – 1 Mai 1915) [FOH2] Paris 1931
Les Armées Françaises dans la Grande Guerre: Tome III: Les Offensives de 1915 – L'Hiver de 1915-1916 [FOH3] Paris 1923
Joffre Maréchal *Mémoires du Maréchal Joffre (1910 – 1917) Tome Second* Paris 1932

Published Works (English)

Military Operations France and Belgium 1915: Winter 1914-15: Battle of Neuve Chapelle: Battles of Ypres [BOH 1] London 1927
Military Operations France and Belgium 1915: Battles of Aubers Ridge, Festubert and Loos [BOH 2] London 1928
Bridger Geoff *Battleground Europe: The Battle of Neuve Chapelle* Barnsley 2000
Bristow Adrian *A Serious Disappointment: The Battle of Aubers Ridge 1915 and the Munitions Scandal* London 1995
Dixon John *Magnificent But Not War: The Battle for Ypres 1915* Barnsley 2003
Hackett General Sir John *The Profession of Arms* London 1983
Hancock Edward *Battleground Europe: Aubers Ridge* Barnsley 2005
Holmes Richard *The Little Field Marshal: A Life of Sir John French* London 2004
Rawson Andrew *Battleground Europe: Loos- Hill 70* Barnsley 2002
Rawson Andrew *Battleground Europe: Loos- Hohenzollern* Barnsley 2003
Sheffield Gary *The Chief: Douglas Haig and the British Army* London 2011
Sheldon Jack *The German Army on Vimy Ridge 1914 – 1917* Barnsley 2008

Index

Aisne ix, 78, 79, 246, 264
Aistermann Leutnant 51, 53, 69
Albrecht Generaloberst Duke of Württemberg vii, 81, 118, 295
Albrecht Reserve Leutnant 266
Alderson LtGen EAH 163
Alderson's Force 155
Alsace 160
Altrock GenLt von 16, 24, 35, 36, 38, 207
Alt-Vendin 223
Alvermann Leutnant 99
Amagne-Lucquy 274
Amiens 206, 293
André Oberstleutnant 180
Angres 127, 205, 207, 212
Annequin 243
Apfelhof 133, 145, 147, 148 – 151
Arbre-Höhe 6, 10, 14 – 16, 21, 23
Ardeuil 264, 269, 275
Argonne Forest vii, viii, xiv, 7, 153, 160, 164 – 202, 249, 296, 300, 301
Argonnenbahn 183
Armentières ix, 55
Armin Gen der Inf Sixt von 223
Arras xi, 93, 103, 122, 128, 136, 140, 148, 182, 205, 206, 207, 252, 256, 260, 272, 299
Attigny 263, 264
Artois viii, ix, 1, 44, 122, 128, 129, 182, 183, 203, 206, 234, 242, 243, 246, 295, 297
Aubérive 24, 246, 250, 251, 262, 271, 274, 276
Aubers 45, 51, 54, 64, 65, 75
Aubers Ridge xii, 45, 75, 122, 129, 137, 160
Aubréville 164
Auchy 207, 209 – 211

Baas Reserve Leutnant 267, 288
Bachschneider Leutnant 138
Bacmeister Oberst 181
Bader Oberstleutnant 168
Bagatelle Pavillon 165, 168, 170, 173, 174, 176, 184

Bagatelle Redoubt 171, 174 – 178, 184, 187, 188, 190
Bahrfeldt Gen der Inf von 10, 295
Bailly 278, 27 9
Bangert Hauptmann 6, 10, 14
Barbot General 125, 292
Bargenda Reserve Leutnant 212, 216
Barricade 182
Barthel Leutnant 15
Barthel Max 188, 194, 197, 202, 296
Bauer Hauptmann
Baulny 194, 195
Bayonville 183
Bazancourt 250, 275
Beaucamps 45, 63
Beaurains 225
Beauséjour Farm 7, 8, 21, 30
Beck Hauptmann 217
Beck Rittmeister von 176
Beck Reserve Leutnant 187
Behr Leutnant 18, 20
Beißbarth Leutnant 188
Belgian Army
  Division
    6th 98
Bellewaarde Lake 115
Berclau 157
Bergh Major van den 23
Berndt Reserve Oberleutnant 32
Bertsch Reserve Oberleutnant 188
Beselare 85
Bétheniville 275
Bethmann Hollweg viii
Béthune 214, 215, 231, 233
Beulwitz Hauptmann von 53
Biez-Wald 47, 49, 50, 52, 57, 59, 61, 68, 69, 78
Biesme, River/Valley 174, 188, 191
Bikschote 86, 88
Billy 157
Binarville 165, 174, 184
Binding Leutnant Rudolf 94, 101, 111, 296
Bockhern Leutnant 132
Boezinge 93, 94, 95, 97, 98, 103
Bois de la Grurie 173, 193
Bolante 181, 182, 194, 195, 200

Bornmüller Leutnant 18
Bössneck Reserve Leutnant 57, 78
Bothmer Gen der Inf von 299
Boyle Lieutenant Colonel RL 99
Brauch Leutnant 134
Brauchitsch GenMaj von 52
Braun Oberst Julius Ritter von 139
Breithaupt Reserve Leutnant 198
Brieger Hauptmann 18
Briesen Hauptmann von 236
Brink Oberstleutnant 88
Brinkard Leutnant 15
Brion Colonel 40
British Army
  Armies
  First 45, 58, 144, 160, 226
  Corps
   I 44, 129, 132; **IV** 48, 57, 129, 137, 234, 245; **XI** 226, 234; **Indian** 48, 57, 129, 132, 159
  Divisions
   Guards 231; **1st** 133, 136, 144, 218, 219, 232, 234, 245; **2nd** 145, 208, 211; **1st Canadian** 44, 163; **2nd Cavalry** 68; **7th** 137, 145, 211; **8th** 48, 137, 144; **9th** 209, 211; **12th** 234; **15th (Scottish)** 217, 218; **21st** 226; **24th** 226 – 228, 230; **28th** 231; **29th** 44; **46th** 44, 234, 238; **47th** 231; **51st (Highland)** 159, 163; **Lahore** 102, 132, 145, 161; **Meerut** 48, 136, 145, 161
  Brigades
   2 Guards 231; **2** 136; **3** 136; **3 Canadian** 155; **5** 145; **6** 148, 208; 25 78; **44** 217, 218; **45** 226, 231; 46 217, 218; **137** 239; **138** 245; 141 215; **Sirhind** 103; **Dehra Dun** 136, 161, 162; **Bareilly** 136, 161; **Garwhal** 145
  Regiments
   Berkshire 78; **Black Watch** 137, 242; **Buffs** 244; **Cameron Highlanders** 242; **Gloucestershire** 232; **Gordon Highlanders** 220, 242; **King's** 219, 232; **King's Royal Rifle Corps** 148; **London** 138, 143, 215; **London Scottish** 219; **Northamptonshire** 134, 162; **Rifle Brigade** 49; **Royal Irish Rifles** 49; **Royal Munster Fusiliers** 161, 232; **Royal Scots** 242; **Royal Scots Fusiliers** 220; **Seaforth Highlanders** 242; **Sherwood**

   Foresters 245; **South Staffordshire** 208;
  Battalions
   8th Canadian 100; **10th Canadian** 99; **15th Canadian** 100; **16th Canadian** 99
Brizy 263
Broodseinde 107
Brüning Leutnant 149
Brunn Hauptmann von 47
Brünner Hauptmann 19
Bürstinghaus Leutnant 39
Büterowe Leutnant 147, 162
Butte de Tahure 258, 259, 263, 272, 280, 284 - 286

Cambrai 145, 206, 243
Carency 123, 125, 140
Cary General de Langle de 252, 292
Cassel 103
Castelnau General de 252, 292
Castendyk Major 147, 151
Central Redoubt 168, 171, 174, 177, 184, 187, 188
Cernay 38
Challerange 250, 264, 275
Chalons 246
Champagne viii, ix, xi, 1, 44, 58, 81, 122, 203, 206, 225, 246, 260, 261, 274, 278 – 280, 287, 292 - 294, 298 - 301
Chantilly xii
Chapigny 47, 65
Charleroi 296
Charme, River 173, 174, 176, 194
Charlepaux 183
Charleville 275
Chatel 190
Chavignon 79
Chemin des Dames 293
Cheppe, River 200
Chipotte 92
Cimitière Redoubt 171, 174, 177, 184, 187, 188
Claer Gen der Inf von 59, 60, 79, 147, 296
Clermont 164, 194
Cliqueterie Farm 66
Courtin Hauptmann 50

Danner GenMaj 138
Dardanelles ix, 39, 44
Daub Oberleutnant 268
Davies Brigadier-General 136
Deligny General 101

Dellmensingen Gen Kraft von 74, 79, 297
Demmering Major 150, 151
Dependorf Oberleutnant 114, 121
Despres 64
Deule Canal 225
Dickson Captain 135
Dieusson Valley/Ravine 165, 167 – 169, 184, 185
Dombois Hauptmann 224
Don 59, 74, 131, 135
Dönhof Leutnant 69
Douai 32, 131, 221, 225
Dourges 244
Douvrin 207, 208, 210, 223
Dreckschlucht 284, 285
Drie Grachten 85
Drigalski Major 97
Duchêne General 174, 293
Dücker Leutnant 237
Dültgen Hauptmann 149
Dumas General 26, 294
Dumas Oberleutnant 88
Dziobek Major 16

Eberhard Major 68
Ecurie 123, 125
Eilers Leutnant 175
Einem GenOberst von 21, 26, 35, 41, 256, 260, 265, 276, 297
Eisenberg 283
Eitel Friedrich Oberst Prinz 206
Eith Leutnant 110
Ekey Leutnant 71
Eksternest 107, 112
Elten Oberleutnant 254, 255
Engländer Wäldchen 215, 228, 233, 245
Englisch Reserve Leutnant 197
Epmeyer Leutnant 137
Elverdinge 92, 93
Engelien Hauptmann 19
Erquinghem 63
Esche Oberstleutnant 125
Esebeck Major Freiherr von 183
Eselsnase 174, 184, 187, 188
Estaires 131, 145
Estorff Oberst von 36
Eulitz Hauptmann 151

Fabeck Gen der Inf von 298
Facius Hauptmann 54, 55
Falkenhayn Gen von vii – xi, 33, 45, 74, 80 – 82, 119, 122, 128, 183, 256, 260, 261, 272, 287

Ferme de Navarin 254, 272, 278, 279, 287
Ferry General 119
Festubert xii, 45, 122, 144, 153, 159, 160
Fither Hauptmann 268
Fleck GenLt 21, 37, 41, 262, 297
Foch General 98, 103, 104, 126, 128, 144, 160, 206, 293
Forstner Hauptmann Freiherr von 236
Fortuinhoek 104, 107
Fosse 8 209, 210, 223, 225, 230, 234
Fosse 9 211
Fosse 11 215
Fosse 12 215
Fosse 13 210, 236
Fosse 14 217, 229
Fosse 15 231
Fournes 47, 52, 55, 63, 143
Franke Hauptmann 254
Frederick the Great 11
French Army
  GQG 24
  Armies
    First 294; **Second** 252, 293; **Third** 7, 294; **Fourth** 3, 7, 26, 252, 292; **Sixth** 293; **Eighth** 294, 295; **Tenth** xi, 44, 103, 122, 123, 125, 128, 136, 144, 160, 182, 206, 293, 295
  Corps
    I 6, 7, 8, 21, 22, 24, 26, 37, 294; **I Cavalry** 6; **II** 6, 24, 26, 37, 165, 293, 294; **III** 205, 293, 294; **IV** 22, 24, 26, 42, 294; **V** 170, 184, 191; **IX** 44, 127, 231, 233, 234; **X** 123, 127; **XI** 286; **XII** 35, 205, 207; **XIII** 293; **XVI** 35, 37, 39, 286; **XVII** 6, 7, 9, 22, 24, 26, 42, 123, 127, 294; **XX** 127, 293; **XXI** 125, 127, 206, 207; **XXIII** 127; **XXXII** 165, 184, 191, 293, 294; **XXXIII** 205, 207, 295
  Divisions
    7th Cavalry 295; **8th** 42; **11th** 119; **13th** 205, 292; **17th** 294; **19th** 293; **24th** 205; **40th** 165; **41st** 294; **42nd** 174, 189, 293, 294; **43rd** 205; **45th** 92, 95, 97, 99; **58th** 144; **60th** 35, 294; **60th Reserve** 7; **70th** 205; **77th** 125, 292; **87th Territorial** 92, 93, 98, 101; **96th** 294; **125th** 184; **152nd** 231; **153rd** 101; **157th** 271; **Moroccan** 123, 127, 160, 294
  Brigades
    4 Dragoon 295; **5** 26; **7** 292; **24** 292;

28 294; 56 294; 90 92; 91 93; 150 184; 186 98
Regiments
1st Rifle 92; 4th Colonial 182; 5th Colonial 182; 8th Chasseur 179; 20th Chasseur 294; 31st 292; 51st 40; 55th 184; 69th 293; 72nd 199; 78th 1; 94th 169, 179; 151st 190; 154th 169; 155th 169; 161st 169; 162nd 179; 255th 184; 402nd 270

French FM Sir John xii, 44, 103, 104, 144, 231
Frese Hauptmann von 28 - 30
Fressel Leutnant 13
Frezenberg 112, 116
Fricke Leutnant 22
Friedrich August King of Saxony 3
Frings Hauptmann 50
Fritsch GenMaj 127
Fritsche Leutnant 195
Fromme Oberst 257, 260
Fromme Leutnant 34
Fromelles 51, 129, 135, 137, 162
Fürst Leutnant 282

Gaedtke Reserve Leutnant 33
Galicia viii, x, 81
Gallipoli ix, 44
Gause Major 217, 218
Gaza Hauptmann von 270
Gérard General 26, 294
Gerlach Leutnant 283, 284
German Crown Prince xii, 183, 191, 200, 287, 298 – 300
German Army
Supreme Army Headquarters 8, 21, 31, 35, 39, 73, 74, 81 – 83, 98, 119, 128, 203, 224, 225, 236, 246, 256, 261, 272, 275, 278, 297, 299
Armies
First 300; Third 8, 15, 21, 24, 26, 31, 35, 38, 39, 41, 43, 128, 203, 225, 246, 249, 250, 256, 260, 261, 263, 271, 274, 276, 280, 286, 287, 297, 299; Fourth vii, viii, 80, 81, 98, 100, 103, 115, 118, 119, 263, 295, 300; Fifth xii, 21, 26, 35, 183, 260, 261, 272, 287, 299, 300; Sixth 26, 73, 74, 77, 122, 125, 127 – 129, 131, 145, 161, 205, 207, 224, 225, 242, 256, 260, 297; Seventh 26, 257, 261; **Eighth** 201, 298, 300; **Tenth** viii; **Seventeenth** 300
Corps
Guard Corps 206, 225, 226, 299, 301; I Bavarian 207; I Bavarian Reserve 123, 182, 205 – 207, 225; II Bavarian xiv, 160; III 300; IV 205, 206, 223 – 226, 231, 260, 297; VI 21, 128, 205, 206, 225, 226, 301; VI Reserve 165; VII 45, 53, 54, 57, 59, 74, 135, 145, 153, 260, 296, 297; VIII 1, 8, 15, 21, 24, 26, 30, 38, 128, 301; VIII Reserve 1, 5, 8, 21, 26, 35, 37, 38, 251, 257, 260, 262, 263, 265, 269, 272, 286, 297, 298; IX 278, 286, 301; X 254, 269, 278, 298 - 300; X Reserve 21; XII 21, 260, 269; XII Reserve 1, 21, 24; XIII 298; XV Reserve 115; XVI vii, 165, 181 – 183, 300; XVII 298; XVIII Reserve 272; XIX 53, 54, 135, 150, 160; XXII Reserve 115; XXIII Reserve 85, 94 – 96, 98, 106, 298; XXIV 297; XXVI Reserve 85, 95, 96, 98, 106, 107, 115, 118, 298; XXVII Reserve 98, 100, 103, 106, 114, 118; **Alpenkorps** 297
Divisions
1st Guards Infantry 6, 26, 32, 206; 1st Bavarian Reserve 123, 127; 2nd Guards Infantry 206, 233, 236, 240; 2nd Infantry 298; 2nd Guards Reserve 38, 147, 149, 153, 156, 160, 171, 223; 2nd Landwehr 165; 4th Infantry 257, 282; 5th Infantry 127, 257, 263, 271; 5th Bavarian Infantry 276, 280, 282, 283, 286; 5th Bavarian Reserve 225; 6th Infantry 301; 6th Bavarian Reserve xiv, 59, 60, 61, 71, 72, 79, 129, 135, 137, 299; 7th Infantry 127, 205, 214, 219, 231 – 233, 257; 7th Reserve 276, 280, 283, 286; 8th Infantry 45, 127, 220 – 222, 224 – 226, 231 - 233; 9th Landwehr 165, 169, 183; 11th Infantry 167, 225, 296; 12th Infantry 225; 13th Infantry 54, 71, 79, 135, 226; 14th Infantry 45, 52, 55, 57, 59, 71, 75, 149, 153, 207, 211, 212, 223, 226, 298; 14th Reserve 45; 15th Infantry 15, 38; 15th Reserve 251, 254, 257, 260 – 262, 264, 271; 16th Infantry

Index   311

24, 127, 128; **16th Reserve** 8, 16, 19, 24, 35, 36, 39, 257, 262, 264, 269, 271; **17th Infantry** 278; **18th Infantry** 278; **19th Infantry** 269, 278; **19th Reserve** 6, 8 – 10, 21, 23, 24, 30, 37, 38, 295; **20th Infantry** 269, 271, 278, 300; **21st Reserve** 271; **22nd Infantry** 296; **22nd Reserve** 257; **24th Infantry** 54, 150; **24th Reserve** 1, 24, 251, 260, 271, 274, 276; **27th Infantry** 165, 167, 169, 174, 176, 183, 186, 200, 300, 301; **28th Infantry** 125; **33rd Infantry** 165, 176, 181 – 183, 194, 195, 199; **34th Infantry** 19, 165, 169, 174, 180, 183, 195; **36th Infantry** 301; **39th Infantry** 298, 300; **40th Infantry** 54; **43rd Reserve** 74, 85, 98; **44th Reserve** 115; **45th Reserve** 94, 98; **46th Reserve** 88, 98; **50th Infantry** 45, 257, 260, 261, 269; **51st Reserve** 89, 98, 99, 104, 116; **52nd Reserve** 86, 88, 91, 95, 96, 98; **53rd Reserve** 100, 106 - 108, 272; **54th Reserve** 100, 106, 110; **56th Infantry** 39, 261, 263, 269, 271, 272, 286; **58th Infantry** 127, 128, 144; **115th Infantry** 144; **117th Infantry** 210, 211, 215, 223, 224, 226; **123rd** 205, 206, 212

Brigades
  2 Guards 301; 3 Guards 301; 4 Guards Cavalry 295; **4 Bavarian Field Artillery** 297; **6 Bavarian Field Artillery** 299; **11** 296; **12 Bavarian Reserve** 70, 139; **13 Reserve** 56; **13 Field Artillery** 54; **14 Infantry** 215; **14 Bavarian Reserve** 59, 68, 138, 139; **15 Infantry** 52, 301; **15 Field Artillery** 127; **26 Reserve** 223; **27 Infantry** 297; **28 Field Artillery** 300; **29 Reserve** 263; **31 Reserve** 10, 32; **37 Infantry** 21; **38 Reserve** 21, 24, 26, 160; **39 Infantry** 301; **39 Reserve** 8, 9; **60** 16, 21; **47 Infantry** 54; **51 Infantry** 295; **53 Infantry** 165, 168, 187; **54 Infantry** 165, 168, 169, 183, 185, 298; **66 Infantry** 194, 196; **67 Infantry** 181, 182, 196; **68 Infantry** 174, 176 - 178; **79 Infantry** 61, 70; **83 Infantry** 298; **86 Infantry** 177, 195; **86 Reserve** 59, 74, 80; **100 Infantry** 45;

112 Infantry 39, 263; **185 Infantry** 257; **192 Infantry** 256, 261

Regiments
Infantry
  Fusilier Guard 296; **Footguard 2** 32, 34, 36, 301; **Grenadier Guard 2** 298, 301; **Marine 2** 117; **Bavarian Reserve 2** 123; **Footguard 3** 39; **Grenadier Guard 3** 300; **Footguard 4** 32, 299; **5** 154; **Grenadier Guard 5** 296; **Bavarian 5** 149; **Bavarian Reserve 7** 125; **Leib Grenadier 8** 264, 286; **Bavarian 9** 72; **Reserve 11** 207, 211, 213, 217, 218, 223; **Bavarian Reserve 12** 125; **13** 45, 47, 48, 50 – 53, 56 – 58, 61, 62, 64, 66, 69, 71, 76; **14** 283; **Bavarian 14** 282; **15** 45, 47, 50 – 52, 56, 79, 135, 219; **Reserve 15** 79, 147, 153, 158, 223, 224, 227, 230, 236, 240 - 242; **16** 45, 47, 48, 50, 51, 53, 54, 56, 68, 69, 135, 207 - 211; **Bavarian 16** 233; **Bavarian Reserve 16** 60, 63, 68, 69, 70, 73, 76, 77, 129, 137 – 140, 142; **Bavarian 17** 245; **Bavarian Reserve 17** 60, 63, 69, 70, 137, 138, 142; **18** 297; **Bavarian 18** 149; **Bavarian 19** 282; **Bavarian Reserve 20** 60, 68, 69, 137; **Bavarian Reserve 21** 60, 61, 68, 69, 137 - 140; **Reserve 22** 182, 207, 212 – 220, 226; **Bavarian 23** 242; **Reserve 23** 182; **Reserve 25** 262 - 264; **26** 128, 215, 226, 227, 233; **27** 214 – 216, 226, 227, 242; **Landwehr 27** 182; **28** 24 - 27; **29** 24, 25, 27, 38; **Reserve 29** 15, 16, 32, 39, 262, 263; **30** 19, 180, 189, 196; **Reserve 30** 36, 263, 264; **Fusilier 35** 264, 265, 269; **Reserve 36** 276, 278; **Fusilier 38** 167 – 169, 184, 300; **Fusilier 39** 45, 257; **Landwehr 39** 123, 125, 225; **42** 297; **47** 269, 283; **49** 283, 286; **50** 264, 283; **52** 257, 276, 278, 286; **53** 45, 47, 272; **55** 45, 71, 131, 135, 144, 145, 147, 148, 151- 153, 160, 162; **Reserve 55** 153, 157, 210, 239 - 241; **56** 45, 50, 53, 61, 149, 153, 156, 160, 207, 210; **57** 45, 50, 53, 61, 69, 133 – 135, 137, 147 – 153, 156, 160, 207, 210, 233, 238; **Reserve 63** 36; **65** 22, 37; **Reserve**

65 18, 19, 21, 36, 262, 263, 272;
Reserve 66 283, 284; 67 169, 174,
175, 177, 178, 190; 68 22, 24, 38;
Reserve 68 19, 22, 263; 69 24, 31;
72 231, 233, 276, 278; Reserve 72
283, 284; Fusilier 73 26 - 30;
Reserve 73 37; 74 278, 298;
Reserve 74 8 – 10, 14 – 16, 37; 75
278; Reserve 77 153 – 155, 159,
172, 182, 210, 233; Landwehr 77
150, 152, 160; Reserve 78 23;
Landwehr 78 100, 156; 79 264; 83
301; Landwehr 83 169, 182; 88
263, 264; Grenadier 89 280; 91
270; Reserve 91 153, 154, 156,
171, 172, 175, 223; Reserve 92 6,
10, 14 – 16, 21, 41; 93 221, 222,
231, 232; 98 182, 195, 199;
Reserve Grenadier 100 276;
Grenadier 101 38; 104 53, 54, 61,
69, 149 – 153, 238, 242; Reserve
102 254; Reserve 104 3, 5; Reserve
106 228, 229, 231, 232; Reserve
107 3, 5, 16, 17, 19, 20, 249, 270,
274; 113 129; 115 76, 80; 118
264, 266 - 268; 120 167 – 169, 183
- 187; 121 298; 122 298; Reserve
122 257; Grenadier 123 169, 177,
178, 187; 124 168, 169, 177, 183,
187, 188; Landwehr 124 182; 125
298; 127 167 – 169, 183 - 185; 130
195, 196, 199, 200; 133 53, 57, 78,
150; Reserve 133 1, 253, 274; 135
181, 182, 195 - 200; 139 51, 53,
54, 61, 150, 153; 140 283; 144 21,
181, 195, 199; 145 176, 177, 188,
190; 147 286; 149 283 - 286; 153
221, 222, 226, 229, 231, 232; 157
18, 19, 207, 212 – 214, 218, 219,
223, 226 - 230; 158 45, 258, 267 –
269, 286; 160 36; 165 219, 233;
173 178 – 180, 189, 195, 198; 178
212, 213, 217, 220 - 223; 179 54,
69, 150; 183 256; 184 257, 270;
192 270; Reserve 203 80; Reserve
204 80; Reserve 205 115, 116;
Reserve 207 115; Reserve 208 115,
116; Reserve 211 95; Reserve 212
94, 95; Reserve 213 88, 95; Reserve
215 89, 94; Reserve 216 97;
Reserve 233 236, 237; Reserve 234
87, 89, 90, 98, 99; Reserve 235 98;
Reserve 236 98, 99, 104, 105, 116,
117; Reserve 239 95 - 97; Reserve
240 86, 91; Reserve 241 100, 272;
Reserve 242 100, 108, 112; Reserve
243 272; Reserve 244 100; Reserve
245 100, 101, 106; Reserve 246
100, 106, 110; Reserve 247 100,
101, 106, 115; Reserve 248 107,
112, 114

Field Artillery
Bavarian Reserve 6 55, 62, 137, 141; 7
47, 49, 50, 69, 72; Bavarian 7 63;
Reserve 15 254 - 256; Reserve 20
21; 22 47, 137; Reserve 24 3; 40
214, 215; 43 47; 49 187; Reserve
54 100, 107; 58 47, 52, 61, 135; 69
180; 75 226, 235; 77 54, 64; 78 54,
66, 75

Foot Artillery
3 287; 7 47

Cavalry
Uhlan 14 297; Uhlan 19 187, 295

Battalions
Foot Artillery 4 251; Jäger 5 195; Jäger
6 197, 199; Pionier 7 300; Foot
Artillery 9 251; Jäger 9 296; Jäger
11 45, 47 – 49, 51, 53, 61, 64, 68,
72, 149, 157, 207, 211, 243;
Reserve Jäger 12 276; Reserve Jäger
15 80; Foot Artillery 19 54; Pionier
7 52, 210; Pionier 16 178; Pionier
29 172, 180; Pionier 35 81, 86;
Fliegerabteilung 3 88

Giersberg Hauptmann 149
Gies Reserve Leutnant 142
Gießler-Höhe 205
Givenchy 45, 135, 140, 156, 206
Givenchy-lez-la-Bassée 207
Goetz Leutnant 148
Goldmann Reserve Leutnant 54
Gonnermann Leutnant 199
Götze Hauptmann 1
Gräber Leutnant 221, 244
Grabbe Reserve Leutnant 34
Graf Leutnant 31
Grahl Hauptmann 114
Gratreuil 34
Grautoff Oberstleutnant 215
Grave Reserve Hauptmann 171, 175
Gravelin 63, 133
Grimm Oberstleutnant 117
Groneweg Hauptmann 214
Gröning Hauptmann 190

Index   313

Gropius Leutnant 34
Gropler Leutnant 69
Grossetti General 35, 37, 294
Guhr Major 19, 212, 213, 216, 217

Haas Hauptmann von 282
Haase Leutnant 54
Hagedorn Leutnant 221
Hagen Major von der 265
Hague Convention 82, 83
Haig General Sir Douglas 58, 129, 144, 159, 226, 231
Haisnes 209, 210 – 212, 223, 236
Haking MajGen/LtGen RCB 136, 226
Halbach Leutnant 114
Halpegarbe 47, 49, 50, 53, 54, 59, 60, 61, 63, 133
Hammerstein Hauptmann von 88, 95
Hanebeek 104
Hanske Reserve Leutnant 151
Hanstein Hauptmann von 210, 211, 243
Hassel Oberstleutnant von 50, 207
Haubourdin 55
Häusler Leutnant 273
Hausser Hauptmann 190
Haut Pommereau 65
Hauviné 249
Hay Leutnant 88, 89
Hazebrouck 104
Heinemeyer Leutnant 10, 11, 41
Heister Leutnant von 34
Heitmueller Reserve Leutnant 29
Hellwig Major 264
Henoumont Hauptmann 176
Hentschel Leutnant 227, 230
Henze Leutnant 15, 16
Herlies 45, 52, 54, 60, 64, 74
Hermann Leutnant 69
Hertzsch Leutnant 54
Het Sas 85, 89, 95, 103
Hiepe Major 19
Hill 29 91, 103
Hill 32 100
Hill 50 112, 114, 115
Hill 60 82, 83
Hill 70 213, 217, 219 – 222, 226, 228, 229, 231, 234, 235, 244
Hill 119 125
Hill 140 125
Hill 171 255
Hill 185 262, 266, 272
Hill 185 (West of Ferme de Navarin) 272
Hill 188 5, 272

Hill 192 286
Hill 196 30, 31 – 33, 36, 38, 39, 263, 264, 283
Hill 199 263, 286
Hill 200 6
Hill 263 194
Hill 285 See *La Fille Morte*
Hindenburg viii, xi
Hirch Leutnant 196
Hoehn GenLt Ritter von 206
Hohenzollernwerk 209, 231, 233, 237 – 240
Höhn GenLt von 261, 262
Hohneck Oberleutnant 108
Hoitz Leutnant 22
Holthausen Hauptmann 20
Holtzendorf Major von 34
Hooge 115
Houthulst Wood 86, 98
Houyette Ravine 188
Hügel Gen der Inf Freiherr von 85, 298
Hugo Leutnant 284
Hulluch 210, 211, 216 – 219, 222, 223, 226 – 230, 234, 236, 237, 245
Hüls Leutnant 133
Humbert General 165, 294

Ijzer – See Yser
Illies 45, 54, 63, 72, 74, 133, 137, 144, 161
Ilse GenMaj 98, 119
Immelmann Leutnant Max 56

Jantzen Leutnant 218
Jersch Leutnant 50, 78
Joffre Maréchal Joseph xii, 1, 3, 7, 21, 37, 40, 44, 78, 80, 118, 122, 144, 160, 203, 206, 207, 231, 252, 287, 292, 293
Johansen Leutnant 199
Junge Leutnant 257 - 260

Kaimberg Leutnant Baumbach von 49, 78
Kanonenberg 264
Kathen Gen der Inf 85, 298
Kayser Leutnant 195
Kellinghusen Reserve Hauptmann 6, 10
Kerselaar 97, 108
Kettmann Reserve Leutnant 284
Kienitz Leutnant von 32
Kiesgrube 210, 223, 233 – 235, 237, 238
Kiesel Major 153, 227, 230
Kissinger Leutnant 104
Kitchener's Wood 99

Kitzling Major von 258, 259
Kitzlinghöhe 283
Klauenflügel Leutnant 235, 238
Klein Reserve Leutnant 216, 244
Klein-Zillebeke 107, 118
Klußmann Leutnant 233
Knobelsdorff GenLt Schmidt von 269, 298
Koch Leutnant Rudolf 226
Koekuit 90
Kohlenhalde St Pierre 215, 233
Kohlmüller Hauptmann 245
König Leutnant 147
Konrad Reserve Leutnant 172
Kortebeek 90
Kortejohann Leutnant 15, 41
Kortekeer 97
Kortemark 81
Kramer Leutnant 190
Kratz Reserve Leutnant 267
Kriege Leutnant 264
Kristen Hauptmann 149
Kuhl General von 242, 243
Kühn Oberleutnant 137
Kuipers Oberleutnant 57, 79
Kuntze Gen der Inf 207
Künzel Hauptmann 150
Küster Leutnant 49, 78

La Bassée 44, 55, 56, 63, 76, 122, 131, 134, 137, 145, 147, 149, 157, 214, 220, 222, 234 – 236, 245
La Bassée Canal 208, 234
Labordère/Martin Redoubt 171, 174, 183 - 187
Labyrinth 123, 125 – 127
La Chevallerie GenMaj von 184
La Cliqueterie 54
La Fille Morte 174, 181, 182, 193 - 195, 197 - 200
La Folie 125, 127, 205
La Harazée 171, 174, 178, 190
La Madeleine 131
Lambsdorff Oberst Graf 225, 242
Lampe Reserve Leutnant 234
Lançon 183, 191
Lange Hauptmann 214, 215, 242
Lange Leutnant 117
Langemark 85, 86, 90, 92, 95, 98, 101, 103, 121
Langer GenMaj 165, 168, 183, 184
Langhäuser Pfarrer 191
Langle General de 3, 5, 22, 26, 37, 40
Lannoy 55

Laon 23
Larenz Hauptmann 16
La Targette 123
La Tourelle 145
L'Aventure 47
Layes Brook 49, 50 – 52
Leckie Lieutenant Colonel RGE 99
Ledebur Oberst von 259, 260
Le Four de Paris 165, 174, 181, 182, 191
Le Fresnoy 139
Legl Hauptmann 114
Le Maisnil 139
Le Marais 47
Le Mesnil 30, 31, 33, 37 – 39, 263
Lennartz Leutnant 91
Lens ix, 78, 80, 207, 212 – 215, 217, 220 – 222, 224, 225, 228, 229, 231, 233 – 235, 243 - 245
Le Plouisch 54
Les Islettes 164
L'Estocq Oberstleutnant von 207, 209
Le Willy 64, 72
Les Brulots 47
Lichtenfels GenLt von 299
Liebert GenLt von 257, 271
Liège 298
Liévin 127, 205
Ligny 74
Lille 44, 54, 55, 60, 63, 78, 150, 225
Linde Leutnant 233, 245
Lizerne 98, 101
Löffler GenMaj 274, 275
Loof Leutnant 240
Loos xii, 55, 203, 205, 206, 212 – 216, 219, 222, 223, 225 - 227, 229, 231 – 233, 242 - 244
Lorette Spur 122, 123, 125 – 127, 140, 144, 217
Lorenz Major 175
Lorgies 131, 133
Lorraine 1, 93
Loßberg Oberst von 260 – 263, 265, 269, 271, 274, 287, 299
Losshagen Leutnant 116
Luckner Reserve Oberleutnant Graf 34
Ludendorff viii, xi, 293, 295
Lüder Major von 273
Ludovici Leutnant 256, 287
Lüttwitz GenLt von 269, 271, 300
Lutz Hauptmann 178, 201
Lys viii

Mainz 298

Maison de Champagne 262, 264, 266
Mamelle Nord (Hill 196) 5
Manre 275
Marne 1, 252, 298
Marquillies 54, 55, 59, 131
Marquis Leutnant 134
Marschall Leutnant Freiherr von 197
Massiges 247, 262, 263
Masuria/Masurian Lakes viii, 40
Mauk Kriegsfreiwilliger Paul, youngest German fatal casualty 129, 161
Médéah Farm 278, 280
Meersmann Oberstleutnant 19
Meinardus Major 22
Meinardus Hauptmann 37
Meißner Hauptmann 112
Melaene Cabaret 88
Mende Reserve Hauptmann 219
Merville 78
Messines 44, 149
Meurisson Ravine/River 181, 191, 198
Meyer Reserve Leutnant Adolf 142
Mezières 73, 183, 257, 260
Mittmann Leutnant 152
Möckel Landwehr Leutnant 34
Mohr Leutnant 49
Mons ix
Montblainville 165, 188
Mont Kemmel 107
Moorslede 114, 121
Mordacq Colonel Henri 92, 120
Moreau Valley 165, 184
Moronvilliers 246, 249
Mouzon 183
Mudra Gen der Inf von vii, 165, 182, 183, 200, 201, 300
Müller Oberst 262
Müller Reserve Oberleutnant Erich 264, 266
Müller Leutnant (RIR 242) 114
Reserve Leutnant Müller (RIR 72) 285
Reserve Leutnant Müller (IR 127) 185
Mund Major 19

Namur 296
Naumann Reserve Oberleutnant 151
Nerée Hauptmann von 50
Nerlich Hauptmann 180
Nesles 74
Neumann Leutnant 257
Neuve Chapelle xii, 44, 45, 48, 49, 51 – 54, 56 – 60, 63, 64, 69, 70, 72, 74 – 77, 80, 81, 129, 131, 133 – 135, 137, 160, 207

Neuville St Vaast 123, 125 – 127, 205
Nicolai Oberleutnant 51
Nieuwpoort 115
Nivelle General xii, 293
Nonebossen 112, 114
North Breastwork 155
Nouart 183
Noyelles 214, 243
Nuber Hauptmann 107, 112, 114

Ober Ost viii
Ohl Leutnant 90
Oldershausen Oberst Freiherr von 269
Onken Landwehr Leutnant 172
Oostnieuwkerke 90
Oscar Prince of Prussia 257
Ostende viii
Otto Reserve Oberleutnant Hermann 30

Packisch Hauptmann von 215
Passchendaele 100, 108, 114, 299
Peiper Major 283
Peitz Leutnant 16
Peltz Hauptmann 228
Perfall Hauptmann Freiherr von 190
Perthes 5 – 8, 10, 21 – 23, 29, 30, 35, 38, 260, 269, 272
Pétain General, 293
Peterson Oberst 85
Petersen Leutnant Hans 240, 241
Pfeiffer Leutnant 270, 271
Pfeil und Klein-Ellguth GenLt Graf von 165, 300
Philippi Leutnant Fritz 71, 79
Piètre 45, 47, 51, 57 – 59, 62, 66, 71
Pijpegale 98
Pilkem 85, 88, 95, 97, 99, 103, 120
Pimple, The 125, 205 - 207
Poelkapelle 90, 100
Polygon Wood 106, 107, 110
Pommereau 71
Pont à Vendin 225
Pont Rouge 64
Pont St Pierre 140
Poperinge 98
Port Arthur 145, 153
Pressenthin Major von 284
Prösch Hauptmann 50, 61
Py, River 269

Quast Gen der Inf von 278, 286, 301
Quesnoy-sur-Deûle 54
Quiquandon General 97, 98, 103, 120

Quittel Reserve Leutnant 155, 163

Ratte Leutnant 134
Rebhuhnwäldchen 228, 229, 231, 234
Red Cross flag, abuse of 70
Reiling Reserve Leutnant 66, 75
Reims xi, 122, 171
Reinhold Hauptmann 19
Reinshagen Oberleutnant 256
Remy Major
Renneburg Hauptmann 149
Reschke Hauptmann 286
Rethel 275
Reuter Oberleutnant Herbert 133, 147, 162
Reuter Leutnant 15
Rheinbaben-Höhe 174, 187 - 190
Richebourg l'Avoue 45, 131, 135
Richter Major 47
Richter Leutnant 221
Richterlein Leutnant 200
Ricken Leutnant 117
Riederer Hauptmann 68
Riemann Gen der Inf 15, 41, 301
Ripont 5, 19, 35, 39, 249, 250, 262, 286
Ritter Hauptmann 19, 218, 219
Robeck Vice Admiral de 39
Roclincourt 123, 205
Roeselare 59, 80
Rogge Oberstleutnant 263
Rohlfing Hauptmann 137
Roller Hauptmann 180
Romer Colonel FC 244
Rommel Leutnant 168
Rose Leutnant 114
Rosenberg Hauptmann von 131
Roth Major 17
Roth Leutnant 9
Roubaix 55
Rouges Bancs 135
Rouvroy 266
Röwe Leutnant 147, 162
Roy General 101
Rudloff Leutnant 51
Runckel GenMaj 98
Ruppenthal Leutnant 148
Rupprecht GenOberst Crown Prince of Bavaria 58, 74, 75, 77, 79, 122, 125, 131, 135, 145, 160, 205, 224, 225, 297
Ryssel Leutnant 218, 221, 244

Sabaß Reserve Hauptmann 214, 216
Sainghin 60, 147

St André 54
St Auguste, Cité 216, 217, 222
St Edouard 214
St Elie, Cité 234
St Hilaire-le-Grand 1, 37, 247
St Hilaire-le-Petit 275
St Hubert-Pavillon 165, 198
St Hubert-Rücken 178, 180, 188, 189, 200
St Juliaan 85, 95, 97 - 100, 102, 104, 106, 118
St Laurent, Cité 215, 217, 220, 221, 228
St Laurent-Blangy 162
Ste Marie-à-Py 5, 21, 269, 271, 279
St Ménéhould 164, 194
St Mihiel 81
St Pierre 214, 233
St Quentin 298
St Souplet 24, 247, 250
Salomé 163
Sandilands Lieutenant Colonel 220
Santhes 225
Sauerbrey Reserve Leutnant 154, 155, 163
Savigny 269
Schabbehardt Leutnant 64, 66
Scanzoni GenLt 71
Scarpe 123
Scharnhorst Leutnant 15
Schauß Leutnants (Brothers) 196
Schele Genmaj 59
Schettler Reserve Leutnant 64
Schlammulde 126, 128
Schmeil Leutnant 229
Schmidt Hauptmann 131
Schmieden GenMaj von 100, 106
Schmidt Hauptmann 147
Schmitt Leutnant 138
Schmitz Hauptmann 139, 140
Schneider Leutnant 273, 279
Schobe Reserve Oberleutnant 64
Schöne Offizierstellvertreter 54
Schöpflin GenLt 94
Schreder Leutnant 255
Schroer Oberleutnant 69
Schulz Major 131, 132, 145, 147
Schulze Leutnant 65
Schumann Leutnant 15
Schwartz Oberstleutnant 223
Schwarze Leutnant 20
Schwarze Kuppe 182
Schweigert Leutnant 196
Schwerin Gen der Inf Graf von 286
Schwerin Leutnant Graf von 34
Schwerling Leutnant 39

Index   317

Seclin 78
Sedan 275
Seeger Leutnant 107
Seltmann Leutnant 232, 244
Semide 278
Semmler Leutnant 116
Serrail General 191
Servon 168, 170, 173, 174, 176, 177, 184, 188, 246, 271
Seydlitz general 11
's-Graventafel 100, 101, 106
Shakerly Major 148
Soden Major Graf 49, 50, 53, 61
Solms Oberleutnant Prinz zu 49, 61
Somme 299, 301
Somme-Py 5, 21, 22, 27, 250, 254, 255, 260, 264, 269, 270, 278, 279
Sommer Leutnant 186
Souain 5, 7, 8, 35, 247, 251, 254, 255, 260, 270, 288
Souchez 122, 125 – 128, 140, 205, 206, 212, 292
Spaer Hauptmann 89
Spamer Hauptmann 89
Speyer Leutnant 90
Spindler Leutnant von 186
Staden 86, 98
Starke Hauptmann 183, 221
Staubwasser 233
Steenstraat 85, 89, 93 – 95, 98, 103
Stein Leutnant 268
Steinmann Reserve Leutnant 233
Steinwald 226, 229
Steuer Major 159
Stever Oberleutnant 273
Stiegler Reserve Leutnant Carl 60, 70, 73
Stober Leutnant Max 88
Stöckhardt Leutnant 239
Storchennest 174, 176, 177, 187, 188
Strauß Leutnant 221, 244
Strippelmann Major 47, 50, 52, 78
Stumme Oberleutnant 254
Stützpunkt III 219, 223, 226
Stützpunkt IV 219, 226
Stützpunkt V 217, 219, 223, 226
Suippes 83
Swart Oberleutnant 50
Sydow Oberst von 174, 176

Tahure 5, 6, 21, 254, 255, 257 – 259, 264, 266 – 269, 272, 276, 283, 285
Tannenberg viii
Tempel Hauptmann 54

Thélus 127, 205
Thesiger Brigadier-General 136
Theyson Hauptmann 156, 163
Thiele Landwehr Rittmeister 196
Totzeck Leutnant 49
Toufflers 55
Tourcoing 60
Trou Bricot 5
Turner Brigadier-General REW Turner VC 155

Ummen Leutnant 13
Urbal General d' 122, 128, 295

Vanheule Farm 104, 106
Varennes 165
Vauquois 160, 171, 181
Velorenhoek 116
Verdun vii, viii, xii, 83, 164, 184, 201, 292, 294, 297, 299
Vermelles 218, 236, 245
Ver Touquet 140
Vetter Leutnant 255
Vienne-le-Chateau 174, 184, 186
Vijfwege 86
Vimy/Vimy Ridge 122, 123, 127, 136, 144, 160, 206, 234, 244
Violaines 134, 148, 155, 156, 224
Vogt Reserve Leutnant 169
Volkmann Hauptmann von 34
Vornkahl Leutnant 215, 216, 228
Vosges 1, 60, 252
Vouziers 8, 33, 40, 247, 262 – 264, 275

Wahlen-Jürgas Oberst von 176
Waldstellung 283
Walker Leutnant 186
Wallemolen 100
Wallmoden Reserve Leutnant von 29
Walsemann Leutnant 14
Warneton/Chateau de Warneton 44, 63
Wartze Leutnant 134
Watter Oberst Freiherr von 167
Waubke Leutnant 147, 162
Wavrin 60, 74
Weber Leutnant (FAR 7) 50
Weber Leutnant (FAR 78) 67, 79
Wegener Hauptmann 197
Weidendrift 93
Weinberger Leutnant 63
Wenbourne Major 50
Wencher GenLt von 165
Wenderoth Hauptmann 89

Werfft Leutnant 230
Westhoek 106, 110, 114
Wetterecke 282
Wicres 60, 63, 79, 135, 162
Wiebel Leutnant 210
Wieltje 99, 104, 116 - 118
Wijtschate 70
Wilhelm II, Kaiser 260, 261, 276, 299
Wilhelm Reserve Leutnant 187
Windhorst Reserve Hauptmann Karl 61, 135
Wingles 223
Winzer Leutnant Richard 272
Wolbrecht Leutnant 61
Wolff Hauptmann 151

Wülfing Major 134, 238
Württemberg King of 200

Ypres vii – ix, 1, 16, 72, 81, 82, 85 – 87, 91, 95, 97, 98, 102, 103, 106, 107, 115, 118, 120, 150, 154, 161, 223
Yser 1, 81 – 83, 85, 89, 92, 94, 95, 102, 103, 115, 294

Ziegler Leutnant 156
Zitzmann Pfarrer 3
Zobel Major 149
Zonnebeke 101, 106, 108, 109